T0244473

PRAISE FOR

The Brazil Chronicles

"Part memoir, part cautionary tale about the hazards of trying to publish an English-language daily newspaper in a foreign country, Stephen G. Bloom's *The Brazil Chronicles* is both entertaining and instructive. With its cast of misfits—ranging from neurotic dreamers and ambitious novices to hard-drinking swashbucklers and smooth glad-handers—it reads at times like a real-life version of satirical novels about journalism like Evelyn Waugh's *Scoop* or George Gissing's *New Grub Street*. But it also zeroes in on the internal conflicts inherent to putting out any newspaper, such as tensions between the business and reporting sides, as well as others that are unique to working under a military dictatorship. I was in Rio de Janeiro at the same time as Bloom, and this book, an engaging combination of thorough research and personal anecdotes, is chock-full of uproarious stories that I had never heard until now. Who knew that Hunter S. Thompson did a stint in Brazil, perfecting the maniacal antics and style that later made him a literary star?"
—Larry Rohter, Brazil correspondent, *Newsweek,* **1977–1982,** *The New York Times,* **1998–2008, author of** *Into the Amazon*

"Reading *The Brazil Chronicles* is like sitting with a bunch of foreign correspondents in some seedy bar drinking questionable local booze as they boast, brag, bust balls and raise hell between deadlines. In his two years in Brazil, Stephen G. Bloom rode the rails of newspaper's golden age, and witnessed the initial stages of print journalism's calamitous demise. This book is a newspaperman's account of a newspaperman's life and dreams. Filled with egos, ruthless competition, exaggeration and envy—elements of the air inside any newsroom—*The Brazil Chronicles* is a first draft of what newspapers once were, and an evergreen profile of the men and women who got off on the clack of typewriters, the smell of ink and the crazy adrenaline of deadlines."
—Anthony DePalma, former *New York Times* **foreign correspondent, author of** *The Cubans, The Man Who Invented Fidel,* **and** *Here*

"Steeped in facts and tropical heat, this memoir will make you young. A budding journalist in 1970s Brazil uncovers a world of expats and adventurers in a historically fraught time. Reading it made me want to have a caipirinha in Copacabana with this vivid storyteller."
—**Andrei Codrescu, NPR commentator, author of** *Too Late for Nightmares*

"In his fun and informative homage to life as an expat on an English language newspaper in Rio, Stephen G. Bloom explores a world teeming with vitality that might otherwise have been lost to the dustbins of history. Unexpected treats abound. On its own the correspondence in the early sixties between staff writer Hunter S. Thompson and Phil Graham, publisher of the *Washington Post*, is worth the price of admission, but there is so much more to admire, to mull and to hail in this recreation of life in what the author calls a "rogue's paradise" as a ragtag group of itinerant journalists live the dream of creating a global-minded newspaper in Latin America. They may have been doomed, but they are never dull. Must reading for anyone who loves newspapers, scoundrels, visionaries and a taut tale well told."
—**Madeleine Blais, Pulitzer Prize-winning journalist, author of** *Queen of the Court* **and** *To the New Owners*

"In 1979 when 28-year-old Berkeley grad Stephen G. Bloom showed up in Sao Paulo, desperate for a newspaper job, no one had heard of BRICS or the Global South; the term was Third World. Staying around for two years until the expat journalism party wound down, meeting a cast of unforgettable characters he likens to Ken Kesey's Merry Pranksters and gathering the yarns that he tells with such verve now in this combination history-memoir, Bloom then returned home to find the U.S. news business in the early stages of its own death spiral. *The Brazil Chronicles* is lively to the point of eliciting belly laughs."
— **Bradley K. Martin, author of** *Under the Loving Care of the Fatherly Leader: North Korea and the Kim Dynasty*

"In this head-spinning 'celebration of what newspapers were and will never be again,' you'll meet a rowdy assemblage of social-justice crusaders, swindlers, bon vivants, revolutionaries, CIA operatives and

itinerant journalists of all kinds, not to mention a world-famous bank robber, a future Hollywood star and a fledgling reporter named Hunter S. Thompson. And at the center of it all, banging away on his broken Olivetti typewriter in a dingy newsroom in Rio de Janeiro, is a marvelous storyteller named Stephen G. Bloom."
—**Miles Harvey, author of** *The Registry of Forgotten Objects,* *King of Confidence,* **and** *The Island of Lost Maps*

"*The Brazil Chronicles* takes us into a magic place and time when spunky young men and women yearning for the life of a foreign correspondent could find it in all its glory—and risks—near the languid beaches of one of the world's most beautiful cities, Rio de Janeiro. Stephen G. Bloom gives us a young reporter's eyewitness account of Latin America's largest country at a tumultuous time, even as he revels in the work he loves, but as the mature observer he is today, Bloom also renders a deeply researched history of expat newspapers serving an important U.S. ally, including their role in Cold War propaganda. A fine read."
—**Mary Jo McConahay, author of** *Playing God,* *The Tango War,* **and** *Maya Roads*

"An entertaining and enlightening journey, this deeply reported narrative unfolds through the eyes of a relatable and passionate Bloom, the older and wiser narrator reflecting upon the choices of his younger self with humor, affection, and remarkable candidness. Embedded within this engaging true tale, Bloom tugs at universal themes: coming of age, identity, the pull of ambition, the power of instinct, and delightful explorations into human nature."
—**Erika Hayasaki, Associate Professor of Literary Journalism, University of California, Irvine, author of** *Somewhere Sisters: A Story of Adoption, Identity and the Meaning of Family*

THE BRAZIL CHRONICLES

THE BRAZIL CHRONICLES

STEPHEN G. BLOOM

UNIVERSITY OF MISSOURI PRESS
COLUMBIA

Library of Congress Cataloging-in-Publication Data

Names: Bloom, Stephen G., author.
Title: The Brazil chronicles / by Stephen G. Bloom.
Description: Columbia : University of Missouri Press, 2024. | Includes
   bibliographical references and index.
Identifiers: LCCN 2024020312 (print) | LCCN 2024020313 (ebook) | ISBN
   9780826223159 (hardcover) | ISBN 9780826275042 (ebook)
Subjects: LCSH: Bloom, Stephen G. | Brazil herald. | Journalists--United
   States--Biography. | Rio de Janeiro (Brazil)--Newspapers. | BISAC:
   LANGUAGE ARTS & DISCIPLINES / Writing / Nonfiction (incl. Memoirs) |
   HISTORY / United States / 20th Century
Classification: LCC PN4874.B554 A3 2024 (print) | LCC PN4874.B554
   (ebook) | DDC 070.92 [B]--dc23/eng/20240523
LC record available at https://lccn.loc.gov/2024020312
LC ebook record available at https://lccn.loc.gov/2024020313

Typeface: Minion Pro and Aktiv Grotesk

Books by Stephen G. Bloom

Blue Eyes, Brown Eyes: A Cautionary Tale of Race and Brutality

The Audacity of Inez Burns: Dreams, Desire, Treachery & Ruin in the City of Gold

The Oxford Project

Tears of Mermaids: The Secret Story of Pearls

Inside the Writer's Mind

Postville: A Clash of Cultures in Heartland America

To Iris

HUTCHESON: *Newspaperman is the best profession in the world. Know what a profession is?*

STUDENT: *Skilled job.*

HUTCHESON: *So's repairing watches. Nope. A profession is the performance of a public good. That's why newspaper work is a profession.*

> Exchange between newspaper editor Ed Hutcheson, played by Humphrey Bogart, and an unnamed journalism student.

— Siegel, Sol C. (Producer), & Brooks, Richard (Director) (1952). *Deadline – U.S.A.* [Motion Picture]. United States: 20th Century-Fox.

CONTENTS

Contents

ILLUSTRATIONS

Illustrations

PREFACE

A Moment in Time

ON SEPTEMBER 26, 1979, when I was twenty-eight, I boarded a Pan Am 747 jet at New York's Kennedy Airport bound for São Paulo, Brazil, to work at a brand new English-language newspaper, the *Latin America Daily Post*. I had bought a one-way plane ticket, thinking that I might never return to the United States. I wasn't a fugitive. I hadn't stolen thousands from the corner bank. I didn't owe alimony, and I wasn't a draft evader. I left for an opportunity I couldn't get at home: a first job in newspapering.

For more than two hundred years, America has been the world's most vaunted destination. Emma Lazarus had inscribed it, and a mighty woman with a torch had proclaimed it. America welcomed everyone (at least it used to). Like my ancestors who had crossed a wide ocean to call America home a century earlier, I, too, was seeking passage, only I was headed in a different direction, south instead of west, leaving the New World for the Third World. The Statue of Liberty would be my guidepost to a departure, not an arrival.

In some ways I felt as though I was getting out of Dodge. At the time, I was living in a potter's studio in Oakland, California. Five years earlier, down the block on Benvenue Avenue, newspaper heiress Patricia Hearst had been kidnapped, joined a group of self-styled urban guerrillas called the Symbionese Liberation Army, and had robbed two California banks. The previous November, nine hundred followers of a San Francisco megalomaniac by the name of Jim Jones had killed themselves by drinking cyanide-laced Kool-Aid in the jungles of Guyana. Nine days after that, San Francisco Mayor George Moscone and Harvey Milk, a member of the city's board of supervisors, had been assassinated by a former supervisor.

Those were strange days for anyone living in Northern California. William Butler Yeats hadn't been far off when he predicted anarchy loosed upon the world, innocence drowned, the center no longer holding. At the time of my exit, I took counsel from San Francisco poet Kenneth Rexroth: "Against the ruin of the world, there is only one defense—the creative act."

In retrospect, those awful events were more an excuse than a reason to leave California and the United States. Exotic Brazil held the promise of a new beginning, a place to live out my dreams of becoming a newspaper reporter.

Before the onset of the internet, cellphones, and blinking computer screens, scoring a job as a reporter was as rare as snow in San Francisco. Newspapers in the late 1970s were just starting to collapse, eventually like dominoes. Why *not* take a chance and move away to Brazil before it would be too late? Disappearing into the wilds of a tropical Shangri-la, doing what I had always dreamt about, seemed like a pretty good idea at the time.

That I would find myself working at the world's least-known global newspaper, where the typesetters didn't have a clue what the words mean that they were so merrily tapping away on their antique keyboards, was just one facet of my new life at the *Daily Post*. I soon discovered I was in good company. Gonzo journalist Hunter S. Thompson had worked as a reporter for an earlier incarnation of the *Daily Post*, as had hundreds of other renegade journalists fed up with the job logjam at US newspapers. If Paris had been the haven for the Lost Generation of émigré artists, poets, and novelists in the first half of the twentieth century, then Brazil would become a New Wave destination for storytellers of a different stripe during the second half. Some of my fellow journalists were brilliant scribes who would make their marks on history; others were deadbeats, ne'er-do-wells, grifters, drug runners, CIA agents, and pornographers (and that's just for starters).

I happily joined this troupe of Merry Pranksters. Brazil has a long tradition of welcoming outliers, spanning more than a century of wily expats, providing a launching pad to those who hadn't been able to lift off at home.

To get anywhere, you have to take a different route. You have to step out of line. You have to be original. Taking a chance often is the only way in. To "light out for the Territory ahead of the rest," as Huck Finn put it, didn't just mean moving west. It meant going *anywhere* for an opportunity, an instinct as American as it gets.

Working at the *Daily Post* would lead to a career at six newspapers, thousands of bylined stories, half a dozen books, and reporting trips to five continents. For me, Brazil was a beginning. It's where I learned a craft, a profession, a way to look at the world and (to try to) make some sense of it. That all started at a sweatbox of a newspaper on the third floor of a firetrap in a down-and-out Rio de Janeiro neighborhood that tutti-frutti, turban-wrapped singer Carmen Miranda had called home.

What follows is a memoir; a breezy, select account of newspaper history, both in Brazil and the United States; and a niche cultural history of both nations. It's multi-layered stories, told in concentric narratives: an insider, dishy, eyewitness, coming-of-age account of journalists far away from home. It's also a previously untold story, the first—and likely the last—book ever written about the tiny, obscure, and forgotten *Latin America Daily Post* and the raft of quixotic expat newspapers that preceded it. But it's more. *The Brazil Chronicles* is a celebration of what newspapers were and will never be again.

PART ONE

CHAPTER 1

Giovanni

I ALWAYS WANTED to be a newspaperman. I was born in 1951 and grew up reading the *Newark Evening News* sprawled out on the living room floor of my family's split-level northern New Jersey suburban home. My family was not a *New York Times* household—the *Times* was too dense, too brainy, no fun. No comics, no political cartoons, no Ann or Abby. On occasion, my father would bring home a treat— the *Daily News, New York Post, World-Telegram,* or *Journal-American.* Those were newspapers! Big photos, crazy headlines, police-blotter stories, crusader columnists. My mother fretted that the ink would rub off my fingertips onto the beige carpet. But I looked at newspaper ink the way Catholics view sooty crosses on their foreheads on Ash Wednesday: a sign of membership. Writing about what landed people in the news (and hot water) seemed a profession too good to be true. To get paid to tell stories, and in the process extract some meaning from other people's lives and maybe my own, where could I sign up?

The first "adult" book I ever read was *The Catcher in the Rye,* a red-and-gold dog-eared Signet paperback that cost fifty cents. I carried around Holden Caulfield's memoir tucked in the back pocket of my dungarees, the same place where students today pack their cell phones. Every evening at ten-fifteen, I'd crawl into bed, Panasonic transistor radio pressed to my ear, and tune in Jean Shepherd on WOR, 710 on the AM dial, who'd spin fantastical tales about growing up in Indiana with Flick and Schwartz and the girls they thought were Venus and Cleopatra, Daphne Bigelow and Wanda Hickey. If I hadn't drifted off to the sandman by Shep's finale, I'd tune in Brad Crandall, another beguiling pied piper on WNBC, whose signoff was, "Until next time, when we sit down by the railroad tracks, open up a can of beans, watch the trains go by, and talk about this crazy world in which we live." These guys could talk about *anything*.

During the summers, I slogged away as a stockboy and apprentice salesman in my father's family shoe store in working-class Union County, where I got initiated into the arcane cosmos of shoe lingo. *Alberts* were A widths; *Bennies*, B's; *Charlies*, C's; *Davids*, D's; *Eddies*, E's; *34s* were *Up*'s (customers) who walked out without buying; to *68* or to *T.O.* meant to "turn over" an *Up* from one *shoe dog* (salesman) to another. *L.Y.*'s were last year's shoes, *double L.Y.*'s were shoes two years old, *triple L.Y.*'s were three-year-old models, and *God-Knows-How-Many L.Y.*'s were shoes worn by Grandma Moses. The *farnaricator* was the end of a broomstick jammed into the toe box to make a shoe longer (usually without the *Up* knowing it). The high point of my day was sitting with Murray, a skinny octogenarian shoe dog who'd regale me with X-rated stories of his youth while sucking on yet another Kent. "Her gams? They stretched to the moon and back! Va-va-va boom, baby!"

In the parlance of the day, I was not cool. Sports didn't motivate me, as either a participant or a fan. It wasn't that I wasn't athletic, it was that I didn't see the point, whether it was tossing a football or swinging a bat. Eager but shy, I grew into a bookworm who worshipped *On the Road*, *The Bell Jar*, and anything by Hermann Hesse. Carlos Castaneda's *The Teachings of Don Juan*, a phantasma about a Yaqui shaman in Sonora, Mexico, took me to places I could hardly imagine. I memorized Ernest Hemingway's *The Nick Adams Stories* ("A Very Short Story" was the best!), and when I discovered that Papa thought *The Adventures of Huckleberry Finn* was the progenitor of all American literature, I studied it paragraph by paragraph. I was seduced by the writerly mechanics of John Cheever, W. Somerset Maugham, John O'Hara, and Irwin Shaw. I had no idea how Truman Capote had pulled off *In Cold Blood*, but the way he wove together the stories of two drifters who murdered four members of the Clutter family in Holcomb, Kansas, gave me goosebumps (it still does).

Joni Mitchell's *Blue* album had just come out, and the song that kept ricocheting in my head was "California." That, and the 1969 dope-smoking-drifter movie *Easy Rider* with Peter Fonda and Jack Nicholson, sealed the deal. I hitchhiked cross-country to California. You could do that in those days. America's nineteenth-century newspaperman Horace Greeley's sage advice, "Go West, young man" updated. Woody Guthrie thumbing his way as far as the continent would allow. I rented a room in a downtown San Francisco flophouse, The Spaulding, on O'Farrell Street, and saved up enough to splurge at Tad's Steakhouse around the corner.

San Francisco and California slayed me. Of course, they did. Why waste away in monochromatic New Jersey (sorry if any New Jersey firsters are reading this) when Day-Glo California, still celebrating the Summer of Love, beckoned? I applied to the University of California, Berkeley, which was *way* out of my league considering what a screwup I'd been in high school. Somehow, a plink plunked my way and I got in. More fortune followed: I drew No. 227 in the 1970 Selective Service lottery, easing worries that I'd be shipped off to Fort Dix and then Vietnam.

At Berkeley, I took a class from poet Josephine Miles, who offhandedly mentioned that writer Joan Didion had taken the same class from her fifteen years earlier and that I happened to be sitting in the same seat in the same classroom as Ms. Didion had sat. I instantly felt encased in a shaft of luminescent light coming from above. Professor Miles, the first woman awarded tenure in Berkeley's English department, who putt-putted around Wheeler Hall in an electric wheelchair due to rheumatoid arthritis, introduced the class to the writing of Kenneth Patchen, who wrote a poem I still love, more than fifty years later, titled "The Origin of Baseball."

At the time, the Free Speech Movement had given way to a pitched battle between Alameda County sheriff's deputies (dubbed the "Blue Meanies") and Berkeley students to take control of a square-block greenspace dubbed People's Park six blocks south of the campus, near where police had killed a twenty-five-year-old African-American by the name of James Rector. "Bloody Thursday" was how everyone I knew referred to the shooting. I worked night and day on the student newspaper, *The Daily Californian,* covering the ensuing riots, prompted by police cars careening and zigzagging down streets that intersected Telegraph Avenue to clear them of protestors. Berkeley students at their best.

As the campus stringer for *Time* magazine in 1972, I got assigned to cover a speech given by beefy, curly-haired novelist Norman Mailer, who spoke in the wake of a misogynist screed he had written, "Prisoner of Sex" that had just been published in *Harpers.* Mailer strutted on the Zellerbach auditorium stage looking like a smug, overstuffed turkey. The mostly female, stridently anti-Mailer crowd showered him with boos. Some had smuggled in tomatoes and heads of cabbage, and threw them at him.

After ducking, Mailer scanned the crowd left to right, up and down, grinning like a lunatic. He adjusted his microphone, waited ten seconds, leaned into it, and over the racket asked the women in the audience to stand if they hated him. A third promptly rose to their feet.

Mailer paused and smiled and then roared: "Now, all you little bitches: Sit down!"

It was outrageous. Some in the audience stormed out; others continued standing, arms crossed defiantly during Mailer's subsequent two-hour fusillade. But most had no recourse. Mailer had put them in an impossible position. Flummoxed, one by one, they took their seats. Mailer had one-upped everyone.

At City Lights Books in San Francisco, owner-poet Lawrence Ferlinghetti introduced the SRO crowd to bedraggled writer Charles Bukowski at a reading so packed that it prompted a last-minute visit from the city's fire marshal, who got pelted with beer cans. Bukowski didn't just look like an unmade bed; he resembled someone who never got out of one. He had spent thirty years toiling in an L.A. post office and had written twenty-five gritty novels and books of poetry documenting it. He was everyman's hero; he gave hope to any scribbler who'd ever dreamed of getting published. In addition to the six-packs he passed out to the crowd, Henry Chinaski's creator shared touts for the next day's races at nearby Tanforan racetrack.

I sat in the front row when Tom Wolfe, dressed in a white linen double-breasted suit, white shoes, and a red four-point-fold tucked in his breast pocket, electrified three-thousand fans by reading excerpts from his forthcoming book, *Radical Chic & Mau-Mauing the Flak Catchers*. Wolfe had singlehandedly invented New Journalism. Breaking stodgy Miss MacGillicuddy rules of grammar and syntax in a precursor to rap and hip hop, Wolfe strung together invented words in meandering, convoluted sentences and paragraphs that sounded like a Charles Mingus jazz riff that made complete sense.

All these happenings were transformative—literary joustings at which ideas, good and bad, reigned supreme. There was no talk of rapacious law, profit-driven medicine, avaricious stock trading, house-flipping real estate, or any other profession deemed "responsible." The pact these prophets had signed onto was to assess the world's chaos by posing questions no one had bothered to ask. What they did resonated with another local literary idol of mine, poet Kenneth Rexroth, who wrote, "Against the ruin of the world, there is only one defense— the creative act."

This multi-ring cerebral circus prompted a return to my earlier obsession with newspapers. Even though I'd been gobsmacked by *Washington Post* cub reporters Woodward and Bernstein's coverage of the developing Watergate scandal, I had little interest in getting myself to the nation's capital. In my mind, most politicians were retooled, updated vaudeville actors; maybe charlatans was a better description. I never saw myself as part of the posse of journalists chasing them around the Capitol for yet one more staged, self-serving comment.

I took to poring through the local newspapers, the *San Francisco Chronicle*, *San Francisco Examiner*, and *Oakland Tribune*, with a deepening admiration for the journalists who made these broad-sheets possible. I diagrammed stories to see how they worked. The

Chronicle's Herb Caen was an amazing word fetishist. He could do things with three-dot journalism I'd never seen before (or since). It was Caen who had knighted San Francisco "Baghdad by the Bay"; the Golden Gate Bridge the "Car-Strangled Spanner"; North Beach poets "beatniks" (back in 1958); and the stretch of sleazy strip clubs along San Francisco's Broadway "Bawdway." As a student reporter for *The Daily Californian*, I interviewed Caen. No disappointment there. He was as witty and debonaire as he ought to have been. A great crime reporter was the *Chronicle's* Carolyn Anspacher. An underrated East Bay columnist was wordsmith Ray Orrock. A morning delight was the fat *Los Angeles Times*, with thumb suckers every day in column one on page one, jumping four or five times inside. I binged on the *Berkeley Barb, Ramparts, Esquire*, and a new magazine called *Rolling Stone*. I gorged on Mike Royko, Pete Hamill, Jimmy Breslin, Murray Kempton, and I. F. Stone, reading out-of-town newspapers late into the night in the reading room at Doe Library.

After I graduated, I worked in a series of dreary day jobs—at Cleo's, a copy store off of Telegraph Avenue; for my landlord, Steve Topol, selling marijuana grow lights to San Francisco plant-store owners and closet entrepreneurs; writing press releases for a sketchy nonprofit Oakland quasi-government agency. After two years of *de minimis* employment, my girlfriend Kirstie and I took a trans-Canada camping trip, only to get busted in International Falls, Minnesota, for transporting half an ounce of weed back into the States.

"Pay me a hundred-and-fifty bucks and we'll git you on yur way," a portly customs agent told us with a wink. I wasn't sure whether he was proffering a bribe or a fine, but we scraped together the dough and hightailed it out, commiserating our loss and rejoicing that we'd gotten off by splurging at the grand Hotel Duluth.

Back in Oakland from a potter's studio I was renting, I was primed to launch my career. I'd been taken by all things newspaper, including an amazing photograph snapped that year by San Francisco Associated Press photographer Sal Veder called "Burst of Joy." Veder had captured a family rushing onto the tarmac at Travis Air Force Base near Sacramento to greet a returning POW from Vietnam. The man's daughter had both feet suspended in mid-air, leaping to embrace her uniformed father. What a moment, what a photo, what a profession!

I freelanced stories for *California Living*, the Sunday magazine of the *San Francisco Examiner*; the *Berkeley Barb*; and a new wire service called Pacific News. I scored big when *The New York Times* published an abbreviated diary of my six-day stint working on the assembly line of a medieval Del Monte cannery in Emeryville, California, processing never-ending clanking cans of fruit cocktail. The story appeared on the *Times*'s Op-Ed Page, then edited by Harrison Salisbury, the first editor of a *Times* innovation, a reader forum that would be copied by nearly every other newspaper in the US. These weren't letters to the editor, but substantial opinion and observation pieces written by the famous and by nobodies like me.

My piece got play. An East Coast labor attorney, outraged that cannery workers got regulated and limited bathroom breaks, wanted to organize them. A radio talk show host in New York City, Barry Farber, from WOR, the same station that Jean Shepherd broadcast from, asked me to be a guest. I flew home, stayed in my old bedroom in my parents' house, took the 107 bus into Manhattan, and talked on air about working the assembly line. I was mostly incoherent, I fear, the victim of radio stage fright.

Earlier that day, I had called Salisbury. Maybe he'd see me. Cordial, gentlemanly, and welcoming but busy, he demurred. Impossible, he said. On deadline.

Could he recommend someone at the *Times* who might be interested in interviewing me for a job?

"You need clips," he said. "But even with clips, it's impossible to get in here. I doubt they'd hire me if I showed up hat in hand at the front door," said Pulitzer-Prize-winner Salisbury.

I visited *Time* magazine in the Time-Life Building across from Radio City Music Hall. My boss at the magazine's San Francisco bureau, Karsten Prager, a former war correspondent who had shepherded my story into *Time* about Norman Mailer, had set up an interview with Marylois Purdy Vega, who headed a department at the maga-zine, Reporter-Researchers, basically fact checkers, a position then almost always filled by women. Vega suggested I wouldn't like the job. "Go out and cover the world; that's what you need to do!" she grandly advised. In the same breath, she cautioned that I didn't have nearly enough experience to get hired as a *Time* correspondent.

Even though I'd been published in both the *Times* and *Time*, my pieces were one-offs, hardly anything to snag a job with. I didn't have what everyone advised I needed, a "rabbi" or "Chinaman." Both terms were appallingly offensive then and today, but unless you had an in-sider willing to die for you, getting a job at one of these powerhouses wasn't going to happen. Those were the rules, and nobody was going to make an exception for inconsequential me.

I returned to California, my meager savings exhausted by my East Coast foray. I had failed miserably. I'd been unable to convert any of these connections and opportunities into anything close to journal-ism employment.

With great deliberation, I assembled an assortment of clips and sent them to David Perlman, the city editor at the *San Francisco Chronicle*, only to get a one-sentence reply a week later: No openings and none were expected. When I asked for my clips back, Perlman wrote that he had thrown them away ("More bad news" was how he put it). After I'd heard nothing from the *Oakland Tribune*, I sat in the newspaper lobby under the *Tribune*'s Renaissance clocktower ready to introduce myself to the managing editor. But after waiting all day, no one resembling the M.E. appeared, and I slunk back to the potter's studio. The features editor at the *San Jose Mercury News*, Jennie Buckner, wrote that if any openings materialized, she'd call. She didn't sound optimistic.

I needed to widen my job-search radius. On a road trip to Seattle in my 1964 VW bug, sleeping and showering in campsites along Highway 5, I set up interviews at six newspapers. The only place hiring was a small daily in southern Oregon, the Medford *Mail Tribune*. Earl Adams, the managing editor, and I clicked; next was the publisher, who did not like me. He frowned when I offered up story ideas about spending a night in the county jail, tracing a year in the life of a rental tuxedo, interviewing petitioners in bankruptcy court about what had gone wrong. He was much more interested in city council meetings, the local forest fire-abatement board, and the Jack in the Box that had just opened.

My ideas were too off the wall. I needed to cut the edge. My rent at the potter's studio, owned by husband-and-wife attorneys, kept going up. I needed to do *something*.

I rebranded myself as a lifestyle/consumer reporter. I took out a position-wanted ad in *Editor & Publisher*: "Looking for the best pastrami sandwiches, dry cleaners, martinis in town? I'll find them and write about them." I'd go anywhere.

I got a nibble from an alternative-weekly newspaper editor in Texas who sounded like he was on crack. We met in Houston, where he plied me with margaritas and nachos, but other than a hangover, nothing came of the trip. Another editor, Stan Strick at the *Minneapolis Star,* flew me to the Twin Cities for a round of interviews, but the editors clashed on whether the newspaper needed such a specialty beat and whether such reporting might trigger blowback from advertisers. They promised to contact me once they'd made a decision.

I wasn't just out of college any longer. I was pushing twenty-seven. My Great Western Savings account was precipitously low. In a fit of frustration, my well-intentioned father called one evening for a come-to-Jesus talk, during which he referred to me as a "literary bum." His heartfelt advice: chuck California, forget newspapers, and take my proper place at Cranford Bootery, two miles off Exit 137 on the Garden State Parkway. Murray had retired and my father needed another shoe dog to fill Murray's size-nine bennies.

Then sunshine.

While visiting my grandmother, I scored the impossible: an interview with Janet Chusmir, the features editor at the *Miami Herald.* I fantasized that Chusmir would be so struck by my portfolio of clips that she'd wine and dine me at Joe's Stone Crab across the bay and over mojitos dangle a job offer.

But the moment I walked into her glass-walled mega-office, Chusmir berated me. "I don't even know how you got in to see me," she fumed, eying me suspiciously. "I have *New York Times* reporters who'd give their eyeteeth to work at the *Herald*!" Then, sounding more like a real estate mogul than a newspaper editor, she shrieked, "Just look at this view!" sweeping her manicured hand toward shimmering Biscayne Bay. "*Everyone* wants to work at the *Herald*! Why are you wasting my time?"

WTF?!

One too many cups of coffee?

In an ill-fated nanosecond, I realized I didn't want to play Chusmir's trapdoor game. Did I really have to grovel for an entry-level reporter's job?

"Well then, I won't waste your time or mine," I replied against all of my interests.

I slid my clips back into my leatherette briefcase, got up, and walked out of her aquamarine office with the hundred-million-dollar view.

Way too direct. On all counts. I had played into the sandbagged hand Chusmir had dealt me from the bottom of her deck. I should have thrown in my cards with a smile and a servile shrug.

Ray of sunshine gone poof.

Back in Oakland, awaiting callbacks from editors that never came, I took a job as a waiter at an Italian restaurant called Giovanni on Shattuck Avenue in Berkeley. Joe, the owner's nephew, a Ph.D. student in English literature at Berkeley, was doing the interviewing, and when I mentioned my former professor, Josephine Miles, he hired me on the spot. All the pasta I could eat, and tips, on busy nights, topped a hundred dollars. What a deal.

At Giovanni, there were two types of waiters: career waiters, mostly first-generation Italians or Chinese who looked at their jobs as a profession, and waiters like me, in-betweeners waiting for a break. Each group looked at the other with a tinge of sadness for their decision to work at Giovanni for however long or short their tenure might be. Whether career or not, all the waiters learned to glide across the dining room floor, never ever stopping abruptly. Otherwise, you chanced a waiter collision and pileup. If you remembered twenty feet after leaving the waiters' station that table E4 wanted a wedge of lemon with a no-ice Tab, you continued cruising to the back of the dining room and *then* returned to slice it at the waiters' station.

Giovanni turned out to be great prep for a wannabe journalist. For one, my notetaking had to be fast and accurate.

"So, you want your Caesar salad with your cioppino? At the same time?"

"No powdered sugar on your cannoli?"

"A *triple* espresso, really?

I also learned what later would be called multitasking, as well as performing on deadline. "I need to get out of here in twenty minutes!"

Waiters had to be personable to diners who are total assholes. The power differential was clear and obvious. On New Year's Eve, I had a diner clap his hands to get my attention as though he was Ali Baba. Being a waiter also was good training for newspapering. Politicians and other publicity seekers similarly commandeer reporters to serve them. This guy was just more transparent about it.

For the moment, I enjoyed the job. I had mornings and afternoons free to look for other work and pitch stories. I took to carrying trays of linguine alle Vongole, lasagna Bolognese, and cannelloni Napoletana high over my head, bobbing and weaving between tables. I learned to wield a corkscrew like Norman Maclean extracting a hand-tied fly from a trout. There certainly was enough material for any aspiring writer: Roger, an elaborately coiffed, high-priced pimp; Sue, a flirty bookkeeper who'd get looped every afternoon on a bottle of Prosecco; Kathy, an experimental-theater actress lubricating her lines with Barolo; Roy, a Hayward carpet salesman who wore too much cologne. "Your usual, sir, a dry martini, two olives? And the lady, what will she be having?" What was his secret?

My time at Giovanni also gave me a chance to brush up on my math skills, also. The waiters added up diners' checks in their heads; no computers. Between lunch and dinner shifts we caravanned to

Golden Gate Fields to pool our tips in an elaborate betting wheel developed by head waiter Bill Tau, even though it seldom paid off.

Meanwhile, I was getting nowhere in reeling in a newspaper job. This was 1978. American newspapers were in free fall. Afternoon dailies had DNR orders tacked to their front doors; my own *Dick and Jane* primer intro into the world of newspapers, the *Newark Evening News*, had closed six years earlier. America's legacy magazines had already been taken off life-support. *Life*, *Look*, and the *Saturday Evening Post* were dead, with scores more on their way. I knew there was no long-term future in print journalism, but when has that nipped anyone's ambition? Or should it? What reasonably well-adjusted person ever chooses a career based on how much money it will return? Surely, no one in their twenties should have such guard rails.

For the moment, journalism didn't want me; it didn't seem to want anyone. Until one afternoon in Giovanni's upstairs break room, just as the dinner shift was about to start.

In the *Los Angeles Times* business section that day, an article jumped off the page and grabbed me by my red waiter's vest with green piping. A start-up newspaper, the *Latin America Daily Post*, modeled after the Paris-based *International Herald Tribune*, was about to start publishing. The newspaper would specialize in coverage of the thirty-four-nation swath that connected San Juan to Buenos Aires. Just as the *International Herald Tribune* was located in Europe's cultural capital, Paris, the *Daily Post* would be published in Latin America's business epicenter, São Paulo, Brazil. Promotional copies of the newspaper had been circulated to influential global readers. Henry Kissinger and William Simon, the US treasury secretary at the time, were photographed reading a mockup. The *Daily Post* would be distributed via satellite to all Latin American capitals, as well as to Miami, New York, and Washington. The newspaper roll-out seemed like a very big deal. The *Chicago Tribune* and *New York Times* followed with their own stories on the new broadsheet.

But the best part was this: The *Daily Post* was hiring.

Giovanni

Why *not* move to Brazil and work for a hot-off-the-presses newspaper that may be destined for greatness?

What did I have to lose?

CHAPTER 2

On My Way

YES, I DESPERATELY wanted a newspaper job. Yes, I was willing to go anywhere. But moving eight thousand miles away to take a shot at a start-up that might or might not get off the ground in a foreign country where I knew no one and couldn't speak the language?

This was smart?

For starters, I had no clue whether I could even get hired at the *Latin America Daily Post*. Thus far my newspaper-employment record hadn't been exactly stellar.

One advantage I had was that I wouldn't be a newcomer to Brazil. For reasons I can't fully explain even today, Latin America has always spoken to me. Maybe in a previous life I'd been a Mayan warrior, an Inca stonecutter, or among the renegades who had followed Butch Cassidy and the Sundance Kid south. A year earlier, I'd taken a break from my job-searching misadventures to embark on a solo trains-planes-buses-hitchhiking trip, starting in Lima, Peru, and ending in Ushuaia, Argentina, the southernmost city in the world. My girlfriend Kirstie was out of the picture by then, and a dozen years after I'd been a high school exchange student in Chile, I set out to visit the family that had taken me in as one of their own.

On this impoverished, helter-skelter pilgrimage, I camped under a canopy of stars in a cocoa field on my way to Machu Picchu. I took a four-day train ride from La Paz, Bolivia, to Antofagasta, Chile, chugging through the moonlit white-sands Atacama Desert that Che Guevara wrote about in *Motorcycle Diaries*. At midnight, I knocked on the door of a tubercular Salvation Army mission in Punta Arenas, Argentina, shivering from the Tierra del Fuego cold, and took refuge with dozens of coughing men in various declinations of morbidity. Ordering me to identify myself, an army guard in Rio Gallegos, Patagonia, fired a shot from his service revolver. I traveled fourth-class in a below-deck hammock from Belém, up the Amazon River to spend a sleepless night in a Manaus caravansary where the front-desk clerk warned me not to leave my shoes unattended (thieves *and* rats). No wonder they called the place a hostel. I limited myself to the equivalent of twenty American dollars a day. As Jack London, John Reed, Nellie Bly, George Orwell, Henry Miller, and thousands of other journalists long before me had done, I wanted to descend to the bottom, but also come up for air to share the joys of everyday humanity.

In Buenos Aires, I hooked up with a pair of spirited Western Canadian girls (Linda and Carole) and the three of us formed an instant, exuberant trio. We crashed for five days in the shell of a house on a volcanic Brazilian island, Ilhabela. In Rio de Janeiro, we stayed in a rooming house in the Catete district, swimming at Ipanema beach and drinking *caipirinhas* (the Brazilian drink of lime, sugar, and *cachaça*, fermented sugar-cane juice). In Salvador da Bahia on Brazil's northeast coast, we took part in a Candomblé ceremony in a shack with a dirt floor where mild-mannered celebrants lapsed into trances and grunted other-worldly lamentations and exultations.

Of all of South America, Brazil resonated the clearest. Portuguese staggered me. In my limited grab bag of skills, language acquisition was one I seemed to have in decent supply. Years of classes and my exchange stay in Chile had provided me with a foundation in Spanish, but outside of a host of cognates, Spanish and Portuguese are wildly different. They may have started out as siblings, but after centuries of separation both had embarked on their own distinct journeys. At first listen, Portuguese sounds as though it had originated somewhere in Transylvania, surrounded by impassable Carpathian mountains. The language sounds faintly Slavic. Unlike Spanish, Portuguese comes forth from deep within the recesses of the larynx. Speakers sound like ventriloquists, hardly moving their lips, bubbles of speech materializing in midair seemingly from nowhere.

Brazil energized me (the coffee probably had something to do with that). The country embraced in equal measure African spiritualism, Catholicism, and evangelicalism; savage capitalism and heart-aching poverty; lilting Bossa Nova, sexual samba, and squeaky choro. No place seemed without lilting melody or song. Music was everywhere. Brazilian skin could be black as onyx or as white as a South Sea pearl, with millions of gradations in between, and every shade seemed to be celebrated. The nation's two megalopolises were polar opposites: laid-back, promiscuous Rio and go-go, business-centric, vertical São Paulo. Working in Brazil as a newspaper journalist would be hallucinogenic.

Even before I had learned about the coming *Latin America Daily Post* in Giovanni's breakroom, I knew that Brazil had been the home to a quirky English-language newspaper that in some ways had rivaled Paris's old trio of English-language newspapers, the *Tribune, Herald*, and *Times*. Founded in 1946 in Rio de Janeiro and called the *Brazil Herald*, the expat newspaper held the distinction of being the last surviving of an assortment of English-language newspapers published in starts and fits in Brazil since 1828. By the time I had arrived in Rio with the Canadian girls, the *Brazil Herald* had fallen on hard times, a *de facto* ad sheet of American baseball and British soccer scores, massage-parlor ads, and, if anyone cared, day-old headlines. With the brand-new *Latin America Daily Post*, the faded *Brazil Herald* would be getting some competition.

In its earlier incarnations, the *Herald* had carved out a rogue pedigree. The newspaper had been the starting gate for scores of reporters who would go on to become megastars. Besides Hunter S. Thompson, Tad Szulc had once worked at the *Herald*. Polish-born, dressed in white linen suits (like Tom Wolfe's), puffing on an African-tusk ivory cigarette holder, Szulc had broken news of the Bay of Pigs affair on the pages of *The New York Times* in 1961. Other journalists who'd taken the leap to Brazil and the pages of the *Brazil Herald* included Edwina Hecht, daughter of famed screenwriter Ben Hecht (half the writing team that produced *The Front Page*, the best play ever written about newspapers); Eric Hippeau, who would become the CEO of the *Huffington Post*; and Don Shannon, who would cover John F. Kennedy's presidential campaign for the *Los Angeles Times*. Much of the AP and UPI Latin America staff got its start at the *Brazil Herald*.

But that was a lifetime ago. Soon the *Latin America Daily Post* was set to knock the wobbly *Brazil Herald* off its precarious perch. A newspaper war in an unlikely place, in Brazil, between two English-language dailies: an upstart broadsheet challenging a three-decades-old rag fallen on hard times.

Back at the potter's studio, I pushed aside last night's tip haul and wrote the executive editor of the *Latin America Daily Post*, offering up my services. Whatever it took, as long as I could work for the new newspaper. No way would I pull a stunt like what I had done in Janet Chusmir's office. I carried a thick manila envelope (clips included) to the post office, bought an assortment of colorful, high-denomination stamps, and pushed my entreaty down the mail slot. A positive omen that afternoon was that between the lunch and dinner shifts, Bill Tau's betting wheel paid on three longshots at Golden Gate Fields, each of us netting $280.

Three weeks later, after my evening shift, waiting for me on at the Hillegass Avenue potter's studio was a response from the *Daily Post*'s top editor, Steve Yolen. He answered each of my succeeding typed aerograms, and by the fourth exchange, Yolen had assured me that as soon as I could get myself to São Paulo, I'd be the first hired at the newspaper. "Your clips are very stimulating, and your experience is quite extensive—I'd be very happy to have you on the *Latin America Daily Post* staff," Yolen wrote, a line that I must have read fifty times.

Finally, a newspaper job, even if it was halfway around the world.

The Canadian girls were happily back ensconced in Saskatchewan, I was tired of waiting for editors to call back once their next year's budget was approved, and no further betting wheels had paid off at Golden Gate Fields. Roger, Sue, Kathy, and Roy, my staples at Giovanni, would become four characters in search of another author.

I came up with a pie-in-the-sky list of story ideas that I'd start on as soon as I arrived in Brazil: clandestine Amazon rubber factories; cotton-growing colonies founded by Confederate diehards; hopscotching Nazis on the run; generals whose pockets were lined with greenbacks; Rio's mirrors-everywhere cult of beauty. Those were for openers. I took my marching orders from George Orwell, who supposedly defined journalism this way: "Printing what someone else does not want printed. Everything else is public relations." I was on a mission. Everything was fair game. I had an entire country to write about.

To be hired at the *Daily Post*, Yolen, the executive editor, advised that I'd need a Brazilian work visa. This would be tricky, he counseled. Because of the vagaries of Brazilian labor laws, I'd first have to get a US news organization to "sponsor" me, even though I'd be working full time for a Brazilian company (the *Daily Post* was a wholly Brazilian-owned entity). I took out another classified ad in *Editor and Publisher*, this time offering my services as a freelance foreign correspondent in South America, and got a bite from a Chicago-based supplementary wire, the Field News Service, which expressed interest in taking me on as a roving correspondent. Field promised no salary or retainer, but would pay me a to-be-determined fee per article. The news service had nothing to lose; it would have an unsalaried reporter who'd contribute stories on spec. A letter on Field letterhead would cut through Brazilian red tape to get me the required work visa.

Next, I needed to learn the fundamentals of Portuguese, the ventriloquist's language I'd gotten an earful of when I had traveled in Brazil with the Canadians. I'd be doing most of my on-the-job interviewing in Portuguese, and I'd need to become, at the least, proficient. That was for starters.

I enrolled in a ten-week, five-day-a-week, five-hour-a-day crash course at Berkeley. I teamed up with Jane, a woman I met while working at Giovanni when she came in with two Brazilians and got seated in my section. We took turns cooking Brazilian dinners while listening to Gal Costa, Gilberto Gil, Maria Bethânia, Milton Nascimento (his 1976 record, *Milton,* was amazing!) and Chico Buarque, Brazilian rock stars.. We played Scrabble in Portuguese. We labeled everything in the potter's studio in Portuguese: lamp, *lustre;* desk, *mesa;* stove, *fogão;* window, *janela;* bed, *cama.* We spoke only Portuguese; our degree of fluency improved bountifully with each bottle of Brazilian beer we drank. Certain words were impossible to pronounce, sober or drunk. *Avó* meant grandmother and *avô* meant grandfather. How could a non-native speaker ever get any of it right?

I quit my job at Giovanni, even though the waiters in the betting-wheel consortium strongly advised against it. One, Jimmy, wanted me to move to Reno, where he'd been hired as the maître d' at a high-end casino restaurant and assured me a job. When I told Jimmy and the others where I would be going, they looked at me like I was nuts.

I sold my VW bug, all my warm clothes, my bed and mattress, the Parsons table I'd refinished and used as a writing and tip-counting desk, and a brass Moderne lamp that had served as a personal torch ever since my college days. I saved a dozen books that I couldn't bear to part with and hauled the rest to Moe's, the second-hand bookstore on Telegraph Avenue. Cashing out never gave you what trade-in credit allowed, but if things went my way, I hoped there'd never again be an opportunity for trade-in credit. From the proceeds of a yard sale, I bought a slimline Olivetti Lettera 32 portable typewriter and a one-way plane ticket.

While Steve Yolen had promised me that I'd be the first hired as soon as the paper had a vacancy, that meant I could be on my own for weeks, possibly months. That I took Yolen's assurances now seems naïve, but I had already made the decision to move. I'd need to find a cheap hotel or rooming house near the newspaper. Any savings I had from my job at Giovanni was long gone, so I'd need to pitch stories to Field News Service to cover rent and food as soon as I got to São Paulo. All of this lay squarely in the category of ultra-high risk. That I'd be moving to Brazil was a leap of faith, based on promises from a faceless editor of a yet-to-be-published newspaper thousands of miles away.

A day before I was to leave the US, Jennie Buckner, the features editor from the *San Jose Mercury News*, called.

"Still interested in working for us?" she asked rather coquettishly.

This was my best and last chance to back out of the Brazil deal. It was what I'd been waiting for. A job as a journalist, this one located in what would become celebrated Silicon Valley.

"Nope!" I answered with as much bravado as I could fake. "I'm going to Brazil to work at a brand-new newspaper, and I'm leaving tomorrow!"

Buckner sounded dubious. I imagined her rolling her eyes.

But I didn't care. I was saying goodbye to everything safe and familiar. I was on my way.

CHAPTER 3

Over the Moon

MY BARGAIN-BASEMENT PAN AM ticket secured me a seat in the center section of a packed 747. During the first four hours, two Brazilian women in their mid-thirties jabbered into the night, speaking in what I was to learn was an extreme Rio accent, the equivalent of Valley Girl talk. I had spoken Portuguese reasonably well in the crash course at Berkeley, even better during the beer-infused Portuguese-only dinners and Scrabble matches with Jane. But our teacher had instructed us in continental Portuguese, not its Brazilian equivalent. The difference was like learning British English in preparation for living in the States. The Brazilian women next to me sounded like they were gargling, speaking buzzingly fast, using slang that our instructor had never bothered with, probably didn't even know. Every one of the women's singsong sentences ended with "SA-be, SA-be," ("ya-know, ya-know"). I tried to follow their run-on monologues about ex-husbands, the suitcases full of clothes they were hauling back home, and the boutique (boo-TEEK-eh was how they pronounced it) they planned to open in Zona Sul, the beachside district south of downtown Rio. "SU-per" was a word they used often.

After a short flight from Rio to São Paulo, on the other side of customs, I stood outside Congonhas Airport in the dusky hours before sunrise and inhaled. Hot vaporous air swelled my nose. I felt as if I had entered a giant steam room. Breathe slowly. This would be my new home. For a year, maybe a lifetime.

25

After a stop-and-go bus ride downtown just as the sun rose, purple pollution haze settling over the lightening horizon chocked with sky-scrapers, I checked into the Hotel Central next to the cavernous main Post Office. My bible, the *South America Handbook*, had assured me that the "Cen-TRAL" was "clean and friendly. With showers." The last part sounded vaguely ominous, but I proceeded. I woke up a sleepy guy sprawled out on the front desk, who groggily led me to a musty room with a lumpy bed and a wrought-iron balcony facing Avenida São João, the city's principal thoroughfare. The stories this room could tell, although I wasn't sure I wanted to hear them. I opened the double doors to the balcony: exhaust belching from honking cars and trucks; bicycles slithering in and out of gridlock; hundreds, maybe thousands of pedestrians moving rhythmically to the staccato of jackhammers. I felt a little like a sash-festooned South American general looking out to a sea of subjects too busy to look up.

Across the street, I spotted a sticky-counter luncheonette, a sand-wich chalkboard out front announcing the day's special, *caldo verde* (creamy soup with kale) for the equivalent of one dollar. I sprinted between the stalled traffic, stood in line, and ordered the caldo and a Coke, which I knew to pronounce "CO-ca." All around me were tradesmen, tool belts girding bellies, hardhats resting on laps; some diners wore boots, others had on flipflops. Men slurping, burping, chewing, and snorting a jumble of words and sentences about whose meanings I didn't have a clue. I tore off a piece of bread from a crusty loaf and soaked it in the goopy soup. No one seemed to make me. Actually, no one seemed to notice me, even though I felt like a lit-up neon sign. The consequences of my actions, saying goodbye to America for a job that might or might not exist, would be mine and mine alone. It'd be either a rollicking adventure or a colossal failure. Nothing in between.

I got back to the Central and asked the comatose clerk if I could make a telephone call. He angled his chin at a gray phone the size of a suitcase.

After several tries, a loud, high-pitched, foreign-sounding dial tone came on the line. The phone made a series of mechanical dit-dit-dit sounds as the plastic dial slid back after each number. On the fifth ring, a woman answered what sounded like "Dilly Poscht-ie!" After several quizzical "eh's?" and more dit-dit-dits, I got transferred to Yolen.

The phoneline suddenly turned staticky. A parallel, crossed-line conversation seemed to be going on, something about shoes, doctors, a massage, or a domestic crisis of monumental importance.

"You there?" Yolen yelled over the chatter.

"Yes, but I can barely hear you!"

"Get yourself to the newspaper. I'll be here till eight, maybe later. You can walk from your hotel. You're maybe ten or twelve blocks away. If it takes more than twenty minutes, you're lost. Ask for directions. See you when you get here. *Tchau!*"

The only suit I owned was the one I had brought with me—a worsted wool plaid jacket and matching trousers. It was wrong on any day in tropical Brazil. But if there ever were cause for such a getup, today would be the day. I wasn't taking any chances.

I marked my route to the *Daily Post* on a page ripped from the *South America Handbook* and set out for 425 Barão de Limeira, housed on the third floor of the *Folha de São Paulo*, a local newspaper whose lobby walls were lined with millions of sparkling aquamarine square tiles.

"Welcome!" Yolen bellowed, hand outstretched. "Good to meet you! Finally!"

Yolen was a compact man in his mid-thirties with a mustache, aviator glasses, and plastered-down auburn hair that flew up at the ends, a casualty of the stratospheric humidity. He had on a white short-sleeve shirt and khaki pants. He immediately insisted that I take off my jacket. "Loosen your tie," Yolen said, scanning my clothes. "You won't need *that* around here."

I noticed three or four reporters eying me as they hunched over manual Royals, pecking at the keys. Yolen took me on a tour of the newsroom: managing editor Ed Taylor in a lime-green guayabera; pipe-smoking, bush-bearded foreign news editor Stan Lehman; fair-skinned feature writer Moyra Ashford, who resembled French actress Simone Signoret; intense Natalie Wood lookalike Karen Lowe, with smoke seemingly spouting from both ears; a string bean business reporter named Eduardo Gentil, a double for Clark Kent. Next were the copyeditors: Alma from the Falkland Islands, sounding as though she'd just inhaled a balloon of helium; and Melva, a tidy woman with half-frame reading glasses hanging from her neck, who informed me with a giggle that she was from "a wee tiny, teeny spit of a town south of Lincolnshire."

Then, suddenly, everything stopped.

A tall, hard-coiffed woman appeared, a spotlight seemingly announcing her presence. Jo Ann Hein, the society correspondent, had arrived, dressed in a canary-yellow bolero jacket, matching pencil skirt, and lemony stilts for heels. Her fingernails were polished shiny pink. Thin, bony, and angular, somewhere between thirty and sixty, it was hard to tell. She looked like June Cleaver on speed.

"Well, hiiii," she purred like a lost kitten.

Everyone looked up, then resumed working without saying a word.

Until a job opened up, Yolen said he'd pay me out of his pocket to write freelance articles for a business journal and to translate editorials from the local newspapers to be reprinted in the *Daily Post*. As soon as someone quit or the publisher coughed up some money, "you'll get the first job," Yolen promised. "We're still feeling our way around. Give us some time." I took this to be either encouraging or alarming. I wasn't sure which.

I celebrated that evening with a beer and cheeseburger (pronounced chiz-BUR-ghur) at the sticky counter across from the Central. I showed up for work the next day, *Novo Michaelis Português-Inglês* dictionary in hand, and started translating formal Portuguese sentences that went on forever. Yolen connected me with a peculiar but otherwise congenial expat journalist in São Paulo who threw some freelance work my way. John Thrall, who played in a bluegrass band with Yolen, edited and owned in part a local computer magazine, *Data News*, for which I would write several articles.

By the end of the week, in preparation for getting hired at the *Daily Post*, Yolen had set me up with a taciturn, enigmatic man dressed in a navy blue double-breasted suit; he looked a lot like Humphrey Bogart. We met in front of the Post Office, next to the Central. I never got his name, but Yolen instructed me to follow him wherever he went. "Don't ask questions. Do exactly as he says. He knows his business. Trust him. Trust me."

Bogie was a *despachante* (roughly, a "dispatcher"), who performs the combined tasks of an immigration attorney, red-tape cutter, and government bureaucrat palm greaser. He was my introduction to the Byzantine world of Brazilian bureaucracy. After standing in front of a black cloth-draped photographer behind a massive Edisonian apparatus to have my photograph taken with an exploding flash bulb, he shepherded me to get a chest x-ray on another antique machine that surely emitted giga doses of roentgens. Next, I got my fingertips rolled and printed to check my criminal history in Brazil (nothing yet). Bogie instructed me to wait in a series of winding queues at a succession of windowless interior government offices, only to be shown to the front of each line after he'd look my way, arch his eyebrows, and motion me forward with a flapping two-finger wave. I felt embarrassed, although no one in front or behind me seemed put off in the least. On the contrary, they appeared pleased that someone, anyone, was getting somewhere in this endless series of serpentine lines that were forever stalled. Bogie carried with him a passport-like book with my name, photograph, and fingerprints inside, and at each stop, yet another government clerk would stamp yet another page in the booklet with fanfare and a flourish, as though I'd just passed an examination of great rigor. By four in the afternoon, Bogie handed me the book full of official-looking signatures, a multitude of affixed chromatic stamps, and numerous blue-boxed formularies. I was to deliver it to Yolen the next morning for processing. My *carteira de identidade nacional* (Brazilian identity card) and work papers were now complete.

For lunch the following day, I went to the corner *lanchonete* with Stan, Moyra, Karen, and Eduardo. Neither Yolen nor Taylor joined us—they were management after all. Someone mentioned something about a newspaper strike or walkout, I wasn't sure which, but no one seemed to want to talk about it. Stan shook his head and winced. It seemed like a sore subject. Lunch was a *misto quente* (grilled ham-and-cheese); *coxa* (breaded chicken thigh); *kibe* (brown-crusted ball of bulgur wheat); *pastel de queijo* (greasy fried cheese-filled wonton); or a *filet* (a grilled slab of beef). For dessert, we all drank *cafezinhos* (syrupy sugary espressos).

Just as we were about to go back to the newspaper, Ed Taylor walked in and sat down at the far end of the counter. Not a word was spoken, just an icy heads-up nod. I noticed Stan clenching his fists. I chalked up the exchange to internal newspaper politics, but about what I wasn't sure.

Back in the newsroom, the Brazilians had no clue how to pronounce my name. Every syllable in Portuguese is vocalized, so Steve came out sounding more like Eh-SCHTEE-vey, pronounced with the authority that Eh-SCHTEE-vey in no way could possibly ever confer. I took this as confirmation that I had descended into a wholly foreign universe. The simplest, most monosyllabic American name altered at its very core.

My first bit of business apart from the newspaper was getting out of the Hotel Central—too noisy and sleazy. No surprise, it was a hot-sheets place, no matter what the *South America Handbook* had advised. After ten at night, Avenida São João was wall-to-wall hookers: women, men, and multitudinous variations in between. Stan, the foreign editor, who had grown up in Caracas and had for a time driven a taxicab in New York City, suggested a *pensão* in the Pinheiros neighborhood, around the corner from where he lived with his wife and infant daughter, on Rua Artur de Azevedo. "I don't know much about the place, but I think they rent rooms upstairs," he said between blue-gray pipe-smoke exhalations. "Downstairs is a restaurant that serves *feijoada* (a black bean and meat stew, Brazil's national dish). It gets pretty noisy, but only on Saturdays. The rooms can't be very expensive. I'll take you there."

The pension was three blocks from a bus stop on Avenida Rebouças, a thirty-minute ride to the newspaper. A room with a bed and desk would cost me the equivalent of seventy-five American dollars a month. I could handle that. I shook hands with Ronaldo, the landlord, and the next day moved in.

By mid-October of 1979, three weeks after I'd arrived, Yolen had come through, hiring me to write feature and news stories, as well as edit the two-page business section (Eduardo had quit to go to NYU business school). The only thing I knew about finance came from working in my father's shoe store and listening to Murray. But the learning curve wasn't steep. I had my pick of hundreds of business-wire stories, many of them smartly written and already edited. I got to write headlines, lay out a daily business section with the help of two paste-up guys who didn't speak a word of English. All of it amounted to a crash course in Portuguese, business, and putting out a newspaper Brazil-style.

I was over the moon. I was working as a journalist.

Finally.

CHAPTER 4

The Operation

THE *DAILY POST*'s page-one, above-the-fold motto—"Latin America's Only Multi-Regional Newspaper"—was more than a little exaggeration. Aspirational, but nowhere close to reality. Beaming satellite images of newspaper pages to printing presses throughout an enormous and fractured Third World continent like South America, and then delivering a daily product in a several-hour window the next day before sunup through traffic-clogged city streets proved totally unworkable. Those plans, for the moment, had been put on hold. It was enough just to get the newspaper printed and delivered to newsstands in São Paulo and to put a thousand copies on a bus to Rio de Janeiro three hundred miles away before sunrise.

Despite any delivery snafus, the *Daily Post* was surprisingly solid and professional, if not a little thin, twelve to sixteen pages. It shared an uncanny resemblance to Paris's *International Herald Tribune* with one at-first-glance difference: the newsprint, which was thick and porous, seemed to turn yellow and brittle in a couple of days. The *Daily Post* ran UPI wire copy, box scores of last night's Major League Baseball games, closing prices of select New York Stock Exchange corporations, along with syndicated editorial cartoons, political columns and crossword puzzles next to recycled Peanuts strips, Dear Abby, and year-old Charles Goren bridge columns.

Fifteen reporters and editors toiled on manual typewriters in various degrees of disrepair atop makeshift desks fashioned from orange crates. As with any assembly of reporters anywhere, there was no small

33

amount of grousing and hushed conversations about assignments, salaries, the huge bonuses management was supposedly pulling in, the
need for a union and collective bargaining, as well as speculation on
whose marriage was failing and the significance of any two people of
the opposite sex going out to lunch together more than twice. Those
on the copy desk took immense pleasure in all forms of lexicography,
vigorously debating and adjudicating homonyms and homophones
that came their way. At 10 p.m., the presses downstairs started rolling,
causing the floor to vibrate. It felt like a rolling California earthquake,
one that I grew to anticipate and appreciate. "That's the press, baby.
The press. And there's nothing you can do about it," as the real Bogie
intoned in *Deadline U.S.A.*

The newsroom was a teetering two-language tower of Babel, its
denizens alternating between Portuguese and English, English and
Portuguese, laughing and arguing, increasingly frustrated in the rising
tropical heat of the day as we approached deadline. The typesetting
computers the newspaper used split syllables per the Portuguese, not
English, so a word like game would get hyphenated to ga-me, plate
would come out pla-te. Editors read voluminous rolls of wire copy,
chose and edited stories, and then oversaw the newspaper's layout with
the help of a dozen highly caffeinated paste-up guys, each armed with
an X-ACTO knife wielded like a switchblade. You learned not to mess
with the paste-up dudes, especially during deadline. They had no clue
what the stories and headlines meant that they so assuredly affixed with
wax to page dummies laid out on glass-and-wood tables with tilted
tops. It made for a landmine of glorious typos, including this headline:

Peace Corpse
Volunteer
Found Alive

A dozen correspondents sent in dispatches from Buenos Aires,
Bogotá, Santiago, Mexico City, and Washington, DC. about upcoming
economic summits, thwarted coups, impending outbreaks of cholera

and meningitis. All possible global crises were bannered on page one. The newspaper's daily editorial page trumpeted multilateral trade, unfettered capitalism, a free press and democracy (neither in practice in Brazil). São Paulo's and Rio's multitude of cultural and entertainment offerings were on full display. If the paper were ever short on copy, Jo Ann Hein, the banana-peel-dressed society editor, filled its back pages with mind-numbing minutiae about consular luncheons ("bananas flambé and hand-cranked vanilla ice cream was served for dessert!"), executive-business soirees ("Mrs. Quincy Taft wore a shimmering chiffon gown!"), and chic hippodromic galas ("the odds-on favorite, Passing Wind, finished dead last!"). Hein covered fashion shows, housewives' cooking lessons, Easter egg rolls, Sunday yacht regattas, and any other event that brought together wealthy American and British expatriates. If any real news ever happened at these alcohol-saturated outings, the newspaper would be sunk.

Every morning, Steve Yolen would stride into the newsroom, rapping his knuckles on the first desk as a kind of starting bell. By noon, Stan Lehman would vanish into a plume of pipe smoke as he unraveled rolls and rolls of blue-ink overnight wire copy. Meanwhile, managing editor Ed Taylor wore a sour, exasperated expression, a visage that seemed to suit him. In Portuguese, Ed was pronounced "edgy." Throughout the day, the paste-up guys bet their salaries on a citywide numbers game called *jogo de bicho*. Throughout the days, teenage runners with fistfuls of cruzeiros would sprint through the newsroom to pick up bets and deliver payoffs (hardly ever the latter). At four in the afternoon, a gnomish lady with white hair and pink flipflops wheeled a cart into the newsroom with thermoses of hot milk and coffee for cafezinhos.

Even without nonstop shots of coffee, I'd have been energized. Every evening after leaving the Folha de São Paulo building, I took to ambulating downtown, walking through the Praça da Sé or Praça da República, two huge forested urban plazas with a rotating retinue of performers: silver-tongued bible thumpers; beggars, some with real, others with doctored, amputated limbs; troupes performing *capoeira*, the Brazilian-African ballet of wits and survival; vendors hawking everything from tube socks and a laundry detergent called Omo to AAA batteries and expandable plastic shoes that *grew* with the wearer ("engineered to last a lifetime!"). Shoeshine boys, each with a pine box and an inclined footprint on top, solicited *graças* (shines). They were virtuosos, snapping polishing cloths to a syncopated rhythm, signaling the end with a squeak at the heel that sounded like a plucked violin string. On particularly humid evenings, I'd duck into one of a dozen refrigerated movie palaces (the Marabá was my favorite). If the film were American, I'd try to match what came out of the actors' mouths with the Portuguese subtitles, a great way to brush up on *giria* (slang) as well as learn assorted cultural tags. When I saw *Manhattan*, the audience roared when Woody Allen put the tips of his thumb and index finger together to form a circle to signal A-OK, a gesture that in Brazil is the equivalent of flipping the bird.

I pushed deeper and deeper into different neighborhoods, going to *feiras* (open-air markets) selling gargantuan prickly fruits and live, clucking chickens ("*That's* the one I want!"). On streetcorners, Artful Dodgers gathered to compare notes. On several occasions, I got dragged into police line-ups when military cops would swoop into a praça and demand from any assembly of men whom they perceived as low-lifes our *documentos*. I'd be released with a huff and a sneer when I'd pull out of my pocket my carteira de identidade. Meanwhile, in neighborhood parks, *empregadas* (live-in maids) would be going hot and heavy with *porteiros* (apartment doormen) on wooden benches, unable or unwilling to find more discreet spots for their romantic assignations.

Week by week, I widened my circumference, taking pleasure whenever I got lost. Back at the pension, partying on the first floor went on till two or three in the morning, and not just on Saturdays, as Stan had advised. A rotund cook from Salvador da Bahia, Dona Luzanete, whose eight-year-old son, Massimo, had the run of the place, took a liking to me and put aside leftover bowls of feijoada or *cozido* (a vegetable and meat stew) for me. I got paid on the first of each month, and after the fifteenth, I'd have to watch my budget. I limited myself to one meal a day, so Dona Luzanete's offerings were welcomed. Once I got my footing and started freelancing for Field, my income would improve. At least, that was the plan.

The pension had its own acoustical personality, demonstrating how much Brazilians love to make music of any kind. Any object could serve as a worthy instrument—forks, spoons, knives, cups, bowls, plates, bottles—all of which, when in spirited contact with each other, made for rousing, combustible chords. To their accompaniment, there'd be singing, banging on tables, and hand-slapping on upside-down plastic buckets that served as makeshift conga drums. By midnight, just as the Tropic of Capricorn humidity had dropped and the city's smoggy haze ascended, the confluence of bop, sweat, cigarette and marijuana smoke, cheap perfume, *cerveja* (beer), and *cachaça* (the local firewater) was enough to entice three or four couples to push the tables and chairs aside to make room for an impromptu dancefloor. Approving men and women would stand in a circle, swaying and clapping, while others would be locked in embraces in darkened corners.

On occasion, I'd join in the festivities, even though I always felt like I had walked into a full-tilt party late. One Saturday, the festivities got so pitched that in the wee hours of the morning a very inebriated couple pushed open my door and tumbled onto my bed. When they realized the bed was otherwise occupied, they were kind enough to retreat to the hallway outside.

Another Saturday, just as the downstairs festivities were cranking up, Dona Luzanete's son, Massimo, banged on my door. "Eh-SCHTEE-vey," he yelled excitedly. "There's an American in the pensão! Downstairs! I heard him speak! What should I do?" Massimo sounded panicked.

"Bring him up," I shrugged.

Massimo returned with a sixteen-year-old boy from Pittsburgh on a two-week soccer-camp program in São Paulo. We nodded, shook hands, exchanged pleasantries. We had little in common. No matter. Massimo looked wide-eyed up at me, then at the other American, then back at me. Two Americans. In one place. At the same time. In his home. Talking in a jumbled, unintelligible language, presumably English. Right before him. Since we were both Americans, Massimo assumed that we likely knew each other, had mutual friends, and surely had relatives in common. At the very least, we ought to have embraced as fellow countrymen and raised a shot of cachaça to toast each other. It was an impromptu lesson in geo-personal politics, that is, the perception of how any two nationally affiliated persons occupying the same distant spot on the other side of the world *must* be connected or, if not, will presently become life-long best friends.

Most evenings, I'd go through a stack of local newspapers and magazines, scouring them for ideas big and small to pitch to Field News Service. For a break, I started reading a turgid Jorge Amado novel, *Capitães da Areia (Captains of the Sand)* in Portuguese about a band of street urchins; alongside the book, I kept a running list of Portuguese slang that I'd try to drop into my conversations. I had an enormous nation to learn about—its language, politics, economy, Iberian-African Third World culture, dictator-to-strongman-to-military-leader history, not to mention immense geography larger than the continental US and distinct, geo-ethnic customs.

One late evening the downstairs partiers got to rocking so loud that I couldn't ignore the racket any longer. I pushed aside the stack of unread newspapers and the Amado novel, pulled out my earplugs, and went down to investigate.

I immediately noticed an African-Brazilian woman in her early twenties with clear blue eyes and hair tied in a ponytail. A blue-eyed Black woman? It was an unusual combination; at least to me, it was. She had on a short denim skirt and white blouse tied in a knot at her navel. We smiled, a mutual invitation.

Her name was Anna Elena, and, like everyone else in Brazil, she was fascinated by mine.

"Eh-SCHTEE-vey!?" she asked, breaking into a smile.

When I nodded sheepishly, she asked in Portuguese, "You mean like Eh-SCHTEE-vey McQueenie, the actor?"

Yes, I said, having heard the comparison more than a few times. I could do worse, an opening I had no part in making.

Anna Elena was from the Northeast port city of Fortaleza. She worked in a beauty salon and hoped to make it as a beautician in São Paulo, where she was staying with an aunt for a two-week-long holiday. Two lonesome newcomers meeting by happenstance.

We had a hard time hearing each other, so I took her by the hand, and we found a stoop a block away, taking turns sipping from a bottle of Pitú cachaça, each of us struck by the prospect of connecting with a foreign-yet-kindred soul.

In front of us, a sliver of a quarter moon illuminated two mangy but otherwise likable dogs humping in the middle of Rua Artur de Azevedo.

"*Vai!*" I said, which means "Scat!"

When the cojoined canines continued to ignore me, Anna Elena let loose a string of Portuguese I was unable to follow, although I was sure it ended with an emphatic "*ow-wow!*"

"Don't you mean *bow-wow*?" I asked.

She most certainly did not. "De jeito nenhum!" (No way!), Anna Elena said, explaining that the sound dogs make doesn't resemble *bow-wow* at all. The closest human approximation was *ow-wow*. There was zero wiggle room in the matter. Anna Elena was absolutely certain.

At which point, we both cracked up, laughing so hard that we nearly doubled over. We couldn't stop howling. Two foreigners to a big city debating the vagaries of North and South American canine sounds. Anna Elena raised a palm toward me, and I gave her a robust high five back. I was pleased that high fives were as customary in Brazil as they are in the United States. A mutual and spontaneous transatlantic gesture of glee.

We waved goodbye to the amorous pooches and stumbled back towards the pension hand-in-hand. After a half a block, we left the uneven sidewalk in favor of the middle of the street. Anna Elena placed her hand on my elbow to steady herself, then bent down to unfasten her sandals to walk barefoot.

After that night, Anna Elena never returned to the pension, at least as far as I knew. That was the last time I saw her. She had talked about returning to Fortaleza to take care of a sick grandmother. Our one-time encounter had come and gone.

Whenever I'd venture downstairs the morning after these Saturday night blowouts, the pension's tabletops would still be wet, a dozen chairs would be turned upside down, empty Antarctica beer bottles would line the perimeter of the dance floor, and several pairs of women's shoes would be unaccountably piled in a corner.

I enjoyed a good time like anyone else, but I was trying to stay focused on why I'd packed up my life and moved eight thousand miles away: to work at a newspaper, to be a journalist, to descend into a wholly different cosmos and write about it. With a news angle dropped in for good measure, my job was to convert whatever I found remarkable into a compelling nonfiction story, as long as there was a prospective audience that could be enticed to be as fascinated as I was with the topic at hand. That was the goal of all good journalism, I figured: To prod a stranger into saying, "Wow!"

To get to the *Daily Post* newsroom every morning, I'd flag down a green-and-beige bus careening down Avenida Rebouças, three or four daredevils hanging onto open rear accordion doors, riding for free. Most buses didn't stop, already filled beyond capacity with passengers from faraway suburbs. When one deigned to stop, I'd step up, steadying myself as the bus lurched forward, angling sideways, pushing into a mass of humanity, enjoying the proximal comfort of strangers. As the driver accelerated, taking a corner wide, passengers would lose their balance in a wave that seismically moved front to back. A woman in her forties juggling two bags of groceries from Peg Pag (a supermarket chain, pronounced Peggy-Paggie), lost her footing, fell into me, and exclaimed, "*Nossa!*" (short for "Our Lady in Heaven!"). "These crazy drivers! They all think they're on the last lap of the Gran Prix, all of them Emerson Fittipaldis," referring to the Brazilian Formula 1 race car driver popular at the time.

The bus drivers generally raced through city streets, accelerating at breakneck speed wherever there was a half-block break in the snail's pace traffic. Maniacally flooring it was one of the few manifestations of power they had. The woman holding the grocery bags arched an indignant eyebrow at the bus driver up front, at the roustabouts hanging onto the rear doors, and finally at me, shaking her head and grimacing. A moment of solidarity forged between two straphangers.

As we passed a church near Largo do Arouche, everyone, including the driver and the guys on their rear-door joy ride, in unison bowed their heads in a spontaneous choreography, followed by the sign of the cross, somehow nary a hand entangled with another. It was such a natural, fluid motion that I almost joined them.

At the newspaper, Moyra, the British feature writer, and I began gravitating towards each other, which prompted the approving paste-up guys to give me the thumbs-up sign. The single mother of a toddler whose absentee father was a wannabe Reggae rock star, Moyra went out of her way to be as Brazilian as possible. Around her neck she wore a small black *figa*, an African-Brazilian amulet of a clenched fist. She had enrolled in an *escola da samba*, one of dozens of local dance troupes prepping for Carnival. She knew capoeira. She spoke flawless Portuguese (albeit with a British accent). Moyra had turned so Brazilian that she showed up late for everything. If she planned to meet me at four on a Saturday afternoon, she wouldn't appear till six. We took to seeing Werner Herzog films together at a local art cinema and sat through *Nosferatu: Phantom der Nacht* twice.

Avoiding the greasy spoon around the corner from the newspaper, we often chose a restaurant down the block run by a tall, moonfaced Chinese man. On a misty December midday, I ordered liver smothered in a tangle of onions, sprinkled with manioc flour. A shock treatment of nutrition wouldn't be bad for me. When the waiter served us cafezinhos, it was a reminder that we ought to get back to the newspaper. Yolen would be furious if we stayed out any longer. The back-page dummies were waiting for us to sign off on, then to be sent downstairs to the pressmen.

As a drizzle turned into sheets of rain, we ran down the sidewalk in a burst of energy. The downpour was enough to soak us to our skin. Suddenly, a sharp pain shot through my side, taking my breath away. I stopped and opened my mouth in an oval embouchure like the hapless soul in the Edvard Munch painting.

"Are you all right, Steve?" Moyra asked.

"Jeez, I dunno," I said, clutching my stomach, trying to catch my breath.

We walked back to the newspaper, drenched. Whatever the stitch was had disappeared.

Thirty minutes later, the pain returned. I reached for a nearby chair in the newsroom but nearly missed it when I sat. "Too much boom-boom, Eh-SCHTEE-vey," said Cashbox, one of the paste-up guys whose nickname came from either running full or empty on payday. I tried to regain my equilibrium, but the color had drained from my face.

Yolen looked my way. "I'll take care of your pages. Go home." I protested, but he insisted.

On the way to the pension, I stopped at the corner pharmacy where I had bought six pairs of earplugs to purchase a bottle of Pepto-Bismol and a roll of Tums.

I stripped off my clothes, crawled into bed, and promptly vomited near but not in the trash can. I slept in fifteen-minute shifts. Everything around me was moving. I blacked out. At least, I think I blacked out. Two, ten minutes, an hour, I wasn't sure.

Food poisoning. The moonfaced man at the restaurant. I had eaten liver, but liver of what?

A grenade had gone off in my stomach. I was gasping for breath. My head felt like it was about to explode.

What a way to die—wayward, forgotten American found dead in a Brazilian flophouse. A junior consular officer with better things to do would claim my body, fill out paperwork in triplicate, and send me home—wherever that was—in a government-issue aluminum casket. My father's advice proven right. I'd score an inside obit in the *Daily Post*, but only if it were a slow news day. I'd depart as stealthily as I had arrived.

I tried getting dressed but lost my balance and collapsed to the floor. I pulled a T-shirt over my head, and only after several attempts was able to put both legs into a pair of jeans. I got down the stairs to the first floor, almost colliding with a late-night couple grinding near the front door.

Where could I go? Moyra's house? Should I call Steve Yolen or Stan Lehman? It was way past midnight.

I put together enough Portuguese and hailed a taxi. "Há que ir al hospital o mais perto. Estou com dor de estômago" ("I've got to get to the nearest hospital. I have a stomach pain"), I croaked to the driver.

For all the cabbie knew, I'd been shot or stabbed: a confused, deranged man mumbling something in a foreign accent, clutching his stomach. This was right out of a bad French *policier*.

The taxi driver seemed primed for his part, whipping a U-turn and flooring it. I held onto the door handle with one hand and my pulsating side with the other. The driver slowed only at intersections. Brazilians don't heed red lights, especially at night—too dangerous, a *ladrão* might break in, point a gun at your head and rob, maybe kill, you. I had no idea where the driver was taking me. I did notice that we sped past a cemetery with banks of kerosene lamp-lit flower stalls serving the bereaved, hardly a salubrious sight given the circumstances.

We skidded to a stop in front of a small brick hospital on a street named Conselheiro Brotero. I gave the driver five crumpled five-cruzeiro notes with as much of an apology as I could muster. It was all I had.

"Vá com Deus!" ("May God be with you!"), he offered, driving into the night.

I turned the key to a bell at an iron gate, and presently a nurse wearing a crisp white uniform and cap greeted me. With hesitation, she helped me limp into an empty waiting room. After forty, sixty, ninety minutes,

I'd lost track, two white-coated interns, repeatedly poking at my inflamed stomach, reached a consensus: an inflamed appendix that had to come out *imediatamente*. My first thought was my grandmother's little brother, Edwin Prenzlauer, who had died of a burst appendix when he was nine. Family lore skipping a continent and a generation.

In the operating room the next morning, as a black rubber oxygen mask was about to be strapped to my face, a surgeon who resembled Raymond Massey in Dr. Kildare instructed me to count from one hundred down—"cem, noventa e nove, noventa e oito"—until I was out cold.

When I came to, I found myself in a sunlit room with a bank of windows. Reaching for my side, I felt a bulky bandage girding my lower torso. A pretty nurse came by and told me that everything had gone as planned. She asked if I wanted to call anyone, and when I nodded, she put her index finger to her lips and handed me a pen and a pad of paper. I scribbled a number and she dialed the *Daily Post*.

Moyra answered on the first ring, announcing in her proper English accent, "*Daily Post!*"

"Where have you been, Steve?" she remonstrated. "Everyone's been worried silly about you!"

By noon that day, Stan had gone to my room at the pension, and when no one answered, he had Ronaldo unlock the door.

I had disappeared!

Steve Yolen was about to call the police!

That evening, Moyra, Stan, Yolen, and one of the newspaper clerks, Margarida, came by my hospital room. Yolen carried a bouquet of flowers, which made him look silly, and he seemed to know it.

"Don't order the liver at the restaurant around the corner," I cracked. "It's a killer."

Everyone laughed, but before I could turn sappy at the outpouring, Stan said they had to get back to the newspaper to sign off on page proofs.

"Gotta put out a paper, you know," Yolen chimed in as Moyra kissed me on both cheeks, Brazilian style.

CHAPTER 5

Confederados

I RECOVERED WHILE staying with Moyra and her one-year-old son, Jubi. They graciously gave me the bedroom in their cottage at the end of a cul-de-sac in São Paulo's Villa Magdalena neighborhood. I protested, but Moyra would have it no other way. My surgery and three-day hospital stay were covered by Brazil's national health insurance. My only out-of-pocket expense was a sixty-cent phone bill for the call I'd made to the *Daily Post*. This was years before arthroscopic surgery was widely available, and I had a neatly stitched three-inch scar on the lower right side of my abdomen. At first, hobbling around Moyra's bungalow sent a galvanic charge through my body, but that began to subside after a week. I returned to the partier's pension, and with my serrated crease on the mend, I was able to get myself back to the newspaper, bandaged and tender. In a couple of weeks, I was sending story pitches to the Field News editors in Chicago. So far, they'd taken only one of my stories, about São Paulo's massive Bienal art exposition with a massive Daliesque series of installations that reminded me of Disneyland's Carousel of Progress but with the animatronic characters on acid.

While still in the Bay Area, before moving to Brazil, I'd been intrigued by a squib I'd read in L. M. Boyd's syndicated Sunday Grab Bag column in the *San Francisco Chronicle* about a community of expatriate Confederate soldiers and their families who had settled in a Brazilian town called Americana following the Civil War. They were proud Southerners; no way were they going to live under Yankee rule, so they set sail for Brazil, where slavery was legal at the time. The Brazilian government recruited these die-hard Confederates to bring their cotton-growing expertise south and start plantations.

By the time I got to Brazil, even though the American Civil War had been over for more than a century, Americana was still a stronghold of Dixie spirit. The tight-knit community of descendants of the original settlers still spoke an arcane variation of English from the American South circa 1865, sipped mint juleps on their bougainvillea-covered verandas, and had rotogravure photographs of Jefferson Davis hanging on their parlor walls.

At least, according to L. M. Boyd, they did.

The account *had* to be fiction, complete journalistic hype. But even if Americana, ninety miles northwest of São Paulo, had nothing to do with a long-lost tribe of wayward Confederates, getting myself there would have a salutary benefit: It'd give me a reprieve from the weekend blowouts at the pension.

When I told the ticket seller at the bus station my destination, I half hoped that he'd nod and smile. Maybe he'd recommend a restaurant that served fried chicken, grits, and pecan pie. Maybe he knew of a kudzu-hidden swimming hole there. But he said nothing, silently sliding my ticket through the half-oval opening at the bottom of the thick glass partition with nary a nod.

Two hours later, Americana didn't look anything like a Confederate outpost seven thousand miles south of Richmond. In the Americana bus terminal gift shop, I couldn't find a single Confederate decal or flag for sale. I walked the central plaza, up and down the grid of commercial streets, passing a Catholic church dedicated to Pope Pius XII. There was nothing reminiscent of the Old Confederacy anywhere. I'm not sure exactly what I was expecting, but downtown Americana was your typical midsized landlocked Brazilian city. The same tacky fluorescent-baked stores that sell cheap luggage, Naugahyde sofas, boom boxes, and vinyl records near any bus depot in the world were bunched together along Avenida Antônio Lobo, flanked by bored barkers doing their best to lure customers. There was zero presence of the Old South. Americana had turned into a total bust.

Before packing it all in, I poked my head into the first car of a three-car taxi queue, the sorry refuge of any out-of-town journalist. "I'm looking for the American community," I said to the driver, not expecting much.

He put down his newspaper and squinted my way.

"Eh?"

"Isn't there a community of American Confederates that live here?"

"Eh?"

"Confederates. Americans. Where do they live? Are there any here?"

That finally got the driver's attention. He flicked out the window a nub of a cigarette. "Os Confederados? Americanos?"

When I nodded, he responded, "Get in. I'll take you."

"Verdadeiro?" I asked. "Really?"

"You ought to go to Villa Jones to meet with the Jones family."

It was the first time I'd heard the name *Jones* spoken in Portuguese. The way the driver said it, Jones came out JOE-ness.

Within ten minutes, we were in front of a gate on the crest of a hilly street, Guilherme de Almeida. The cabbie pointed towards the terra cotta tile roof of a one-story house on the inside of a thick white-washed wall.

"Ring the doorbell. They'll answer it."

"Are you sure?"

"Absolutely. Ring the bell. You'll see."

I pressed the buzzer, not knowing who or what to expect, and soon a white-haired man with black metal-frame glasses appeared. My first impression was that Colonel Harland Sanders himself was standing in front of me. After I mumbled something in Portuguese about my being an American who had come to inquire about descendants of Confederate émigrés but wasn't sure whether this was the place, the man flashed a big, toothy grin.

47

"Well, yaw cum raht in. I'll git mah whife, and we'll set us down and have us a rail nahce vis-i-ta-shun."

SAY WHAT?

The man spoke an English that, while wholly fluent, came out fractured like nothing I'd ever heard before. It was part Portuguese accent and part molasses drawl that sounded like it came from deep within the bowels of Georgia, just north of where the gnat line begins in Macon. There was something all wrong about the words he spoke and how he strung them together, not to mention the man himself. He seemed like he could have been whisked from a hundred years earlier and somehow had been hurled into the present. His voice had a scratchy quality to it, as though it came from a Victrola spinning at the wrong speed.

In a mild state of shock, all I remember thinking was this:

Listen to how this man talks because you will never hear anything like it ever again.

He introduced himself as Jim Jones (pronounced just as the taxi driver had said, in two syllables, JOE-ness), and soon his wife, Judith MacKnight Jones, joined us, and then Mrs. Jones introduced me to *her* mother, Elizabeth MacKnight, a woman in a cotton-print dress with a mass of fine white hair gathered atop her head in a tidy bun. Mrs. MacKnight proudly told me that she was ninety-nine years old. She stopped there, waiting for my reaction, and when she got it, she beamed.

The four of us took seats in white wicker chairs on the veranda, three pairs of hands neatly folded on laps, three faces staring at me like I was from Mars.

"Yaw jus en tahm fer hour aftah-noon ahced-tee pahty," Judith said with a hiccup of a titter.

At any moment, I was expecting Rod Serling to step out from behind the yard's grove of magnolia trees and announce that I had just entered The Twilight Zone.

Judith handed me a frosty glass, garnished with a sprig of mint that, she pointed out, she had just picked from her garden "ovah yondah."

Fig. 5.1 Elizabeth MacKnight. Photograph by the author.

Her smile was so welcoming, so inviting, that I thought she surely must have known me, or my family, or at the very least, *of* my family. Why else would she be so hospitable to a stranger—a Yankee stranger, no less—who happened to show up unannounced on her doorstep?

For the next two hours, Judith (she pronounced it the Portuguese way, Ju-DIT-ah) and Jim talked in the same archaic, cadenced accents about their lives and the lives of their parents, grandparents, and great grandparents. All the while, I kept chiding myself for ever doubting the veracity of L. M. Boyd's Sunday Grab Bag column. I got the distinct impression that Jim, Judith, and Mrs. MacKnight had been waiting for someone like me to come by for quite some time.

"Oh, yes, sir-ree," Judith said, confirming that more than ninety Confederate descendants still lived in the area, and although none had been born in the United States and few had ever visited, almost all spoke the same anachronistic variant of English among themselves.

Their speech, I was to discover, was a linguistic phenomenon, a language spoken nowhere else in the world but in and around Americana and the adjacent municipality of Santa Bárbara d'Oeste. In recording how they spoke, I hesitated whether to relate it phonetically or to "fix" the dialect so it might be more easily understood. I chose the former, with apologies to readers for how challenging the below passages will be to follow, as well as to respect the authenticity of the language Judith and Jim used. In no way did I want to disparage the Joneses in doing so; the following passages were just the way I heard them.

That afternoon Judith related the Confederate colony's history as though I was the first to hear it. Immediately following the Civil War, Brazil was as much a land of opportunity for American Southerners as the United States would become for Europeans. Within five years, as many as twenty-five thousand Confederates emigrated to Brazil, a nation at the time twice the size of the United States. While the US had outlawed it in 1865, slavery remained intact in Brazil till 1888 and in effect in some remote areas for at least another decade. The Brazilian government, under the rule of Emperor Dom Pedro II, took out advertisements in US newspapers and sent representatives to the American South to persuade disgruntled and well-off white Southerners to live out their dreams in Brazil.

The Brazilians guaranteed the Confederates arable land at twenty-two cents an acre. Most of the Southern emigrants went to interior areas surrounding São Paulo, but several shiploads landed at the port of Rio de Janeiro and were so taken by the city's knock-out geography and profligate culture that they promptly assimilated and disappeared. At least one shipload docked in the Northeastern port of Belém, set sail down the Amazon River, and survived on berries and monkey meat, only to perish from malaria.[1] The sole community of Southern immigrants that survived past 1900 was the group that got to the place called Americana, which they chose because it reminded them of their home in Georgia.

The Joneses' story *seemed* to make sense, but my face likely betrayed me because when I said that I hadn't read much about this *Gone with the Wind* Camelot, Jim looked at me kind of pitifully, then stretched out his hands, palms up. The reason for my ig-nor-ahnce, as he put it, was because, "Ya'll's his-tah-ree buks don't whant ya'll Yan-keys tah know what hour brave Con-fed-a-rit ancestahs dihd. Dhat's dah reason! Doze ah Yan-keys who wroht doze buks—dint ya know dhat, Stephen? Ain't dhat right, Ju-dit-ah?"

Jim was dead serious about this literary conspiracy, even though at that moment I still held out the reasonable possibility that what I'd seen and heard thus far was an elaborate hoax and that I was being punked as though I had stepped into some future David Mamet play. Jim, though, was a true believer, a card-carrying member of the Sons of Confederate Veterans. That—or he'd spent too much time imbibing basement-distilled bourbon mash.

For her part, Judith nodded in a guardian-of-the-secrets way, which said she knew all there was to know about the Southern Migration after the War of Northern Aggression, including family names, dates of births and deaths, who owned which plots of land (and how many hectares each was), what each descendant did for a living, who slept with whom, and who wasn't worth a doodly damn, as Jim put it. Judith and Jim were keepers of a flickering flame—fliker-in' was what Jim said. "Whe're dah ox-ah-gin dhat keeps dah flame fruhm goin' out."

Right about this time, Judith's mother, Mrs. MacKnight, rose stiffly and got herself to the cushioned swing gently swaying on the veranda. Judith filled my glass with more iced tea, suhn tea she called it. She brought out a plate of soft white goat-cheese sandwiches cut in little triangles without the crusts, and as I sat there in this cocoon of Southern hospitality, I realized I had indeed stumbled upon the remnants of a lost battalion of Confederate soldiers who had never quite figured out that Appomattox was more than just a forgotten town in Virginia.

Judith pulled up her chair next to mine. I needed a history lesson, and by golly, she was going to deliver one. Those who left the American South after the Civil War had the most to lose by staying. Among the Confederates who set sail for Brazil's sandy shores were attorneys, architects, farmers, plantation owners, physicians, and businessmen, all fine men from fine families, she said. "I'll 'ave yaw know," all of them from families educated at some of the finest Southern institutions of higher learning. Jim here, Judith said with no small amount of pride, was a retired dentist, and one of "dah best dah folks of Americana evah 'ad," to which Jim dipped his head modestly, registering Judith's praise, but also to remind her that we don't go bragging about ourselves in these parts.

Our ancestors owned slaves, Judith said with more than a tincture of defiance, and "by Golly, day whas good tah dhose slaves." Then, I suppose anticipating some reaction from me, Jim added, "Now, don't yaw go makin' hour ancestahs out to be mean, not fer one secon'. Day treated dhem slaves as dough day was fam-e-lee." I surmised this had been a touchy subject that had come up before with other visitors.

The migration to Brazil, Judith said in a voice that had grown emphatic, was one of the largest exoduses in "dah his-to-ree of dah Younigh-ted States of Am-er-i-ca!"

Jim wasn't about to let his wife go on without putting in his two cents. After the War of Northern Aggression, leaving America for Brazil meant that thousands of Confederates could live with honor, something in dwindling supply to Southerners at the time. "It's even en Ghone Wit Dah Wind, dhat book dhat dhat Margarit Mit-shell 'rote 'bout dah wahr. Didja even know dhat dah O'Hara fam-e-lee thought o' leavin' Tarah fer Brasil? She menchons it twhice in dhat buk. Ju-dit-ah has it inshde," Jim said, peering at me like a preacher over the top half of his black-frame glasses.

We visited for another hour or so, trading stories, talking about President Jimmy Carter (their idol, who in several months would lose his reelection bid to Ronald Reagan) and whose wife Rosalynn's ancestors had been part of the Great Migration South. In 1972, then-Georgia Governor Carter had visited Americana and had posed for a photo with Jim. "'Ere, lemme git it and show yah."

Fig. 5.2 Jim Jones and President Jimmy Carter. Photograph courtesy of Jim and Judith Jones.

When I mentioned Reagan, Jim slapped his right knee and started chuckling. Judith seemed more focused on her mother, who by now was snoring on the veranda swing while holding onto a black cane with a knobby hand. Regarding Reagan, Jim flung forth a string of invectives I couldn't follow, which ended with, "Dhat dohg don't hunt! No, sir-ree!"

"Dog?" I asked.

"What dohg?"

"The one that doesn't hunt."

"Oh, dhat dohg! Dhat's an expreshon mah granpappy yoused to youse all dah tyme. Ray-gun fer Pres-i-dent? Whaz wrong with youse A-mer-i-cans? An act-tah fer Pres-i-dent? Howze an act-tah gonna be Pres-i-dent? Ain't dhat a good 'ne!"

When I pointed out that Carter, while not an actor, was a peanut farmer, Jim shot back with the fact that Carter was an engineer, a graduate of Annapolis, the Naval Academy, and had been elected governor of the great state of Georgia.

Reagan had been governor of an even larger state, California, I said, to which Jim laughed as though I had proven his point.

"Whaddayah espect? What whas 't dhat I red 'bout Cal-e-forn-e-ah? I red 't just dah othah dhey. Dhat Cal-e-forn-e-ah is dah 'and o' fruits 'n nuts? Dhat's 't! Dah 'and o' fruits 'n nuts. So, mah-be dhem Cal-e-forn-e-ahns, dhey deserve a guvnur like Ray-gun!"

Then, as though he himself had been the brunt of similar jokes and wanted to lay all of them to rest, Jim moved on to another Californian, this one, in Jim's mind, even shadier than Ronald Reagan. "Nowh, don't go gittin' me confhused with dhat crazy Jim Joe-ness," referring to the cult leader. "I got nutin' tah do wit dhat fellah. Nutin! He was no rela-chon to mah kin. Nahn at all. He whas a Yan-key!" Another practiced line, I'm sure, which led to more general knee slapping and guffaws.

I let the laughter settle down, but wanted to ask Jim and Judith about something that had been on my mind: Where were the original Confederate settlers and their families buried? They did not return home and had to have died in Brazil. Where were they?

I didn't want to sound too forward. No matter how warmly the Joneses had welcomed me, I still was a newcomer. A stranger asking Jim and Judith about the local cemetery might strike them as rude, something a Northerner might be expected to do. But there had to be a Confederate cemetery in Americana. If the Southern separatists had led their lives in Brazil so apart from everyone else, they surely would have wanted to be commemorated for eternity with other like-minded expatriates. Bodies, or at least tombstones, would be proof that I wasn't experiencing some post-appendectomy delirium. So, I asked.

Jim and Judith turned towards each other and nodded, then looked back my way.

"If yaw wanna go, we cahn," Judith started, "but we bettah 'urry or we'll nevah git to da campo beforh suhndown." She gently shook Mrs. MacKnight, who opened her eyes and presently rose, steadying her-self with the cane. "She gits awful turd 'bout dhis tyme a dey," Judith announced as the two padded into the house.

Judith, Jim, and I proceeded to a mud-splattered white Ford parked out front, with Jim driving, Judith in the passenger seat, and me in the back. We drove past the city limits and soon we were passing fields of tall, undulating green stalks. "Dhem dare's shu-gah cahne. Dhat's what 't is fer as fahr as yawl cahn see," Jim said, glancing back at me in the rearview mirror for a reaction.

Judith volunteered that when she went to the United States for the first time a decade earlier, she felt as though she'd just about gone to heaven. "Dees were mah re-lay-shons, but I'd nevah met 'em before, and nevah thought dhat I'd evah git tah meet 'em, and dhere dhey all were, all con-versin' like I 'ad just come 'n frum dah parlah tah git outtah dah aftahnoon suhn. Mah was 't evah sum-in!"

Our voices rose and fell as Jim steered the Ford around a series of potholes on roads that had gone from tar to loose gravel to dirt. He was probably going faster than he should have been, and as he sped to beat the sunset, miniature spinning tornados of red-clay dust swirled behind us. He took the first left, the third right, then another left, but I wasn't able to follow the rest, and instead tried to keep one eye on the car's odometer. After eleven miles, just as the sun was nearing the broad equinoctial horizon, we reached our destination.

"We ain't got much deylight 'eft, Stephen," Jim advised. "We bettah git ah move on dhit!" As the three of us made our way into the cemetery, I noticed that some of the headstones were cracked and crooked, pushed into the ground at oblique angles, which, with the crepuscular sun sinking, gave the graveyard a spooky, Halloween atmosphere. Added to that, almost all the faint engravings were etched in English. One after another, Americans with purpose and design who had ended up in a long-forgotten Brazilian cemetery.

It was while tiptoeing between two aboveground plots—Gibson Harris and his sister, Maglin Harris—when a mass of chilly air greeted us as though we just walked into a refrigerated vault, which prompted goosebumps on both my arms. Then, just as abruptly, the air turned warm and fetid. The unmistakable odor of decay made my nose twitch and before I could scratch it, I sneezed twice.

Fig. 5.3 Tombstone of John Henry Wheelock. Photograph by the author.

Jim and Judith were a full five strides ahead of me, but they must have felt the same seesaw in temperature. And the smell—how could they not have noticed it?

Past the Harris plots, several graves looked as though vandals had opened and ransacked them. The names and dates on some of the headstones (which totaled 440) were barely legible. Some were crusted with so much grime and discoloration that it seemed no amount of cleaning would be able to restore them.

Judith seemed on a mission, striding with purpose, and I soon found out why. She was headed for the tomb of her father—Mrs. MacKnight's husband, John Calvin MacKnight, who had died in 1932 at age forty-seven. Judith knelt down, and in a way that showed she had performed the same act of contrition many times before, pulled at errant weeds crowding the edges of her father's sepulcher.

"Yes, suh! Dhis 'ere's mah daddy. 'nd rhaht next tah 'im," she said, patting the soil, "is where mammah's gonnah be buried. And dhen Jim 'nd I, we'll be buried rhaht 'ere next to 'er. Aint dhat rhaht, Jim

Joe-ness?" who nodded in a way that was as equanimous as could be considering the subject at hand.

It was time to leave, and as we walked back to the Ford, savoring the purple-blue twilight sky descending over what Judith and Jim surely thought was sacred land, this time I felt no sudden temperature drop nor did I smell anything malodorous, but we didn't pass the Harris family plots. At the cemetery entrance stood a weathered obelisk with ninety-four names engraved on the base—the original Confederate families who had founded the Confederate colony a hundred and eleven years earlier. The twelve-foot tower was a scaled-down replica of the monument at Confederate President Jefferson Davis's birthplace in Todd County, Kentucky.

In the car, with Jim driving, the three of us conversing about this-that and whatnot, with Judith elaborating on the finer points, when all of a sudden Jim drove in and out of a pothole that must have been the size of a moon crater, and all of us went jiggly. I sank into the backseat's sprung springs, then shot upwards so far that my head banged against the Ford's ceiling liner.

"Sloooow dowhn, cowboyh!" Judith scolded her husband. "We ghot cum-pan-nee, Jim Joe-ness. Yaw'll raht back thare, Stephen?"

"Yes, mahm!" I replied, thoroughly enjoying the ride and unscripted thrills and chills.

As we sped past silhouettes of sugarcane with leaves that formed a canopy over the one-lane washboard road, I was transported to a world neither completely Brazilian nor American. Where exactly was I? What year was it? For a moment, I wasn't sure.

Halfway back to town, Judith mentioned that many of the descendants of the original Americana settlers had never gotten married and never had children, which may have accelerated the demise of the Confederate enclave. The sanctioned circle they socialized in was small and select, which in turn made it smaller and more select. "Yaw real-lee cud count 'em on yawr fingahs, on one 'and, mabe two." Many of the offspring of the original founders were brought up to be "ver-ee par-tic-u-larh" was how Judith put it. "We stayed amongst hourselves. Aftah all, 't's what bound all o' us to-gethah."

As a result, the core of Southern descendants dwindled from several thousand to what it became, fewer than a hundred. As they grew older, many children moved to the big city to launch their lives, and few returned. An example, Jim mentioned, was Rita Lee, a Brazilian mega popstar, descended from Confederates, distantly related to him.[2]

As we came into town, I noticed the names of many of the streets—Rua Cicero Jones, Rua Roberto Norris—were reminders of the influence of the long-ago settlers. Judith and Jim owned sixty acres of their ancestors' original estate, twenty of which had been developed and turned into a housing complex. On forty remaining acres, four blocks from their house, they raised water buffaloes.

Back home on Guilherme de Almeida, while Judith attended to Mrs. MacKnight, I wanted to get deeper into the issue of race, this being Brazil where there was so much intermarriage between Blacks and whites that few families could—or would—claim any degree of racial purity. The separatist Confederate community in that way seemed thoroughly anti-Brazilian.

Jim pulled no punches. "Nig-rahs," he said, wasn't the reason "at all fer hour ancestahs tah come 'ere." There were manifold motivations to leave America, but mostly, Jim said, it was for "one thang: op-'or-tune-a-tee."

"Yaw don't take no of-fense to dhat word, nig-rah, do yaw?" Jim asked as an afterthought. "We don't mean nutin' by 't. 'ats how mah gran pappy 'sed to call cah-lid folk, and 't's just what we call 'em. I know yawh don't use dhat word,' but yawh can't blame us. At least, I 'ope yawh don't. We nevah did live 'n dhe You-nigh-ed States, remembah."

I was enjoying the Joneses so much that I thought it impertinent to correct Jim's mea culpa. They had been such hospitable hosts, and I felt an immediate guilt for not saying anything. Maybe a precursor to what would be called white privilege.

Jim glanced down at his watch and said he'd better drive me downtown or I'd never catch the last bus back to São Paulo. Judith appeared on the veranda, and as Jim and I prepared to leave, she kissed me on both cheeks. "Yaw cum back 'ere enah-tyme yaw whant!"

When we arrived at the bus station, Jim let the Ford's engine run as he and I both got out. We faced each other and shook hands, but that didn't seem quite right, so we hugged the way Brazilian men do, in an *abraço*. "Don't yaw forget: Yaw ain't no strange-ah 'ere no morh. Yaw as close as fam-e-lee."

I didn't for a second doubt Jim's sincerity then or now, forty-four years later. Despite how different they were from me, Jim and Judith Jones (could they possibly have had more American names?) had served as genial yet unlikely greeters to my new home. In the United States, the three of us would have had little in common, like the American kid attending soccer camp whom Massimo had brought to my door. We likely never would have had occasion to even meet, let alone spend a cordial afternoon and evening together. But the Joneses had been as gracious as possible, certainly more than most Americans would have been to a wayward stranger materializing at their front door one Saturday afternoon. Maybe it was just Southern hospitality carried forth through three generations.

But I think it was more than that. I came to realize that the reason for Jim's and Judith's generosity of spirit—besides the fact that they were genuinely gracious and probably a touch lonely—was that, in some sense, they needed me. They reveled in their Confederate Americanness and, whenever they had the opportunity, they rejoiced in celebrating it, even if just for several hours welcoming a stranger.

Like the Jones's ancestors, I, too, had left the country of my birth for opportunity. But unlike Jim and Judith, from the moment I had stepped off the plane at Congonhas Airport, I *wanted* to blend into Brazil. When someone on the street asked me for the time or directions, I felt a sense of satisfaction. My attempt to go undetected had succeeded. I hadn't been made.

The Joneses, though, wanted to stick out, and were proud to do so. In a land of beige, brown, and black, with all shades in between, Jim and Judith prided themselves on their fair features, their white skin and blue eyes. That their community took such pains to preserve these physical characteristics, as well their Southern dialect, was further evidence that they had little interest in diluting their ersatz Gone-with-the-Wind culture. On paper, Jim and Judith were one hundred-percent Brazilian, born and raised, but they resolutely refused to be like everyone else. That would have given them no pleasure at all.

Then, a wild sci-fi vision overtook me. If I ended up staying in Brazil, living out the rest of my life there—marrying, having children, eventually dying in this faraway land—could my encounter with Judith and Jim Jones have become a harbinger of what a visitor in a hundred years might find if he or she happened onto *my* descendants? Could the Joneses have been the equivalent of my grandchildren or subsequent generations, talking to a curious stranger about how long, long ago, their ancestor had left America for the shores of vast and bountiful Brazil for the opportunity to get—what had it been?— *newspaper* work, whatever *that* was?

CHAPTER 6

Cidade Maravilhosa

FINALLY, A WOWZA of a story to pitch to the Field News editors in Chicago.

It took several takes to get it right on my Lettera 32, and the following Saturday, I got myself to the Reuters office near the Anhangabaú metro stop and asked the overnight Telex operator to wire my story. The editors liked the piece, and within days Field moved the story to its clients, including the *Los Angeles Times*, which printed it in the lower righthand corner of page one. The Confederates story was an oddball entry, a blot on the romantic notion central to the American cultural fabric that everyone around the globe wants to make the United States their home. No one *leaves* America. That, in part, was why it was news.

I was thrilled by the story's play, although my colleagues at the *Daily Post* didn't share that enthusiasm. Some were furious that I had written the piece at all, and its popularity back in the States didn't help matters. My account was lightweight and simplistic, an evergreen story that had already been reported all too often. It wasn't a trenchant analysis of the life-and-death issues confronting Brazil. Those were the stories that Americans needed to read about Brazil, not a retold puff piece that lionized racists.

Almost every reporter at the *Daily Post* was a stringer for some newspaper or magazine in the US or Britain with various side deals to contribute stories on spec, just as I had set up with Field, and in that sense, I posed a threat to them. I was their competition. My co-workers had a valid point about the Americana story, even though I had thoroughly enjoyed meeting the Joneses and trying to make some sense out of their lives, language, and a cemetery spun out of a Stephen King novel. But to many English-language journalists in Brazil, my piece was a superficial curio of the past. There was nothing cutting edge or new about either the Joneses or Americana. The story was a freakshow I had showcased, front and center, on the midway.

Unless they were business journalists or wire-service reporters, the mandate of most Third World foreign correspondents was to write about weighty, doctrinaire topics: soaring poverty and illiteracy, graft and corruption, International Monetary Fund vultures circling the quicksand economy, greedy multinationals monopolizing essential services and gouging those who needed such services the most, CIA meddling in another nation's affairs, deforestation, subtle and not-so-subtle forms of racism, genocide of indigenous Indians, human-rights abuses, the jailing of political opponents, divorce and the Catholic Church, abortion. The list went on and on. If you were a correspondent working in a developing nation like Brazil, breaking news of coups, earthquakes, plane crashes, train derailments, mega-fires, and sinking ferries were the stories your bosses and colleagues expected of you first. But between those parachute stories of death and destruction, serious journalism was the mandate. Per that algorithm, my piece on Americana was lightweight with zero gravitas.

Worse, I had squandered the limited number of stories the English-language press would absorb on Brazil. The American and British public's appetite for news from Brazil was finite, and I had just blown every newspaper's or magazine's monthly quota, maybe yearly quota. Worse, the more play my story got, the more editors would want to match it with similar soft, fuzzy features, which would do even more to undermine any attempt at so-called important journalism that came with a Brazil dateline. I was a novice interloper whose story had played to veteran correspondents' worst fears of a naïve newcomer among their ranks. I had broken the rules.

I weathered the criticism, copping a wide-eyed, new-guy-on-the-block response, pledging to write more significant pieces as I picked up speed.

I followed the Americana story with a more predictable, topical piece—Brazil's transition from a suffocating dictatorship to burgeoning democracy. That was more like it, but that piece didn't get nearly the play as my account on Americana had. For a geographically-challenged American audience that knew and cared little about Brazil, the Americana story had legs. It had struck a chord. That exercise in giving customers what they wanted—or might be convinced what they wanted if I could work the story right—turned into a lasting lesson for me.

Field didn't pay me much, seventy-five dollars, but the clip was the thing, despite any blowback I got. Moyra, Stan, and Steve Yolen generously chalked up my infraction to being a rookie.

Eight months into my São Paulo adventure, in early 1980, Yolen convened a staff meeting. Since when did Yolen show up for work in a jacket and tie? And why was Mauro Salles, the newspaper's pint-sized, slicked-back-hair absentee publisher, who looked like a 1940s movie mogul, in the newsroom?

With a helping hand from Yolen, Salles precariously climbed up onto the rickety copy desk, prompting raised eyebrows from Alma and Melva, and announced the news. Since Salles had bought the competition, the *Brazil Herald*, the longtime English-language six-day-a-week newspaper published in Rio de Janeiro, the *Daily Post* would be relocating to Rio to take over the *Herald's* newsroom, back shop, and printing presses. The two newspaper staffs would merge. The *Herald* would be converted into a daily insert of the *Daily Post* and would carry local staff-written feature news under its motto, "Brazil's Oldest English Language Daily." All of the *Daily Post's* editorial and business operations would be consolidated in Rio. It was a move to strengthen both newspapers. That at least was how Salles explained it.

As part of the merger, Yolen, Ed Taylor, and I would immediately be transferred to Rio; Stan, Moyra, and Jo Ann Hein would remain in São Paulo. Natalie Wood lookalike reporter Karen Lowe and her husband, the local UPI correspondent, were moving to Puerto Rico, so she wouldn't be affected by the merger.

There were hugs all around, but everyone knew the ax had fallen. Alma and Melva shrugged their shoulders; they'd surely be able to pick up translation or copyediting work locally. Melva squeezed in with the rest of the editorial staff for beers at the corner lanchonete that afternoon. To hell with proofing tomorrow's copy.

That weekend I took the bus to Rio to find a place to live. I splurged, paying for an *executivo* with reclining seats and a *rodo moça* (literarily, a "road girl") who passed out sealed cups of water, foil envelopes of peanuts, and cellophane-wrapped blankets to warm passengers from the frigid air conditioning. As I remembered from my previous trip with Linda and Carole, the Canadian girls, Rio was eyes-wide-open, coming-at-you gorgeous. The beaches stretched for miles. Gloria, Arpoador, Copacabana, Botafogo, Ipanema, Leblón, Barra. Beaux-Arts downtown Rio was bisected by an adjacent wide, majestic esplanade with stately Art Moderne and Art Deco buildings on either side. A clean, limpid breeze vitalized the city. No way could grimy São Paulo compare to what the locals called *Cidade Maravilhosa*.

I found an apartment at the end of a steep one-way street in a neighborhood called Laranjeiras, which means "orange groves." It backed up to Corcovado, the forested urban peak from which Christ the Redeemer, one of the New Seven Wonders of the World, blessed his minions, everyone, it seemed, including me, a Jewish guy from New Jersey.

PART TWO

CHAPTER 7

The Ark of the Southern Journalistic Covenant

EVEN THOUGH THE *Latin America Daily Post* was the newest newspaper on the block, I was to discover that English-language newspapers in Brazil pitched to expatriates were nothing new. The *Daily Post* was just the most recent of dozens of newspapers dating back more than one-hundred-and-fifty years. Little had been written about them and no one ever talked about them. I had stumbled upon an obscure but indisputable wrinkle in another country's history, a long-lost Ark of the Southern Journalistic Covenant.

Some of these long-defunct expat newspapers had been founded by fly-by-night flimflam operators hoping to tap into a slice of the emerging demographic of Americans and Brits who had forged a southern and across-the-pond route to Rio as adventurers, smugglers, naturalists, tourists, diplomats, maritime officers, medical practitioners, bankers, engineers, preachers, and wannabe entrepreneurs. When I picked up and moved to Brazil, I was hardly the first. I was just one in a cast of tens of thousands spread over two centuries. I was another variation of Jim and Judith Jones's long-lost Confederate relatives, only I hadn't moved to strike it rich in the cotton-growing business. I was to learn that I had joined a long line of journalists before me who had not left home just to jump the job queue, but because we wanted to satiate a mega dose of wanderlust. Exotic Brazil had been our vaunted destination.

Most of these English-language newspapers were short-lived ventures, lasting no more than a year or two. Others kept going for decades, for as long as their owner-editors could reap financial rewards and professional stardom from spreading news and opinion to far-away-from-home readers hankering to read all about it in English.

There were sound reasons for the proliferation of such newspapers. Ever since the "discovery" of Brazil by Portuguese explorer Pedro Álvares Cabral in 1500, the country's development and transformation from an agrarian to an industrialized economy was built on international investment. Brazil's emerging infrastructure—transportation, energy, water, finance, communication—was dependent on infusions of capital primarily from the United States, England, and, to a lesser extent, Portugal and France. Shepherding these investments came educated, well-off stewards, administrators, and professionals who sheltered themselves in walled-in enclaves. Like the Joneses' ancestors, these early expats started their own schools, churches, social clubs, hospitals, cemeteries—and newspapers.

Relocating to Brazil for these pioneers, however long they would stay, proved to be easier and more seamless than it had been for me when I moved to São Paulo in 1979. Nineteenth century luxury passenger steamers connected North America and Europe with regularity to Rio de Janeiro. Once in the capital city, life for monied expats was pampered and privileged, a world apart from the realities shared by most residents of a developing country. Most had servants, cooks, and chauffeurs. Before Brazil's emancipation, some had slaves.

During the second half of the 1800s, life in Rio was a far cry from the rugged Wild West that American settlers would experience during the same time period. While cultured, sophisticated Buenos Aires was known as "the Paris of South America," Rio would earn the sobriquet "the Marvelous City," and for many expats, the local social circuit was much more demanding than it had been back home: a full season of fashionable engagements, elegant dinners and parties, pampered outings to the nearby cooler countryside, then a first-cabin steamer home for the unbearable summer months of December and January (remember, the seasons are reversed in the Southern Hemisphere), which allowed for visits to stateside relatives and friends from Thanksgiving through the New Year. To the less fortunate, Rio could be a teeming, fetid, and primitive backwater outpost, but to wealthy foreigners, the city was glamorous and exhilarating, grand and providential. They could live staggeringly well in Rio or São Paulo. Fluttering *Daily Post* society columnist Jo Ann Hein, whom I had met during my first day at the newspaper, was just the latest chronicler of the in crowd of wealthy expats and what they did to while away their leisure hours.

That expansive sense of living large still happened for multinational executives platooned to Brazil when I moved to there in 1979, but certainly not for lowly journalists who had to budget every week what little they made.

More than a hundred years earlier, after word of mouth, the basic mode of information exchange was the printed word, and once settled in their new home, literate newcomers craved newspapers printed in a language they could understand to learn details of the events and causes they cared about. Judith and Jim Jones's Confederate ancestors were no exception. To serve their burgeoning community at least four English-language newspapers, *The Brazilian Immigrant, Brazilian Reflector, Brazilian World,* and *Emigration Reporter,* were founded in the late-1860s with varying degrees of longevity.[1] Newspapers were essential to conveying vital information, circulating commercial notices, relevant political happenings, news from back home and abroad, comings and goings within the expatriates' communities, a variety of opinion, and, of course, the constant mainstay, gossip. A thorough reading of a daily newspaper was a hard-to-break habit.

The first English-language newspaper in Brazil with any intent of regularity was the weekly *Rio Herald,* which started publishing on March 8, 1828, and lasted eighteen issues, the final one July 5, 1828. Its publisher, Thomas B. Hunt, was a well-to-do Brit; his newspaper was typeset and printed by Pierre Plancher, another immigrant, who a year before had published Brazil's first French-language newspaper, the *L'Indépendant,* serving the growing French immigrant community.[2] In a front-page, first-issue editorial note titled "To the Public," Hunt laid out the *Rio Herald*'s raison d'etre:

The benefits which have resulted to Europe and the United States of North America from the diffusion of useful information, by means of Public Journals, are so obvious; and the certainty that the same causes operating in Brasil will produce the same effects, induces us to undertake the publication of a weekly Journal in the English language. The receipts arising from such a publication cannot for some time be adequate to our labors; but from the indulgence and protection of an enlightened Public we hope much, especially when we see that the knowledge of the English language is becoming general in Brasil, and that its study now forms a prominent part of a liberal education.

Our pages will be open to communications upon every useful and scientific subject; but our attention will more particularly be directed to Politics, interesting foreign and domestic news, maritime intelligence, statistics, and instructive miscellaneous articles. No communications on religious controversial subjects, or those of an immoral tendency can be admitted.

Resolved are we are to establish our Journal upon independent principles, our pages will be at the disposition of all parties on political subjects so long as their communications are consistent with the true liberty of the press; but we reserve to ourselves the privilege of refusing the publication of any article by which that liberty would be violated.

Our Journal will be published every Saturday under the title of the Rio Herald, and from our own assiduous attention and unwearied efforts to make it respectable together with the assistance which we may derive from the communication of our friends, we trust that our publication will merit the support and protection of the Public.[3]

Hunt's newspaper was cheeky and irreverent, snarky and opinionated by today's standards. It carried a lively exchange of letters to the editor. It published poetry and travelogues. It regularly took to task the local press with formidable hauteur. The *Rio Herald* pulled no punches. Consider this broadside editor Hunt waged against another newspaper, the *Gazette*, published in the fifth issue of the *Herald*:

The Gazette, the servile and toad-eater of the late ministry, died an unnatural death; the natural end of all such low unprincipled periodicals, published for the express purpose of forcing down the throat of the nation ... whatever issued from the Government, whether unconsitucional [*sic*], unjust, or flagrantly infracting the established Laws was right, And why! Merely because it was an act of government—Such was the Gazette which on the appointment of the present administration, from innumerable natural causes, fell immediately into disrepute, and came to rather an untimely end, and was burnt in effigy by every true friend to his country, his Sovereign, and his constitutional liberty.[4]

Hunt's garrulous, pointed opinions were too harsh for the local press to sit by idly, particularly since he was a foreigner. He got into a contretemps with the editors of two Rio newspapers, the *Astrea* and the *Aurora*, who condemned his creation, in part, because of Hunt's nationality, which ultimately led to the *Herald*'s demise. In shuttering his newspaper, Hunt wrote:

[O]ur only fault is being foreigners, the *Aurora* raised the hue and cry, and the *Astrea* follows up the scent with the keenness of a blood-hound. We shall close this unpleasant subject with the sincere recommendation to the *Astrea* never again to let malice subvert her judgment or bias the equipoise of her scales, and above all never let her attempt to separate herself for a moment from her sister Goddess, without whom she cannot exist; and to the *Aurora* to invoke the assistance of truth and justice, and to remember that it is not the tragical exit of the Rio Herald that will strength her cause, that such an idea can only be the child of cowardice, or conscious error, her assertions and insinuations. . . .[5]

Not to be deterred, Hunt followed with another English-language newspaper, this one grandly titled *The Literary Intelligencer and Universal Gleaner*, "[d]evoted to News, Commerce, Manufacturing, General Literature," with offices down the street from the *Rio Herald*'s old operations. Befitting its mast, Hunt's second try at newspaper publishing produced an eclectic English-language journal with tracts on astronomy, glaciers on Montblanc, Italian hot springs, and coverage of an assortment of bizarre crimes and accidents.[6] To supplement *The Literary Intelligencer and Universal Gleaner*, Hunt published commercial guides in English and Portuguese that served suppliers importing goods into Brazil with pricing data of luxury items such as beeswax, codfish, cheese, cotton, American gin, Cephaelis ipecacuanha (a homeopathic elixir), olive oil, and writing paper.[7] Hunt would eventually become a press lord in Brazil, printing an assortment of newspapers and magazines, including the Brazilian Crown's own publications, women's magazines, and satirical tracts on politics.[8]

Another English-language newspaper, this one entirely business-centric, the *Rio Mercantile Journal*, started in 1847. Edited by Isey Levi, a British-born Jew who arrived in Rio in 1838, Isey first worked for the Portuguese-language business daily, *Jornal do Commercio*, but realized there was a market for US and British businessmen who didn't speak the local language and needed access to price tables of stocks, futures, and commodities.[9] Levi sold the *Rio Mercantile Journal* in 1856, at which point the paper changed its name to the *Rio Commercial Journal*.

The weekly *Anglo-Brazilian Times*, described under its mast as a "political, literary, and commercial newspaper" debuted on February 7, 1865, was edited by William Scully, an Irishman, with this pledge:

Taking up the Editorial pen for the first time in a new Country and plunged headlong into the sea of criticism, it behoves [*sic*] us as we make our first bow, to ask our readers to judge us kindly and to bear with our faults, failings and shortcomings in the outset of a new undertaking.

Readers, we crave your charity, critics we crave your blindness, and all be assured we will do our utmost to merit your kindness and deserve your support.

We intend this little sheet to be the means of conveying information, and as such, not open for political or personal discussions, although, on all occasions, we will insert Political articles that may convey interesting intelligence, whether from one side or the other. This is our salaám, we could say more only we fear to try your patience and it behoves [sic] us to look around when *girding up our loins* to start on, we hope, a prosperous and agreeable journey.[10]

Like much of the English-language press in Brazil, Scully's *Anglo-Brazilian Times* was beset by typos, the subject of a sympathetic and collegial note published overseas by the *New York Daily Herald*.

Criticism injurious to the Anglo-Brazilian Times are plentiful among the English speaking community of this place; but, as the French would say, 'What would you have, gentlemen?' It is a matter of considerable difficulty—greater difficulty than the uninitiated can possibly understand—to get out a number of the *New York Herald*, despite its efficient staff of writers of all kinds, compositors and proof-readers. What, then, must be the botheration of the man who has to write in English "stuff" (I use the printer's word) to be set up by Portuguese compositors, who do not understand one word of the language in which his 'copy' is written? Even when the compositor sets up type in his own language he is troubled with particular words, which can only be arrived at by the context. In a language where every letter must be known by itself, the difficulty is obviously increased a hundredfold.[11]

Despite the typographical blunders, Scully's paper proved to be a rousing success, lasting almost two decades. Scully's die-hard editorial cause was—no surprise—immigration. He championed mass European immigration to Brazil as a way to render Brazilian slavery obsolete, as well as an unapologetic fix to boost the nation's white population in a kind of reverse Great Replacement Theory, which right-wing ideologues more than one hundred and fifty years later would intone. "[W]ith the European immigrant comes progress, wealth, and empire; that he brings with him skill, knowledge, enterprise, and advanced ideas, and has full right to demand, as a condition of his advent, equal consideration with the children of the soil he attaches his fortunes unto," Scully editorialized.[12] The publisher advocated for "free workers," as Scully called emancipated Afro-Brazilian slaves, based on the rationale that they would be more productive since they'd be paid for their labor, and the increase in their productivity would, in turn, lead to greater wealth for merchants, industrialists, and landowners. The pay "free workers" would earn would create purchasing power, thereby expanding the national economy. Thus, everyone would benefit. Slavery, Scully wrote, perpetuated flat economic growth since slaves were separate and apart from the capitalist system of necessary growth and expansion. Further, he preached, slavery dampened the necessity for technological innovation, further thwarting economic development.[13]

Born during the potato famine in Tipperary, Scully arrived in Brazil in 1861, at first working as a calligrapher, later as a shipping clerk, then as the local representative for the National Bolivian Navigation Company. Like other editors of English-language newspapers in Brazil, he got into trouble for what he published. Scully was sentenced to three months in prison for libeling Rio de Janeiro's police chief, a sentence commuted by the Brazilian monarchy.[14] He eventually sold his newspaper to James M. Wright, a transplanted Baltimore entrepreneur, but Wright was unable to keep the publication going, and its last issue came out on September 24, 1884.[15]

Following the *Anglo-Brazilian Times,* the stridently anti-abolitionist *Brazilian World,* owned and edited by Memphis native J. H. Freligh, a Mississippi steamboat captain and friend of Confederacy president Jefferson Davis, began publishing weekly. In a letter in the *Memphis Daily Appeal,* titled *"A Memphian Abroad,"* Freligh swelled with pride as he waxed euphoric about the post-Civil War influx of American Southerners into Rio, ". . . [N]ow we have quite a show. Merchants, doctors, dentists, ferry owners, city transfer companies, etc., etc.—the Brazilians saying that the *Nord Americans* are smart in getting the thing that pays best."[16]

Four years later, on Christmas, a charismatic former priest and businessman, Charles F. de Vivaldi, started yet another English-language newspaper, this one titled *The American Mail,* which would later change its name to *The South American Mail.*[17] Vivaldi deserves more than a mention because his story, while unconventional and remarkable, reflects some of the imagination and grit of expats who moved to Brazil and started publishing newspapers.

Born Carlos Francisco Alberto Julio Lorenzo de Vivaldi in 1824 in Sardinia to an aristocratic family and ordained as a Catholic priest in Turin, Vivaldi turned to political agitation as a youth and was forced to flee the Italian state for France in 1848. From there, he sailed to North America, proselytizing Winnebago Indians in the Minnesota Territory. He renounced the priesthood, married Mary F. Meade, a wealthy Protestant widow, and then moved to Manhattan, Kansas, where he started a weekly newspaper, the *Western Kansas Express.* A staunch supporter of anti-slavery Union forces, Vivaldi joined the Kansas militia and became active in the then-emerging Republican Party, led by a tall, craggy-faced congressman from Illinois named Abraham Lincoln. After reneging on a series of loans and disappearing, some said by faking his own death, Vivaldi resurfaced in 1861 as the US consul general in, of all places, Santos, Brazil, having been appointed by newly elected President Lincoln. Vivaldi moved to Rio, where he started two Portuguese-language magazines, *Ilustração do Brasil* (1876-1880) and *Ilustração Popular* (1876-1877) edited by his daughter, Corinna. Both contained rotogravure photographs, at the time new to Brazil.[18] With success from the magazines, Vivaldi founded *The American Mail*. By 1882, he had left his wife, resumed the priesthood, and repaired to a Salesian monastery in Argentina's Chubut Province. After returning to the American Midwest to claim forty acres of land, Vivaldi traveled to California, then to the Vatican and Europe, where he died in a French convent in 1902.[19]

Along the way, Vivaldi sold *The South American Mail* to James Edwin Hewitt, a Brit who brought the revamped newspaper out under the reworked title, *The British and American Mail*.[20] In a note of introduction to readers, Hewitt published this august manifesto:

None can estimate more highly than ourselves the importance and responsibility of the Herculean task which we have this day undertaken. . . .

But, after mature consideration, we have decided to avail ourselves of the present opportunity to publish what our experience has taught us to believe is a great desideratum, viz: a good newspaper in the English language, a newspaper such as the merchants and residents of this city will feel they may send home to their correspondents and friends, a faithful representative of affairs in Brazil.

The newspaper, as it has passed to English hands, will of course be published as an English newspaper, as we wish to sail under no false colours. But, at the same time, we feel we can with all confidence appeal for the support of American residents, for, having early imbibed the advanced ideas of those who see in the independence of the great American nation a providential movement by which in its reaction upon the Old world Liberty rested upon broader based, and having further resided for several years in the United States, and known intimately how much Americans and English are at heart alike, we feel that our course will be such as they will approve. The slight modification which the newspaper will undergo in this respect is represented in the title which will henceforth be, *The British and American Mail.*[21]

Hewitt, a literary figure in his own right, capped his welcome this way: "The bark is launched, the die is cast, the Rubicon is crossed, and we are pledged to success, for a worthy task, well and faithfully performed, cannot fail the necessary encouragement."[22] He gave away the first two issues as an inducement to subscribe.

In addition to publishing *The British and American Mail*, Hewitt directed two English-language day schools in Rio; he also published the first English-language translation of *Os Lusíadas*, the Homeric poem written by Portugal's most famous poet, Luís Vaz de Camões, about Vasco da Gama's sea route to India. In his newspaper, Hewitt republished English-translated excerpts from *Os Lusíadas*, as well as his own poetry, along with a self-serving plug from American poet Henry Wadsworth Longfellow touting it. After a decade, Hewitt sold *The British and American Mail* to Oliver James, who changed the paper's name to the more manageable *The Rio Mail*.[23]

From the beginning, almost all of the English-language press in Brazil, in the best tradition of American and British journalism, served as an oppositional voice to whatever sanctions at the moment the Brazilian Monarchy was imposing, including tariffs, taxes, bureaucratic red tape, or press censorship. Because government censors had little or no command of any language other than Portuguese, these newspapers often escaped censorship, allowing them more freedom of expression than the national press.

By far the most famous of all English-language newspapers in Brazil was founded and operated by a starry-eyed renegade journalist who had left America to strike out on his own. Andrew Jackson Lamoureux published the inaugural issue of *The Rio News* on April 5, 1879, and quickly his newspaper caught on in American and British circles in the nation's capital. Lamoureux's paper was lively, literate, and progressive. It would become required reading for all Americans and Brits in Rio, as well as anyone in Brazil who could read English.

As I would learn, Lamoureux's bittersweet story would become inspirational and prescriptive for any American journalist with the temerity to move to far-away Brazil. His story, for better or for worse, could serve as a harbinger for my own.

CHAPTER 8

Not All Beer and Skittles

WHILE THE ECONOMIC imperative of *The Rio News* skewed to well-to-do Americans and Brits in Brazil, A. J. Lamoureux (as his byline read) used his sparkling, literate newspaper as a pulpit to preach the evils of slavery. This was by no means either a popular or profitable editorial stance since the readers and advertisers Lamoureux sought to attract were some of the same people who had the most to lose should slaves in Brazil ever be emancipated. Because of this dogged and deserved pursuit, Lamoureux's legacy ought to be secure, but his saga is one of anguish—a cautionary tale of adventure, daring, accomplishment, and, ultimately, despair, told through the backstory of a musty collection of thirty-three letters Lamoureux wrote to a life-long friend, which I happened to discover in the hermetically sealed recesses of a seldom-visited California archive seven thousand miles from their origin.

Lamoureux became a newspaper owner and editor during an era when journalists could be heroes—or villains—by printing tracts of uncomfortable truths. At the time, Lamoureux was part of a global network publishing news and commentary, not to make money, but because its members believed the public needed be informed and enlightened. Such activity was considered a subversive political act. It still is today.

An overview to put Lamoureux's courageous conte in context:

As noted, Brazil has always been a destination for expats looking to make their fortunes, and depending on the industry in which they were engaged, such fortunes historically were dependent, directly or indirectly, on the exploitation of African slaves. The discovery of gold, silver, diamonds, and other precious stones in the Portuguese colony's interior in the late 1600s created a lucrative international market for such commodities, extracted by slaves from mineshafts in the Brazilian state named *Minas Gerais* (General Mines). By 1819, the population of Brazil was 3.6 million, a staggering one-third of whom were enslaved men and women of African descent. The worldwide popularity of coffee, as well as sugar processed from sugar cane, dramatically increased slave trade to Brazil in need of laborers to harvest these profitable crops. Brazil's northeast coast at Salvador da Bahia, just eight hundred miles west of the horn of Northwestern Africa, made slave trafficking between the two continents particularly feasible. And following the American Civil War, the recruitment of American Confederates to Brazil, such as the Joneses' ancestors, further increased the exploitation of enslaved persons to cultivate another lucrative commodity that came from the ground—cotton.

Fig. 8.1 A. J. Lamoureux. From *The Lamoureux Record: A Study of the Lamoureux Family in America* (April 1939).

Full of enterprise and adventure, Andrew Jackson Lamoureux, Ajax as his friends called him, arrived from New York via steamer at the Port of Rio de Janeiro in the fall of 1877 when he was twenty-seven.[1] A descendant of French Huguenots, Lamoureux was born in Iosco, Michigan, on the shores of Lake Huron, the oldest of three brothers. He had been a capable undergraduate at newly founded Cornell University in Ithaca, New York, from 1870 to1874.[2] There, Lamoureux rowed crew, served as president of the First Boat Club, and was a member of Delta Upsilon fraternity, an organization of independently minded students opposed to what they called "aristocratic secret societies." The *Star-Gazette* in nearby Elmira wrote that bespectacled Lamoureux, with his trademark thick, drooping mustache, was "known during his undergraduate days for his fine literary abilities."[3] In 1873, he became editor of the *Cornell Era*, the student newspaper. But ill health forced stick-thin Lamoureux to leave the university before graduating.

The illness turned out to be non-ulcer dyspepsia, or general stomach pain, although the recurring ailment did not deter Lamoureux from plunging headfirst into newspaper work. He was smitten with journalism and became a reporter for the *Utica Morning Herald*, editor of the *Ithaca Herald* and *Weekly Ithacan*, followed by a position as associate editor of the *Chicago Advance* and assistant editor of *Rowell's American Newspaper Directory*. In 1876, Lamoureux moved to New York to take a job as associate editor of the *New Century*, a short-lived progressive literary journal.[4]

The next year, Lamoureux sailed to Brazil on a packet steamer, first working as a clerk in the US Legation in Rio, during which he also was a parttime correspondent for the *New York Evening Post* and *New York Tribune*. Three months later, he got hired as editor of *The British and American Mail*, and within a year ended up borrowing enough money to buy the newspaper and changed its name to *The Rio News*.[5]

In a welcome to readers, Lamoureux showcased both his commitment and personality:

There is a time-honored custom among newspaper makers and newspapers readers which requires that the opening and closing of a journal's life, its purposes and results, shall be accorded the honors of a public reception. The Rio News seeks no such honor. It comes into existence in obedience to a recognized necessity; when that necessity no longer exists, should that time ever come, it will discontinue publication. In the meantime, its patrons may feel assured that its work will be done impersonally and conscientiously on the part of its conductors, and with all the thoroughness which its means and surroundiugs [sic] will admit.[6]

For a brief time, a revitalized version of *The British and American Mail*, now shortened to *The American Mail*, and Lamoureux's *Rio News* went head to head in an out-and-out English-language-newspaper war. There was no love lost between the editors of the two expat journals. In August 1879 editorial, Lamoureux scolded his competition for stealing the *News*'s editorial copy and reprinting it with neither permission nor attribution.

We regret the necessity of calling the attention of our contemporary, *The American Mail*, to one of the little courtesies of journalism which it should never have forgotten.

There is a certain class of items which from their character and wide circulation, become common property; but when it comes to the local work of a newspaper, upon which it spends time and money, there is proprietorship in it which other journals should not fail to recognize. We are pleased to have the Mail make full and free use of our columns, but we expect it to give us due credit such as the Commercial Bulletin and other reputable journals are scrupulous in doing. We are accustomed to using care and discrimination in our editorial work, and we expect to be held fully responsible for it.

The Mail knows perfectly well how unjust the scissors can be in journalism, and how it is sometimes characterized. We cannot but believe that its failure to credit us for extracts in its July number is an oversight, which will not occur again.[7]

When the *American Mail* went out of business, the *News* promptly bannered itself bold-faced and on page one with no small amount of glee: "The Only English Newspaper Published in Brazil."

Lamoureux's *Rio News* was cleanly laid out and designed. The writing was fresh, original, and snappy. As was the custom at the time, the front page partially consisted of advertisements, followed by inside pages chock full of news. Lamoureux was a one-man band laboring around the clock to make the compendious *Rio News* a staple in the expat community. The newspaper covered exports and imports; agriculture; mining; banking; railroads; shipping; politics on the international, national, provincial, and local fronts; sports (including local cricket matches as a nod to the British community); births, weddings, and deaths; ship arrivals and departures, all with particular interest to the expat English-speaking population.

Lamoureux was not timid about publishing his opinion on seemingly everything, in particular, about emancipation. He wrote passionately against the pro-slavery politics of the Confederates who had settled in the western region of the state of São Paulo to grow cotton. He criticized the Brazilian monarchy for not following the United States' lead in abolishing slavery more than a decade earlier. He rejected modest, conservative timetables for freeing Brazilian slaves, editorializing, "We believe the great evil should be abolished now and forever." Slavery, Lamoureux wrote, promotes "stagnation in industry, decadence in business, uncertainty in enterprise, checks in national development, and that when it shall be abolished then and not until then will there come that true and permanent prosperity which this country so much needs."[8]

Lamoureux was unsparing in exposing slavery's brutality. In the May 24, 1880, issue of *The Rio News*, Lamoureux wrote, "A slave was buried at Jundiahy on the 12th who had been literally whipped to death. His wounds, which were seen by many people, were frightful, the bones being exposed in places by the gashes. The published note of this brutal occurrence does not gives [sic] the name of the master; it is simply given as a matter of news. The curse of these unpunished brutalities will someday [sic] overwhelm the people who permit them."[9]

Labeled a radical for his crusading editorial broadsides in the *News*, Lamoureux's contrarian advocacy catapulted him to the forefront of progressive Brazilian politics. In addition to his newspaper, he translated and published anti-slavery pamphlets and tracts of abolitionist politicians, circulating them in the United States and Europe in an effort to bring international pressure for global emancipation.[10] He was a frequent contributor to *The Anti-Slavery Reporter*, a monthly publication of the London-based British and Foreign Anti-Slavery Society.

When Lamoureux started publishing *The Rio News*, Black Africans in Brazil outnumbered whites 6.7 million to 5.5 million.[11] The nation was faced with twin issues: the potential integration of so many enslaved Africans into Brazil's minority-white population, and the prospective loss of so much slave labor, which ant-abolitionists contended would decimate the national economy.[12]

Lamoureux called such caution racist nonsense. Those with vested interests in maintaining slavery countered with fear-mongering: the inevitability of looting, vagrancy, lawlessness, out-and-out anarchy— scare tactics Lamoureux rejected and rebuked. Because *The Rio News*'s readership largely comprised well-to-do expat businessmen and their families, Lamoureux's anti-slavery stance curried little favor, even though at the same time, more and more readers and advertisers were turning to his newspaper. Fearful of the economic impact of abolition, few mainstream Brazilian publications followed Lamoureux's editorial lead. Only two other Rio de Janeiro newspapers joined Lamoureux in supporting the cause of emancipation: the *Revista Illustrada*, published by an Italian expat, and the *Gazeta da Tarde*, run by abolitionists. The *Revista Illustrada* labeled *The Rio News* "a model of energy and sincerity."[13] The *Gazeta* published this all-out encomium:

The roar of the interests fed by the immoral traffic in human flesh does not frighten this independent sheet which sees every day an increase in the number of its readers and earnest panegyrists. The whole English colony of Rio de Janeiro prize the Rio News, and there are already many Brazilians who seek it for its very exact appreciations and judicious commentaries on all questions relating to the prosperity of Brazil. . . . We wish the Rio News success and congratulate ourselves in seeing that it fights, with great valor and excellent judgment, to save Brazil from the disgrace of possessing slaves in the last quarter of the nineteenth century. The existence of this important organ of the press is a splendid proof that it is not alone by the support of the slave-holders that a journal can live.[14]

By 1881, Lamoureux's newspaper, with offices at 79 Rua Sete de Setembro in the city's commercial district, had doubled in size from four to eight pages of densely packed type, published on the fifth, fifteenth, and twenty-fourth of every month, a schedule that coincided with the departure of American and French mail ships for New York and Le Havre, and a British steamer destined for Southampton. In an editorial note on the paper's expansion, Lamoureux wrote optimistically, "With this issue The Rio News makes its appearance in a new and enlarged format. The generous support and encouragement which we have received in the brief time since this journal passed into our hands, has rendered this step both easy and necessary. . . .Our success thus far has fully demonstrated the fact that an independent English commercial newspaper can be published in this city on its own merits and without any extrinsic aid or influence whatsoever."[15]

With more pages to fill, Lamoureux needed help putting out the newspaper. The editor-publisher not only had difficulty finding competent journalists fluent in English, but also assistants who would hew to his exacting standards. In 1880, one of the Ithaca newspapers back home ran a tart item in its unbylined Town Talk column that didn't create much of a welcome to anyone thinking of following the former Ithacan's journey to Brazil: "An aspiring young journalist with the right amount of energy and one not afraid of yellow fever can obtain a situation on the News, a commercial paper published at Rio de Janeiro and edited by A. J. Lamoreux [sic]. The pay is good and the privations many."[16] Perhaps the newspaper was seeking to settle an old score with a former competitor.

To raise funds to support his budding enterprise, Lamoureux wrote, edited, and published other English-language publications in Rio, including a detailed 225-page tourist's guide to the city, which *The New York Times* called "convenient, carefully written and well-arranged."[17] In 1892, Lamoureux published an English-as-a-second-language textbook for secondary-school students.[18] He published a sixty-four-page volume in English written by lawyer-physician-adventurer Frank Cowan, titled *The City of Royal Palm, and Other Poems*.[19] Under the imprimatur of his own publishing company, Aldina Books, he printed dozens of volumes by Brazil's leading anti-slavery politicians, diplomats, and intellectuals, including André Rebouças, Joaquim Nabuco, and Ruy Barbosa.[20] Lamoureux translated and published Barbosa's sixty-page appeal to the Brazilian Supreme Court for habeas corpus in response to the government's imposition of martial law following the arrests of protestors in October 1890.[21] He took on contract printing jobs for the central railroad and post office, and published forty thousand copies of a national almanac, as well as a half dozen other periodicals, including a 128-page national travel guide. Lamoureux took on all these publications to offset the rising costs of publishing *The Rio News*, from the start a loss leader.

Reflecting the *News's* editorial stance, Lamoureux became an ardent supporter of American journalist, pamphleteer, and politician Henry George, known for his reformist economic initiatives, including a single tax levied on landowners, not renters, which George advanced in his 1880 global bestseller, *Progress and Poverty*.[22] Lamoureux published Nabuco's Portuguese-language interpretation of George's philosophy in which the Brazilian politician railed against Britain's monopoly interests in Brazil. Nabuco's book helped spread George's

populist views so thoroughly in Brazil that the American writer's philosophy earned the Portuguese moniker, *georgismo*.[23]

In every issue of *The Rio News*, Lamoureux continued publishing
stinging editorial notes condemning social and economic injustice.
An example from July 5, 1879: "[T]he practice of stealing Indian children on the tributaries of the upper Amazon and selling them into
slavery is openly carried on and under the eyes even of Brazilian officials. . . . [I]t is the duty of the Brazilian government, indicated by
every sense of humanity, honor and good faith, to inquire into these
charges without delay and to suppress with unsparing hand every ves-
tige of this inhuman traffic."[24]

Lamoureux, it turned out, had become the social conscience of not
just the American and British expat community but also all of Brazil.

Following an 1888 decree that finally abolished slavery, Lamoureux
and Angelo Agostini, owner and illustrator of the weekly *Revista
Illustrada*, were feted for their decade-long campaign demanding
emancipation.[25] At a testimonial held in the grand ballroom of the
Hotel Globo, Lamoureux was awarded a diamond-inlay gold pen,
crafted by Brazilian metalsmith Valentim da Fonseca e Silva, with
the inscription, "*A. J. Lamoureux—Redactor-Proprietario do Rio
News—13 de Maio de 1888— Os Abolicionistas Brasileiros*."[26] In a notice under the headline, "An American Honored in Brazil," *The New
York Times* noted that Lamoureux and Agostini, "rank as pioneers in
the memorable work of achieving emancipation in Brazil. They began
their assaults on slavery in 1879, and have kept them up continuously ever since. This statement can be made of no other journalists in
Brazil."[27]

That same month, Lamoureux wrote his friend Nabuco a letter that
might serve as a credo for journalists anywhere then and now:

It is true that I began advocating the abolition of slavery in
1879, and that I have kept up the discussion continuously and
untiringly ever since; and it is true, also, that for a great part
of the time, *The Rio News* was the only advocate, so far as I am

informed, of immediate and unconditional emancipation, but I cannot think that any special credit is due to me on this account. Abolition was with me simply a question of principle; it was an act of abstract justice and sound political economy.

Believing, as I do, that it is the highest duty of the journalist to lead and instruct public opinion, to condemn everything unjust and hurtful and to commend and aid everything right and beneficial, I simply had no other policy to pursue.

I should like to feel certain that my influence as a journalist had been of service to you and your friends, but I cannot flatter myself that this had been the case. Indirectly, however, I may have been of some service by making the questions of Brazilian slavery and emancipation better understood and by convincing foreigners resident in Brazil of the justice and urgency of the immediate abolition of slavery.

However that may be, it is my good fortune to have seen this great revolution peacefully accomplished, and to have rendered even the slightest service toward that happy result. And it is both my duty and my pleasure, as an American who has seen this same controversy solved in his own country only by means of one of the most terrific struggles of modern times, to congratulate you and your countrymen on the peaceful abolition of slavery in Brazil. The record of this great event will be written in characters of gold on the imperishable pages of your national history, and will be, let us hope, an inspiration and example through all time for the peaceful solution of similar questions.[28]

By no means was *The Rio News* a single-issue newspaper, though. Despite Lamoureux's strident editorial advocacy on emancipation, the newspaper was a full-service periodical. It presaged what would become mandatory reading in the combined *Latin America Daily Post* and *Brazil Herald* when I started working as an editor there a century later.

Lamoureux's *Rio News* covered crime, and did it in a distinctive, laconic manner. Crime coverage became a tradition at the *News*, to be continued by another expat journalist seventy-five years later, also with a singular name, Herbert Zschech, who would start working for the *Brazil Herald* in its first year of publication, and, like Lamoureux, would serve as its long-term editor and political columnist.

A police-blotter sampling from *The Rio News* of December 15, 1879:

—At a place called Melancias, province of Bahia, Felippe da Silva Pimpim was shot by his brother, Victor da Silva.

—A soldier of the 11th battalion, accompanying the Brazilian boundary commission on the upper Rio Negro, recently assassinated a comrade.

—On the 6th ult, at a place called Illhetas, near Limoeiro, Pernambuco, a certain Joaquim Matheus met Manoel Rodrigues da Silva whom he knocked down and afterwards stabbed through and through.

—According to the Dario do Maranhão a boy of 13 years was re- cently brought before the police authorities for committing a rape on a girl of 9 years. Both were Cearenses.[29]

Under the headline, "Provincial Notes," a regular feature, the news- paper ran these terse, free-form poetic news items:

—A Brazilian lady died recently in Paraná at the age of 123.

—The cattle trade at River Plate is animated and prices pretty high.

—The usual number of murders, suicides and robberies are being committed in the provinces.

—A soldier of the 1st regiment named Villar was found in a bath- ing place at S. Gabriel do Sul, one day last month, strangled, stabbed and shackled.

—Counterfeit street-car tickets have appeared in Pará.

—A valiant officer of the guard at the palace in São Paulo punished a soldier by chopping his head and face open with a sword.

—A boy was killed at Faxima, S. Paulo, on the 24 ult by a hailstone.

—Two men named Francisco Rodrigues de Almeida and Fidencio Soares de Menzes got into a fight at Resinga do Araça, Rio Grande do Sul, on the 11th ult. The first will fight no more; the other will if he recovers.

—They are having bullfights in Santos.[30]

In addition to crime and political coverage, Lamoureux sprinkled the *News* with common-sense wisdom. He was an early practitioner of the kind of "everyman's" newspaper-column writing that had drawn me into journalism when I was growing up in New Jersey and later at Berkeley.

To show contempt for the proliferation of meaningless higher-education degrees, as well as to poke fun at the Brazilian practice of bestowing honorific titles on seemingly anyone who graduated from high school (and perhaps because he never graduated from college), Lamoureux published this tongue-in-cheek editorial aside:

Degree of Doctor
University of Philadelphia

Persons who desire to obtain the degree of doctor in Law, Philosophy, Surgery, Dentistry, Theology, Arts, Sciences, Letters, etc., from the American University of Philadelphia will find in the office of the *Diario* the precise information sought.

We can conscientiously recommend these degrees to every young man who feels the necessity of possessing the title of 'doctor' and yet is either too lazy or idiotic to work for it. The title of 'doctor' is, naturally, a necessity of life. To the aspiring noodle it is an indispensable as long finger nails and corns. The terms of course will be proportionate to the relative dignity of the degree conferred, that of Law and Medicine ranking the highest. That of Theology is more difficult to classify, owning to the very limited demand for it in this country. The terms will probably be very high. The degree in Sciences is a very popular one and is in great demand. As it doesn't mean anything, and as the 'doctor' will never be called upon to classify anything more difficult than a tadpole, the price will be appropriately low. The cheapest and best degree in the whole list for those who feel include to resort to this manufactory, is that of 'etc.' The boundless possibilities comprised in the title 'Doctor of Etcetera,' the charming vagueness, the subtle inferences, the plastic adaptabilities and the total irresponsibilities, are all in its favor. It affords the title, but it imposes no burden upon the wearer, neither intellectual nor social. As far as dignity goes it answers all existing purposes, but it binds its possessor to the defense of no system nor theory. It conveys no idea of special training nor occupation; its application is universal. For these reasons it should be highly popular among young men of weak intellects and subdued physical activity. It is to be regretted that the branch office of the Philadelphia doctor factory is so far away. If a similar agency could only be established in Rio, we are confident that it would be actively patronized.[31]

In another editorial note, Lamoureux wrote, "The São Paulo law school has 454 students on its rolls, of which 56 are to graduate this year. It makes one tremble for the future of the country."[32]

Lamoureux made his first trip back to the United States in 1884, six years after his arrival in Brazil. Traveling by steamship to New York, he wangled an interview with a reporter for *The New York Times*, plying his South American expertise to share insights about an incipient war between Brazil and Argentina. The interview was widely syndicated, strategically spreading word of both Lamoureux and his increasingly influential expat newspaper.[33] On the same trip, after visiting his parents in Michigan, Lamoureux called on *The Detroit Free Press,* which ran a lengthy question-and-answer interview with the thirty-four-year-old Michigan native. The article started this way:

The Rio News, published three times a month, is as handsome a paper as you would wish to see. It is an eight-page paper with four columns to the page, printed on fine white paper, and published in the interests of the commerce of Brazil. Mr. A. J. Lamoureux, its editor and proprietor, is a young man of rather Bostonique appearance, who wears glasses and a St. John mustache and whose face is bronzed with the Brazilian sun.[34]

At the same time, the New York-based weekly magazine, *The Illustrated American*, had taken notice of Lamoureux, and ran a plug for him and his enterprise. "There is no English-speaking writer in Brazil who understands Brazilian affairs so well as Mr. A. J. Lamoureux, the editor of the *Rio News*. He is an American by birth and instinct, and a citizen of the world."[35]

By 1892, Lamoureux had moved from his Botafogo apartment in Rio to a house on the water's edge in the Jurajuba neighborhood in the city of Niterói, across Guanabara Bay. The house was owned by Clement Heatherly Wilmot, a British civil engineer and wealthy textile industrialist. "It is one of the most charming places that can be found anywhere," Lamoureux wrote to his lifetime friend, geologist John "Jack" Casper Branner, whom he met at Cornell as an undergraduate and who would become president of Stanford University in 1913.

A two-decade-long exchange of letters between the two men would reveal Lamoureux's musings on life, his career, and his intimacies. The letters, all but one handwritten in elegant penmanship, are contained in a box in an archival depository at Stanford, which Branner donated to the university prior to his death in 1922.

Tennessee-born Branner would lead three geological expeditions in Brazil, one of which was financed by Thomas Edison to investigate vegetable fibers as filaments for his invention, the incandescent light bulb. Branner became so learned in Portuguese that he wrote the textbook, *A Brief Grammar of the Portuguese Language with Exercises and Vocabularies*.[36] He translated Portugal's Alexandre Herculano's landmark book, *History of the Origin and Establishment of the Inquisition in Portugal*, which revealed how the monarchy and church had conspired to confiscate property of so-called "New Christians," or converted Jews.[37]

Lamoureux's cache of letters to Branner amply indicates—and as other publishers of English-language publications in Brazil would discover—that while owning and editing a newspaper pitched to expats could afford its proprietor political influence, the business seldom proved lucrative on a long-term basis. Lamoureux's operations were beset by chronic newsprint shortages, imported machinery that broke down with maddening regularity, unreliable and underqualified personnel, advertisers who reneged on bills, readers ticked off at the newspaper's editorial stances, not to mention government interference, as well as an erratic national economy ravaged by chronic inflation. Identical travails would surface nearly a century later when I would work at the *Latin America Daily Post*.

To Branner in 1893 Lamoureux complained, "The truth is I am no longer my own master. I am the slave of my debts and other obligations, the hod carrier of my own ambition. I am working as I never worked before, conscious that I am throwing away time, opportunity and life, and yet unable to break the bonds. That's the diagnosis of my case, Jack, as I see it."[38] In another letter, Lamoureux wrote Branner, "Personally I am not at all well; am overworked and played out."[39]

Lamoureux was a crusading journalist-intellectual first, publisher-businessman second, so it came as no surprise that he would butt heads with anyone in authority, Brazilian or American, in public or in private. In August 1900, he and Charles Page Bryan, the US envoy to Brazil, clashed when Bryan publicly condemned *The Rio News* for its "pessimistic attitude." The ensuing imbroglio was classic push-pull between government official and journalist. In a scorching seven-page rebuke to Bryan, Lamoureux, assuming the role of the loyal opposition, fumed:

I must protest and I do protest against this pernicious and wholly unwarranted criticism of my work. My criticisms are not pessimistic, unless we agree to believe that mischievous legislation and bad administration represent the true and progressive interests of the country. Under a bad and reactionary government, the man who protests against blunders and abuses is not a pessimist. Were he such, he would declare the situation hopeless, throw up the sponge and retire from public life altogether. The simple fact that he continues at his post, reclaiming against abuses, perhaps for the moment without the slightest prospect of success is the best proof that he is an optimist, that he still hopes for the regeneration and prosperity of the country.[40]

Combative Lamoureux maintained a small and seemingly contracting circle of friends. Editorially, he spared no one. Anyone who deserved a reproach got it in the editorial columns of *The Rio News*. But there was a price to be paid for such public candor. Along with his fame—and notoriety—Lamoureux garnered a reputation as prickly and difficult. As he wrote to Branner on his forty-second birthday, "I am getting to be a solitary old fellow, and there are but few friendships during these latter years which take hold of my heart like the old ones." [41] In another letter to Branner, Lamoureux lamented, "Even my own countrymen condemn me because I will call a spade a spade. But, my dear boy, I was built that way and I can't do otherwise. Do you know I am so hated by Brazilians that they refuse even to give work to my printing office, or even to speak kindly of me. Were I to smash up, I doubt if they would have a kind word for me, or even a crust to keep me from starvation."[42]

With the Brazilian economy once again in freefall and the nation's political stability fractured, Lamoureux's imperative to keep *The Rio News* solvent became a daily struggle. The editor's love affair with Brazil began to cool. "If the government will let matters alone, and the agitators and military idiots will only keep quiet, we shall soon see the difficulty righting itself. . . . I am sorry to say, however, that there is but little hope of inducing the doctors to keep their hands off. There is hardly an honest and decent man in public life. Rio is over-run with speculators and parasites, and men of the worse type are apparently the most influential," Lamoureux wrote Branner in the summer of 1892. [43]

The next year, in response to an attempted insurrection in Rio, Brazil's military president-strongman, Floriano Vieira Peixoto, known as the "Iron Marshal," placed the nation under martial law, which included stringent press censorship. Peixoto issued a directive to Lamoureux to cease all political commentary or face indefinite suspension of *The Rio News*. Predictably, the government directive had the opposite effect on Lamoureux. The strongman Peixoto administration countered by closing down the *News*.[44]

To a newspaper in New York, Lamoureux smuggled a message past the censors: "How the struggle will end, no one can foresee, but it is anything but comfortable for us here. We have had the shells flying over us occasionally and some casualties have occurred in the city. It is now said that the British government will interfere, but as we are not permitted to use the telegraph ourselves, we never know what to believe."[45]

The *Chicago Tribune* followed with a report on the crossfire, which noted, "Lamoureux, editor of the Rio *News*, is said to be in personal danger of assault because of his boldness in printing the truth about the situation in the city and the progress of the revolution."[46]

As Lamoureux explained to Branner, "When the News was suspended, I planned to make a short visit to the River [Rio de la Plata], but I am not now certain I can manage it. There is a scarcity of money in this office which seriously interferes with such plans. When I first thought of going, there was some indications that an attempt would be made to assassinate me, but I think that has now blown over."[47]

Lamoureux went underground, never staying in the same location for more than several days. This way, he wrote Branner, he "avoided my customary haunts and streets, and thus escaped notice." Lamoureux was able to secure second-class passage on the Royal Mail steamer, SS *Clyde*, to Buenos Aires. "What my future movements will be I do not at this moment know," he wrote. "I shall not return to Rio until I know something definite as to the movements of those who are seeking my ruin. The prisons are still crowded with 4000 to 5000 prisoners, and I am not at all hungry for that species of martyrdom."[48]

Six months later, Lamoureux wrote Branner, "The gov't is now allowing some of the suspended papers to resume, and as the American minister has been using his good offices on my behalf, of his own volition, it may be that I may also be permitted to resume. However I am not building a very large air-castle on that. I do not propose to eat any humble-pie, whatever may occur, for the paper was suspended without assigning a reason for it, and it will resume on exactly the same terms—or not at all." [49]

When Lamoureux returned to Rio and was able to resume publication of the *News* with press restrictions for the moment temporarily lifted, he wrote Branner, "I am wretchedly busy . . . and am miserably ill. . . . I have no assistant either, and am doing all the *News* work alone, except trifling assistance from an inexperienced Com. Editor.[50] And I assure you, it keeps me tied down to my desk all the time."[51] With a new Marinoni press, *The Rio News* started coming out weekly, expanded to twelve pages, soon sixteen pages. Even though the newspaper was filled with advertising and seemingly flourishing, it was still losing money.

So busy was Lamoureux that in 1895 he wrote Branner to enlist his help in finding an American journalist who might relocate to Brazil. "Do you know a young man who would work with me, accept my ways, be contented with moderate success and slow methods, and not want the whole earth to begin with? I must have an assistant. I must come home next year if I can, and I want someone to leave in charge." Lamoureux also allowed that he was ready to say goodbye to Brazil. "I have a splendid chance of starting a daily paper in Buenos Aires, leaving the News in the hands of my assistant. I feel the tide has turned, and I think I can give the right man a good start," he wrote Branner.[52]

This was not to happen. The illness that had caused Lamoureux to drop out of Cornell, dyspepsia, continued to beset him. Admitted to Rio's Stranger's Hospital, a local medical facility he had helped found, Lamoureux wrote, "I'm thin and weak enough to frighten a ghost. My business has largely outgrown my ability to supervise it."[53]

In a succeeding letter, Lamoureux called dyspepsia, "the mother of all my physical troubles." He wrote Branner that he was adhering to a strict diet of milk, oatmeal, beef bouillon, eggs, chicken-and-rice soup, roast chicken, and apple slices. Lamoureux described himself as "thin as a state pencil, and as weak as I was in the starvation days of our college experience."[54]

Still, he continued as manically as ever, putting out the newspaper, translating manuscripts, publishing books, running a bindery and metal foundry that manufactured type forms. Indefatigable Lamoureux moved from Wilmot's Niterói house to a room above the newspaper office as a matter of economy and efficiency.

When Branner wrote back that he had found an assistant for Lamoureux, the newspaper editor was overjoyed, noting that he'd pay passage from New York to Rio for the new hire, as well as allot a financial interest in the newspaper to a deserving candidate. Within months, though, Lamoureux withdrew the job offer, citing yet another downturn in business, the erratic Brazilian economy, and advertisers defaulting on their bills. "So you can see, my dear Jack, it is not all beer and skittles with us down here. I never saw worse times than we are now experiencing. My presses are idle a third of the time. Business everywhere is stopped. Prices, rents, everything, are high, money is scarce, and everyone discouraged." Through it all, determined Lamoureux and colleague Joaquim Nabuco were still cooking up plans to publish a progressive Portuguese-language daily newspaper in Rio, but that venture went nowhere.[55]

On July 12, 1896, forty-six-year-old Lamoureux finally shared with Branner some good news. "Yes! It's a fact! I'm going to get married! Not tomorrow, nor even next month, but if all goes well about the end of the year. The sweet little woman (this is for Mrs. B's ear) is a trained nurse, an Englishwoman, and will know exactly how to manage an old fellow like myself." Ironically, Lamoureux asked Branner for his discretion in sharing the news. "I haven't told anyone here as yet and do not intend to for some time, so please don't advertise."[56]

Lamoureux's fiancée was Sarah Cross, a nurse fifteen years younger than he, born in Warwickshire, England, who worked at Stranger's Hospital, where the two had met while Lamoureux had been a patient. Cross had been trained at Swansea General and Eye Hospital in Birmingham. "I am counting on much happiness with her—and I am inclined to believe I deserve it," Lamoureux wrote Branner.[57]

Lamoureux and Sarah, whom he called Sallie, sailed to England, where they got married in Swansea during the summer of 1887. To Branner, the new groom wrote, "You will like Sallie I am sure! She is not of the 'new woman' type at all; she is only a quiet, loving, little woman, sunny of temper and always solicitous for those she loves." Lamoureux added preemptively, "Of course, I am happy! How could I be otherwise. In spite of my Cornell reputation, I was destined for the life I have now begun."[58] Leaving the News in the hands of a temporary protégé Lamoureux had managed to find, the newlyweds honeymooned in Britain, visiting Canterbury, Ramsgate, Dover, Deal, Turnbridge Wells, Hastings, Deal, and finally, London.

The couple would become parents of four children. Of their first, Mabel, born in 1898, sleep-deprived yet euphoric Lamoureux gushed, "She will be a fortnight old tomorrow, and already she sings melodiously. One can lie awake nights listening to her."[59] Within a year, Sallie was again pregnant, and she and Mabel (whom Lamoureux described to Branner as "the prettiest little girl you ever saw") took the cargo steamer SS Gothic to England, where their second child, Vincent, was born.[60] To honor his Cornell friend, Lamoureux gave the boy the middle name, Branner.[61]

While Sallie and their two children were abroad, Lamoureux wrote Branner again of his business woes back in Brazil. "Am literally on the ragged edge. The "News" is barely holding its own, and the printing office is really not paying expenses. . . . I'm between the devil and the deep sea, and there's no escape."[62]

Now, actively looking for a buyer of the News, Lamoureux allowed, "I shall leave here without a moment's regret."[63] In a subsequent letter to Branner, he added, "I do not see how I can keep it up. I want to come home and spend the rest of my life in a white man's country."[64] Writing of his desire to travel to California, where Branner was living, Lamoureux said, "Of course, I must come, even if there is no money. What is money anyhow, when a friend is concerned? If I had nothing better to do, I would walk 3000 miles any day just to see you."[65]

Lamoureux's newspaper was to come to an abrupt and inglorious end. On August 2, 1901, Lamoureux, Sallie, Mabel and Vincent, sailed to New York on the British steamship, the SS *Buffon*.[66] In a family genealogy pamphlet, a relative wrote that Lamoureux had left Brazil, "when a series of reverses coupled with a break-down in health obliged him to return to the United States."[67]

To announce the newspaper's change of ownership, *The Rio News* buried this sleeper inside on page four:

Notice is hereby given that Mr. A. J. Lamoureux has given his procuration to Sr Arnaldo José Dias de Miranda for the administration of The Rio News, and to Sr. Manoel Joaquim Moreira Maximino for the administration of his printing office, known as the Typographia Adina during his absence. The procuration given to Mr. Frederick Pfeffer is hereby revoked.[68]

It seems that Lamoureux had been the victim of fraud when he tried to sell the newspaper. "Early in the present century 'The Rio News,' through a series of misfortunes in which its subsequent purchasers were not above suspicion, underwent a forced sale," read the only story in *The Rio News* about the fate of Lamoureux's twenty-two-year-old creation.[69]

The newspaper's final issue came out December 3, 1901. In a note to readers, a new publisher explained inconclusively, "When the editor of The Rio News left for the United States, he informed the public through this journal that he could not insure the publication of the paper on established lines during his absence, but that efforts would be made by his office employes and some of his friends to publish the customary commercial information and local news as circumstances would permit. The publication is now resumed and will, we trust, hereafter continue without interruption. Under these circumstances we renew the editor's request to his old friends for indulgence and support."[70]

The last page of the last issue of the *News* carried this last-ditch solicitation: "As an advertising medium The News occupies an exceptionally advantageous position. It circulates widely throughout Brazil, and also in Europe and the United States. Its subscribers are principally business men interested in Brazilian trade, industries and investments. No other periodical, even with much larger circulation, can offer better inducements to advertisers who seek the attention of these classes."[71]

With *The Rio News* shuttered, Lamoureux was ready to reset his once-promising career back in America. The previous twenty years had been taken over by owning and editing a lively, topical, albeit insolvent, newspaper in Brazil. Except for reading about the United States and visiting on occasion, Lamoureux had severed himself from much of American life and culture. Returning to the country of his birth, Lamoureux was now free of the burden of editing and owning a newspaper under constant duress. He would no longer have to dodge creditors or government officials, nor would he have to chase advertisers whose accounts were overdue. Set to impart his vast knowledge and experience to a new and eager audience, Lamoureux at fifty-one was far from ready to retire from his life's work. He was primed to immerse himself in the heady mix of US newspapers, the promising career he had cut short to leave for Brazil when he had been a tyro journalist of twenty-seven.

Lamoureux telegraphed his return to America by writing an ambitious thirteen-part, twenty-thousand-word series that appeared in the *Boston Evening Record*, titled "Regeneration of South America."[72] Besides a journalistic tour de force, the series served as a newsflash to the stateside newspaper industry that a uniquely qualified voice would soon be looking for a job.

Writing in the third person, as was the journalistic convention at the time, Lamoureux candidly wrote about his experience as editor and owner of *The Rio News*:

Something more than a score of years ago an American Journalist undertook the publication of a small newspaper in one of the larger capitals of South America. He had had no experience outside the United States and had no conception of the difference in habits, taste, customs and morals between his own people and those among whom he had come to reside. Naturally he began work just as he would have done in the United States: he adopted a defined policy for his paper, he criticized freely and frankly, he warmly defended the interests of his patrons, and he assaulted every Government project that ran counter to his opinions. To his great surprise this policy gave offence, not only to the Government and its supporters, but also to many of the foreigners whose interests he had espoused. They feared that open criticism would bring official resentment upon them, while many of them argued that the foreigner was only a guest and had no right to criticise.[73]

Despite the reveille, Lamoureux didn't have it easy back in the States. It wasn't that the invitation he had crafted for himself never got delivered—worse, it had been received and rejected. If Lamoureux had flown high in Brazil as an influential editor, publisher, and preeminent voice of reform, back home he was about to crash.

A year after his return, still looking for full-time newspaper work, Lamoureux contributed a piquant essay to the influential journal *Out West*, edited by famed naturalist Charles F. Lummis. Lamoureux's geopolitical discourse turned into a rant on how little North Americans know or care about their southern neighbors. The journalist who had championed a platform to end slavery in Brazil was unable to conceal his dismay at his own fall from leading figure in Latin America to persona non grata back in his own country.

> After a residence of many years on the eastern coast of South America, an American journalist recently came home with the idea that there would be a demand for his knowledge and experience, but he was mistaken. In London, his position would be secure and influential, for there they take a live interest in South America. Here he is of much less account than the reporter who can write up a racy sketch of a baseball match. He tried to find an opening in the newspapers for a discussion of South American topics, but, although the Pan-American Exposition had just closed, and a Pan-American Congress was in session, he was told that "no one Wants to know anything about South America."

In an editor's note, Lummis backed up Lamoureux, calling him "one of the most competent and reliable living authorities touching the eastern slope of South America."[74] It was high praise coming from an editor as distinguished as Lummis.

Despite the billboard endorsement, Lamoureux was unable to secure newspaper work in the United States that would match his talent. Lamoureux had returned during the golden age of newspapers. Every metropolis had a raft of competing quality broadsheets. New York and San Francisco each had fifteen dailies fiercely competing for readers at the time. And those were just two cities out of dozens with an array of flourishing, battling, vibrant newspapers. Lamoureux surely should have been able to convert his deep journalistic experience into a significant stateside position. But no one wanted to hire him.

Perhaps he was exhausted from the accumulation of two decades of never-ending deadlines. Maybe newspaper work no longer gave him the satisfaction it once had, having turned into an onerous obligation, a voracious, self-serving beast to be fed constantly. The collapse of *The Rio News* surely had contributed to an economic sense of burden and encumbrance, as had his worsening case of dyspepsia. Two more children, Emily Elizabeth and Clarence Eugene, would soon be born to Lamoureux and Sallie. Lamoureux was no longer a pliable young reporter-editor.

Lamoureux worked briefly at the *Harbor Springs Republican* in his home state of Michigan, then traveled to Maryland, Canada, and New York. For a time, he was a cataloger at Stanford University Library, a position his friend Jack Branner helped him secure.

Without any promising newspaper offers, Lamoureux and his family moved to Ithaca, New York, to a house adjacent to Cornell's botanical gardens on the Byway in the Forest Home district.[75] In 1913, with four children to provide for, Lamoureux took an anonymous job as assistant reference librarian at Cornell's agriculture college.

Journalists as outspoken as Lamoureux aren't easily silenced. Without a ready outlet to publish his work, the once-prolific newsman became an inveterate writer of letters to the editor about issues specific to Latin America, the Panama Canal, railroads, trade, and the Monroe Doctrine. From 1902 to 1906, *The New York Times* published fourteen letters he had submitted to the newspaper.[76] When the *Times* would no longer print his rambling missives, Lamoureux turned to *The Ithaca Daily Journal* and wrote letters about the US gold standard, corporate monopolies, Germany's invasion of Belgium, the value of the League of Nations, and magnate John D. Rockefeller, whom Lamoureux called "inimical."[77] He contributed seventeen entries to the *Encyclopedia Britannica* on matters of Brazil and South America.[78]

Lamoureux died unheralded in Ithaca on February 25, 1928, at age seventy-seven.[79] A one-paragraph obituary that appeared in an African-American newspaper, *The Western Outlook*, published twenty-eight hundred miles away in Oakland, California, on page eight, carried the page-one-worthy headline: "He Stopped Slavery in Brazil," but few other newspapers published notices of Lamoureux's death.[80] His hometown newspaper, *The Ithaca Journal-News*, buried an obituary on page five, even though it contained this provocative first paragraph: "Although the latter part of his life had been spent in the comparative quiet and retirement of a university community, his early years offer an unusual story of danger, hardship, and achievement in a foreign land."[81] The obit neglected to go into further detail. Lamoureux's grave is located at Pleasant Grove Cemetery in Ithaca, next to Sallie's, who would die at age eighty-two in 1949.

Lamoureux's legacy *ought* to have been inspiration to any American journalist seeking recognition by emigrating to Brazil. He had been a giant in the annals of another country. What ultimately happened to him was disheartening, but also cautionary. Hailed as a hero in Brazil, he returned home vanquished.

Lamoureux and I had had a surfeit of differences. To compare us is an injustice to him. I never aspired to be a pivotal figure in another nation's history, nor did I possess the instinct, talent, wisdom, intellect, or courage that Lamoureux amply demonstrated. Our lives were separated by a century. He was a publisher, entrepreneur, *and* newspaperman. I never imagined realizing anything close to what Lamoureux had accomplished.

But we did share more than a few similarities. Lamoureux and I were just a year in age apart when we left America, both of us hoping to live out our dreams through newspapers. We looked to the same foreign country to secure a toehold. We weren't satisfied with staying put. For both of us, what lay around the bend was more beguiling than what was straight ahead. We both had more than a small dose of wanderlust. However much we both wanted to descend into a foreign culture, we both resolutely retained our American identity. A. J. and I even shared proximal ailments—mine was brief and singular, erupting as appendicitis; his lasted a lifetime.

Surely Lamoureux had wrestled for years with how more than two decades in Brazil had seemingly undermined what would have been a stellar journalistic career in the States. A. J. Lamoureux had absolutely been on the right side of history, but back home no one seemed to care.

CHAPTER 9

Ralph, Betty, Zschech, Vic, Lee, Joe, and Frank

HOWEVER PROPHETIC A. J. Lamoureux's professional life may have turned out, I don't think the cold-shoulder reception he got when he returned to the States, even if I had known about it before I had left for Brazil, would have dissuaded me from packing up and leaving California. Like Ajax, I had made the decision to embark on something wild, unpredictable, surely reckless. Nothing would have stopped me. I was at a point of no return. That Ajax and so many others had taken a chance on Brazil would have been reassuring, no matter what would happen to them and what would happen to me.

With the void created by *The Rio News*'s closing, other enterprising expat American and British journalists bought, borrowed, or rented printing presses to fill the English-language newspaper vacuum in Rio and beyond. Their creations included the *Brazilian American* in 1918, *Times of Brazil* in 1919, *Anglo-Brazilian Chronicle* in 1921, the *News* in 1939, and eventually the *Brazil Herald* in 1946 and *Latin America Daily Post* in 1979, where I would work. None sought to reach the hearts, souls, and ire of readers as Lamoureux's bold creation had. All were foremost commercial ventures that covered whatever their owners, editors, and reporters deemed newsworthy.

After I arrived in Brazil, when Mauro Salles precariously climbed atop the copy desk in São Paulo and announced that the *Brazil Herald* and *Latin America Daily Post* would be consolidating, I already knew that the *Herald*, the newspaper Salles had bought, had a raucous reputation. While in Rio, the Canadian girls and I had read the *Herald* as beachside entertainment to get a sprinkling of back-home news. The *Herald* was rip-and-read, capricious, splashy, an unpredictable mix of college newspaper, headline tip sheet, government-business press release, Hollywood tattler, and *National Enquirer* knock-off. It was a Mixmaster of wire copy, half-baked columns, society fluff, and plugola sandwiched between advertisements for tourist traps and massage parlors. About the only thing the *Daily Post* and *Herald* had in common was that they were both newspapers printed in English in the same nation far from America shores. That these two very different newspapers could be combined into one caused no small amount of handwringing among the journalists at the new up-and-coming *Daily Post*.

Founded forty-five years after Lamoureux had closed *The Rio News*, the *Herald* for decades had been known as a way station for wayward itinerant journalists—some manifestly talented, others who couldn't stitch together an English sentence, all employed under the same leaky roof, working on the same creaky wooden floorboards littered with cigarette butts, beer bottles (full, half-full, and empty), and teetering stacks of yellowed newspapers. Some of these scribes had presented themselves at the newspaper's hotbox of a newsroom, were directed to one of several broken-down Royal or Underwood typewriters, and told to crank out instant copy about anything they fancied. Many arrived with letters of introduction, some legitimate, others noticeably forged. A few had been CIA operatives, seeking cover as journalists, the oldest beard in the espionage business. Many were drifters, carousers, grifters, alcoholics, government informers, drug dealers (and users), smugglers, dreamers, and self-styled prophets—not all that different from personnel at any newsroom of the same late-1940s vintage.

Rio has always been a rogue's paradise. It's where conman Charles Ponzi ended up after being deported to Italy from the United States. While few were as successful, many *Herald* journalists were like-minded exiles hellbent on either making a name for themselves—or desperately seeking to disappear into the newspaper's termite-infested woodwork. Some were real-life incarnations of characters from classic newspaper movies such as *The Front Page, His Girl Friday, Deadline U.S.A.*, or *Ace in the Hole.* More than several could have been spun from the pages of a three-card-monte Damon Runyon short story.[1] This, by the way, wasn't bad for any newspaper dependent on the daily output of a team of wily and spirited reporters and editors.

Before I left São Paulo for Rio to work at the newly combined newspaper, I never saw a copy of the *Brazil Herald* in the *Daily Post's* newsroom. I thought this odd. Journalists usually devour print materials, especially their competition. Not so the *Herald*, in part, because no one at the *Daily Post* viewed the *Herald* as competition. Whenever somber *Daily Post* managing editor Ed Taylor deigned even a mention of the *Herald*, he'd shake his head and effect a rather painful, thin-lipped, rubbery smile, as though to say the *Herald* was hardly a newspaper at all. As for the *Herald* editorial staff in sybaritic Rio, Taylor would only allow, "The editor wears a Micky Mouse watch" without elaboration. I wasn't sure whether Taylor meant this literarily, but it seemed to sum up the *Daily Post's* collective sentiment about the *Herald* and its hang-loose, pell-mell staff that barely kept the newspaper coming out day by day.

Taylor and the other journalists Steve Yolen had assembled for the *Daily Post's* startup were committed to the lofty ideals of a noble profession, given added purpose by Bob Woodward and Carl Bernstein's uncovering of the Watergate scandal, which had led to a Pulitzer Prize for *The Washington Post* seven years earlier. Not that the *Daily Post* could ever summon anything remotely close to the kind of resources and impact such intrepid shoe-leather reporting on rare occasions delivers. Still, that was what journalism was all about for the rookies at the new *Daily Post.* All Ajax Lamoureuxes in the making. Like journalists everywhere, we had taken a sort of oath. We could have made more money in any number of allied professions, but that would have meant going to the dark side, working in commerce, PR, or worse—the government. What Woodward and Bernstein had pulled off gave journalists stature, respect, and no small amount of attitude. We considered the lightweight *Brazil Herald* an ad sheet masquerading as a broadsheet. Its staff of misfits ought to have been elated that Salles had bought the throw-away rag and we were coming for its rescue.

That these two oppositely charged newspapers were merging thoroughly energized an upbeat Yolen, who viewed the combined venture as a once-in-a-lifetime opportunity. The Manhattan-born executive editor played country guitar and blue-grass banjo on the side, and had been a boy-wonder UPI correspondent in Latin America. A smart and nimble journalist, he was giddy with anticipation at Salles's acquisition of the Rio newspaper. "The *Herald*'s got only one way to go, and that's up!" Yolen crowed to anyone who'd bother to ask.

While the *Herald* had been an irascible Rio de Janeiro institution for more than three decades and had never been anything close to a stellar newspaper, neither had the Paris *Herald*, the fulcrum of the trio of English-language newspapers during the so-called Lost Generation of the 1930s. The Paris *Herald*'s night city editor Al Laney recalled that the European paper wasn't "very good, often quite bad." Copyreader Kenneth Stewart was less charitable: "The *Herald* was worse than any paper I had ever worked for." Eric Sevareid, who started out his career at the newspaper and who would become one of the twentieth century's most influential journalists, called the Paris *Herald* a "rather absurd little house organ for the diminishing American colony, which made ample room for the resort and fashion-house advertisements and as a kind of afterthought squeezed in the news."[2]

In that way, the Paris and the Brazil *Herald*s were kindred spirits. Both were English-language newspapers located six thousand miles and an ocean apart, non-consanguineous siblings who found themselves the byproducts of two dizzying and intoxicating foreign-city cultures, chronicled by expats merrily ensconced abroad. Both the

Paris and Brazil *Herald*s had limited circulations, abbreviated page counts, nonstop typography migraines, and a finite number of journalists on their staffs, not to mention a natural cap on readers. That they both managed to come out daily was something of a miracle.

Despite these limitations, the *Brazil Herald*, like its counterpart in Paris, brought with it a heady literary provenance. In addition to such luminaries as Edwina "Teddy" Hecht (famed American playwright and screenwriter Ben Hecht's talented daughter), Hunter S. Thompson, Tad Szulc, Don Shannon, and Eric Hippeau, hundreds of other *Brazil Herald* reporters and editors would go on to become well-known journalists. Some would join the AP, UPI, Dow-Jones, Bloomberg, Reuters, Agence France-Presse, Knight-Ridder, *The New York Times*, *Washington Post*, and *Los Angeles Times*. Others would become leaders in the world of arts as critics and entertainers. Several would turn to the US Foreign Service. Working at the *Brazil Herald* was a passport. It conferred brio, guts, and gusto to any holder. It was a calling card with which to launch a career.

That's ostensibly why itinerant, journeyman journalist Ralph Bisett Ross had moved to Brazil and resurrected Andrew Jackson Lamoureux's defunct *Rio News* on September 19, 1939, and eventually turned it into the *Brazil Herald*.

Born in Moberly, Missouri, in 1889, Ross hopscotched reporting jobs at the *Moberly Monitor*, then as city editor at the *St. Louis Republic*, followed by a stint at the *St. Louis Post-Dispatch*, as well as working for United Press in Washington, DC. There, he met Argentina's first ambassador to the United States, Rómulo S. Naón, and followed him in 1918 to Buenos Aires to serve as the ambassador's home secretary. In Argentina, Ross worked as a stringer for the *New York Herald* and *Washington Post*, then landed a job at the Buenos Aires daily, *La Nación*, before launching in 1921 his own ad weekly, *El Suplemento Semanal*, and with his brother, Claude, creating a company that sold advertisements in the Argentine capital's new subway system, the first in South America. Busy Ross was a business representative for

Hearst News Services and International News Services in Argentina; he also was one of several owners of an English-language newspaper in Buenos Aires called the *River Plate-American*, as well as founder of an expat weekly, *America*.[3]

In 1939, Ross moved to Brazil to restart Andrew Jackson Lamoureux's *Rio News*, only to be shut down two years later when populist Brazilian dictator Getúlio Vargas imposed a wartime ban on newspapers and magazines printed in any language other than Portuguese.[4] Vargas's edict closed more than fifty foreign-language newspapers and magazines published at the time in Brazil. Of those shuttered, the largest (in descending order) were printed in Italian, German, French, and English, a snapshot of the relative size of the Brazil's expatriate pre-war population.[5] To abide by the Vargas decree, instead of closing during the war years, some foreign-language newspapers in Brazil converted to Portuguese. That's what the *Times of Brazil*, primarily serving the British expat settlement, did.[6]

Five months after the end of World War II, on February 1, 1946, Ross and three partners renamed *The Rio News* the *Brazil Herald*, thus becoming the first newspaper following the war to be published in Brazil in a language other than Portuguese. The men who joined Ross in the publishing enterprise were Joseph Folsom Brown and Frank Mario Garcia, both well-traveled American expats in Rio de Janeiro, and Otto (Vic) Hawkins, an Argentine-born advertising executive whose American father had worked as an executive with the Argentine national railroad. Prior to partnering with Ross, Hawkins had worked in Buenos Aires for International Harvester, United States Rubber Company, and as the local representative for the German publisher Rudolf Mosse.[7] Each partner invested the equivalent of $5,000 to launch the *Brazil Herald*.[8] Each brought singular, distinctive talents to the fledgling English-language daily.

In the case of Brown and Garcia, both had ample political connections, along with financial acumen and journalistic expertise respectively. Brown was an American-born, Harvard-educated attorney and local business fixer; Garcia, a Puerto Rican-born journalist, was the longtime *New York Times* correspondent in Brazil. Both enjoyed a cordial, personal relationship with Brazilian President Vargas, and on several occasions had personally discussed with him their vision of a pro-business English-language daily in the nation's capital. "He considered the idea unworkable though personally he had no objections," Brown would write. "But if we really persisted in the plan, he personally would offer no obstacle. Knowing the president as we did, we felt certain that we could count on him."[9]

With the end of World War II in sight, Brown and Garcia had begun lobbying Foreign Minister Osvaldo Aranha, the former Brazilian ambassador to the United States, to ease Vargas's wartime foreign-language press ban. Aranha, who would become Brazil's ambassador to the U.N., made personal entreaties to Vargas, proffering that a newspaper touting Brazilian and American commercial ties, published in English, would benefit postwar Brazil. Six months before Vargas would lift the prohibition, Brown and Garcia joined Ross and Hawkins, and got back-channel assurances from Aranha to begin planning the *Brazil Herald*'s launch.[10]

The February 1, 1946, inaugural issue of the *Herald* was a six-page broadsheet that carried a banner headline announcing Vargas's hand-picked protégée and presidential successor: "Dutra Inaugurated as Brazil's President."[11] That lead story about the installation of Eurico Gaspar Dutra carried the byline, Betty Dyer, a newly arrived cracker-jack newspaperwoman from the States.

Just as Lamoureux may have personified the timbre of American expat journalists in Brazil, so did trailblazer Dyer fifty years later. Born in Carson City, Nevada, Elisabeth Townsend Dyer grew up in San Francisco and graduated from the University of California, Berkeley, where, like me, she'd been a reporter for the student newspaper, *The Daily Californian*. She got hired at the *Berkeley Gazette*, then the *Oakland Post-Enquirer*, where she met the man who would become her husband, Richard Dyer. Both were early organizers for the American Newspaper Guild, and during her vacation days Betty traveled across the United States to convince newsroom personnel to join the journalists' labor organization. Fearless in spreading word of the union, Dyer was a remade incarnation of Mary G. Harris Jones, the turn-of-the-century labor activist known as Mother Jones.

In 1939, Betty and Dick moved to New York, where Betty became the first female "rewrite man" for the *New York Post*. She also was

Fig. 9.1 Betty Dyer. Courtesy of *The Tico Times*.

assistant city editor of the newspaper *PM*, a daily magazine financed by Chicago department-store tycoon Marshall Field II.[12] In what little spare time she had, Betty wrote a children's book, *Johnny and His Wonderful Bed*. While working for the *New York Post*, then a pro-labor tabloid owned by Theodore Olin Thackrey (whose widow, Dorothy Schiff, would sell the newspaper to Australian press baron Rupert Murdoch in 1976), Betty developed a hard-ball reputation for covering traditional male beats, notably crime. She scored a journalistic coup when she wrote a series on the blockbuster murder of gold-mine millionaire Sir Harry Oakes, bludgeoned to death in the bedroom of his Bahamian estate in 1943. Writing from Nassau, Betty explored the curious underpinnings of the slaying. At the time, the island's governor was the Duke of Windsor, formerly King Edward VIII, who along with his wife, Wallis Simpson, lived in the crown paradise known as a decadent haven for tax dodgers and Nazi sympathizers.[13]

Betty and Dick moved to Rio, where Dick became bureau chief for International News Service and King Features Syndicate while Betty worked for the brand new *Brazil Herald*, and later as assistant bureau chief for the Associated Press. Six years later, the couple, now with a daughter, moved to San José, Costa Rica, where Dick became United Fruit Company's public relations director and Betty, in 1956, founded the *Tico Times*, an English-language newspaper still published today online.[14]

The bannered story that Betty Dyer wrote for the inaugural issue of the *Brazil Herald* was played above the fold under the newspaper's mast and boldfaced motto, "Brazil's Only English Language Daily," a replay of A. J. Lamoureux's 1880 front-page epigram in *The Rio News*, "The Only English Newspaper Published in Brazil." Alongside Dyer's story was the new newspaper's welcome to readers:

Brazil Herald makes its bow to the English speaking communities of this country and gratefully takes its place as a member of the Brazilian family of newspapers. It appears after months of preparation, effort and struggle. It carries the full wire services of the Associated Press and the special service of International News Service. It has four comics—although the ones appearing today are not the ones chosen; they will be along in a few days—from King Features Syndicate and United Features Syndicate and Chicago Tribune Feature Service. Louella Parson's Hollywood column will appear daily. Crossword puzzles, fashion pictures and other features of interest to women will be found on the proper pages.

As a preview of editorial snafus down the road, the unbylined greeting carried this preemptive apology:

To the people, institutions and agencies who have assisted in getting the paper under way Brazil Herald founders are grateful and they pledge themselves to respond to the confidence of these persons and organizations by getting out the best newspaper in their power to produce: They are not amateurs at the business but, needless to say, unusual problems must be faced and surmounted in the manufacture of a daily newspaper in Brazil. The body matter will be set by linotype operators who do not understand a word of what they are composing. In other sections the same conditions prevail so it is extremely unlikely that the paper will reach the hands of the readers without typographical errors. Patience is indicated. Proofreaders are and will continue to be on the job but when the operators correct one error in a line another is likely to crop up. But every effort will be taken to publish as bright and clean a paper as possible.

The success or failure of the venture, commercially speaking, depends exclusively upon the cooperation or lack of it from the public and business world. The reception to date has been more almost than could be hoped. Subscriptions and advertisements have been pleasingly abundant and everything points to an interesting future for all concerned.[15]

Herald co-owner Frank Garcia had a connection with an editorial writer at the *Washington Post*, and shortly after the *Herald*'s debut, the *Post* published a collegial greeting. "The first issue of the newspaper is, considering the great mechanical difficulties that had to be overcome, a surprisingly workmanlike job. Although the typesetters' lack of knowledge of English, the *Herald*'s Volume 1, Number 1 is remarkably free of typographical errors. There is excellent coverage of news from Brazil, the United States and the world. We welcome our new Rio contemporary," read the backslapping editorial.[16]

The *Herald*'s start-up circulation was tiny, touted at five thousand, although no audited assay would ever verify this. However many copies were actually sold, the *Herald*'s circulation was minuscule compared to Rio's mass of dailies at the time, but the quartet of owners steadfastly believed that the newspaper's affluent, English-reading demographic would make up for the lopsided deficit. The *Herald*'s newsstand price was one cruzeiro, about a dime per copy. The first issue's page-one layout resembled a vintage American newspaper of the era: six columns with seven stories, which in addition to Dyer's article, included wire pieces on atomic fallout in Japan, a denial from soon-to-be Argentine President General Juan Perón that he and his military allies would attempt a coup, and pretender-to-the-Spanish throne Juan de Borbón's five-point do-or-die ultimatum to fascist Generalissimo Francisco Franco. All typical fare.

From its beginning, in addition to chronicling the comings and goings of wealthy expats living in Rio, the early years of the *Herald* showcased Hollywood gossip. That among the newspaper's original syndicated columnists was popular Hollywood tattler Louella Parsons indicated the *Herald*'s pedigree as a newspaper pitched to Americans, or at least those interested in American entertainment, culture, and manufactured dish. Parsons's column in the *Herald* also made financial sense to the newspaper's owners: US movies (with Portuguese subtitles) were a booming postwar business in Brazil, and the *Herald* carried prominent display advertisements touting them.

The story that generated the most play in the *Herald* a month after its first issue was the arrival of twenty-five-year-old Hollywood pinup Lana Turner on a publicity tour to Brazil to top off movie-ticket sales for her first femme fatale role, playing opposite John Garfield in the box-office hit, *The Postman Always Rings Twice*. The *Herald* reported the so-called "Atomic Bombshell" disappointed legions of fans in São Paulo when she refused to leave her Pan American airplane parked on the airport's tarmac. Turner's alleged tantrum, the *Herald* speculated, triggered "crew members to fear the crowd would wreck the plane."[17] The choreographed episode fit nicely within the *Herald*'s dawning editorial contours.

In March 1947, the *Herald* ran on page three the feverish headline, "Goldwyn Girls Coming to Rio!" with photographs of two comely chorus girls, Karen X. Gaylord and Diana Mumby, appearing alongside a reader advisory that the newspaper would print two additional photographs of more arriving Goldwyn Girls, labeled "the most beautiful chorus girls in the world" the following day and two more the day after.[18] When all of them showed up, the *Herald* breathlessly enthused:

Six tall, slim, incredible, fantastic dreams dropped into Rio yesterday. And as they stepped from the plane one at a time, beautiful, beautiful, more beautiful not bad, otimo, mas ou menos (that makes six) I immediately wondered how the pilot could go about his business knowing that all that gorgeous pulchritude was aboard.

The sextet was part of a tour to plug a new musical-comedy movie, *Wonder Man*, starring Danny Kaye and Virginia Mayo. The writer of the *Herald* story, seemingly a short man struck by the vertical stature of the starlets, crowned his story with this notice: "I warn all of you, get elevator shoes or have your head set up a few inches, cause they're kinda tall. It sorta does something to one's manliness to have to look at a gal that tall."[19]

Fig. 9.2 Bob Hope in Brazil, Flanked by *Brazil Herald* partners Frank Garcia to the *left* of Hope, and Lee Langley to the *right*. Courtesy of the *Brazil Herald*.

Three months later, Bob Hope made a Paramount Pictures tour to Rio, and the *Herald* ran on page three a photo of the funnyman mugging with newspaper co-founder Frank Garcia, along with a young *Herald* editor, Lee Langley, at the city's elite Jockey Club.[20]

In another *Herald* issue under the groan-worthy front-page headline "A Fitting Title," a photograph of a busty woman appeared with this caption:

Lovely and shapely Carroll Brooks has been awarded the title 'National Sweater Girl of 1947' after winning the unanimous decision of the judges in a recent contes [*sic*] in New York City. Carroll's dimensions are: height, 5 feet, 10 inches; weight 120 pounds; bust, 35 inches; and waist, 24 inches.[21]

At about the same time, actor Tyrone Power (or most likely, a press agent) wrote a letter to the *Herald*, which the newspaper gleefully published with the headline, "Tyrone Power Through Brazil Herald Gives Impressions of Rio de Janeiro," in which the Hollywood star waxed, "Even though so much as happened since I was here last, I was glad indeed to discover my memory not only had not played tricks with me, but I find Rio even more beautiful than when I saw here last."[22]

The *Herald* published recipes, fashion notes, and interior-decorating tips on an inside page titled "Mainly for Women," syndicated editorial cartoons, comic strips Dick Tracy, The Gumps, Smitty, and Blondie, as well as a local horse-racing column written by someone who went by the onomatopoeic penname "Typhoon." On the feature page, expat Marybelle Metzleur Weldon wrote a quizzical column called ". . . Did You Know . . . ," citing obscure but mildly interesting facts about Brazil. Weldon and her husband, American businessman Leslie G. Weldon, who worked in Rio for the multinational shoe manufacturer G. R. Kinney Co., were competitive world-class contract bridge players.[23] For a time, Charles Anderson Weaver, an American-born missionary in Brazil, also wrote another head-scratching column, "Kindred Words," about the etymology of English-language terms.[24] Soon, two columns, "People We've Met . . . " signed simply "By Joan," and "Window Shopping," which carried the byline "Mlle. Footsore," started appearing. It's unknown whether the columns were written by one person or were the products of whoever happened to take on the assignment *du jour.* The former were About Town profiles of expat newcomers who struck the columnist's fancy ("When I walked into the Reuters office last Thursday afternoon, I found Charlie Lynch staring out the window disconsolately and muttering to himself, 'Well, what do they do in Rio when it rains?'"); the latter was advice to expat housewives and mothers ("With the servant problem being as it is, there's no reason on earth why angel children shouldn't learn to wield a broom early in life."), as well as shopping tips on hard-to-find foods and fashions of particular interest to North American and European homemakers.[25]

Following Betty Dyer, among the *Herald*'s first hires was a forty-year-old German émigré with the jigsaw-puzzle last name of Zschech (pronounced *Check*), at the time an out-of-work foreign correspondent who'd been scraping by as a clerical assistant to a local professor of Greek literature, as well as by dabbling as a chemist in a makeshift laboratory of test tubes and petri dishes in his cramped Rio de Janeiro kitchen. Educated at universities in Germany, France, and Italy, and

118

having earned degrees in political science, economics, and philosophy, Herbert Zschech was a polyglot who spoke (in descending order of fluency) German, French, Russian, Portuguese, Dutch, Spanish, Italian, English, ancient Greek and Latin, along with a smattering of a half-dozen other languages.

Prior to joining the *Herald,* Zschech had worked during the mid-1930s for a financial newspaper in Berlin owned by a Jewish

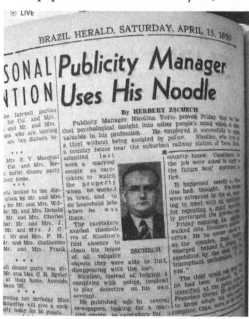

Fig. 9.3 Columnist Herbert Zschech, 1950. Courtesy of the *Brazil Herald.*

family. When Nazis shut down the paper, Zschech left Germany for the Netherlands, but with Europe on the brink of war, he boarded a steamer bound for Buenos Aires via Rio. Arriving at Guanabara Bay, Zschech was sufficiently taken by the local sights that he never got back onboard.

Settling into a new life in Rio, Zschech concocted facial creams and cosmetics, which he sold under the shingle of a Rio beauty salon. He called his company Cosmetics Alemã, Ltda. (German Cosmetics, Limited), and worked alongside a Russian-born woman who would become his wife. In an article extoling Zschech's esthetic-enhancing elixirs, the Rio newspaper *O Jornal* wrote of the "inauguration of an important Scientific Institute of Beauty," under the "technical direction of Mme. Vera," a specialist in "scientific beauty treatments." Another *O Jornal* article plugged the salon's first anniversary, and alerted readers that the beauty parlor was the "exclusive vendor of the famous products of the German scientist, Dr. Herbert Zschech." The newspaper shilled Zschech's rejuvenating creams as "the best that exist," and "the sensation of the feminine world in Paris and New York." An advertisement for Zschech's potions guaranteed patrons "immediate results!"

Zschech got out of his kitchen laboratory when he found work as an editor of a German-language newspaper published in Rio, but with President Vargas's edict outlawing foreign-language newspapers, he once again found himself unemployed and forced to return to formulating "one-of-a-kind" beauty creams that guaranteed elimination of "wrinkles, dry or oily skin, thinning hair, receding hairlines, and premature aging," according to a recurring advertisement in two Rio newspapers.[26]

During the spring of 1946, while taking a break from his cluttered apartment laboratory, the five-foot, four-inch jack-of-all-trades was having drinks with a visiting American student at a busy café on Rua Santa Luzia in Rio's downtown Cinelândia district when the pair spotted a beleaguered man downing whiskey shots at a nearby table.

"'That's the owner of the *Brazil Herald*,' the girl said to me,'" Zschech would write. "'You know, that paper which is not only Brazil's only to be written in English but the world's only to have more misprinted words than correctly printed ones in each number. I'll introduce you to him and ask him to show you his editorial circus. I'm sure you never met with anything like that.'"

The coed steered Zschech to Ralph Ross, the Missouri-born co-owner and editor of the *Herald*. "Waiters appreciated him for his generous tips and not insignificant daily consumption of whisky. The latter was the source of his inspiration for writing headlines," Zschech would write of Ross and the encounter.

After a woozy toast to the virtues of journalism, Ross invited Zschech for a tour of the *Herald* newsroom, where, as the German chemist-cum-journalist would recall, "they just couldn't get the wire service machinery working properly. Everything came over garbled. So, I spent a few minutes with the machines, and I managed to get everything working. They were amazed and hired me a few days later."[27]

In three weeks, Zschech found himself promoted to editor.[28]

A squat, square-shouldered man whose daily uniform consisted of a baggy suit, wide silk tie, voluminous trousers pulled high on his waist, and a porkpie hat dipped rakishly above his right eye, Zschech would stay affiliated with the *Herald* as editor and columnist for four decades, "trapped like a bear," as he inimitably would put it.[29]

Zschech was a doppelgänger for either a gnome or a leprechaun. When I worked for the *Latin America Daily Post* after it had acquired the *Brazil Herald*, Zschech would materialize at the newspaper offices between 10:00 and 10:30 a.m. every day (due to his train schedule from the Rio suburbs) to hand-deliver his typed column with numerous amendments and penciled-in revisions contained in multiple, connecting balloons, all of which was virtually impossible to decipher.

As editor of an English-language daily (the *Herald* came out six days a week with the exception of Monday), how Zschech, whose eighth language was English, could have edited copy and improved it was questionable. In addition to assigning stories, Zschech wrote meanderingly and turgidly about politics in a Sunday column initially titled "Here and There Last Week," which carried the byline "Probex." Despite his limitations as a writer of English, Zschech maintained a voluminous mental Rolodex of mid- and upper-level government officials within the federal and state bureaucracies in Brazil, whether headed by generals or civilians depending on the year, whom he quoted anonymously on political matters. Some readers swore by the veracity of Zschech's insider access; others just swore, frustrated by his impenetrable prose.

In addition to creams and politics, Zschech had a macabre fascination with grisly crime. He covered an assortment of flagrant, seemingly Biblical misdeeds with the same succinct flare that editor-publisher Andrew Jackson Lamoureux had mastered a half century earlier. Zschech's crime copy, lifted and improvised from Brazil's panoply of lurid tabloids, became a staple in the *Herald* as much for its content as for its execution. Here's a Zschech story, complete with one-of-a-kind diction and original typos:

Slaying Orgy

Between the railroad stations Coroa Grande and Itacurussá, in the state of Rio, there is the Tinguassú water fall, a sport well-known to tourists. A certain religious sect, practicing a low form of spiritualism, meets there several times a year for their religious ceremonies during which small animal are sacrificed. The inhabitants of the nearby villages complained several times to the police, because the ceremonies were always accompanied by a great deal of drinking and all sorts of immoral goings-on. But the police authorities answered that they had no grounds on which to stop the whole thing.

Saturday night a group of members of this cult went on their periodical pilgrimage to the Tingussú waterfall. The festivities were beginning when a suden downpour threatened to stop htem. They sought refuge at the house of a stone mason nearby, a man called "Zé da Viola", who rented them a room for several cruzeiros, so that they could continue their cerimony.

Early Sunday morning "Zé da Viola" got fed up with the noise, and threw the pilgrims out. All of them drunk, they left, promising to revenge themselves. They were not far from the place, when "Zé da Viola" appeared on the road, armed with a knife, and looking like a madman. The pilgrims hid in the surrounding woods, and began to throw stones at the man.

Infuriated by this, he got hold of one of them, stabbing him. A woman, who ran to his rescue, was also stabbed. Finally all of them were wounded, including the criminal, who lost consciousness because of his wounds which were caused by the stones thrown at him. When the police arrived on the spot a man and a woman were dead, and "Ze da Viola", was in a comatose state.[30]

And another:

Because of a Pair of Hands

A girl's beautiful hands were the source of all the evil in a tragedy which yesterday occurred in Petropolis, when a couple killed themselves on the steps of the Cathedral by taking poison.

The man was an official of the Police Identification Department in Rio. He was married and had children. His life was going on normally until the day an 18 year old girl came to his office to have her fingerprints taken for an identification document. The man was fascinated by the girl. His infatuation led him to take inconsiderate steps, which brought about family trouble and financial, difficulties and made his life complicated to the utmost degree.

The corpses of the two lovers were found yesterday morning on the steps of the Petropolis Cathedral. Witnesses said they had spent the night dancing and drinking in restaurants and hotels, and they apparently were in a very cheerful mood. At dawn they killed themselves.[31]

Still searching for an identity, within two months of its debut, the *Herald* began mimicking the layout of Brazilian newspapers, crowding its first page with a kaleidoscope of abbreviated stories. The April 25, 1946, issue had an eye-straining nineteen short articles on page one, with jumps to inside pages for five of them.

Among the longest stories the *Herald* ran during its first year was an obituary of Vic Hawkins, one of the newspaper's four original partners, who died unexpectedly at age forty-four. In an unbylined front-page article, presumably written by Ralph Ross, the obit read: "I have known him for sixteen years and worked with him under the closest possible circumstances during the past six. He and I ran [the *Herald*'s forerunner] 'The News.' Help was scarce and we were forced to dig in sixteen or more hours daily. We perhaps became as close together as two male creatures can be."

Ross's heartfelt tribute went on for thirty-three paragraphs. "Don't think life with Vic Hawkins was dull. Not for a second; it was hectic; it was screamingly funny; it was tragic, because he was given to exaggeration and any situation was exploited to its fullest. And that was one reason he was a fine correspondent and newspaperman."

Ross wrote that Hawkins, seldom without a cigarette, was "the most energetic individual I have ever met. Even when he hadn't much work to do his nightly rest seldom passed five or six hours." Hawkins, Ross wrote, was a large man, about six-foot-four-inches tall, and two hundred and forty pounds, but "he carried all this bulk as if it were feathers. He never seemed to tire. He was ready for fun, frolic or work at any time." Hawkins died of esophageal varices, a ruptured vein between his throat and stomach commonly associated with liver disease.[32]

Perhaps prompted by Hawkins's premature death, Ross soon quit the *Herald*, "fed up with his seemingly impossible plan to publish a foreign-language paper in circumstances apt to exhaust a saint's patience, and which no doses of whisky could cause to look brighter," Zschech would write. Ross would return to Buenos Aires, "never again to have anything to do with the newspaper business which he now viewed with horror."

Before he left, though, Ross invited a man who'd been hanging out at the *Herald*'s newsroom to his regular outdoor bistro table in Cinelândia for several animated rounds of whiskey shots. It was there where Ross convinced Lee Langley, an American in his late twenties who favored sandals and open-collar shirts, to take his place and join the newspaper's two remaining partners, Brown and Garcia, and help Zschech edit the *Herald*. There is no record of any monetary exchange;

it's unknown what Langley paid or was paid or what percentage of the newspaper's shares he was given or bought.[33]

Like seemingly everyone else associated with the *Herald*, new co-owner Langley, who was a part-time correspondent for ABC in Rio, had a pocketful of sui generis credentials, particularly so for a newspaperman. Born in Philadelphia, the blonde and fair Langley had earned a bachelor's degree from UCLA, followed by a master's degree from Stanford, and a Ph.D. from Yale in physiology. Joining the Navy Hospital Service Corps, he shipped off to Brazil as a researcher at the Instituto de Biofísica, a medical institute that would become part of the University of Rio de Janeiro. In between shifts at the institute, Langley worked at the *Herald*, editing and writing stories, including an illuminating multi-part series on the history of medicine in Brazil, as well as a weekly column titled "On Second Thought."[34] After he

Fig. 9.4 Columnist Herbert Zschech and Mrs. Lee Langley in the *Brazil Herald*, 1946. Courtesy of the *Brazil Herald*.

left the *Herald*, Langley would go on to earn a law degree, serve in Turkey for the United Nations, become a professor at the University of Alabama and University of Missouri, write a medical textbook, and work for the National Heart Institute and the National Library of Medicine in Bethesda, Maryland. He also played competitive tennis and traveled the world in search of his favorite operas.[35]

Dropping in occasionally at the newspaper office was original partner Joe Brown, whose father had been editor of the *Hammondsport
Herald* in the Finger Lakes district of New York. The younger Brown
arrived in Brazil in 1911, dispatched by Ford Motors to scout the
developing nation as a market for cars and trucks. Brown soon
found himself working in Brazil for Standard Oil, then as a fixer for
American firms seeking a foothold in the fast-industrializing nation. From 1936 to 1942, he worked for the American Chamber of
Commerce in Rio, where he was the editor of *Brazilian Business*, the
Chamber's magazine. During World War II, Brown worked for the
Inter-American Affairs Agency, a quasi-government organization
headed by young Nelson A. Rockefeller, whose family had extensive
holdings in Brazil.[36] The IAAA secured loans to bankroll large economic development projects as a precursor to today's World Bank
and International Monetary Fund.[37] Brown had a bulging portfolio of
connections in Latin America and used them, particularly among the
expat community, to circulate interest in the fledging *Herald*.

Garcia, the remaining partner at the *Herald*, was a balding man
with round tortoise-shell glasses and a long poker face. Garcia's father
had been a Spanish Army officer who had immigrated to Puerto Rico,
where the younger Garcia had grown up. Garcia dropped out of college and moved to New York, where he was hired as a correspondent
for a San Juan newspaper. In 1904 Garcia married Mabel Cross, an
heir to the Singer Sewing Machine fortune, and twelve years later, the
couple boarded a steamer to Brazil, where Garcia would become a
correspondent for the *Public Ledger*, a Philadelphia newspaper, and
later was named *The New York Times* correspondent in Rio, a post he
would keep for decades, more a sinecure than a steppingstone.

Garcia was a member of just about every expat and insider club
or association in Rio, including the Brazil-United States Institute,
American Society of Rio de Janeiro, American Chamber of Commerce,
the Gávea Golf and Country Club, and the Rio de Janeiro Country
Club. In 1921, when the first Rotary Club was established in Brazil,

Garcia was a founding member (along with local American power-brokers in Brazil Herbert Moses and Richard Momsen).[38] In 1948, he was awarded the Order of the Southern Cross by the Brazilian government, the highest honorary title bestowed on a non-national in Brazil. A two-block-long street, Rua Frank Garcia, in Rio's Tauá neighborhood is named after him.[39] While working as the *Times*'s correspondent, Garcia wrote a daily column in the *Herald* titled "Brazil." More understandable than Zschech's garbled prose, Garcia's column was nonetheless plodding. It dealt with obscure, often inaccessible topics such as fiscal policy, government infrastructure, and import-export regulations.

Neither Brown nor Garcia was Brazilian, but both were thoroughly Brazilian. Both spoke Portuguese with ease and both circulated among the upper crust of the local and expatriate glitterati, entertaining the shifting cast of diplomats, politicians, and business executives shuttling in and out of Rio. Ink-stained newsmen Lee Langley and Herb Zschech were left to get the newspaper out as best they could.

Despite Brown's and Garcia's connections and Langley's and Zschech's around-the-clock labor, the *Herald* was a losing proposition from the start. By September 1946, seven months after its first issue, the newspaper was perilously close to shuttering. The four owners convened a meeting of the American Chamber of Commerce and the local American Society, at which they floated a last-ditch proposition. In exchange for an immediate infusion of funds, investors would earn a six-to-nine percent return on the *Herald's* annual profits (if there were any). "It was the feeling of the group that there was a place and need for an English-language daily in this community," read an account published in the *Herald* of the fund-raising effort. "To allow the newspaper to fold up and disappear would not only mean the loss of a franchise for printing an English-language daily (which was not easy to get) but it would also mean loss of face and prestige to the English-speaking community."

At least twenty-three individuals and business entities chipped in to bolster the *Herald's* near-depleted finances, including Moore-McCormack Shipping, Gillette, Kibon (a Brazil-based ice-cream manufacturer), Kodak, Columbia Pictures, ITT, and General Electric. [40] There likely were other multinationals, local subsidiaries, and donors, although no records exist today to document any roster of investors.

The funds went toward the purchase of several used presses, as well as renting space for a printing plant, located on a circular street behind Rio's main railroad station. This allowed the *Herald* to save the cost of renting press time at another Rio daily, *A Noite*, where the newspaper had been printed since its inception.

The influx of capital did little to improve the newspaper's editorial quality, which continued to be blotted by so many typographical errors that in its first Christmas issue, the editors ran this page-one explanation:

This is the first Christmas in the life of the BRAZIL HERALD. Characteristic of all infants we have made mistakes, we have made many false starts, we have moved ahead with unsure steps; and, occasionally, you have laughed at us just as you laugh at the amusing actions of any child. But we honestly believe that we have progressed, that despite these obvious signs of immaturity, adolescence and maturity are not too far off.

Now, with all of this behind us, now, when we are able to laugh ourselves, we pause, this Christmas day, to look ahead and to make a vow. It is our desire not only to serve you, but to make you justly proud of this paper, which, actually, is your paper.

And that we shall do.

May we be one of the first, this Christmas morning to come into your home and wish you a Very Merry Christmas. [41]

The financial angels' holiday wish was that the new year would bring to the newspaper proofreader talent, advertising, subscribers, and a modest return on their investment. But the benefactors' bail out bought only so much time, and soon the *Herald* found itself once again on the brink of a financial precipice. Owning and operating a printing press, which broke down regularly, it turned out, went only so far to avoid economic disaster.

To the rescue came a wealthy patron in the visage of a dazzling new US ambassador to Brazil.

Enter dapper William Douglas Pawley, known to friends simply as "Cuba."

CHAPTER 10

Cuba, Teddy, Dawn, Tad, and Marc

THE NEW AMERICAN ambassador was a flashy international million-aire who had made his far-flung fortunes in Florida real estate, private bus companies, and aviation enterprises in Cuba, Nationalist China, and India. Born in Florence, South Carolina, but raised in Caimanera, Cuba, where his father had been a contractor for the nearby US Naval fleet at Guantánamo Bay, Bill Pawley had helped create a mercenary squadron of civilian American flyers, the Flying Tigers, led by former US Air Corps pilot Claire Chennault, to go to war on behalf of the forces of Chinese Nationalist leader Chiang Kai-shek against the Japanese during World War II. After he divorced his first wife of twenty-three years, Pawley married his secretary, Edna Earle Cadenhead, of Tulsa, Oklahoma. The newlyweds honeymooned in a teakwood forest in India, where they rode maximus indicus elephants and hunted Bengali tigers as guests of the Maharaja of the Kingdom of Mysore. In 1945, Pawley served as US ambassador to Peru, but resigned that post to accept the more prestigious Brazil appointment a year later. He arrived in Rio with fanfare befitting royalty, showing up with his own fleet of air-lifted Cadillac limousines, along with a private airplane and a saluting uniformed crew. Pawley and his wife created an instant stir in Rio, a city well-acquainted with international razzmatazz. As *Life* magazine would describe Pawley, he had a knack for "being in the right place for a few minutes before the right time."[1]

The hubbub surrounding the new ambassador couldn't have hap-pened at a better time for the struggling *Brazil Herald*. In breaking the news of Pawley's confirmation, the *Herald* ran this klieg-lighted front-page headline, "New American Ambassador to Brazil Has Had Exciting and Romanic Career."[2] It was a precursor to how the oleaginous *Herald* would embrace Pawley and all that the ambassador would offer the pro-business newspaper.

Fig. 10.1 Front-page coverage of US Ambassador William D. Pawley. Courtesy of the *Brazil Herald*.

Pawley's predecessor had been nerdy Ambassador Adolph Berle, a penny-pinching Columbia University law professor and savant who'd been admitted to Harvard when he was fourteen. The US embassy in Rio's Botafogo district was shabby and rundown, in part because regal trappings were never a priority for Berle. Threadbare carpets, dingy furniture encased in frayed slipcovers, and faded drapes had underscored the wartime finances of the US State Department and its run-dry consular budgets, particularly in forgotten Latin America. Ambassador Pawley was Berle's opposite, running a "grand embassy" in the words of his assistant, John Howard Burns. Immediately upon arrival, Pawley decorated the embassy at 388 São Clemente Avenue with his own Persian rugs, Oriental antiques, and Indian furnishings.

Although Pawley spoke Spanish, he made no effort to learn Portuguese. He was too busy filling up his social calendar. As consular official Burns remembered, the ambassador "was popular with the government and with everyone else, a very likable individual and exceedingly generous."[3]

Pawley brought the same panache to Rio that he had flaunted in Miami Beach, his home in the States. He and wife Edna enjoyed hosting gala soirees at the ambassador's residence in the shadow of Rio's Corcovado. The Pawleys' dance card their first year included General Dwight Eisenhower; General Mark Clark, under whose command the Brazilian air division had served in Italy; and Henry Luce, the right-wing publisher of the Time-Life empire, and his firebrand wife, playwright, journalist, anti-communist ideologue Clare Boothe Luce.[4]

In one of his last bylined stories, outgoing *Brazil Herald* co-founder Ralph Ross wrote a front-page walkup to the Eisenhower visit, which read, "Never since the visit of President Franklin D. Roosevelt in 1936 has this country received such a distinguished American. He will be accorded honors and given attention which few countries other than this hospitable nation knows how to bestow."[5] The fawning coverage demonstrated the *Herald*'s servitude to courting Pawley and thus being accorded a front-row seat to the future President's touring retinue. The day after Eisenhower arrived, the *Herald* ran this soapy lede: "In an interview characterized by Dr. Herbert Moses, President of the Brazilian Press Association as the best ever given by a visitor to local journalists, General Dwight D. Eisenhower further expressed his conviction that the elimination of future wars was in the hands of the citizens of democratic countries."[6] The gratuitous mention of local American-Brazilian fixer Moses, as well as Eisenhower's pie-in-sky assessment of how world conflict might be prevented, seemed a clumsy attempt at reminding American expat readers that the *Herald* was their go-to source of so-called "news."

Ross would soon leave Brazil to return to the US to work for a government-assistance initiative cloaked under the guise of improving Third World economic conditions under the direction of US Secretary of State Dean Acheson. In reality, the so-called Four Point Program was a transparent strategy of American self-interest to expedite the importation of rare raw materials, and at the same time, counter growing Soviet political influence. The program was akin to the modern US Agency for International Development.[7]

Meanwhile, rabid anti-communist Pawley's tenure as ambassador was a whirlwind, culminating in the summer of 1947 with the Inter-American Defense Conference, a multinational Monroe Doctrinesque summit that convened in Rio. The summit was a public-relations coup that Pawley had employed his ample political portfolio to successfully pull off. It brought to Rio US President and Mrs. Truman and their twenty-three-year-old daughter Margaret; Secretary of State George C. Marshall; a raft of US congressmen; and the three-football-fields-long USS *Missouri*, the battleship on whose deck the Japanese had surrendered to the Allies two years earlier.

"The President, riding in an open car, saw a thick and continuous storm of paper and ticker-tape raining down on him," the *Herald* enthused in an unbylined page one story with a banner headline. "People jammed every window of the tall buildings and as the President passed they broke into enthusiastic, spontaneous applause."[8]

Although Margaret Truman wore a daring off-the-shoulder evening gown for a gala state dinner at the American embassy the next evening,

Miss Truman was overshadowed by the show-stopping, twenty-eight-year-old blonde wife of newly elected Argentine President Juan Perón, recognized globally by her first name, Evita. Under a page-one photo of the Argentine first lady, the *Herald* trilled, "Dressed in a baby blue outfit, the famous wife of President Peron looked rested, animated and quite up to her well-publicized beauty."[9]

To cover the star-studded conference came a bevy of high-powered media luminaries, including Eric Sevareid, the CBS radio commentator who earlier in his career had worked at the Paris *Herald*. Mixing pleasure with business, Sevareid stayed at Pawley's home as the ambassador's guest.

A master of orchestrated drama, Pawley signed off on Truman's surprise appearance at Rio's grand beaux arts Municipal Theater, where the opera *Tosca* was playing. Just as act one ended and a thick red-velvet proscenium curtain descended, the audience recognized the American president sitting front and center. The thrilled crowd responded by giving Truman a ten-minute standing ovation. The event would be typical of the way Pawley would operate during his tenure as ambassador.

Pawley made for instant copy in the new *Brazil Herald*. The international conference and visiting delegations were ready-made events happening down the block from the *Herald*'s newsroom, located on the fourth floor, in cluttered room 401, at 257 Rio Branco Avenue. The around-the-clock buzz couldn't have happened at a better time to bang the drums for the financially strapped newspaper. It didn't hurt that two of the three remaining *Brazil Herald* partners, Joe Brown and Frank Garcia, got along famously with Pawley. The third partner, Lee Langley, with editor and columnist Herb Zschech, anchored the newsroom, leaving the glad-handing to Brown and Garcia, who introduced the new ambassador to Rio's receiving line of business executives, consular officials, Brazilian politicians, and otherwise go-to influencers.

The technology to deliver the *Herald* to these stalwarts was cumbersome and costly. Heavy metal plates of the newspaper's pages were created in a second-floor pressroom, then transported to the base-ment in a clanking elevator that often got stuck between floors. This made for the backbreaking work of transporting heavy printing forms from the pressroom to flatbed presses down a flight of narrow stairs.

That was only one problem associated with the *Herald*'s antiquat-ed printing process. Another was the location of the pressroom and presses, near the British cemetery in the Gamboa section of Rio, sit-uated in an asphalt gulch that even moderate rainstorms thoroughly inundated. As editor-columnist Zschech recalled, "Gamboa Street became a navigable river whenever it rained, with water sometimes rising above an average person's head. One day, I entered the building through a second-floor window, after tipping a strong man in a near-by bar to carry me on his back through the rolling waves in front of the premises."[10] One can imagine stout and sodden Zschech, dressed in suit, tie, and hat, atop the broad shoulders of a stranger wading through cresting flood waters to arrive at the printing plant.

Getting the newspaper into the hands of readers through home de-livery or through *bancas* (sidewalk newsstands) the following morning also courted disaster since the paper's arrival depended on a tenuous chain of part-time intermediaries, none employed by the *Herald*.

Neither Brown nor Garcia had started the *Herald* to make money, and it's doubtful that either Langley or Zschech was making much either. Still, the *Herald* earned a hearty welcome in several thousand American and British households in Rio on the days that it arrived before noon, if at all. Filled with bold sans serif headlines, fluffy so-ciety news, back-home sports scores, and manufactured Hollywood drama,[11] the newspaper assiduously covered Ambassador Pawley's comings and goings as though it was the diplomat's personal publicity machine, which in a sense it was.

When Brown informed Pawley that the newspaper might be forced to downsize to twice weekly, the ambassador promptly opened his own checkbook and wrote out a personal check for $17,000. Pawley's donation was a stopgap measure to ensure another month or two of publishing. He likely could have accessed backdoor funds through the

State Department since the *Herald* was an unabashed supporter of US-Brazilian business ties and cultural cooperation, but Pawley used his own resources to throw the newspaper a life ring.[12]

Unlike A. J. Lamoureux's combative *Rio News*, the *Herald* was a cheerleader for all things American and US-government endorsed. In doing so, the newspaper also served as a vehicle for co-founders Brown and Garcia to remain preeminent, in-the-know players in Rio's expatriate community. Garcia made use of his political and business connections, and wrote about them effusively in his daily column, seemingly paying back a plethora of favors.

When Brazil's former President Vargas was elected a federal senator in 1946, Garcia's front-page story might have come directly from Vargas's own press office, as the *Herald* had demonstrated with its coverage of Pawley.

"Senhor Vargas is still the same jovial man whose easy and happy smile has become so familiar to Brazilians," Garcia's page-one account read. "Wearing his equally familiar gray, double-breasted business suit, he smoke [*sic*] his big cigars, his healthy appearance is enviable, and his mind is as alert as always."[13]

Garcia followed several months later with another valentine, this one about a resolution before the Brazilian Chamber of Deputies nominating politician Oswaldo Aranha, recovering from pneumonia, for the Nobel Peace Prize. Garcia's story seemed to be payback for Aranha's lobbying Vargas to permit the launch of the *Herald* a year earlier, even though Aranha had little chance of being awarded the coveted prize.[14]

While the *Herald* was doing whatever it could to gain standing in the local expat marketplace, typographical errors continued to undercut the daily product. The paper offered a series of apologies, once again suggesting to readers, "We need to have a few more people about in critical positions who know the language in which this paper is reputed to be. Plans are rapidly moving ahead to do just that, but it will take time, a few months, we hope. In the meantime, grin and laugh and bear it, and if you are still unconvinced come down to the print shop some night and we feel sure you will agree with us that The Brazil Herald is, after all, quite a miracle." As though to make the point, the story contained a host of mistakes, particularly words incorrectly split at line breaks, such as hea-ding, ans-wer, bu-siness, li-nes, re-present, we-ars, bur-ning, sh-op, establishme-nt, betwe-en, whi-ch, we-re, pa-rts, ra-ck, and diffe-rent.[15]

Even with Ambassador Pawley's lifeline of funds, the *Herald* seemed perpetually on the brink of folding. "Aside from cards, drink and women, two popular ways to lose money are poultry raising and restaurant operating," Joseph Brown would reflect. "Mortality is high. But unquestionably, the most certain way is to start an English-language daily in a foreign country."[16]

Finances aside, some prodigious talent found its way to the newspaper during these perilous first years. Many were Americans, Brits, and a host of other nationals with varying degrees of English fluency who had traveled to Rio de Janeiro as tourists, pinched themselves, and decided to stay. Others had arrived through family ties, marriages, or assorted business ventures and showed up at the *Herald*'s newsroom to experience the romantic yet penurious notion of working at a newspaper. There was little planning of what went into tomorrow's paper, none for next week's. Few *Herald* editors and reporters had been trained as journalists. Some picked up the craft as they went along, others decidedly did not. That made little difference. Well-written and informative dispatches appeared next to news accounts that were thoroughly unreadable. Both became trademarks of a spectacularly uneven newspaper.

One talented *Herald* staffer during these years already had a famous name—at least through her father she did: Edwina Hecht, the first daughter of Chicago journalist, screenwriter, playwright Ben Hecht, who had enshrined himself in the hearts of the American public with his (and Charles MacArthur's) 1928 smash Broadway tribute to the newspaper business, *The Front Page*. Ben Hecht was twentieth-century America's most prolific screenwriter. As an accomplished nineteen-year-old journalist herself, Edwina had already shared a byline in a "Talk of the Town" piece in *The New Yorker* in 1935.[17] That same year, she had appeared in a movie, *Once in a Blue Moon*, directed by Hecht and MacArthur, in which she, as Princess Ilena, co-starred with Broadway clown Jimmy Savo, along with six hundred extras in a film about a group of Russian aristocrats disguised as a traveling circus troupe fleeing the Bolshevik revolution.[18]

Fig. 10.2 Edwina (Teddy) Hecht. Reprinted by permission of Mirim Tullis.

Teddy, as she was affectionately called due to a childhood attachment she had for a toy stuffed bear, grew up in Chicago, and once her father's writing career took off, in Nyack, New York. Two years after the dissolution of her first marriage, Teddy married French-born Brazilian Mario Nicholas Barboza-Carneiro in New York, and the couple moved to Rio, where Teddy was named editor of a slick, thick, and sophisticated fashion magazine called *Sombra*, a *Vogue* clone.[19] Although written in Portuguese, oversized *Sombra* (shadow in English) was truly an international publication. In 1940, it showcased a whimsical, wavy-lined cover drawn by a young Romanian-born artist, Saul Steinberg, who three decades later would create *The New Yorker*'s most famous cover, that of a satiric map of the world as seen from the eyes of a jaded Manhattanite.[20]

In addition to her editing duties, Teddy contributed several stories to *Sombra*, one of her impressions of Rio, another on the New Orleans jazz scene.[21] For *Sombra*, she wrote in English and translators rendered her prose in Portuguese. In one story, she was photographed by French photographer Jean Manzon in Guanabara Bay, lounging in a two-piece bathing suit on the deck of a seventy-two-foot schooner, the *Regina*, owned by Herbert S. Polin, an American coffee-roasting magnate and chemist who lived part-time in Rio.[22]

Teddy had a nasty split with the owners of *Sombra* and was fired, which resulted in a protracted legal battle that never got fully resolved. Energetic and able, she then teamed up with *Newsweek*'s Latin America correspondent John G. Nasht to create a prototype for another glossy, high-end Brazilian fashion magazine to be called *Senhorita*. That publication never took flight, so on and off through the late-1940s Teddy worked alongside Herb Zschech as an editor and reporter at the *Brazil Herald*.[23]

Like A. J. Lamoureux and other expat journalists who found their way to Rio, Teddy Hecht's professional life was filled with flashes of literary brilliance played against the backdrop of a vibrant, exotic port city seemingly constantly beset by runaway inflation and nonstop political instability. Teddy was smart, attractive, sophisticated, fashionable, and vivacious, a young American woman abroad who might well have served as the protagonist of an Irwin Shaw or Mary McCarthy short story of the same era. A trove of two dozen typewritten letters I came across in Chicago's Newberry Library written to her famous father paints a composite of a spectacularly talented but unheralded journalist juggling multiple familial and financial balls while thoroughly enjoying expatriate life in Rio. In many ways, the letters—witty, literate, and self-deprecating—all typed on onionskin paper, contained as an overlooked addendum in her father's voluminous archived correspondence, are significant because they so fully describe the lively yet challenging life of a female American journalist living abroad during the 1940s and 1950s.[24]

In one letter dated April 20, 1945, Teddy informed her father and his second wife Rose (Ben Hecht and Marie Armstrong, Teddy's mother, had divorced in 1925), living in Oceanside, California, and New York, "I got your letter this morning and was as pleased and thrilled as if it were a communication from Mars." Teddy described her 6,500-mile New York-Rio passage on four DC 3 TACA airlines planes as "an impassable distance and nothing short of magic. . . . Don't let anyone tell you that flying 5 days in a plane is any fun. My fanny was so stiff and sore that it literally hurt."[25]

As a minimally paid journalist and frugal newlywed in the mid-1940s, Teddy fretted about properly outfitting the Rio apartment she shared with her husband. "It is absolutely no use trying to use the chintzes and linens and cretonnes they have here now. They are frightfully expensive and so horrible that no one but some high class Riverside Drive bitch would be caught dead with them," she typed to her father, whom she addressed as Daddy.[26]

In another letter, Teddy wrote, "[I]t is impossible to get nice inexpensive things here. Expensive, yes, but too expensive. The $15 dress that is wearable doesn't exist. Nor do a lot of household things that we can get for next to nothing in the States. . . .I haven't bought a thing here for a long time." In the same letter, she confessed a longing affection for an au courant French perfume called Tabu.[27]

After her marriage to Barboza-Carneiro unraveled, Teddy found herself single in a drawn-out separation that led to a protracted divorce. "Since I know Mario is doing his best to run me out of the country, I prefer to stay and try to annoy him, Our relations are those of the Hatfields and the Coys [sic]—shoot on sight. I haven't seen him, even accidentally, for some weeks, but when we do talk over the phone, once in a great while, it ends up in a fine screaming match."[28]

To earn money, Teddy got hired at the Herald at a salary of sixty dollars a month. In addition to editing the newspaper's "Woman's Page," she solicited ads for the "Movie Page," and "from this, I get a commission and, with my salary which is minute, I should be able to get enough. The Herald is ok except that instead of 2 hours, it takes about 4 hours a day." She wrote, "I've got the B. Herald down to a kind of system so that I find time to do something else besides that every day."[29]

Teddy volunteered to her father that she was involved in "a fairly gay social life, though I had to stop that business of going to bed late and getting up for work, which went on with some visiting firemen for a couple of weeks."[30]

While working at the Herald, Teddy's preoccupation was finding a reasonably priced apartment. To economize, she often stayed with friends or housesat. "I had an apt. for 3 weeks that was pure charm—on Ipanema beach and the top floor of an old Portuguese-Moorish house with columned terraces et al," she wrote her father. "It saved my life, financially, for that period, and it is only sad that the guy came back from NY too soon."[31]

On another occasion, Teddy found temporary housing at another apartment in Rio's beachside Zona Sul district.

I've played Wandering Jew and moved once more. This time I've a darling one room, balcony, kitchen, hall and bath in Copacabana overlooking the ocean though one block away. The only drawback is, it's only for 2 months, unless the girl decides to stay away longer. I would like that, if I have to stay here, because it is one of the most comfortable places I've been in and has a decent bed. After that piece of stone in the hotel, this is a relief. I moved only last week, so still have some time to look around. But Lord, am I sick of packing those damn suitcases! Anyway, I have a maid, a laundress and no trouble at all with the place.[32]

When short-term housing opportunities dried up, Teddy stayed in a boardinghouse, The Central, the same ubiquitous name as the hot-sheets hotel where I stayed when I arrived in São Paulo three decades later.

Like seemingly every newcomer to Rio, Teddy was drawn to the beach. "It's pure heaven to go out there on Sat. or Sundays. A rainy Sunday here is misery. And tragedy. I'm very brown and look horribly healthy. Two weeks ago I spent some 6 hours on the beach and burned one little spot right in the middle of my back. A regular 3rd degree burn."[33]

In another letter she wrote:

Socially, I am having a marvelous time. . . . My 5th column tells me that Mario is sulking in his tent and saying that he can't go out because of our odd situation, so I sent back a message that he'd better stop thinking that way because it didn't stop me ever. I haven't seen or spoken to him for about a month. I go with a very nice, gay group of people and we manage to dream up something amusing almost every week. Weekends are what we live for—beach, of course. And when it rains, like today, we wander desolately around the Riding Club, the Botanical Garden and other places thinking whom we can annoy. Usually we have huge Sunday lunches which Dorothy and I cook, and, while it all sounds silly from here, it is fun.[34]

In taking the *Herald* job, Teddy had taken a 60-percent pay cut from what she'd been making at *Sombra*. She soon was to get a raise at the *Herald* to "the magnificent sum of $75 a month." She wrote her father: "Obviously, one does not live on this! Especially here wher [sic] living is now known to be higher than NY."[35]

Like many journalists in Brazil, Teddy picked up occasional side jobs. One was for businessman-banker Nelson Rockefeller. "When Nelson was here, I was sort of ex-officio advisor on people, and it was wonderful fun to watch every crook and blackmailer or anyone with a square foot of land for sale descending on the hotel where Nelson was. I had to fill him in on all the characters. . . ."[36]

Outside of work at the *Herald* and whatever other jobs she could hustle, Teddy's bustling days included ballet lessons three times a week, as well as all things equestrian, which, she wrote her father, caused her body all kinds of aches and pains. "The first time I went riding it was almost impossible to walk the next day, much less do 'pliers' [the plié position in ballet]." She added that she had a Finnish masseuse come to her apartment for massage and gymnastics.[37]

Teddy rode dressage at the local hippodrome on a series of horses, Champagne, Avahi, Bismuth, Czardas, and Morfeu, and became accomplished enough to win a trophy case full of medals, to be nationally ranked, and for the *Gazeta Esportiva* to run dozens of articles on her with photographs and interviews.[38] Teddy went on to win first prize for dressage "Grace and Elegance" at São Paulo's Santo Amaro Clube Hipico.[39]

But come Monday morning, it was back to work, or, as she wrote, "off to the races" to edit "recipes, beauty and fashion and movies. . . . What a chore filling 3 pages a day. . . . Whew!" It's likely she contributed to the *Herald*'s regular women's feature, "Window Shopping," which carried the anonymous byline, "Mlle. Footsore."

Teddy called her hectic daily routine, "this radio serial life of mine. . . .I haven't been lost in the wilds of the jungle. Just busy as hell, moving, working, playing, etc."[40] She occasionally asked her well-off father for financial help. "Contributions are always gratefully accepted in this parish. And this year, we had so many presents to buy for so many people, and so many more tips to give that the sum was a rather staggering one."[41]

In almost all her letters, she made references to her father's prolific writing, particularly stories that had appeared in *P.M.*, *Colliers*, and *Red Book*, as well as his meteoric career in Hollywood, which would include screenplays for Alfred Hitchcock's *Notorious* and *Foreign Correspondent*, as well as for *Scarface*, *Gunga Din*, and collaborations on *Gone with the Wind* and *Gilda*. In another letter, she made mention of her father's 1946 Broadway play, *A Flag Is Born*, starring Paul Muni, Celia Adler, a newly discovered actor by the name of Marlon Brando, as well as a musical score by German-American composer Kurt Weill. "How many movies are you working on at once, Daddy?" she asked in another letter.[42]

Teddy seldom mentioned her own literary talent, even though she pitched freelance articles to *Vogue*, *Elle*, *Glamour*, and *Mademoiselle*, as well as to a host of Brazilian magazines and newspapers. To her father, she volubly wrote about fashion, a manifestation of carefree mirth from a sophisticated American woman living large abroad following World War II.

After she left the *Herald* and moved to São Paulo, Teddy wrote:

The other day I bought two suits and a top coat and a terrific bright red cape. An export man has just come back from visiting America and since we know him I got them at almost New York prices. The suit is blue wool (French blue, a color I always fell for) with bright yellow checks. The top coat matches it, and is quite pretty. The other is just a very plain little black suit to wear around and the cape, as I said, is terrific. One needs those things actually as the nights are very chilly and, like California in winter, winter here is cool the minute you step out of the sun.[43]

As a follow-up, she added:

I have a lion's mane which is the envy of the town. The hairdresser is a big bore, so I wash it myself and hang it out to dry. I don't

145

always look like the well-groomed editor, but my hair is clean which is more than they get done anyplace else. I think I weigh about 120 or so—it's hard to translate from kilos—and I don't look too poochy. I still have 3 precious pairs of unopened Nylon stockings which I shall ice slightly and serve when Armistice is signed.[44]

At about this time Teddy started dating American businessman Dee William Jackson, another expatriate living in Brazil, and during a trip back to the United States, the couple got married in Juárez, Mexico. They eventually had two children, Mirim and Benjamin (named after Teddy's father).

In Nyack with her parents, Teddy had grown up with a menagerie of dogs, and in her letters she often inquired about her father's brood of canines. Teddy supplemented her income in Brazil by importing and breeding championship dalmatians and boxers, and it was from those funds that she and Dee, who for a time worked for the Brazilian subsidiary of GM, sent Mirim and Benjamin to Graded, a pricey American school in São Paulo.

After leaving the *Herald*, Teddy joined the J. Walter Thompson Agency as an advertising executive in charge of accounts of the Brazilian department-store, Mappin, as well as of the American healthcare-products subsidiary, Johnson & Johnson ("They get you from womb to tomb," she wrote her father[45]) and of Sherwin-Williams paints. She happily called herself a "huckster on a grand scale," working in the world of advertising. "[A]ll they say about the profession is true. However, so far, it's a pack of fun."[46]

In another letter, she wrote, "I have decided that a one-armed paper hanger is an unemployed little fellow compared with myself."[47] At some time, she left J. Walter Thompson, and joined another agency, Grant Advertising. "I am among other things, traffic manager . . . copy writer, campaign planner, feminine touch, general aide to the boss, and God knows what else. I am also, I guess, what is known as an account executive, and have more responsibility thrown on me than I'm used to. I know this must all be hard for you to imagine, since I'm sure you still think of me as 16 years old and playing on the hockey team."[48]

In São Paulo, she managed to ride horses early in the morning, then commuted an hour each way to work. She spoke Portuguese, but, as her daughter, Mirim Tullis, would remember, "it was kinda broken. When she'd forget the word for something, she'd just say, '*coisa*,'" which means *thing*. During weekends, Teddy took to drinking heavily, her beverage of choice, dry martinis, recalled Tullis.[49]

The cooler weather in São Paulo, Teddy wrote her father, "makes a huge difference in the amount of work one is able to get done and still stay alive and feel like a human. The climate here for us Northerners is delightful. Downright cold, in fact. 3 blankets at night and woolen suits plus coat is nothing. Frost in the mornings and you can see your breath almost any time." Ever the fashion arbitrator, Teddy noted, "all the girls are walking around in flat feet and wide gray skirts . . . and black blouses or jerseys." [50]

Teddy, Dee, and their children lived in an out-of-the-way neighborhood, Santa Amaro, far from downtown, at 1000 Estrada da Zavuvus, down an unpaved, dirt road in a rented ramshackle compound with stables, a horse ring, small lake, and a bocce ball court, for which they paid $175 a month. The couple had hens to lay eggs and grew their own vegetables. At times, the family had two dozen dogs at the *fazenda*. They lived a charmed, bohemian life and had friends over often, including famous Brazilian musician Dorival Caymmi. Every Sunday was reserved for a *churrasco*, an outdoor party of grilled meats.[51]

On a visit to her father's house in Nyack in the late-1950s, Teddy fell down a staircase and fractured her coccyx, which necessitated a complicated surgical grafting of her tailbone to her vertebral column. The surgery was successful, but as Teddy resumed dressage riding, the activity aggravated the injury. She needed a second grafting, and it was while recovering at Albert Einstein Jewish Hospital in São Paulo that she died of pneumonia on August 18, 1972, at age fifty-six.

Well before then, Teddy had given up any pretense that she would ever return to the United States as a resident. Among her possessions when she died was a long-expired US passport.[52]

Along with Teddy Hecht, another young reporter drawn to the *Herald* during the same period was Dawn Addams. Born in Suffolk, England, and raised in Calcutta, India, her father, an RAF captain, packed eighteen-year-old Addams off to Rio to live with relatives after she declared she wanted to be an actress. "I had a friend on the Brazil Herald who said: 'Look you're going to all the parties. How about writing a social column for us?" Addams assisted *Herald* columnist and entertainment writer André Fodor with his "Rio at Night" column, but as Fodor later would put it, "she was too good looking to stay in Brazil."[53] After a yearlong stint at the *Herald*, Addams returned to England, then moved to Hollywood and went on to a marquee career as an MGM contract actor. Her first big roles were in *Night into Morning, Singin' in the Rain, Young Bess, Plymouth Adventure,* and the *Hour of 13*. In 1957, she played opposite Charlie Chaplin in *A King in New York*, Chaplin's last leading role. Addams was a leading lady to Spencer Tracy, Christopher Jones, Van Johnson, Alan Young, and Peter Lawford. She was Roger Moore's love interests in the cult-classic TV show, *The Saint*, variously as Magda Varnoff, Countess Audrey Morova, and Queen Adana. In Otto Preminger's 1952 *The Moon is Blue*, Addams played David Niven's catty socialite daughter, ending up in of all places, Rio de Janeiro, rather than home in the arms of her married beau, William Holden. The film became a footnote for film scholars because it defied the Hollywood studios' morals code at the time by mentioning two words: "virgin" and "mistress."

Addams's personal life after she left the *Herald* would get splashed in tabloids and movie magazines. She carried on assiduously publicized spats with a raft of alleged suitors, including Farley Granger, Ray Milland, Tab Hunter, Peter Lawford, and French actor Claude Dauphin. She was often photographed socializing with girlfriends Shelley Winters and Zsa Zsa Gabor. For a while, Addams appeared to be fashion mogul Oleg Cassini's love interest, but when she married

Vittorio Emanuele Massimo, Prince of Roccasecca di Volsci in 1954, the wedding became a spread in *Life* magazine. Living in the prince's castle in Cortona, Italy, the couple were intimates of actress Gina Lollobrigida and husband Dr. Milko Skofic; the foursome frequently showed up photographed skiing in the Alps together. Addams and the prince divorced, and she made the Mediterranean island of Malta her home, where she met retired American businessman Jimmy White, whom she subsequently married. Addams died in London of lung cancer in 1985.[54]

Perhaps the most notable of all *Herald* hires, at least journalistically, during the same era as Teddy Hecht and Dawn Addams, was Tad Szulc (pronounced *Schultz*), who would go on to leave an indelible mark on American journalism and world affairs. Born in Warsaw in 1926, Tadeusz Witold Szulc's well-to-do parents emigrated from Poland to Rio de Janeiro in the mid-1930s, where Tad's father, Seweryn, was the Polish consul, during which he secured visas for hundreds of Poles fleeing their homeland, either anticipating the German invasion of Poland or fleeing after the Nazi occupation and resettling in Brazil. The senior Szulc's influence "accounted for a substantial urban Polish

Fig. 10.3 Tad Szulc. Reprinted by permission of *The New York Times* and Redux Pictures.

colony in Brazil," recalled Joseph Novitski, *The New York Times* correspondent in Rio who would follow Tad Szulc in the same journalistic
posting.[55]

Szulc's parents sent Tad to the premier Swiss boarding school, Le
Rosey, before he rejoined his family in Rio in the mid-1940s, ma-
triculating at the newly founded University of Brazil (to be renamed
the Federal University of Rio de Janeiro). Like Andrew Jackson
Lamoureux, Szulc never graduated from the university, but a college
degree then (or now) was not a prerequisite to enter the journalism
profession and flourish in it.

One of Szulc's college friends, Brazilian Nahum Sirotsky, who
would go on to become a prominent journalist and diplomat, remembered Szulc as a Jewish refugee who carried a patrician, aristocratic
air about him. He was not known for modesty, recalled Sirotsky. Like
Herb Zschech, Szulc was a polyglot, with varying degrees of fluency
in Polish, English, French, Spanish, and Portuguese. Sirotsky remembered Szulc in his late teens and early twenties as associating with
two groups: journalists and members of Rio's relatively sizeable Jewish
community. Sirotsky recalled Szulc as "energetic, persistent, of difficult temperament, ambitious, and an exceptional writer."[56] He spoke
Portuguese with a heavy accent, and because of that had a difficult
time getting hired at a Brazilian newspaper. Szulc's English was mar-
ginally better than his Portuguese, which made him a natural for the
newly launched *Brazil Herald*.[57]

Szulc, twenty at the time, wrote a daily column for the *Herald* re-
ductively titled "World Today." Ponderous and verbose, Szulc wrote
about issues before the United Nations, Brazilian politics, the global
threat of communism, and assorted international crises, pending or
anticipated. He took special interest in the new Argentine president,
General Juan Perón. He often sneered at the state of post-World War
II global affairs, and in one column wrote that his *Herald* editor at the
time, presumably Zschech, had urged him to impart more "constructive" opinions.

"The editor's orders are orders and little can be done about it, so I took Sunday to meditate over his recommendation," Szulc wrote. He then concluded:

> There is a big tribe of reporters and columnists who write not what they think they should write but what they are told to. They receive bribes or are simply hired for this kind of writing. They are the so-called official writers whose job is to sing tributes to the rulers. They remind me a little of the old-age court poets who in lengthy stanzas described the king's merits. . . . These men certainly bring shame to the rest of us who try to be honest. I hope that I will never be forced to write things against my beliefs. It would be, if nothing else, cheating the man who spends a nickel for the paper to find out what really is going on in this world of ours.[58]

The column was Szulc's letter of resignation. Zschech's editorial mandate to write positively and optimistically had been similar to the rebuke US Envoy Charles Page Bryan had given A. J. Lamoureux more than fifty years earlier. Both journalists, similarly obdurate, bristled at the admonition and proceeded to carry on editorially just as they had before their knuckles had been rapped.

Unlike Lamoureux, though, Szulc didn't own the newspaper he was writing for. To protest Zschech's scolding, Szulc abruptly left the *Herald* and began freelancing for the Associated Press.[59] By May 1947, he had moved to the Rio bureau of the French wire service then known as France Presse, followed by a full-time job at the local AP bureau. Szulc roused the interests of American intelligence officers in Rio at the time, and according to declassified CIA documents, agents opened a file on him that suggested Szulc was connected to a local communist newspaper called *Directrizes*. "There is little doubt that Szulc is pro-communist," the government file read without elaboration or apparent provocation.[60]

Like Lamoureux, chain-smoker Szulc was driven, tenacious, and ambitious. Visiting relatives in New York, he landed work as United Press's United Nations correspondent from 1949 to 1953. US intelligence agents, following the budding journalist's ascending career with alarm, suggested that Szulc had been hired by the wire service through the influence of his uncle, John Wiley, US ambassador to Portugal and later Panama. However he secured the post, Szulc's reporting at the UN, an international organization whose transactions prompted yawns from most American readers, attracted the attention of *New York Times* columnist Arthur Krock, who recommended Szulc for a slot on the newspaper's night copy desk. Szulc's first byline appeared in the *Times* in 1954, a year before he would become a naturalized US citizen.[61] Later he would be named the newspaper's correspondent in Rio, followed by Buenos Aires.[62]

Ultimately, Szulc would become one of America's premier foreign correspondents—certainly one of the most dogged. On a layover in 1961 in Miami, he chased down a seemingly preposterous yarn that Cuban exiles were planning to invade their homeland and that the rebels were being trained and funded by CIA operatives in the Florida swampland. The Bay of Pigs exposé was a seemingly fanciful story that turned out to be true. At the behest of the Kennedy Administration, the *Times* held Szulc's explosive account for several days, and when it ran, portions were deleted as demanded by the government.

Szulc seemed sprung from an Ian Fleming novel. He was a wine connoisseur who started an invitation-only Tuesday-evening gastronomical club, La Société Secrète des Mangeurs de Mardi. He showed up at the *Times* newsroom on 43rd Street in custom-tailored linen shirts and suits with a plethora of pockets, some hidden. On overseas assignments, he wore a dark trench coat and carried with him multiple packs of American cigarettes (good for bribing sources as well as feeding his own habit), a dinner jacket, and white tie.[63] His drink of choice was a martini. "He liked to whisper from the corner of his mouth and this habit, overlaid by his accent made his observations even more mysterious than they were," wrote *New York Times* colleague Harrison Salisbury, the famed *Times* chronicler who would publish my diary of cannery assembly-line work when I got out of Berkeley. "He had a passion for meeting odd strangers in ill-lighted bars in ill-frequented parts of town—any town."[64] Szulc left the *Times* in 1972, fittingly over a disagreement with editors. He became a prolific book and magazine-article writer, dying of cancer in Washington, DC, in 2001 at the age of seventy-four.

Another *Brazil Herald* writer at the time was Marc Berkowitz, the newspaper's arts, music, and cultural critic, a position he would keep into the mid-1960s. Like seemingly everyone else at the *Herald*, Berkowitz had an unusual pedigree. His parents were Jewish refugees who fled the Russian Revolution for Rio when Berkowitz was ten. Like Zschech and Szulc, Berkowitz was a polyglot who spoke Portuguese, Russian, German, English, French, and Spanish. Like Szulc, Berkowitz was a gourmand, serving grand lunches at his Botafogo home, accompanied by vodka he fermented, distilled, and bottled himself.[65] Berkowitz wrote thousands of reviews and essays for the *Herald*, as well as for international arts publications and catalogues, ultimately becoming an influential critic of Brazilian sculpture, painting, and printmaking.

As a critic, Berkowitz was unsparing. In an *ArtNews* review of the XIII São Paulo Bienal, Berkowitz wrote that the grand prizewinner's work "lacks the impact of great art. The word 'craftsmanship' comes to mind"; he called another prizewinner's art "rather dreary," labeled West Germany's entry into the international show "poor and empty," Italy's and Belgium's submissions "very disappointing," and the US bid as "endless and tiresome."[66] Prolific Berkowitz, bombastic and self-assured from his *Herald* perch, was instantly recognizable by the impossibly large black rectangular spectacles he wore. He got the opportunity to interview hundreds of international celebrities passing through Rio and wrote about them in his daily *Herald* column, generically titled "Cultural Activities," later called "The Arts."

When American novelists Erskine Caldwell and Frank Norris visited Brazil in 1946, Berkowitz took both authors to the cozy bar adjacent to the lobby of the Glória Hotel, where I was to stay when the *Latin America Daily Post* moved to Rio to combine with the *Brazil Herald*.[67] "Erskine Caldwell talked and I listened," Berkowitz wrote of their hours-long conversation, in which the critic proceeded to write paragraph after paragraph of his own thoughts about, of all things, classical music.[68] In another column, Berkowitz effused about a Canadian poet, Ralph Gustafson, visiting Rio in 1947, whose short fiction that year in *The Atlantic*, "The Human Fly," Berkowitz wrote "belongs to the not so many really good short stories I have ever read."[69] Berkowitz's eye for spotting emerging artistic genius became a well-deserved hallmark. He was an early admirer of Brazilian architect Oscar Niemeyer, who went on to design the nation's avant-garde capital, Brasília, and sang his praises often in the *Herald*.

Hecht, Addams, Szulc, Shannon, and Berkowitz were role models who also had colored way outside the lines and gotten themselves to Brazil.[70] Even though *Herald* salaries remained low, that hadn't deterred any of these writers from walking into the *Herald* newsroom and asking editor Zschech for work. Even with the paltry remuneration and a surfeit of talent, the newspaper continued to bleed financially, and as a cost-cutting measure, the newspaper downsized from a broadsheet to a tabloid with this front-page boxed announcement:

Brazil Herald in New Dress

Here we are in our new dress. It is our first day in the new print shop and the first time we have tried ou [*sic*] hand at editing a tabloid. We have tried hard and perhaps the errors which occur—we are supposing in advance that there will be some— may be corrected for succeeding issues. Tell us what you think of this issue and send us suggestions you may have which will enable us to do a better job.

In less than two years, the *Herald* would lose its primary benefactor when US Ambassador Pawley resigned, citing poor health after taking a leave of absence from his Rio post and spending five months in the States. In reality, Pawley quit because in a meeting with Brazilian President Dutra he had promised forty thousand tons of American wheat, a deal that would be nixed by career bureaucrats in the US State Department, even though Pawley had said the exchange had been approved by President Truman. To protest the back-channel veto, Pawley resigned.[71]

But before Pawley would retire to his Virginia horse ranch and steep himself in a two-decades-long obsession with ferreting out communists wherever he saw and imagined them, he made sure the *Herald* was in safe hands.

CHAPTER 11

John D., Hugh, Stu, and Margaret

ON OCTOBER 31, 1947, John D. Montgomery, a garrulous and charming publisher who owned a small chain of newspapers in Miami and Kansas, paid $40,000 to acquire the nearly bankrupt, twenty-one-month-old *Brazil Herald*. Montgomery bought the newspaper "more as a favor to the Truman administration than as a realistic business investment," *The New York Times* reported.[1]

That seems to be a ready case of journalistic hyperbole. It's doubtful that Truman or his administration cared one way or another about the fate of a relatively inconsequential newspaper five thousand miles south of Washington, DC. What is not disputed is that US Ambassador Pawley was a friend and business associate of Montgomery's, and that he personally brokered the deal for Montgomery to buy the struggling expat newspaper.

"When Mr. Pawley was U.S. ambassador to Brazil, he invited me to rush to Rio de Janeiro 'on important business,'" Montgomery would write. "When I arrived there, he told me that an English-language newspaper, the *Brazil Herald*, was in bad financial trouble with poor standing and would probably have to shut down unless I bought out three partners who owned it and provided operating capital and management. He explained that it was most important to the American colony in Brazil to have a credible newspaper and that it was my patriotic duty to 'rescue' the paper so that it could continue to operate and reflect a non-communistic image."[2]

There may—or may not—have been more to the transaction. Montgomery's son, John Grey Montgomery, would recall that "While President Truman was in Brazil in 1947, Harry saw some photos of slums in Chicago that were in the *Brazil Herald* and told Pawley about it. There was some talk about the paper leaning communist, or that someone there might have been communist, I'm not sure which."[3]

At the time, in a letter Ambassador Pawley wrote to Montgomery, Pawley expressed his dislike of Lee Langley, the young pathologist and editor-columnist who had joined *Herald* founders Joe Brown and Frank Garcia after the death of Vic Hawkins and the exit of Ralph Ross. Editor Herb Zschech would describe Renaissance man Langley as "a hippie type. His unorthodox opinions on many subjects and his uninhibited ways of expressing them confirmed this impression."[4] Ambassador Pawley apparently shared this vague assessment of Langley, but whether the two ever even met is unclear.

"Gradually, and to our dismay, the paper took on an extremely anti-American slant, and upon some investigation it appears that this young man had a grudge against the U.S.," Pawley wrote without ostensible foundation to Montgomery.[5] It's unclear what Pawley was referring to in disparaging Langley or what the *Herald* may have printed that had so incensed the ambassador.

Once again, as A. J. Lamoureux had discovered five decades earlier, American officials possess thin skins when it comes to newspapers printing anything perceived as even mildly critical of the United States. Whether President Truman had ever mentioned to Pawley what he may have seen in the *Herald* is wholly speculative. At the time, American media, whether home or abroad, that didn't routinely present the United States as an indefatigable beacon of opportunity and racial equality were often labeled unpatriotic and by extension, "communist." Particularly during the mid-to-late 1940s and during the 1950s, patriotism seemed to mandate that journalists report unabashedly positive news about America. Communist baiting accelerated with the advent of McCarthyism at the time and would continue to persist for decades (and in some ways continues today). Such an agenda of national boosterism at the *Brazil Herald* was a replay of why Tad Szulc had left the newspaper when editor Zschech had criticized the journalist's column for not being "constructive," as Zschech had put it.

An ambassador griping about what the local newspaper printed, or complaining about the political views of the newspaper's personnel, was to be expected, but Pawley went further when he personally brokered the deal to sell the *Herald* to an American publisher with whom he had numerous business dealings. To Pawley and the local expat community in Brazil, the *Herald* was *their* newspaper. Pawley and a like-minded coterie of pro-business Americans had financially supported the newspaper and had contributed enough to keep it from going under. That dealmaker Pawley went searching to sell the *Herald* to a vetted buyer was a matter of protecting their investment, as well as making sure the newspaper continued to hew to their political and commercial interests.

As for why Pawley wanted to oust Lee Langley from the *Herald's* owners, no one today knows for sure. What was it that Langley could have written or directed to be published that might have so inflamed the ambassador?

There are some tantalizing clues. Two weeks after Pawley had arrived in Brazil, in Langley's weekly editorial-page column "On Second Thought," Langley wrote an essay disparaging US Navy Admiral William F. "Bull" Halsey Jr. for an article Halsey had written for *Collier's* magazine in which the American war hero had called for the public execution of one Japanese military officer for every GI killed by Japanese soldiers. In the article, Halsey labeled the Japanese "just plain dumb" and threatened to ride a white horse into Tokyo, celebrating the Allies' victory.[6] Langley reasonably responded in his *Herald* column that such statements "are typical of Admiral Halsey, they are typical of the average American, and they illustrate a characteristic that foreigners, without exception, find so repulsive. Hitler ignited his country and the world by preaching German superiority but the superiority he taught, and the superiority his people felt, did not, in any respect, exceed the feelings that most Americans [espouse] so blatantly."[7] Such editorial reflections may seem tame by today's standards, but during the years following World War II, they were incendiary.

Whatever Langley's alleged infraction was, partners Garcia and Brown agreed on a backchannel plan to purge the moonlighting pathologist from the *Herald*'s leadership triad and replace him with someone more politically allied with their views. If Langley's replacement had access to financial resources and had newspaper publishing experience, that would be even better. When brought into the cabal, Pawley readily suggested his friend Montgomery as a candidate, and thus it was agreed that the ambassador would approach Kansas-native Montgomery to gauge his interest in buying the *Herald* and keeping Brown and Garcia as his local point men.

"I had several talks with some of the other partners, but it was difficult to find any solution as the others were busy earning a living and could not take over the responsibility of running the Brazil Herald," Pawley proposed in a letter to Montgomery. "It was at this point that it occurred to me that you, as an old friend and newspaperman, might come into the picture by buying out at least three of the stockholders, thereby enabling you to take over control and, under those circumstances, the undesirable partner would very likely want to sell also."[8]

The ambassador felt so strongly about getting rid of Langley and keeping the *Herald* afloat that he secured a cashier's check from Bankers Trust so that in the event Montgomery balked at buying the newspaper, Pawley would step in, purchase the *Herald* for Montgomery, and give it to him outright as a gift. As Montgomery's son, John Grey Montgomery, would recall, "Pawley called my dad and asked him, 'Why don't you buy this newspaper? I'll pay for it!'"[9]

That wouldn't be necessary. Pawley had hooked Montgomery, forty-three at the time, with a shiny lure impossible to ignore. It didn't take much for Montgomery to buy out the three partners, a little less than $15,000 each, for the *Herald*'s title and assorted assets to be transferred to Montgomery, who for a bargain-basement price had become an international newspaper publisher.[10] The fire sale also bailed out Brown, Garcia, and Langley from the newspaper's long queue of creditors.

As it turned out, few publishers were more suited to assume ownership of an English-language newspaper in Latin America than

Fig. 11.1 *Brazil Herald* publisher John D. Montgomery. Courtesy of the Bill Williamson Collection.

Montgomery. Before they ran the *Herald*, neither Brown, Garcia, nor Langley had any experience operating a newspaper, whereas printer's ink coursed through Montgomery's veins. He was a third-generation Kansas publisher whose grandfather had bought the *Junction City Daily Union*, the family's flagship newspaper, in 1888. But what made Montgomery such a well-suited choice to take over the *Brazil Herald* was his south-of-the-border experience. Through his publisher father's connections, at the age of twenty-seven, Montgomery had been the United Press correspondent in Rio, living like no other correspondent out of an apartment at the opulent Copacabana Palace, constructed with imported Carrara marble and patterned after grand hotels in Nice and Cannes, France. The hotel, which resembles a multi-story ice cream sheet cake, faces an expansive stretch of Atlantic Ocean beach. It was where the dancing team of Fred Astaire and Ginger Rogers would be first paired in the 1933 movie, *Flying Down to Rio*.

Ambassador Pawley's political and business acumen along with publisher Montgomery's journalism and public-relations knowledge dovetailed to serve the two men's mutual interests well. Their association went back to Montgomery's early years in Miami, when he worked for Pawley's real estate firm, Williams and Pawley, which owned and operated small hotels in the area today known as South Beach.[11] Montgomery worked as general manager at Miami Beach's Roney Plaza Hotel and the Tower Hotel, as well as at the Biltmore Hotel in Coral Gables, and at Nassau's British Colonial Hotel, built by Miami industrialist Henry Flagler. By 1930, Montgomery had returned to his family's publishing roots, but this time in a place about as far away from Kansas as he could get. Montgomery started his own chain of neighborhood newspapers in the Miami area, which would include the *Coral Gables Riviera, Coconut Grove Times, Florida Sun, Florida Star*, and *Miami Beach Sun-Tropics*.

For a time, Montgomery and his wife, Mary Liz, lived in Cuba, where Montgomery was general manager of the English-language *Havana Daily Post and Evening Telegraph*, and Mary Liz wrote a society column, titled "Incidentally," about the comings and goings of the expatriate American colony there. At the time, Montgomery pursued purchasing another English-language expat newspaper, the *Caracas Journal* in Venezuela, but that deal fell through.[12]

Pawley's and Montgomery's large lives shadowed each other. Both maintained stateside homes on two of four exclusive Miami Beach islands. Pawley and his wife lived in a waterfront estate on Lake

Avenue on one Sunset Island; Montgomery and Mary Liz owned a home on 24th Street on an adjacent Sunset Island. In 1945, Pawley had been elected president of Miami Beach's tony La Gorce Country Club at the same time Montgomery served as a director on its board. Montgomery served three terms as president of the Miami Beach Chamber of Commerce, was a member of the inaugural Orange Bowl steering committee, and was president of the Miami Rotary Club.[13]

The Pawleys and Montgomerys often dined together; a favorite of theirs was Miami's French restaurant Maxim's. Both couples attended charity benefits at Miami's Hialeah Park Racetrack, whose trademark pink flamingos fluttered their plumes in the infield. Montgomery got approval from the Florida State Racing Commission to open a jai alai fronton in Fort Lauderdale, a natural extension of his business portfolio since he also was vice chairman of the Florida State Advertising Commission, but he never completed the transaction.[14]

All the while, Montgomery and eventually his son, John Grey, would add more than a dozen community newspapers to the family's portfolio back in Kansas, where they maintained homes.

As Montgomery entered his mid-forties, the Miami papers had become as much business enterprises as excuses for him and Mary Liz to spend time out of the Kansas winters. Now, with the *Brazil Herald* among his holdings, salubrious Miami would become a convenient base from which Montgomery would fly to Rio, ostensibly to oversee his newest acquisition, as well as a coffee plantation he would buy near the Brazil-Paraguay border.

Upon purchasing the *Brazil Herald*, Ambassador Pawley praised Montgomery with all the requisite encomia, calling the native Kansan a man of "foresight and vision in wanting to produce a first-class publication for the benefit of the Americans and those of other nationalities."[15] US businessmen in Brazil shared that assessment, optimistic that Montgomery would ensure the longevity of the financially imperiled newspaper, deepen its resources, and above all, maintain it as a house organ for their interests.

It wasn't an inopportune moment to invest in Brazil. The post-World War II national economy was booming, growing at an accelerated pace, 9.7 percent in 1948 and 7.7 percent in 1949.[16] Brazil, labeled the "sleeping giant," was charging ahead to take its place as a modern industrialized consumer nation. Montgomery's initial vision was to capitalize on that bonanza by taking over a newspaper pitched to affluent Brazil-based expats leading the charge, and then expand to other monied expat readers (and advertisers hoping to reach them) in other Latin American nations.

As John Grey Montgomery recalled, "My dad had a vision to do the same thing that the *Herald Tribune* had done in Europe. That was my dad's dream. After he bought the *Brazil Herald*, he spent time in Buenos Aires and in Caracas, thinking he could unify all the English-language newspapers on the continent into one. But he never was able to get the national ads, so we kept the *Herald* a paper focused on Brazil."[17] The same grand hemispheric plan, it turned out, would be the template Mauro Salles would envision when he conceived of the *Latin America Daily Post* and I started working at the newspaper in 1979.

A third well-heeled associate of the Pawley-Montgomery axis was Pan American Airlines founder Juan Trippe. Pawley had sold two airlines, one based in Cuba and the other in China, to Trippe, who folded the aviation companies into a worldwide network of routes and aircraft that would become known as Pan Am. The trio of men provided each other with invitations to the limited number of social circles of which none was already a member.[18] A fourth associate was Florida Democratic politician Claude Pepper, who would serve multiple terms, from 1936 to 1989, as US Senator, followed by a long-held seat in the US House of Representatives from the Sunshine State.

To congratulate Montgomery for his purchase of the *Brazil Herald*, Trippe gave the publisher a lifetime pass to fly on Pan Am.[19] With that evergreen ticket came an implicit quid pro quo: that the *Herald* would be in Trippe's and Pan Am's debt for however long Montgomery owned the newspaper. Not that the publisher needed such an incentive; even without the largesse, the *Herald* would have accorded front page booster coverage to the airlines, as it did all US business interests in Brazil.

Helping to secure Montgomery's purchase of the *Herald* was long-time Rio power broker Richard P. Momsen, a Milwaukee-born attorney who had been the US consul general in Rio, as well as founder of Rio's American Chamber of Commerce. Along with *Herald* co-founder Joe Brown, Momsen was a fixer for American firms seeking to create or expand their footprints in Brazil. Momsen and Frank Garcia, the *Herald* co-founder, were longtime friends; Garcia had been an usher at Momsen's wedding in 1921, and like Garcia, Momsen had been awarded the Order of the Southern Cross by the Brazilian government.[20]

The way Momsen structured the newspaper transfer from Brown, Garcia, and Langley to Montgomery was that the new publisher would own all but twenty of a total of 442 shares of the newspaper. Those remaining minority shares would go to a Brazilian native, George H. Newman, the in-house counsel at IBM's subsidiary in Rio. In reality, Newman's role was to act as a frontman for Montgomery. Newman would assume the legal entity of *Editor Responsável*, Editor in Chief, on the newly constituted *Herald* masthead to satisfy a legal stipulation that no foreign national could occupy the top business or editorial slot at any Brazilian media company. Not only had attorney Newman never worked for a newspaper, he seldom, if ever, would set foot inside the *Herald's* offices.[21] As an additional political backstop, another Brazilian national, Samuel Waxibaum, was named on the masthead as the *Herald's* printing plant manager.

Atop Newman's name on the *Herald's* page four masthead was the official designation of the newspaper's newly created holding company, Editôra Mory, a nifty neologism that while sounding vaguely Brazilian was a contraction of publisher Montgomery's name, starting with "Mo" and ending with "ry."

Under Montgomery, Frank Garcia would continue writing a daily column to backslap Brazilian politicians, consular officials, and

American businessmen. Editor and columnist Herb Zschech would remain at the paper, but as a reporter and columnist, not as top editor. Montgomery promptly fired Langley, whose tenure in Brazil was over anyway and who would go on to a global career as a pathologist. To replace Zschech and Langley as the newspaper's editorial supervisors, Montgomery hired Hugh Parks Rusk Sr., a veteran newspaperman from Atlanta and Miami, as the *Brazil Herald's* general manager. Like seemingly everyone else at the *Herald*, Rusk had a one-of-a-kind pedigree. His father had been a rural Presbyterian minister in Cherokee County, Georgia; his younger brother, Dean Rusk, would become President Lyndon B. Johnson's secretary of state and preside over much of Johnson's failed Vietnam War policy; another brother, Roger, was a physics professor at the University of Tennessee.

Hugh Parks Rusk Sr. had been managing editor of Montgomery's *Miami Beach Sun* and *Miami Beach Morning Star;* he'd also been a reporter for the *Atlanta Constitution*, as well as an Atlanta city councilmember. In addition, Rusk had worked as director of publicity for the La Gorce Country Club, where Montgomery and Pawley had both been board members. In addition, Rusk had been a flack for the Biltmore Hotel in Coral Gables while Montgomery had worked in the executive suite.

Rusk's first triumph at the *Herald* was to create the July 4, 1948, edition, an eighty-page commemorative issue with more than one hundred and seventy display ads. It was the fattest *Herald* ever.[22] As Frank Garcia had done when the *Brazil Herald* first came out in 1946, securing a congratulatory editorial in the *Washington Post*, Rusk leaned on a friend at the *Miami Herald* to run a similar laudatory editorial, which read, "John D. Montgomery of Miami Beach is to be congratulated for his acquisition as principal partner of an [sic] unique enterprise in Latin America, the English-language Brazil Herald. Reminiscent, on a smaller scale, of the Paris editions of New York Herald-Tribune, the Brazil Herald is read in Rio de Janeiro by thousands of Americans and other residents of the Brazilian capital."[23]

Rusk stayed at the *Brazil Herald* for less than two years. He never adjusted to life in Rio, liking neither the Southern Hemispheric heat nor the accumulated stress of putting out a daily newspaper in it. On his way out, Rusk suffered a nervous breakdown and for several days lay ill in a hotel room at Rio's Galeão Airport, unable to fly back to the States.[24]

To replace Rusk, Montgomery hired a newly married husband-and-wife team: Harry Stuart Morrison, who'd been telegraph editor at the *Miami Herald* and managing editor at two of Montgomery's Florida newspapers, and Margaret Mercedes Miles Morrison, an ex-Women's Army Corps (WAC) officer and Key West native who had worked at the *Miami Herald*. Harry Morrison, known as Stu, became the *Brazil Herald*'s general manager and chief ad salesman while Margaret took over as managing editor.

"We arrived in July with a flourishing deficit," Stu Morrison told Ernie Hill, the *Miami Herald*'s South American correspondent in the fall of 1949, "and managed to bring it just a shade out of the red in September. October will be all right." Outside of cutting costs and increasing circulation and advertising lineage, the *Brazil Herald*'s most pressing problem was personnel—finding and keeping qualified journalists. "What we need is for an American desk man or former news editor to show up in Rio. Boy, he would have a job in 10 minutes," Hill quoted Morrison as saying.[25]

The Morrisons amped up the newspaper's editorial chorus for the expat community, running recurring display ads seeking volunteer correspondents to report on expat parties, clubs, and cultural events. "This should interest some housewife who has had a least school newspaper experience. Duties will be chiefly covering social and civic notes in American and British colonies," the house ads read. In subsequent issues, the *Herald* would run ads seeking similar volunteer correspondents in Brazil's secondary cities, including Recife, Santos, Goiania, and Salvador da Bahia.[26]

As Teddy Hecht and others at the newspaper had experienced, the newly arrived Morrisons' most challenging domestic challenge was finding suitable housing, made more complicated by the presence of their Irish Setter, Choo-Choo. Margaret, who wrote a Sunday column for the *Herald*, explained the predicament, with or without Choo-Choo:

> We read the ads in the paper—The Brazil Herald, naturally. We advertised in the paper—The Brazil Herald, of course. A friend who knows Portuguese searches the advertisements in the Brazilian- language papers.
>
> "Ah!" he ah's "here is one. Just right for you." We leap into a borrowed car and start driving. We keep on driving. And driving. It is just this side of Buenos Aires, we think, or possibly Lima. We are not yet familiar with the geography of our new country.
>
> Eventually the hello box rings and someone says, "You are looking for a place to live? This one will be just right for you."
>
> We take the address, learn that the apartment is close to town. It is luxuriously furnished, is close to busses [*sic*] and lotaçoes [trains], in case we do not have a car, and even has a telephone. Bliss, indeed we think.
>
> Until we see it. The bed is closer to the floor than a flea's hop. It is fatal to advance forward into the kitchen for then one must back out or knock elbows. But then, you've seen them, too.
>
> However, our new friends counsel 'paciencia', and we are quite willing to practice that small virtue in return for eventually finding, as everyone promises, that 'place just right for you'.
>
> The lovely lady that is the city of Rio de Janeiro can't hold out forever.[27]

In an ode to her heartthrob, Margaret wrote in another column, "They're saying Bing Crosby is through, finished, done—that the golden well has been sung dry, that he's worn out his voice, lost his sense of rhythm, discarded his sincerity and verse for languorous indifference. . . .For who can add up the hearts he has soothed, the loneliness he has assuaged, the inspirations he has encouraged, the pure enjoyment he has brought?"[28]

With the Morrisons taking on dual roles as top salesman and top editor, Herb Zschech was able to turn to his forte, political and crime reporting. Zschech resurrected his political column, Probex, but it was his police-blotter stories, which ran daily with a thumbnail photo of fastidious, square-jaw, diminutive Zschech in a jacket and tie that drew particular attention from readers. Zschech's crime sagas were word equivalents of the grisly crime photographs of famed New York tabloid press photographer Arthur Fellig, better known as Weegee, of the same epoch. An assortment of Zschech columns from 1949 to 1954 included these haiku-worthy headlines:

Two Boyfriends, Same Name
One Jailed on Murder Rap[29]

Confession by Girl
of Poisoning Father[30]

Should A Husband Slay
an Unfaithful Wife?[31]

Enamored with Neighbor,
Suitor Kills Her, Himself[32]

Sleepwalker Blows
His Kitchen Apart[33]

Sandwich Swindlers
Sadder But Wiser[34]

Floor Sweeper Saw
No Future In It[35]

Result Bad
Whatever
The Cause[36]

Rejected Lover Stabs
Girlfriend 10 Times[37]

After 14 Years, Man
Yearns for Lost Love[38]

Lifeguard Attempts
To Kill Whole Family[39]

Puzzled Boy Robbed
Of 32,000 Cruzeiros[40]

Four Girl Singers Mix
In Tropical Tempest[41]

Hillbillies Swap Wives,
Storm Rages in Parana[42]

Mystery of Stolen
Streetcar Solved[43]

Intrepid Congressman
Dares Risk 44th Scar[44]

Judge Aghast, Jury Frees
Religious Sect Murderers[45]

Bewitched Umbrella
Missing[46]

Lioness
Dies In
Rio's Zoo[47]

So one-of-a-kind were Zschech's diction and the subject matter he
wrote about that the American poet Richard O'Connell would write
three poems, published in consecutive months in *The New Yorker*,
each titled "Brazilian Happenings," based on the bizarre news items
reported by Zschech.[48]

Under the Morrisons, the *Herald* developed an eccentric personality, particularly with Zschech's compulsive crime forays alongside
Margaret Morrison's homespun domestic dramas. In doing so, the
Morrisons did whatever they could to solidify the *Herald*'s relationship with, and coverage of, the expat English-speaking community.
An example of that was the seventh anniversary of the newspaper's
founding, when the *Herald* ran a half-page reproduction of a typewritten letter from American Ambassador Herschel V. Johnson.[49]
The letter, likely written by an underling whose facility with English
was limited, read: "As spokesman of the great press traditions of the
United States and the other freedom loving nations, you enjoy as all
of us do the genuine hospitality of Brazil. I assure you of my very
sincere appreciation of the unremitting effort required to fulfill successfully your very important mission and that my earnest wishes for
the growing success of yourself and of those on your staff are always
with you."[50] The wholesale duplication of the missive underscored the
newspaper's relationship with consular officialdom more as shills than
as journalists. In the same issue, Stu Morrison reiterated the *Herald*'s
central mission: to represent expats "playing an ever increasingly important role in Brazilian achievement" even though they often were
considered, as Morrison, without explanation, put it, "second class
citizens."[51]

Speaking directly to the *Herald*'s demographics, Margaret Morrison
wrote in 1951 a column directed at idle expat housewives. It was

either a woman's manifesto or an apologia for the status quo. It's unclear which:

> The plight of some of the women in the colony here is a sad thing to contemplate and my heart goes out to them. At least, three of them—at widely separated times and places—have told me that they are bored and unhappy because their housekeeping duties are relegated to a maid or maids and they have no notion how to occupy their time. They would like to get jobs—but their husbands object, pleading prestige as the reason. . . .
>
> The woman without children or whose children are grown or in The States in school—and who is energetic and ambitious—has a vacuum to fill. Some can do it with bridge and tea parties and clubs and golf or swimming or tennis or social work with the poor, and if they are content with those things, who would deny them their right to them?
>
> Sometimes I get tired and irritable and think, "Gee, I wish I'd gotten married at 16 and had 10 kids and never heard of the newspaper business. I wish I could stay home and be a housewife." And yet I know I'd get bats in the belfry within a week. And so I sympathize with the woman who wants to work but whose husband is a director of this or that and feels it would hurt his business and social prestige if she did.
>
> And I also think these husbands are making a mistake which may cost them more than the penalty of Mrs. Jones whispering to Mrs. Brown, 'Did you know Mrs. Green has gotten a JOB? X company must be in bad shape.' Or whatever it is that the men think would go the rounds.
>
> I think it has cost some and will cost others their marital happiness—because a frustrated wife with no outlet for her energy and intelligence is an unhappy wife. And an unhappy wife—unless she's a saint with a golden halo—takes out her irritation on her husband. And where does that lead to? Quarrels, separation, divorce—you name it. At any rate, a most unhappy home life.

And what does that lead to? A man who can't relax and feel loved and at peace with the world in his home. . . .So look, Joe— get smart. Your wife says she wants to get a job to occupy her time, you betta letta.

As a matter of fact, Joe, you should be proud of her.[52]

With the Morrisons in charge, a *Herald* staple became page one vanity photographs of publisher Montgomery, whether he was in town or not. In one, he appeared with Elmer F. Johnson, head of the American and Foreign Power Company's electrical subsidiary, the largest American investor in Brazil at the time.[53]

In hopes of attracting additional financial backing for the *Herald*, Montgomery went out of his way to try to foster a relationship with New York businessman Nelson A. Rockefeller, one of the heirs to the Chase Manhattan Bank and Standard Oil fortunes, the same industrial titan Teddy Hecht had worked part-time for when he was in town. In 1950, Montgomery crony Herbert Moses gave the publisher his business card to present to Rockefeller on a visit to New York. On it, Moses had penned an introduction. When that went nowhere, Montgomery tried to leverage his connection with Karl Bickel, a Florida developer and former president and board member of UPI, to make an introduction to Rockefeller whose family had extensive multi-generational holdings in Latin America.[54] A New York advertising agency, Pedlar & Ryan, at the time under contract with the *Brazil Herald*, solicited from a Rockefeller aide the names of potential advertisers from the Rockefeller galaxy of companies. When Montgomery got no nibbles, Montgomery redoubled his efforts to reel in Rockefeller's support, and sent Rockefeller a *Brazil Herald* editorial column that Stu Morrison had written urging Rockefeller's appointment as President-elect Eisenhower's secretary of state, with Montgomery's scrawl on top, "I hope so."[55] While such appeals would never connect Rockefeller and his family's businesses to the *Herald*, it didn't stop the newspaper from running photographs of Rockefeller family members whenever they were in Rio.

In a similar entreaty, the *Herald* prominently played any positive-spin story in which Pan Am Airways was mentioned. Pan Am was the principal US air carrier serving Brazil, so news coverage of the airline was certainly topical. Lurking in the back of such coverage, of course, was publisher Montgomery's lifetime Pan Am travel pass. Typical *Herald* valentines were non-stories such as a page one, above-the-fold photograph of bronzed and blonde Pan Am stewardess Judy Reid in a bikini and a model Pan Am Clipper perched on her left knee (". . . in case you are paying any attention to such things," read the caption), basking on Copacabana Beach with Sugar Loaf mountain in the background.[56] As John Grey Montgomery would recall, "There were *all* kinds of trade-outs, including those with Pan Am. That's one of the reasons my father enjoyed owning the newspaper."[57]

Such payback went deeper than commercial deals the *Herald* publisher and his lieutenants could wangle. Like mainstream Brazilian newspapers at the time, the *Herald* gleefully celebrated the inauguration of Getúlio Vargas for a second term as Brazil's president in 1951. Vargas's heralded return to lead the country certainly was news, but not couched this way: The *Herald* ran in 106-point type the headline, "Brazilians Happy, Getulio Returns," with a purple-prose lede written by Stu Morrison. "Getulio Vargas returned to the Presidential Palace Wednesday literally borne there on the cheers of the people who thronged the streets hours ahead of time waiting for a glimpse of their beloved 'Geto.'"[58]

Under the Morrisons, the *Herald* returned to publishing verbatim press releases from Hollywood as a staple. Another page one, above-the-fold photograph showed actress Rita Hayworth with caption that read the actress denied press reports of a possible reconciliation with her husband, socialite and racehorse owner Prince Aly Salman Khan.[59] Another *Herald* nonstory was a bannered page one birthday greeting to filmmaker Cecil B. de Mille with the headline, "Movies' Vet Producer Just 70 Years Young," a not-so-subliminal message for readers to go see Hollywood movies playing in Rio's multitude of movie theaters, which happened to advertise in the *Herald*.[60]

One editorial feature the Morrisons retained from the earliest days of Lamoureux's *The Rio News* was noting in the newspaper the names of Americans and Brits who had checked into Rio's major hotels (providing a souvenir for the visiting tourists, as well as a plug for the hotels), those who had arrived on passenger liners and commercial airplanes (more commercial plugs), as well as the frequent comings and goings of US and British business executives (good will, potential reader subscriptions and display advertising).

Alas, as Hugh Parks Rusk had experienced, the around-the-clock stress of publishing a daily newspaper in the tropics became too much for Stu and Margaret Morrison, who would leave the *Herald* and subsequently divorce. Stu was fired by Montgomery in 1954. Margaret returned to the States, where she would go on to editing positions at the *Milwaukee Sentinel* and *Chicago Daily News*. In 1964, at age forty-eight, she remarried a *Chicago Daily News* reporter. Margaret would die in Chicago at age fifty-eight in 1974.

In 1961, Stu Morrison got work as the coordinator of a high school foreign-exchange program between Latin America and the US, primarily funded by the *Miami Herald*. As described before Congress in a hearing titled, "Winning the Cold War: The U.S. Ideological Offensive," Morrison's job was to coordinate bringing "planeloads of Latin students to see democracy in action at U.S. homes and schools for a 2-week period."[61] His job at the *Herald* seemed a fitting walk-up to such an initiative.

Morrison soon left the so-called Operation Amigos program without employment or focus. Ed Miller, an AP correspondent who arrived in Brazil in 1961, recalled the former *Herald* general manager as "rather down on his luck. He was still on the diplomatic A-lists and turned up at all the embassy receptions for free food and booze. I remember seeing him at a party stuffing his coat pockets full of food. He usually wore a rumpled white linen suit. He was something of a loner."[62] Future *Brazil Herald* managing partner Bill Williamson remembered Morrison as "frequently drunk to the point of near incoherence."[63] Morrison died at Hospital Souza Aguiar in Rio of pulmonary edema at sixty-two on February 1, 1964, the eighteenth anniversary of the *Herald's* founding.[64] Miller and Williamson were among Morrison's pallbearers at the Cemitério dos Ingleses in Rio, located around the corner from the old *Herald* printing plant.

Depending on the newspaper's personnel at any given time, the *Herald* was able to strengthen its reporting, but even at its best, the quality of the editorial personnel remained spotty, and the newspaper hobbled along. In 1962, the newsroom moved to a small suite of offices on the eleventh floor of a fourteen-floor office building at 31 Rua Mexico. As in its earlier days, the overwhelming task facing the staff wasn't so much selecting what would appear in the newspaper, but getting the newspaper out every day. With Margaret Morrison's departure, dependable Herb Zschech was reappointed editor and given the title on the masthead as Supervisor. Reporters and subeditors honorifically referred to him as "Mr. Zschech."

Zschech remembered the staff this way: "The two small rooms were crowded with a motley bunch of people of either sex, talking several languages including some English, which seemed to be a minority. I soon got the impression that their main activities, besides telling jokes and discussing local subjects, were fighting for one of the three typewriters—one of which was badly broken—which were the most prominent items of office equipment. None of these people seemed to have any definite assignment. They showed up and left as it suited them, wrote or edited according to the whims of the moment, discussed or read aloud to each other funny passages from original."[65]

One of that disparate staff was David Hume, a dual British-Argentine citizen who had grown up in Buenos Aires, where his father had been an engineer for Standard Electric/ITT's local subsidiary. When the senior Hume got transferred to Rio, David showed up at the *Herald* during a break from high school, telling Zschech he was eighteen when in fact he was sixteen. Zschech hired Hume on the spot, instructing him to take a seat at a desk with an ancient black Underwood typewriter on it. "Zschech would spend a lot of time scouring the pages of Brazilian newspapers, from which he would cull stories for me to translate and provide inspiration for his columns," Hume would recall.

The process of putting out the newspaper wasn't just translating, writing, editing, and proofing copy, but also creating hot-type metal set by press operators and then operating archaic Linotype machines apt to break down in a stifling plant without air conditioning. Even with a battery of rotary fans, the Rio climate was challenging enough. A pressroom with hot, melting metal made conditions nearly unbearable. Hume recalled:

> My copy would go down to the composing room where shirtless typesetters sitting at Linotype machines would spit out metal lines of text the width of the newspaper's columns. The lines of text would be set in a galley the size of the *Herald*'s pages and a proof of the page would be obtained by placing a sheet of newsprint on the page and rubbing on it with an ink-soaked roller. To speed things up, I learned how to read upside down and from right to left after the typesetter changed each line that I had pointed out had a typo. They'd lift the line of metal type out of the galley, insert a metal placeholder vertically instead of horizontally until the corrected type was ready to be replaced."[66]

By the time the paper got put to bed and papers sputtered off the presses, bleary yet wide-eyed Hume would fall in with a posse of ink-stained pressmen lumbering over to nearby Praça Mauá for early-morning beers while prostitutes paraded around strip clubs on Rio's waterfront before Hume would head home exhausted and exhilarated.

All this was prologue to the most essential function of any newspaper: getting the product to customers in a window of just two to three hours. If that didn't happen, then the accumulation of all previous sequential steps would be for naught. The man in charge of the *Herald*'s circulation at the time, Giovanni Manfredi, had been hired by the original quartet of owners, Ralph Ross, Vic Hawkins, Joe Brown and

Frank Garcia. Manfredi's monumental task was getting the newspapers to subscribers' homes, as well as to hundreds of sidewalk bancas to be displayed early the next morning. Some days the *Herald* was stacked side-by-side with Brazil's premier dailies, *O Estado de São Paulo, Jornal do Brasil, O Globo, Folha de S. Paulo, Correio de Manhã,* along with the nation's largest-circulation newspaper, the sensationalist *O Dia.* Other days, the *Herald* wouldn't be delivered till noon, if at all, depending on a series of reoccurring miscues the night before.

Publisher Montgomery rarely made appearances at either the printing plant or newsroom. Montgomery and Mary Liz took one or two annual trips to Rio, where they stayed in a suite of rooms on the eleventh floor of the Swiss-owned Hotel Ouro Verde on Avenida Atlântica, not far from the Copacabana Palace, where Montgomery had lived two decades earlier when he was a correspondent for UPI. The Montgomerys welcomed friends and business associates for pre-dinner cocktails in a terrace bar before adjourning to the hotel's dining room. While in Brazil, Montgomery would visit the coffee plantation he owned near Pedro Juan Caballero, a Wild West town on the other side of the Brazil-Paraguay border.

Bookkeeping at the *Herald* remained a convoluted mess, one complicated by myriad side deals common in many Brazilian businesses. Because of that, it was impossible to keep anything close to an accurate record of the newspaper's expenses and accounts receivable, as well as actual profits and losses. At first, that didn't seem to bother publisher Montgomery. The *Herald* was an incongruous curio that seemed to suit the absentee publisher, who took no small amount of pride in owning a newspaper in faraway Brazil. If not providing a reward of financial profits or editorial excellence, the newspaper gave Montgomery cachet. How many small-town publishers could boast ownership of an English-language newspaper outside the United States, particularly one in exotic Rio de Janeiro?

CHAPTER 12

Senhor Bill

ANIMATED AND VOLUBLE, John Montgomery loved being at the center of an ever-expanding covey of friends and associates, regaling them with yet another story, whether set in Rio, Havana, Miami, or Junction City, Kansas. Chivas Regal in one hand, smoldering ash-tipped Marlboro in the other, Montgomery, a former collegiate boxer, was a natural raconteur. He especially enjoyed attending Inter American Press Association (IAPA) meetings held annually in a different Latin American capital. With other publishers and a select sprinkling of editors, Montgomery held forth through a variety of leadership roles in the newspaper lobbying group. In 1961, as both a board member and publisher, he attended the gala inauguration of Brazilian President Jânio Quadros in the nation's striking new capital, Brasília.

By the mid-1960s, Montgomery began to retreat more and more to his native state of Kansas, where he would dive headfirst into politics. Montgomery's flagship newspaper, the *Junction City Daily Union*, was the only newspaper in the state that could be relied on to endorse Democratic candidates every election cycle, from state representatives to US presidents. At some point it occurred to Montgomery that owning a chain of newspapers ought to allow him to flex his own political muscle. A staunch supporter of President Lyndon Baines Johnson, Montgomery announced his own candidacy for Kansas's second congressional district seat in 1964, but he couldn't muster enough support in the Republican-dominated state, so he dropped out. News of the Montgomery's announcement was dutifully carried on the front page of the faraway *Brazil Herald*, even though it held little relevance to readers, except, of course, that the newspaper's publisher was the candidate.[1]

Dipping his toe into electoral politics accelerated Montgomery's interest in raising his public persona back in Kansas, who had by now retreated from Miami Beach. He served on the state Board of Regents, as a director of the state Highway Commission, and state chair of the Democratic Party. He and banker Robert Docking, a fellow Democrat who would ultimately break the state's Republican stronghold and get elected governor in 1967, became friends and political allies. Ten years later, Montgomery would become state chair of US Senator Henry M. Jackson's failed bid for the Democratic nomination for President. "Scoop" Jackson and Montgomery were cut from the same political cloth. The two men even bore a hefty and uncanny resemblance to each other. Jackson supported increased military spending and a hard line against the Soviet Union while endorsing mainstream social-welfare programs and expanding civil rights.[2] It was a political agenda that coincided with Montgomery's own reformist business-centric philosophy.

In Rio, once Stu and Margaret Morrison had departed from the *Herald*, Montgomery turned to Joe Brown to serve as interim-caretaker manager of the newspaper. Herb Zschech resumed as editor, political columnist, and deft crime-writer, while Frank Garcia kept up with his column of all things Brazilian-American. The newspaper was steady and stagnant. Montgomery left it to his head-scratching accountants to assess the paper's convoluted finances. Montgomery seldom made extended trips to Rio, leaving day-to-day operations up to whoever was in charge that week or month. Still, in Montgomery's constellation of business and political pursuits, the *Herald* remained a star, if a distant one.

When Joe Brown opened the *Herald's* financial ledgers in the Morrisons' absence, he was shocked. At least, he said he was shocked.

Under Stu Morrison's bleary-eyed watch, the paper had been hemor-rhaging cash.

"An examination showed that the paper was covered by many liens, taxes unpaid, and creditors about to take over," Brown would write. "Fortunately, the victims willingly granted us time to work out a solution. The actual losses were never clearly known. Economies were adopted, collections paid promptly, and within a few years, we were able to return the paper to Mr. Montgomery with all debts paid and a balance in the bank."[3] Brown found pages and pages of unpaid accounts receivable, as well as scores of outstanding bills for every-thing from newsprint to printing equipment. Zschech squeezed as much copy as he could from the revolving door of *Herald* reporters to fit between the newspaper's display and classified ads. He did ev-erything to ensure that the *Herald* was delivered to subscribers and news bancas at a reasonable morning hour, although on some days, he just threw up his hands in frustration.

The newspaper was, for all practical purposes, rudderless, once again precariously close to folding. If Montgomery intended to keep the porous *Herald* afloat, he needed to find a competent, full-time, on-site manager to batten down the hatches. Montgomery had put off for too long what he now knew he had to do. The editorial staff was an ad hoc troupe of polyglot part-timers who some days convened in the Rua Mexico newsroom and other days did not. Columnist Frank Garcia remembered that at one time more than twenty languages were spoken in the newsroom, with little direction given in any. Garcia charitably labeled the *Herald* on its eleventh anniversary in 1957 "still a teenager though already wearing long pants."[4] To many, it was wearing no clothes at all.

Within a year, co-founder and columnist Garcia would be dead. He died at Stranger's Hospital, the same medical facility that Andrew Jackson Lamoureux had helped found, and was buried in Rio at the Cemitério dos Ingleses, the same cemetery where Vic Hawkins and Stu Morrison were buried, as would be *Herald* art critic Marc

Berkowitz. Joe Brown wrote Garcia's laudatory obit for the *Herald*, its content and style indicative of how Brown viewed expat journalism in Brazil:

In the passing of Frank M. Garcia, Brazil lost a tried and true friend who had dedicated much of his life to bettering the relations between the United States and his adopted home. His opinions were always definite—often expressed in critical terms—but behind his thoughts was only the purpose to help the country in which he had spent so many years. And thoughtful Brazilians recognized his worth. His Brazilian friends were legion and it is doubtful any American had such wide and close relations with Brazilian officialdom.[5]

If *Herald* publisher Montgomery had ever needed a tap on his shoulder to find a competent full-time editorial supervisor for his drifting newspaper, with Garcia's death he had received a shove in the small of his back. From Kansas, in Rio, and during IAPA summits in Latin America, Montgomery interviewed an array of potential managers. Some were international businessmen unfamiliar with the newspaper industry; others were publishers at small US weeklies and dailies who wouldn't make a long-term commitment to living in Brazil. To Montgomery, US nationality, American newspaper experience, and English fluency were essential qualifications. If the newspaper supervisor didn't already speak Portuguese, the successful candidate ought to express a desire to learn. These were the minimum requirements.

As a capper, Montgomery's new hire shouldn't expect much in remuneration. Instead of a commensurate salary, Montgomery's pitch would be the promise of an assortment of business and social perks—as many as could be leveraged using the *Herald's* editorial and advertising space in exchange for personal freebies, discounts, and kickbacks. While such exchanges in the news business in the US might strike some as unethical, the practice in Brazil was commonplace, and expected. An additional incentive for the right manager would be that the new supervisor could be given stock in Editôra Mory, the *Herald*'s holding company. Montgomery wasn't interested in giving away the store, but allotting the *Herald*'s on-site supervisor a minority interest, Montgomery figured, might foster loyalty and longevity.

Through Rio fixer Richard Momsen, who had put together Montgomery's purchase of the *Herald* twelve years earlier from William Pawley, Montgomery was introduced to a likable and ambitious ex-Marine who at the time was editor of the Rio-based American Chamber of Commerce's publication, *Brazilian Business*, while stringing for McGraw-Hill World News Service and hustling to create a Brazilian wire service of his own.

Fig. 12.1 Bill Williamson and John D. Montgomery. Courtesy of the Bill Williamson Collection.

Born in Des Moines, Iowa, William Paul Williamson Jr. was the son of a single mother who was a Cedar Falls schoolteacher. While in the Marines, he had been editor of the *Station Daily News Bulletin*, in El Toro, California. On the GI bill, Williamson had earned an undergraduate degree from what would become the University of Northern Iowa, followed by a master's degree in journalism from the University of Iowa. His graduate thesis was a comparative analysis of newspapers in Mexico City and Chicago, which earned Williamson fellowships at the University of Havana and the University of the Americas in Mexico City. In 1952, Williamson worked as assistant managing editor for the English-language *Mexico City News*, after which he enrolled in Memphis State University to earn a Ph.D. in journalism; his dissertation was to be an analysis of the Brazilian newspaper industry, a subject he researched with vigor, visiting more than one hundred fifty newspapers in Brazil's then twenty-five states on a US State Department-funded trip in 1956-57. Williamson's goal was to become a journalism professor back in the US.

With Momsen's endorsement, Montgomery got to know Williamson through a series of letters the two men exchanged during the summer of 1959. Williamson met all the requirements Montgomery had set forth and then some. Both Montgomery and Williamson were Midwesterners who had spent time in Cuba. Not only was Williamson an American, but he was also thoroughly familiar with newspaper journalism *and* already in Rio *and* he wanted to stay there for the foreseeable future. Additional pluses were that Williamson had recently married a Brazilian woman and spoke Portuguese reasonably well.

Could there possibly be a better candidate to take over the wobbly helm of the *Brazil Herald*?

Williamson had met his wife, Vânia Tôrres Nogueira, on his first day in Brazil, during which he paid a courtesy visit to the US Embassy. As soon as Vânia, who was working in the embassy's library, laid eyes on the blond, blue-eyed Iowan, she turned to a coworker and whispered, "I'm going to marry that man!"[6]

Montgomery invited Williamson to Kansas, and as a twofer, Williamson and his new bride took their honeymoon in the American Midwest, first to meet Williamson's mother in Iowa and then to get to know Montgomery in Kansas. On the day after Christmas, during which Vânia saw snow for the first time, Williamson borrowed his mother's new Chevrolet Impala, and the couple drove from Cedar Falls, Iowa, to Kansas City to join Montgomery and Mary Liz for dinner at the Muehlebach Hotel. The next day, they caravanned west to Junction City, where Montgomery and Williamson agreed on terms for Williamson to take over as general manager of the *Brazil Herald*.[7]

In Williamson, Montgomery had found what seemed a perfect executive to run his Southern Hemisphere publishing enterprise. Not only did Williamson know his way around a newsroom, he was thoroughly familiar with the newspaper printing-press process. He had started his career delivering the *Waterloo Daily Courier* door to door when he was eight. As a teenager after school, he worked at the *Rockford Register*, operating a sheet-fed Platinum printing press, and later, for the Woolverton and Holst Printing companies in Cedar Falls and the Albee Printing in Waterloo, where he learned to handset type. Williamson had been a "printer's devil," newspaper lingo for an all-purpose apprentice.[8] For someone who had grown up milking cows at cousin Roy's farm and cleaning chicken coops at Uncle Lee's ranch, Montgomery's offer was too good to be true. Williamson had gone from rural Iowa to urban Brazil, to become editor and manager of a small but promising daily newspaper in the twentieth largest city the world.[9]

With Williamson's hire, Joe Brown was elated to be relieved of overseeing the *Herald*'s financial mess. "While we hated to leave, we were pleased that we could turn over to our successor a newspaper worthy of its name," Brown would write, understating his glee and overstating the *Herald*'s reputation.[10]

To augment the *Herald*'s bottom line and in hopes of elevating the newspaper's profile, Williamson rented out a spare office in the *Herald*'s newsroom to the American television network CBS to house its new Latin America bureau and correspondent, Charles Bishop Kuralt. With Kuralt down the hall, Williamson figured that the *Herald*'s reputation might improve, at least among American correspondents based in Brazil, and through them, the expat paper might be able to establish some needed credibility back home. Kuralt's proximal presence at the *Herald* also would give affable Williamson the opportunity to squire the folksy TV correspondent around town.[11]

In the internecine world of office politics back at CBS headquarters in New York, the head of CBS television at the time, Jim Aubrey, had launched an anti-Kuralt campaign, complaining that Kuralt was "low-key, slow, not what you want.'" Kuralt and another on-air CBS newsman at the time, gravitas-laced, authoritative Walter Cronkite, were vying to be named anchor of the network's marquee offering, the CBS Evening News. When Cronkite got the job, "Kuralt was shipped out of the country," according to Ralph Grizzle in his biography, *Remembering Charles Kuralt*. Grizzle quoted CBS executive Les Midgley, producer of the network's program "Eyewitness to History," who said, Kuralt was "the only correspondent the network had on the whole continent. It was a bad thing to do to him after he had worked so well and so hard. Brazil was not at all where Kuralt had thought his career was going, and he was lonely there."[12]

Just before leaving the States for Rio, Kuralt had gotten married, the second marriage for the twenty-six-year-old journalist, to Suzanna "Petie" Baird, who had been fellow newsman Douglas Edwards's secretary at CBS headquarters in New York. Baird seemingly did not adjust to life in Brazil. Ed Miller, the Rio correspondent for the Associated Press, remembered, "Charlie's wife had white hair, but she wasn't old. She was very strange. And she always wore a black dress. Never any color. Very standoffish."

Thirty-five years later when Kuralt died in 1997 at sixty-two, he would make news for something other than his journalistic talent. Kuralt had led a double life, still married to and living with wife Petie in New York, but also maintaining a long-term clandestine relationship and part-time home with another woman, Pat Shannon, in Montana.[13]

Petie seemed to be the opposite of florid Rio and amiable Kuralt, whom Miller described as a "helluva correspondent."[14] With the backdrop of beguiling Brazil, Kuralt, despite being banished to the outer reaches of CBS's galaxy, had a ready-made palette for his budding reportorial elegance and rich narrative skills for which he would become renowned, especially with his long-running *On the Road* TV series, exploring rural America.

One of Kuralt's first reports from Brazil would be an assessment of the local press, required reading for any foreign correspondent seeking to learn the intricacies and idiosyncrasies of a new assignment. Kuralt sent back home a Sunday piece on Rio's robust newspaper scene, which he found nothing short of remarkable.

"[E]ven though Rio, as a city, is only about a third the size of New York City in population, and even though about half the people of this country don't know how to read, the fact is that there are more than twice as many daily newspapers in Rio de Janeiro as there are in New York. And I have to start by admitting to a prejudice. I love them.

"It's hard to find their match for enterprise, for the hard work of good journalism; it's impossible to find their match for wild irresponsibility," Kuralt intoned in his twangy drawl that Americans would come to savor for four decades. "The most cheerfully libelous of these newspapers will take your breath away. The newspaper reader in Rio has his choice of gravity or libel and thus he's a blessed man."

In the fifteen-minute Sunday noon report for New York's WCBS-TV, substituting for regular Charles Collingwood, Kuralt singled out Rio's mainstay, the *Jornal do Brasil*, pronouncing it "the most lovable paper I have ever read." Kuralt especially liked how JB, as it is called, published splashy, large photographs (his affection for the oversized black-and-white images may have had something to do with the fact that Kuralt didn't speak Portuguese and couldn't read what was under and alongside the photographs). "This newspaper has the best photographers in Latin America and it uses them, and it plays their pictures the way newspaper pictures are supposed to be played, the way photographers all over the world dream of."

In his report, Kuralt took to task Rio's daily newspapers at the time for their apparent lack of press ethics. "All these papers are full of the most incredible blather about the 'wonderful new line of watches at such and such super honest jewelry store.' Nothing special about those watches, of course, except that some reporter is now wearing one."

Kuralt included a mention of the *Brazil Herald* in his report, characterizing it as "a brave little newspaper but it isn't much good. It does, thank Heaven, carry PEANUTS and POGO and [political pundit] Walter Lippmann but for the rest it is all Associated Press copy—no local reporting at all, except for what's been stolen from the Rio press the day before. But it's getting better, and it does —I forgot—carry DEAR ABBIE! [*sic*]"[15]

Herald manager Bill Williamson never heard Kuralt's assessment, and perhaps that was a good thing. Williamson was a natural and unabashed cheerleader for the *Herald*, eating as many churrascos and downing as many caipirinhas as he could with businessmen and merchants in Rio and São Paulo in hopes of attracting advertising in the newspaper. Williamson joined every local, regional, and national organization open to him in Rio. He went out of his way to meet publishers and editors of any newspaper throughout Brazil, a courtesy arranged by Herbert Moses, the president of the Brazilian Press Association and a founder of Rio's *O Globo* newspaper. Williamson was popular with the corps of foreign correspondents and promptly got elected president of the local Overseas Press Club in Rio. He and publisher Montgomery attended each of the hemispheric Inter American Press Association annual meetings, where the pair would pal around with other publishers and newspaper managers over cocktails, spreading word of the invigorated *Herald*.

To a degree, Williamson's infectious enthusiasm worked. He became well known and liked as the *Herald*'s convivial general manager. Within two years, Montgomery would promote Williamson to managing partner, giving the native Iowan a twenty-five percent share in the *Herald*'s privately held stock, along with a contract clause that provided Williamson with first right of refusal should Montgomery ever choose to sell the newspaper.

Williamson, whom the Brazilians in the *Herald* newsroom addressed as "Senhor Bill," elongating "Bill" to a two-syllable-long singsong "BEELL-il," did whatever he could to increase visibility and spread word of the "new and improved" *Herald*, which ran from twelve to twenty-four pages a day. Williamson managed to increase circulation to between twelve thousand and fifteen thousand, although circulation figures of the newspaper were never reliable.

Under Williamson, the *Herald* finally had reached a modicum of financial stability. That was paramount for Williamson and Montgomery, who in more than fifty letters I reviewed between the two men never once discussed the content of the newspaper's editorial product. Both were businessmen first, journalists perhaps third or fourth, if at all. In all their handwritten correspondence, neither ever mentioned a single news story the *Herald* had published. As the younger Montgomery, John Grey, would recall, "I don't remember any conversation about content, except maybe promotional material. Their emphasis was on sales or PR."[16] Perhaps to prove the point, *The New Yorker* would occasionally publish bemused, curious fillers from the *Herald* at the bottom of the magazine's columns.[17]

As the *Herald*'s bottom line began improving, Williamson was able to enjoy the assorted perks that went along with being an executive in Rio, advantages the young newspaper executive never would have had in the States as a general manager of a similarly-sized newspaper. Williamson had a chauffeured car at his disposal to take him between his office and his oceanfront apartment, as well as on the town in the evenings; he and Vânia had a live-in maid (although this was common, even for middle-class Brazilians); they would be able to send their three children to the private and elite American School in Rio. The fifth-floor apartment in which the Williamson family lived was in an elegant building, the Edificio Iguassu at 1588 Avenida Atlântica, down the block from the Copacabana Palace, where publisher

Montgomery had once lived, facing the beach and the azure waters of the Atlantic. The Williamson home was among the premier addresses in all of Brazil. It was where *New York Times* correspondent and former *Brazil Herald* reporter Tad Szulc and his wife, Marianne Carr, had once lived. The apartment came with a telephone and working phone number, a coveted domestic commodity at the time.[18]

Williamson soon became the *Herald's* leading man, the newspaper's No. 1 salesman. He was a member of two yacht clubs, two regatta clubs, a golf and country club, all necessary affiliations, he argued, for the *Herald* to compete with other Brazilian newspapers for upscale retail and corporate advertising, not to mention affluent, influential subscribers.

Part of Williamson's intuitive appeal came from his natural good looks and aw-shucks, easy-going personality. He was a combination of Cary Grant and Jimmy Stewart in appearance and stage presence. He carried himself with understated savoir faire. Bill and Vânia threw

Fig. 12.2 Bill Williamson and Army Marshal Artur da Costa e Silva, President of Brazil, 1967-1969. Courtesy of the Bill Williamson Collection.

fabulous parties to welcome consular officials, business executives, and American correspondents to town, another way to build goodwill for the *Herald*. Bill owned an oft-used tuxedo and Vânia was a knockout in fashionable evening wear, which included a closetful of gowns. The couple were guests at as many as five engagements a week. Rio is a party town, and the Williamsons seemed to be on everyone's A-list, at least among the monied expat set.

"Bill really enjoyed life," recalled Ed Miller, the former AP correspondent. "He really made a point of it. He loved to go to parties. He was elegant. He was dashing—you can't use that word with many men. Was Bill a ladies' man? Only in the sense that the ladies threw themselves at his feet. Bill was like a movie star. I remember once in São Paulo, we were in a restaurant and it had booths and this lady, if you can call her that, came over and sat with us and she was all over Bill. She wouldn't leave him alone. And finally, Bill had to push her out of the booth. That was the only way he could get rid of her."[19]

Walter Colton, who would become managing editor of the *Brazil Herald* in the mid-1970s, would recall that Williamson "always had these gorgeous, buxom secretaries, and we were all salivating over them. He had a door to his office, and a private bathroom and shower. Bill was handsome, he was virile, he was a physical guy. The guy exuded charm."[20]

In the newsroom Williamson was approachable, well-reasoned, and usually open to anything new and different as long as it didn't cost much and might appeal to *Herald* readers. He chatted up everyone, from pressmen wearing grimy T-shirts, shorts, and flipflops to the newspaper's society columnists off to soirees, wearing gloves and gowns.

In 1962, publisher Montgomery made another purchase of an English-language newspaper, the weekly *Times of Brazil*, which had primarily served Rio's British expatriate community intermittently since 1919. Williamson folded the new acquisition into the *Herald* as a weekend features insert. By doing so, he neatly consolidated readership of the only other non-specialty English-language daily in

Brazil. In an effort to comply with extant Brazilian laws prohibiting foreigners from owning or holding top positions in media firms, Williamson made Vânia, a Brazilian, the nominal publisher, or Editôra Responsável, of the *Herald*'s acquisition.

In 1967, Williamson moved the *Herald*'s newsroom and printing presses, this time to a classic, turn-of-the-century, three-story building at 65 Rua do Resende, in a colonial district of Rio called Lapa, where Brazilian singer and actor Carmen Miranda had grown up. On the corner was Gugs (pronounced *Goo-gues*), a sticky-counter restaurant that would become a popular lunch hangout for the newspaper staff. Across the street was an assortment of hole-in-the-wall funeral-supply stores with elaborate arrays of caskets that drew a steady stream of grieving customers. Around the corner was the Instituto Médico Legal, Rio's morgue. *Botânicas* were scattered throughout the neighborhood, brimming with ceramic statues of deities, soaps, and incense that guaranteed everything, from getting rid of your mother-in-law and increasing sexual prowess to winning the national lottery and growing curls on a bald pate. These dispensaries sold myriad offerings related to Candomblé, Umbanda, and Macumba, Brazilian-African mélanges of Catholicism and native spirits. Down the street from the *Herald* was Bar Brasil, a down-at-its-heels 1940s watering hole that became a mandatory stop-off after work for *Herald* and, later, *Latin America Daily Post* reporters and editors. All these landmarks were places I got to know when I started at the newspaper in early 1980.

The acquisition of the *Times of Brazil* expanded the number of the *Herald*'s Linotype machines to four, along with a photo plate-maker. While the additional printing equipment made publishing more efficient, the *Herald* still had its share of technical headaches.

As Mary A. Lenz, a *Herald* staffer, noted in a letter to her parents at the time, "You can't put -30- at the end of the story because the Brazilian staff will set everything up in 30-point type." In journalism as practiced in the United States, -30- traditionally signified to editors and typesetters the end of a reporter's story.[21]

Just as Montgomery had realized that he needed a skilled newsroom supervisor, Williamson also knew that he had to find an English-and-Portuguese-speaking foreman to oversee the newspaper's keyboard operators to minimize the multitude of egregious typographical errors that still bedeviled the newspaper, as well as to manage the back shop. He did so with Igor Tsvik, a hefty Russian who had arrived in Brazil via Manchuria in the early 1950s. In the tradition of the *Herald*, Tsvik spoke multiple languages, including English, Portuguese, Mandarin, Russian, and an assortment of Slavic dialects. Tsvik's English had been good enough to get him hired first as a proofreader at the newspaper, but he also was so savvy and mechanically inclined that he soon became the go-to fix-it man in the pressroom.

With the addition of a Goss Community printing press manufactured in Chicago, the staff held its collective breath when the *Herald*'s first edition rolled off the new press with this announcement on page 1 in the summer of 1968:

If part of today's copy looks neater, nicer and better printed, it is because it was printed on our fabulous high speed web offset press. If part of today's copy doesn't look neater, nice and better

Fig. 12.3 Igor Tsvik (*left*) and Bill Williamson. Courtesy of the Bill Williamson Collection.

printed, it is because no one really knows how to run our fabulous high speed web offset press yet."[22]

As the paper's mechanical hiccups began to abate, the *Herald* started utilizing new offset technology and cold type to publish color advertising circulars. The first came out July 4, 1969, an ad for Coca-Cola. The paper followed with other color ads for Mesbla, the same department store chain that Teddy Hecht had created advertisements for as an account executive, along with supplements for Brazilian retailers Ultralar, Sears, Peg Pag, Mar e Terra, Merci, and Casas de Banha.

Always on the lookout for side jobs to utilize the *Herald*'s printing presses when idle during daytime hours, Williamson secured contracts that included *GIL Modas*, a fashion magazine that printed sewing patterns; a music magazine called *CD em Revista*; the *Gazeta da Farmárcia*, the bible for Brazilian pharmacists; and *Gira da Umbanda*, a guide to popular Brazilian occultism. The *Herald* also printed *O Pasquim*, a weekly satirical newspaper that ran articles and cartoons produced by some of the nation's most well-known journalists and illustrators. Other side jobs included *Opinião*, a left-wing political journal edited by Fernando Gasparian, along with a neighborhood ad sheet, *Jornal de Ipanema*, and a magazine showcasing one of Rio's premier soccer teams, Vasco da Gama. Williamson was following the same course that *Rio News* owner and editor A. J. Lamoureux had charted eighty years earlier by printing an array of publications designed to offset the cost of putting out a daily newspaper.

Like his predecessors, Williamson had difficulty increasing with any regularity the *Herald*'s circulation outside of Rio and São Paulo. The wholesale cost per copy to deliver the newspaper to distant destinations didn't justify the expense to get it there. A more pressing problem was the *Herald*'s continued inability to establish a reliable infrastructure that would guarantee daily delivery each morning in Rio.

Though their relationship was mostly long-distance, Williamson and publisher Montgomery shared a genuine affection for each other. On the surface, Williamson seemed everything Montgomery could have hoped for in his local man in Rio. Both were chain smokers (Williamson was up to three packs of Brazilian Hollywood and Continental cigarettes a day; Montgomery's smokes were Marlboros), and when together in Rio, the men would talk into the late-evening hours sipping Chivas and drawing on cigarettes. Montgomery wasn't a big man, five-foot, eight inches, but he was stocky and overweight. Like Williamson, he wore black-frame glasses. And like Williamson, he had a placid, what-me-worry manner, seldom, if ever, troubled. Together, the men complemented each other's tact and warmth. Montgomery's son, John Grey, was adopted, and in some ways, Williamson was more like Montgomery than John Grey was.

Williamson's and Montgomery's wives were close, too, so close that Bill and Vânia named their first-born daughter Mary Liz, as a tribute to Montgomery's wife. Once AT&T international rates started going down, Williamson and Montgomery often talked on the phone late into the night. Montgomery sent Bill's aging mother, who by now had moved from Iowa to Los Angeles, *Brazil Herald* clippings of Bill and Vânia being feted at parties and events, with congratulatory notes scribbled in the margins. To both men, the *Herald* was part of a grand adventure that had taken them from the provincial American Midwest to cosmopolitan Rio de Janeiro.

It was during the fall of 1962 that Williamson received a rather curious letter in the mail from a US journalist vagabonding through South America, seeking to join him in that high-flying adventure.

CHAPTER 13

Gonzo

WHILE *HERALD* JOURNALISTS Betty Dyer, Herb Zschech, Tad Szulc, Teddy Hecht, Marc Berkowitz, and Margaret Morrison were dependable professionals whose work counterbalanced the newspaper's lopsided reliance on amateurs, they were in a completely different league when compared to an untamed reporter Bill Williamson hired in the fall of 1962 with the rather long byline of Hunter S. Thompson.

Thompson worked for the *Herald* for only a few months, but his experience in Brazil helped form the basis of a body of work that would rock global journalism to its core. Hunter Stockton Thompson would become the cult writer who would introduce the world to his singular brand of stream-of-consciousness, profanity-laced, participatory journalism known as "Gonzo." To Thompson, the circuitous process of *getting* the story was as important as the story itself. In fact, it *was* the story.

Thompson had figured in my own trajectory as a budding writer, and his wild "fear and loathing" tales of sloth, politics, American culture, depravity, sex, violence, and drugs would rock my own world, as well as that of every journalist I knew. That he had his beginnings in Brazil and at the newspaper where I would work would be an encouraging nod that I had made the right move.

Thompson had long considered reporting from South America, and in October 1961 came up with a skeletal itinerary he shared in a letter to a friend, Eugene W. McGarr, while he was going broke trying to finish his first novel, *The Rum Diary*, in Big Sur, California.[1] Thompson's idea of embarking on a headstrong reporting trip through the Southern Hemisphere's asphalt jungles picked up speed, and in a rambling letter to another friend, Paul Semonin, the following February, Thompson wrote, "I am becoming more and more certain that this South American venture is my last chance to do something big and bad, come to grips with the basic wildness. . . . I am going to write massive tomes from South America. I can hardly wait to get my teeth into it."[2]

To writer Lionel Olay, a week before he was to leave, Thompson wrote about his upcoming odyssey, referring to himself in the third person. Most itinerant writers can relate to the sentiments Thompson expressed, with the possible exception of HST's case of hemorrhoids.

Mr. Thompson will shove off for South America and begin the long hot agony of trying to keep alive on free-lance journalism. That's my plan in a nutshell. I've been long delayed here, fighting with that stinking book, and now when I sit down to read these 366 pages that took me 18 months to create, it simply seems like a waste of time. Right as I was finishing mine, I read a book called Out of Africa by Isak Dinesen, and it almost broke me down. I am going to do a lot of thinking before I start another book, which maddeningly enough, is already creeping into outline form. This writing is like cocaine and I'm damned if I can figure out why people keep at it. Aside from everything else, sitting on my ass all that time gave me a whopping case of piles. Where is the percentage?"[3]

The idea for Thompson's tropical peregrination had come through a journalism connection he'd made in his thus-far short-lived newspaper career. In 1961, Thompson had worked with journalist Bob Bone at the *Middletown Daily Record* in upstate New York. Thompson had the habit of not wearing shoes in the newsroom, which his supervisor did not like, but what got him fired from the newspaper was kicking in a vending machine and destroying it after the offending machine

failed to deliver that candy bar that he had paid for. "[H]e just beat
it—'savagely' to use his word—until it dislodged his candy bar," recalled Bone.⁴

Bone left the *Middletown Daily Record* soon after Thompson, first
going to San Juan, Puerto Rico, then to Brazil for fun, adventure, and
a little work, which he found with Bill Williamson's former employer,
the American Chamber of Commerce in Rio, writing the business organization's magazine, *Brazilian Business*. Thompson contacted Bone
in Rio and asked if he would connect him with Williamson to ask
about a job at the *Herald*.

Always on the lookout for American journalists willing to relocate to Brazil on their own dime, Williamson replied with a letter to
Thompson that while he couldn't make any promises, if Thompson
showed up at the *Herald's* newsroom, Williamson likely would be able
to make some use of him. It was the same no-strings commitment
Steve Yolen had made to me when he dangled the possibility of a job
at the *Latin America Daily Post*.

That was just the opening Thompson had been waiting for. He'd
leverage Williamson's promise of work to reel in other journalistic
assignments on the road to Rio, his ultimate destination. That's what
I had done when I connected with the Field News Service to write
freelance pieces. Thompson contacted an at-the-time new, general-
interest weekly newspaper, the *National Observer*, published by Dow
Jones, where he got a vague commitment, this one for pickup work
along the way. Founded by editor Barney Kilgore, who would take
the *Wall Street Journal* from a small, insider's financial newspaper to
a publishing powerhouse, the *National Observer* would be known for
synthesizing events and trends in a stylized and breezy format.⁵ An
editor at the new weekly, Clifford A. Ridley, wrote back to Thompson,
saying he'd consider publishing Thompson's dispatches from South
America.⁶ As Williamson had done, Ridley made no promises, but
encouraged Thompson to send him any and all of his dispatches.

To twenty-four-year-old Thompson, these two quasi-commitments
from Williamson and Ridley were more than enough to send him

packing. Thompson would start his southern pilgrimage, like Bone, in Puerto Rico, where he got a job for a soon-to-be insolvent bowling magazine. In San Juan, Thompson would meet William Kennedy, who'd go on to win the 1984 Pulitzer Prize for his masterful novel, *Ironweed*. At the time, Kennedy was managing editor of another expat English-language newspaper, *The San Juan Star*, and struggling with his on-the-side fiction writing. Bone had worked at the *Star*, and Thompson asked Kennedy to hire him at the *Star*, but Kennedy demurred, saying there wasn't an opening, but even if there had been, Thompson wouldn't have been a good fit.[7] Thompson stayed in Puerto Rico for several months, during which he got arrested for his involvement in a brawl prompted by an unpaid bar tab; Kennedy arranged bail to get Thompson sprung from jail.[8]

From Puerto Rico via a roundabout trip to Bermuda, Aruba, and Honduras, Thompson got himself to Bogotá, Colombia. By then, he was a month into what would become a crazed, diarrhetic trek across the northern third of South America. From Lima, Peru, Thompson sent *Brazil Herald* manager Bill Williamson another letter, inside a wrinkled envelope, which carried the protracted August 3, 1962, dateline: "From the extra bed in the flea-ridden hotel room of Hunter S. Thompson." The letter advised Williamson, "I will proceed as planned from here to La Paz to Rio . . . . It will involve a mad, headlong poverty-stricken rush across the continent."

Either Thompson was flexing his unorthodox writing chops or warning Williamson (whom he had never met) that if he ever got to the *Herald* newsroom, he'd be a resoundingly unconventional hire. It likely was both. Thompson's scattered correspondence read:

If Rio is no better than the places I have visited thus far I will beat a hasty retreat to the north and write this continent off as a lost cause. For the past month I have felt on the brink of insanity: weakened by dysentery, plagued by fleas and vermin of all sizes, cut off from mail, money, sex and all but the foulest of food and hounded 24 hours a day by thieves, beggars, pimps, fascists, usurers, dolts and human jackdaws of every shape and description. If these are Pizzaro's ancestors, you are goddamn lucky he never got to Brazil. All this time I have had in the back of my mind an unreasoning certainty that Rio is a decent place where a man can sit in the sun and drink a beer without having to put on a frock coat and carry a truncheon to ward off the citizenry. If this is a delusion I will probably have a breakdown when I arrive and the Embassy will be forced to ship me home like an animal, with "No Dice" scrawled across my passport.

At any rate, your note was the only ray of optimism I have found in as long as I dare remember. My last communication from [Robert] Bone was a letter threatening my life, I believe, and the rest of the mail has been no cheerier. I will be here long enough to divine the nature of Peruvian politics, then push on to La Paz for a bout with whatever diseases are currently fashionable in that country. After that, train trip to Rio, which should just about finish me off. If there is an Alms House in Rio, I trust you are on good terms with the proprietor, so I can enter without delay.

Thompson signed the unhinged letter, "Until then, I remain, yours for the broadening aspects of travel, HST."[9]

If there ever were a moment in which Gonzo journalism was born, Thompson's letter to Williamson might have been it.

Not scared off by Thompson's letter, Williamson replied with a positive-but-guarded response: Show up at the *Herald* once you get to town. Williamson was careful not to promise Thompson anything specific, just as Yolen had done with me.

Holed up in Lima, Thompson had just sent off a piece to Ridley at the *National Observer* (to be headlined, "Democracy Dies in Peru, But Few Seem to Mourn Its Passing") and was primed for what Thompson had optimistically construed as a firm job offer from. Rio de Janeiro would be the shimmering pot of gold at the end of a thus-far faded South American rainbow. To friend Paul Semonin, Thompson wrote:

I have been getting steadily more depressed until I am seriously beginning to wonder if my personality is being undermined. As a matter of fact, every place I have been except Cali, Colombia has been a pure dull hell and full of so many nagging discomforts that I am tempted at times to write this continent off as a lost cause. Lima is the worst so far; I have done nothing but sit in my hotel room, which is like something on the main street of Flora, Illinois, and smoke. Now and then I go out to eat or to be snubbed at the Embassy. I have spoken to no one except the AP man in four days. Perhaps I should say I have talked to no one; there is a lot of talking done here but it means absolutely nothing—in a way that makes it an easy place to write about, because all you have to do is line up all the facts, note how they refute everything you are told, and simply ignore all the shit people ram in your ears.

In the letter, Thompson continued, "I retain a mad faith that Rio is better, primarily because I have heard it is bad from people who would not know a good thing if they swallowed it. . . . So I hope to be in Rio by September 1, probably in rotten shape but with things looking up. I hope. (It is a good sign that I remembered to say this; maybe my brains are warming up.)" [10]

Thompson wrapped up the letter by overstating Williamson's promise of a job. "I have also had a good exchange of letters with the editor of the paper there, saying flatly that I need not worry about money although he is not sure where it will come from. But he sounds hip and the atmosphere is at least that uncertain and besides he says it is cheap even by my standards." [11]

Thompson arrived in Rio more or less on schedule on September 15, made a beeline for the *Herald* and met Williamson, who hired him on the spot. In a letter to Ridley at the *National Observer*, Thompson boasted two days later, "I definitely mean to base here, for a while, anyway. The Brazil Herald offered me a job at a ridiculous salary—adds up to less than $100 a month, U.S.—but I told them I couldn't tie my-self down here with local reporting & still get around enough to send you a varied assortment. I have all intentions of staying here as much as possible, but I want to be free to move around to the other countries as soon as I get rested and cured. It is about time I lived like a human being for a change. . . . This is a fine town & pretty cheap to live in if you're careful."[12]

The sentiments seemed spun from *A Moveable Feast*, in which Hemingway wrote, "In Paris, you could live very well on almost nothing and by skipping meals occasionally and never buying new clothes, you could save and have luxuries."[13] They were similar to my own upon arriving in São Paulo. What more could a young, eager journalist new to a big foreign city want?

During his first week in Rio, Thompson paid a visit to the local AP bureau as a wannabe professional courtesy, which seemed to be his practice when arriving in South American capitals. Ed Miller, the AP correspondent, remembered meeting Thompson, but not with any affection. "I kicked him out . . . with the blessing of my boss, and he never came back," Miller recalled. "I honestly can't remember what it was that pissed me off so much. I think he may have been drunk. I just remember him from that brief visit as being really obnoxious. A complete pain in the ass."[14]

Thompson was soon joined in Rio by his girlfriend and future first wife, Sandy Conklin. The couple stayed in a budget hotel in Copacabana, and by November had moved to a nearby apartment, which they rented for the equivalent of thirty American dollars a month. Thompson boasted in a letter to a friend that he was thinking of buying a Jeep, having his Doberman flown from his mother's home in Louisville, and buying a country home on the outskirts of Rio. These were grandiose fictions that Thompson would become famous for. "Right now I have more money than I can reasonably waste. Rio is a hell of a city and impossible to describe in a few lines. I'll be here another six months, anyway. Same address. Living is cheap but it may not last," he wrote.[15]

Thompson didn't do much socializing with other reporters or editors in the *Herald* newsroom. That might have been because stern Herb Zschech was the newspaper's editor at the time or that the cliquish staffers were jacks of all trades for whom the *Herald* was a side gig. Outside of Conklin, Thompson's only friend in town seemed to have been Bone, the local Chamber of Commerce flack who had connected Thompson to Williamson and the *Herald*.

Bone recalled that while driving along Copacabana Beach one afternoon in an MG convertible, he spotted Thompson loping along Avenida Atlântica, near the Williamson apartment. Bone beeped his horn and Thompson hopped in. "Hunter was a little drunk," Bone remembered, "but he said, 'That's nothing. The thing that's drunk is in my pocket,'" and proceeded to produce a small monkey to Bone's amazement.

Fig. 13.1 From *left*, Bob Bone, Hunter S. Thompson, and Sandy Conklin on Copacabana Beach. From Robert W. Bone, *Fire Bone: A Maverick's Guide to Life in Journalism* (Walnut Creek, CA: Peripety Press, 2017).

Thompson and the monkey would become inseparable, so much so that Thompson would take the simian to taverns, although this may be creative fabrication on Bone's part, a case of one too many monkey-says-to-the-bartender jokes, which Bone imported into his memory, even though Bone steadfastly maintained in his memoir, *Fire Bone*, that the monkey, whom Thompson named Ace, was actually a coati who was house-broken and washed his hands with soap after using the toilet.[16]

While Thompson's only newspaper job as a reporter for the *Middletown Daily Record*, had not ended well, his tenure at the free-wheeling *Brazil Herald* turned out to be more conducive to the budding writer's personality. Thompson's most memorable bylined story appeared on October 23, 1962, on page two of the *Herald*, under the headline, "Sen. Talmadge Stresses Self-Help, Voices Concern Over L. America." The article ran when Williamson was off attending that year's annual Inter American Press Association convention, this time in Santiago, Chile, where he and Montgomery, per their usual, drank Chivas, smoked cigarettes, and held court.

Herald editor Zschech had assigned Thompson to cover what ordinarily would have been a standard *Herald* valentine. The event was a business luncheon sponsored by Bone's boss and Williamson's former employer, the American Chamber of Commerce, held at the Hotel Glória, where a dozen US congressmen were being feted, the same place where *Herald* arts critic Marc Berkowitz had regaled the writer Erskine Caldwell with his erudition on classical music, and where I would stay when I would move to Rio from São Paulo. The bloviating politicians at the meeting included Virginia Senator Absalom Willis Robertson (the father of future televangelist Pat Robertson) and Georgia Senator Herman E. Talmadge. They were on their way to attend a snoozy boondoggle, the 51ˢᵗ Inter-Parliamentary Conference, in the new inland capital, Brasília. The cadre of conservative Southern politicians on a slap-happy junket played perfectly to what would become Thompson's out-there literary trademark.

Robertson, Talmadge, and the other US officials in attendance were upset by the recent expropriation of a tract of land owned by the Brazilian subsidiary of International Telephone and Telegraph in the southeast Brazilian state of Rio Grande do Sul. The politicians expressed growing fears that such government mandates were tantamount to stealing, a harbinger of populist Brazilian President João Goulart's increasingly strident one-year-old leftist administration. At the Chamber luncheon, hardliner US Ambassador Lincoln Gordon was seated at the head table, nodding in agreement with other American officials and expat executives appalled at what they viewed as a government-sponsored land grab. How would such private-property seizures end? To them, the answer was clear: communism in neon lights.

In the article's lede, Thompson quoted Talmadge drawling to the Chamber attendees, "We know from readin' the Bible and readin' the scriptures that neither the United States nor God can help people who cannot help themselves."

Thompson followed with the junior senator intoning, "'Let me tell you in all frankness and all candor that people in Congress and all over the U.S. are concerned about recent events in South America. Great social change is taking place (in South America) and will continue . . . but if the people change faster than their governments it will benefit nobody but Moscow.' Not all observers were sure just what he meant by this, but all agreed it had an ominous ring."

Talmadge was invoking the canard of the threat of communism, the rallying cry of legions of American officials past and future as justification for meddling and intervening in another country's internal affairs, and Thompson was inside the Hotel Glória ballroom documenting it all. Whether anyone at the luncheon realized that a reporter was jotting down these and other rants is unknown.

Thompson followed Talmadge's remarks by quoting some folk wisdom spun by the host of the gathering, Richard Fallon, the Chamber president, CEO of General Electric's subsidiary in Rio, and drinking buddy of *Herald* managing partner Williamson:

In closing, Mr. Fallon tossed in an analogy of obscure and indeterminate import. He noted that when Yankee Stadium was constructed in 1923, it was decided that seats of from 17 to 19 inches wide would be adequate for the average spectator. But when the new [Washington Senators] stadium was constructed last year in Washington DC, it was deemed necessary to install seats of 20 to 23 inches in width. At least one spectator interpreted this to mean that if Brazilians refrain from harassing American business, Rio's man in the street will be three inches fatter 40 years hence.[17]

As Thompson wrote it, the baseball stadium-seat reference made little sense, except to say that the unwashed masses will do whatever feels good, that eating too many hot dogs and Cracker Jacks has consequences—and that unless someone or some country, namely the US, rightfully intervenes in what surely was happening on a national scale, feel-good communism will ravage America's largest southern-neighbor and de facto mercantile colony.

Fallon's comments seemed to resonate with the visiting US politicians consorting with multinational executives and Brazilian officials yucking it up inside the corridors of power in a neoclassical Rio de Janeiro hotel. The sentiments and context gave Thompson the ability to make the assembled powerbrokers sound like morons, an enduring hallmark of the writer's poison-pen prowess.

The *Herald*'s Zschech, himself a late arrival to the English language, edited the early-Gonzo preternatural account, and would remember that Thompson's story had been "tongue-in-cheek and no doubt accurate, but its ridicule did not meet with approval of the local businessmen."[18]

And how!

Upon his return from the publishers' jamboree in Chile, Williamson fielded calls from irate American businessmen who charged that Thompson had taken Talmadge's and Fallon's quotes out of context. Thompson's coverage of the businessmen's luncheon ought to have been a puff piece. What exactly was this? And who the hell was this new reporter with the unfamiliar byline? The *Herald* had always curried favor with American interests in Brazil. Hadn't Williamson or Zschech clued the new guy in on what was expected of him?

Thompson's account had placed Williamson in an uncomfortable position. He and chamber president Fallon often took the evening train from Rio to São Paulo for American Chamber luncheons together. Williamson and Vânia socialized with Fallon and his wife, Mavis. Maybe it had been fortuitous that Williamson had been away on business when the offending piece ran. At least, he had an excuse to explain it away to his friends.

When Williamson read the piece upon his return, he recalled, "I thought the article was hilarious, but I could never say so publicly to my business friends and advertisers."[19]

Williamson placated Fallon and the others by inviting them out for happy-hour caipirinhas on the *Herald*'s cruzeiro. Pay no attention to that man with the reporter's notebook, Williamson told them. He'll likely be here for only a short while. The executives breathed a sigh of relief.

Privately, Williamson remembered that Thompson "turned out to be a pretty good reporter." Suit-wearing Zschech would characterize hang-loose Thompson in a similar manner as how he had described *Herald* partner Lee Langley, as "a pre-hippie type," but would allow that Thompson "turned out some good copy for the *Brazil Herald* for several months."[20]

To author Brian Kevin, who traced Thompson's continental odyssey in *The Footloose American: Following the Hunter S. Thompson Trail Across South America*, Williamson volunteered, "At the time, Hunter was the best reporter we had," which perhaps said more about the *Herald* than about Thompson.[21]

Williamson would recall that Thompson "smoked a lot, but didn't drink any more than any other journalist did in those days." Williamson would also remember that Thompson talked a lot about guns and hunting, but not about drugs. At least to Williamson, he didn't.[22]

While in Rio, Thompson got a hold of a revolver and on at least one occasion took to shooting scurrying rats in a vacant lot overgrown with weeds. A neighbor called the police, and while being interrogated at the local police station, Bone recalled, "Hunter put his feet up on the cop's desk, and bullets rolled out of his pocket....It blew over somehow."[23]

In fact, for much of his adult life Thompson would be obsessed with guns. His South American pilgrimage stoked that fascination. Before leaving the States, Thompson had joined the NRA in search of information about gun laws in South America. He wrote friend Paul Semonin, loosely quoting from a Portuguese-language book called *Tigrero*, "'In Brazil a gun or a knife is considered a fair weapon, and there is no dishonor in being wounded or even killed. But to hit a man with your fists is to insult him beyond remedy. He can only avenge the humiliation by killing you.'" Thompson went as far as contacting the author of *Tigrero*, Sasha Siemel, whom Thompson described as "a tiger hunter in the Mato Grosso." Siemel advised him "to bring the gun into the country in a shoulder-holster because Brazil customs men do not search bodies, only luggage." To Semonin, Thomson wrote, "This man seemed to think it was very important that I get my gun in with me and I tend to agree."[24]

As for his life in Rio, Thompson would recall in his 2003 book, *Kingdom of Fear*, "All things considered, Rio was pretty close to the best place in the world to be lost and stranded when the World finally shuts down."[25]

Thomson freelanced a total of five articles for the *National Observer* during his time in Rio, while working for the *Brazil Herald*. Always manically prolix and ceaselessly on the lookout for outlets for his writing, just as he was about to leave Brazil and return to the States in 1963, Thompson engaged in an extraordinary letter exchange with Philip L. Graham, then publisher of *The Washington Post* and *Newsweek*.

Thompson initiated the correspondence by taking Graham to task for a story *Newsweek* had published on Brazil. Graham had never heard of Thompson, and as publisher, he had nothing to do with day-to-day editing of either the newspaper or magazine. To most, Thompson's letter would have appeared to have been written by a lunatic and surely would have gone unanswered and discarded.

Thompson wrote:

God only knows who wrote the rotten thing; the only explanation that seems reasonable to me is that it was slapped together by a committee of buffoons whose ties were too tight on their necks on whatever morning they gathered to hash the thing together. . . . The thing that really surprised me about the story, however, was not that it was shot through with errors, but that it appeared at all. Your normal South American "coverage" is a silly joke, and about as nourishing as a month-old hamburger. In the past eight months I have been through every country on this continent except two, and I have met only two people even vaguely connected with *Newsweek*— both in Rio. It is a goddamned abomination, a fraud, and a black onus on American journalism that a magazine with *Newsweek*'s money and circulation so slothfully ignores a continent as critical to American interests as this one.

With that vast, driving, stiff-necked staff of yours, I'll bet a bottle of Old Crow that, over the past eight months, you haven't even equaled my published output in words, much less insignificant stories. And, hell, I'm only a young, inexperienced and underpaid punk.I'm beginning to think you're a phony, Graham. You hired Walter Lippmann, and his debut—that thing on John Kennedy —was the coldest hash I've read in a long time. If you hired the Marquis de Sade, he'd come out bland. Maybe you should loosen your tie a little bit and consider your own hash— because, dollar for dollar, it ain't so tasty, and you're sufficiently old, experienced and overpaid to have no real excuse at all.

Sincerely,

Hunter S. Thompson

Thompson couldn't have realistically expected a response to such a screed. But his off-the-wall lure worked. Six weeks later, Thompson received a typewritten reply from Graham, sent in care of the *Brazil Herald,* in which the publisher tried to match Thompson's bluster point by point. He did a pretty good job.

Dear Mr. Thompson,
For the past few weeks I have been mainly away from my office enjoying the normal sybaritic pursuits of proprietorship, and so have only today come across your moderate and shy letter of February 8th, in which you say that "I'm beginning to think you're a phony, Graham." This displays a very notable cultural lag on your part. Many intelligent leaders have long ago got themselves to the conclusion that you are only beginning to think about. Now, why don't you write me a somewhat less breathless letter, in which you tell me about yourself, and don't make it more than 2 pages single space—which means a third draft and not a first draft.
    Sincerely,
    Philip L. Graham

Media mogul Graham, one of the most powerful men in American journalism, had nibbled at nobody Thompson's bait. Thompson's insults had piqued Graham's curiosity enough to egg him to answer. That Graham, forty-eight, had deigned to read, lest respond to, Thompson's litany of insults is the stuff journalists' fantasies are made of.
    Thompson replied immediately.

Dear Mr. Graham:
Well . . . two pages, single-space, catch my breath, define myself . . . that's a tall order for a man of my stripe, but I'll give it a go. I doubt I can match the olympian spleen of my last effort, but what the hell?

You may be a phony, Graham, but I admire your spirit. Your letter of March 25 had a cavalier tone that in some circles would pass for a very high kind of élan. The only real flaw I found was that it was written in English, instead of French. But, again, what the hell?

Actually, I am more interested in your reason for answering my letter, than in anything you had to say. Mine (the "moderate and shy" one of February 8th) was written in a pure, rum-flavored rage at about four in the morning. Needless to say, it was not re-written the next day, as most of my stuff is.

It meant, as I recall, exactly what it appeared to mean. There were no ulterior motives—except, perhaps, that of prodding you into a reply.

Certainly, I would not want you to interpret it as a devious means of applying for a job on the assembly line at *Newsweek*, or covering speeches for *The Washington Post*. I sign what I write, and I mean to keep on signing it.[26]

As for me, I'm a writer. I came to South America to find out what it meant, and I comfort myself in knowing that at least my failure has been on a grand scale. After a year of roaming around down here, the main thing I've learned is that I now understand the United States and why it will never be what it could have been, or at least tried to be. So, I'm getting ready to come back and write what I've learned. With luck, I will be in New York and Washington by June. Perhaps you'll be able to afford that bottle of Old Crow by then. As I recall, I offered to bet you a bottle of Old Crow that my published output, since coming to South America, would surpass the entire output of the *Newsweek* staff—on South America stories published over the course of the past year. You did not mention either the bet or the bourbon in your letter, so I assume you are weaseling out.

My relationship with the *National Observer* has been excep-tionally decent. They have published all my articles—even my letters (*NO* 12/31/62)—and paid me well enough so that I don't have to write unless I feel like writing, or have something solid to write about. In return, most of the things I've sent them have been incomparable.

I don't know what all of this means to you, but the fact that you answered my letter leads me to believe that you now and then take a break from the "normal, sybaritic pursuits of proprietorship," and devote a few idle moments to pondering the meaning of your days and your time. How old are you? Maybe that's a clue. Have you come to that point where you suddenly realize you're afraid of people as young as I am? Or have you passed on, into a sort of crotchety, good-humored resignation?

Now, to change the subject, I've been forced to modify my hardnose line of February 8, for several reasons: 1) I recently had dinner with Milan Kubic, who tells me he's about to open a *Newsweek* bureau in Rio; a good move, but not quite as laudable as it is overdue; 2) Lippmann's piece on Rockefeller was Grade-A stuff, as was the *Newsweek* cover story on unemployment in the U.S. Since I knocked you on your South America coverage, I'd be acting like a newsmagazine editor if I ignored your best efforts; 3) Your letter came on the heels of "recent reports" that you were seriously ill.[27] After being down here for a year, I have little faith in "recent reports," but if that one happens to be true, I'm sorry and I hope you're back in shape. Judging from your letter, I assume you are. At any rate, I felt vaguely uncomfortable about sending that kind of a letter to a man who was "seriously ill." Hell, I haven't used up my two pages. What else can I tell you? Height 6′3″; Weight 190; Age 25; Politics: opposed to Nixon, Norman Mailer & George Lincoln Rockwell; Draft Status: Vet; Religion: Seeker. At this point it gets difficult. . . .

Oh yeah, I like a good tavern, sun on grass, a lean white hull, a beautiful woman, fine writing, fine whiskey . . . I could carry on here, but there's not much sense in it. I guess I'll owe you that other half-page.

Chao,[28]

Hunter S. Thompson

A month later, Thompson left Brazil and the *Herald* for Lima, and then flew back to the States. Williamson and Zschech were left one reporter short. Sandy Conklin returned to the US, and the couple would get married by an Indiana justice of the peace, across the Ohio River from Thompson's hometown of Louisville, Kentucky, on May 19, 1963.

As for Thompson's pet monkey or coati, no one seemed to know what happened. Bob Bone would write that Ace committed suicide when he jumped off a ten-story balcony from an apartment building. Such animals seldom fall to their death, and he wasn't pushed, Bone wrote, speculating that Ace must have drunk too much too often from an open bottle of cachaça and was likely suffering from DTs, delirium tremens.[29]

The day before Thompson's and Conklin's wedding, Philip Graham answered Thompson's second letter to him, seemingly smitten with his new pen pal. To Graham, Thompson wasn't a chronicler of others' achievements, but an agile and adept, if not skewed, observer of the human condition, who might turn out to be an exceptional hire.

Dear Mr. Thompson:
Your letter of April 8 got to Washington just after I left for a month in Europe. And I must say it is a welcome relief to read yours among the banal pile of accumulated correspondence I am digging into. If you get to Washington in June, would you let me know, as I would like to have a visit with you and have you meet our Managing Editor, Al Friendly. We have nothing at the moment that I think would at all interest you, but I always like to keep in touch with young people possessed of such overriding humility and shyness.

Sincerely,
Philip L. Graham[30]

Alas, Graham and Thompson never were to meet. Diagnosed with clinical depression for more than a decade, Graham's personal and professional life were collapsing by the time Thompson had connected with him. Earlier that year, Graham had been admitted to a psychiatric hospital in Rockland, Maryland. Upon his release, he announced his intention to seek a divorce from his wife, Katharine; marry Robin Webb, an Australian stringer for *Newsweek* with whom he was having an affair; and assume unilateral control of the Washington Post Company.

With the exception of an extra-marital affair, the announcement sent shock waves within American media circles. The accumulation of erratic behavior caused Graham to be confined a second time to another psychiatric hospital, and after being discharged to his Virginia farmhouse, Graham took his life with a 28-gauge shotgun on August 3, 1963.[31]

Within the year, Thompson would make a pilgrimage to the Ketchum, Idaho, home of Ernest Hemingway, another journalist fascinated with Luso-Iberian culture, guns, and death. Two years earlier, Hemingway had killed himself in a similar manner as Graham, with a long-barreled .22 pigeon gun he had used in shooting competitions in Cuba, duck hunting in Italy, and a safari in East Africa.[32]

Forty-four years after his South American journey and his hopscotch employment at the *Brazil Herald*, Thompson, at age sixty-seven, would kill himself with a 45-caliber pistol at his home in Woody Creek, Colorado. His suicide note read:

No More Games. No More Bombs. No More Walking. No More Fun. No More Swimming. 67. That is 17 years past 50. 17 more than I needed or wanted. Boring. I am always bitchy. No Fun— for anybody. 67. You are getting Greedy. Act your age. Relax— This won't hurt.[33]

By the time I arrived at the newspaper, everyone knew who Hunter Thompson was, but besides Bill Williamson and Herb Zschech, hardly anyone knew that he had once worked there.

CHAPTER 14

André, Rita, Eddie, Humphrey, and Jean

OUTSIDE OF AN occasional walk-on hire like Hunter S. Thompson, when Bill Williamson took over in 1960 as the *Brazil Herald*'s on-site manager, he had inherited a patchwork of editorial employees and a slew of non-English-speaking pressmen and factotums. In addition to Herb Zschech, who continued filling in whenever and as often as an editor-in-charge quit, Williamson discovered another reporter on the payroll who would also become a steady fixture at the *Herald*: André Fodor.

More an impresario than a journalist, Fodor was a facile writer up for sale. He traded favors for most of the items he inserted in his daily column, providing reams of copy that *Herald* readers grew to expect and enjoy. Advertisers appreciated mentions in Fodor's column tailored to wealthy expats and tourists, but they also paid him for such plugs. Williamson had never before seen as prolific a self-promoter as Fodor. There was little he could (or wanted to) do about Fodor and how he operated.

Born in Budapest in 1905, Fodor arrived in Brazil in 1946 from Le Havre, France, on the ship *Formose*.[1] In Hungary, he had worked in advertising and publicity for Standard Electric until he was drafted into the army and emigrated to Brazil. Once in Rio, Fodor discovered that his surname in Portuguese slang meant "fucker," and because of that, depending on the circumstances, he opted to substitute André *Todor* for his *Herald* byline. Enterprising Fodor inherited the popular *Herald* column, "Rio by Night," heretofore written by an

217

Fig. 14.1 André Fodor's Brazilian identity card.

ever-changing roster of contributors who had started at the newspaper's inception. Bon vivant Fodor amended the all-purpose column's title to "Rio by Day and Night." In it, he nonstop name-dropped his own advertising firm, Duo Publiçidade, whose slogan was "The Biggest Little Agency in Rio."[2] Fodor's company took on a variety of jobs, really anything that came over the transom, from publicity for products, bars and night clubs to booking cabaret appearances, tours, and promoting an annual beauty pageant Fodor originated but never actually held.

Fodor called the phantom event, *Miss Estrangeira* (Miss Foreigner). It worked—or, more accurately, did not work—like this: Each week in the *Herald*, Fodor published photographs of prospective Miss Estrangeira contestants he had solicited in his column. As an initial come-on, Fodor wrote:

> So please young ladies of the Distrito Federal [the federal district, Rio de Janeiro] if you want to participate in the contest, send me a good picture of yourself, with all the details (address, telephone, etc.) to the Brazil Herald or call me 52-0799 (Duo Publiçidade) to arrange an interview. The contest will take place in a big downtown fashionable place sometime at the end of January, 1956, together with an interesting show. The total receipts of the show and contest will be given to an important Rio

charity. About the prizes for the winners all I can tell today is that I wish I could be the happy winner. There will be film contract, etc., etc. So come on girls, if you have some foreign blood in you. But you must be good looking, intelligent, talented, no more or less.[3]

All of it was a come-on. That year after year the pageants never materialized, no charity ever received anything, no film contracts were ever signed, and no show ever got staged, and no prizes ever were given came as no surprise to those who knew Fodor. Tanned to the point of appearing bronzed, he drove around town in an instantly recognizable white Mercedes convertible, which any salary he got from the *Herald* surely didn't pay for. The head-turning automobile served to announce Fodor's arrival at movie premieres, gallery and nightclub openings, and symphony and opera galas.

Fodor was a well-traveled man-about-town, charming and worldly. Like seemingly everyone else at the *Herald*, he spoke a string of languages. He prided himself on being a gourmet, enjoying the best food, usually for free, at Rio's plethora of five-star restaurants. Every afternoon, he had a standing reservation for his usual tennis court at the Paissandu Athletic Club, where before and after he transacted business. Fodor was married to a fellow Hungarian émigré, but as future *Brazil Herald* columnist Harold Emert would note, "only his wife knew it."[4]

At least Fodor was transparent about the purpose of his *Herald* column. "I tried to cover almost everything—like tourism, shopping, arts, films, stage, shows, parties—everything except politics. But the idea behind it was—and many who could read between the lines realized it—to boost advertisers and at the same time give advice to local foreigners and tourists where to go and what to see or buy. Or even where to fly," he would write in 1971.

As for his provocative surname, Fodor added that at first he was ashamed to use it in Brazil, but as profanity became more accepted, "I became proud of my funny name, which no Brazilian ever forgets."[5]

Williamson, genial to everyone, considered Fodor as a kind of procurer. "That, I think, would be the best way to put it. He played around like you wouldn't believe. He often hired women for tourists and VIPs. [*Herald* publisher] Montgomery once had a party at a big hotel suite, and André produced a few gorgeous Brazilian gals who on cue suddenly appeared—and soon disappeared. He had his hand in everything."[6]

Joining Fodor at the *Herald* was another longtime columnist, Rita Davy, who led the newspaper's society coverage of the expatriate British community and wrote a popular feature called "Rio Social Spotlight." When Montgomery acquired the *Times of Brazil* in 1962, Williamson also acquired the services of Davy, who lived with her sister, Marjorie, and a series of well-nourished cats in Rio's bohemian, hilly Santa Teresa district. In a past iteration of history, spry and slight Davy might have been called a "spinster." She arrived in Brazil in the early 1950s from London, but that wasn't her first time in the South American nation. Her father had been a civil engineer employed by the Rio de Janeiro City Improvements Company, and Davy and Marjorie had grown up in Rio.

Born Winifred Rose Davy, she clung to her British heritage like creeping English ivy on a country cottage. Davy held high tea at the *Herald*'s offices at four p.m. daily, and invited, usually without success, anyone in the newsroom to join her for steaming cups of Earl Grey and imported British shortbread biscuits served on Wedgwood Willow Blue China. She adored Queen Elizabeth, Prince Philip, Buckingham Palace, Windsor Castle, and everything else Royal. The pinnacle of her career at the *Herald* was covering the Royal couple aboard the royal yacht *Britannia* moored in Rio's Guanabara Bay.

White-blonde and fair-skinned, as a young woman Davy moved back to London, where she worked for the C.P.R. advertising agency, handling the Elizabeth Arden cosmetics account. As a perquisite of her job, Davy was offered a beauty treatment administered by beauty icon Arden herself, but as soon as Arden laid her eyes on Davy, she

Fig. 14.2 Bill Williamson, Rita Davy, unidentified man, and Vânia Williamson (*left* to *right*). Courtesy of the Bill Williamson Collection.

refused, saying Davy's creamy skin was so flawless that it couldn't possibly be improved.[7] Davy returned to Brazil in 1952, and ultimately was awarded the MBE (Member Excellent Order of the British Empire), outside of knighthood the third-highest degree of appointment in the British order of chivalry. Her main job at the *Herald* was to attend as many parties as she could and record the names of guests, who had accompanied them, what they wore, and what they ate. Jo Ann Hein, the yellow-skirted June Cleaver gadabout I met on my first day when I walked into the *Latin America Daily Post*, was Davy's nominal counterpart in São Paulo. Davy held a variety of positions at the newspaper, as columnist, receptionist, librarian, switchboard operator, proofreader, and de facto mother, sister, aunt, or grandmother, depending on the age of the staffer.

Tom Murphy, who would become a workhorse *Herald* reporter when I joined the combined newspapers, remembered Davy this way:

I had the feeling that she had looked the same for the last twenty years and would look the same for the next twenty. She tended toward friendly chatter and non-sequiturs. One day she approached me as I entered the newsroom: 'Oh, he can't *possibly* stay, can he? What do you think? I mean, he's become such an *embarrassment.*'

It took me awhile to realize she was talking about the Shah of Iran [who at the time had sought temporary refuge in Mexico]. One could imagine similar conversations among British expats in dozens of countries over the previous hundred years.[8]

Fodor and to a lesser degree Davy were prime examples of where the *Herald* situated itself when it came to the thorny issue of newspaper ethics. Though owned and operated by Americans, the paper was a thoroughly Brazilian enterprise, and as such operated within the contours of the Brazilian business and journalism worlds. Unlike in the United States, where reputable newspapers erected a firewall between the publication's business and editorial functions—sometimes impermeable, other times variously porous, depending on the importance of the violator—no such separation existed in most Brazilian media. This played out in ways small and large when it came to the *Herald*, including the practice of what amounted to bribing journalists. As newsman Charles Kuralt had noted, journalism ethics Brazil style meant that freebies were routinely offered to editorial employees in exchange for positive coverage and spin. Following André Fodor's lead, other critics and reviewers on the *Herald*'s payroll routinely plugged restaurants, gallery exhibitions, cabaret performances, theatrical events, and nightclub acts in exchange for cash or freebies. Such a practice was necessary, apologists suggested, as a way to offset journalists' meager wages. Management went along with this self-serving scheme.

Assorted perks to *Herald* staffers ranged from comped meals to free airline tickets in Brazil and around the world. In Portuguese, such plugola is known as *permutas*. Management did nothing to prohibit these exchanges or "side deals." In some ways, these freebies indicated a newspaper's worth in terms of who was reading it and how far local, national, and global businesses would go to court readers based on the publication's clout, reach, prestige, and demographics.

Not everyone was on the take at the *Herald*. Most journalists never had occasion to affect commercial businesses with the stories they wrote, and thus were not candidates for such kickbacks. Favorable coverage in the paper, of course, wasn't limited to just the entertainment section. Since its founding, the *Herald* had traded positive coverage of politicians, multinational and local companies, government policies, and causes the newspaper's owners and managers sought to champion. This was borne out in headlines, content, tone, and where stories and photographs were played in the newspaper. Williamson and Montgomery were willing players in the quid pro quo schema.

On occasion, the *Herald* could muster resources to be a competitive newspaper with an edge, coming up with significant stories, although when that happened, it seldom was the result of planning, usually the byproduct of serendipity. *Herald* exclusives often were about embezzlers, swindlers, and other fortune-seekers who had spirited themselves to Brazil. Just as Hunter S. Thompson was leaving Rio, the *Herald* landed the first in a string of such scoops.

One of the biggest bunko artists ever to flee the United States for Brazil was Eddie M. Gilbert, known as the "Boy Wonder of Wall Street," who showed up unannounced at the *Herald*'s offices in 1962 and sang his story of avarice to an incredulous Bill Williamson, who scribbled as fast as Gilbert talked. Williamson seldom wrote for the newspaper, but when Gilbert stopped by, Williamson was the only person the native New Yorker would talk to.

Gilbert had "borrowed" two million dollars from a company he headed, Tennessee-based E. L. Bruce Co., a manufacturer of flooring. Gilbert owned a massive Fifth Avenue apartment overlooking New York's Central Park, as well as a villa in Monte Carlo, both decorated with priceless art. Gilbert's first wife, Rhoda, described in society columns as "one of the best dressed women in the world," was Christian Dior's number-one global customer. The couple were chauffeured in a custom-designed Rolls-Royce limousine. Gilbert, who claimed friendships with writers John Dos Passos and Jack Kerouac, had produced two plays on Broadway, including a production of *Peter Pan* starring Jean Arthur and Boris Karloff.

Gilbert's travails began when he used money from E. L. Bruce to cover his own stock-margin calls. At the time, the federal government had assessed Gilbert with a lien on unpaid taxes of $3.5 million while Gilbert was claiming he was $14 million in debt. Gilbert maintained he intended to return the borrowed funds to the publicly traded flooring company, but when pressed by stockholders, Gilbert hopped on a Pan Am red-eye to Rio. The international press promptly amended Gilbert's nickname from "Boy Wonder" to "Fugitive Playboy."[9]

In scoring the world's first interview with on-the-lam Gilbert, Williamson had been tipped off by none other than *Herald* columnist André Fodor, who happened to be on the same Pan Am flight as Gilbert and had chatted up the fleeing financier midair. Once in Rio, Fodor steered Gilbert to the *Herald* newsroom days before other press could get to him. Sitting on the couch in Williamson's second-floor office, Gilbert tearfully promised "to pay everyone back and make everything whole someday."[10]

As a fugitive in Rio, Gilbert would go on to play the Brazilian stock markets and dollar-cruzeiro float rates to his advantage. *Life* magazine published a nine-page spread on him. A Louis Auchincloss novel, *A World of Profit*, would be based on Gilbert and his calculated financial miscues. Gilbert eventually returned to the United States, pled guilty to three counts of grand larceny and served two years in federal prison, where he cornered the black-market in cigarettes. Gilbert's conviction would be overturned, but he subsequently was convicted of stock manipulation and served another two years in federal prison, followed by a reborn, high-flying career, this time in New Mexico real estate.[11]

Other *Herald* fugitive exclusives followed, including a story about Texas financier Ben Jack Cage who had jumped bail and landed in Brazil. Like Gilbert, Cage was drawn to the *Herald* to tell his side of the story; in Cage's case, the disgraced financier chatted up co-founder

Joe Brown, who remembered Cage as "one of the most charming men I've ever met."[12]

A scoop of another sort came the *Herald*'s way in September 1969 while Williamson's wife Vânia was eating lunch with the wife of US Ambassador Charles Burke Elbrick and the wives of four other American executives at the ambassador's home.[13] The five were busy labeling canned fruit to be sold at the American booth of an upcoming charity event when word got back to them that left-wing kidnappers had ambushed Elbrick's Cadillac on a Rio side street and had taken the sixty-one-year-old diplomat hostage. Coincidently, Elbrick had been scheduled to drop in at the *Herald* for a courtesy visit with Williamson that afternoon. From the Elbricks' living room Vânia hurriedly rang Williamson, giving the *Herald* yet another international scoop.[14] Elbrick was released unharmed seventy-eight hours after the abduction in exchange for the release of fifteen political prisoners flown to Mexico, where they were granted asylum.[15]

In 1973, the *Herald* published another news flash, this one claiming that Norma Levy, a twenty-six-year-old London prostitute caught in flagrante delicto in succession with two members of British Prime Minister Edward Heath's cabinet, had slipped into Rio via Morocco. Levy counted numerous politicians and industrialists as her clients, including oil magnate J. Paul Getty, who paid for her to lie in an open coffin while he watched, wearing only his underpants. After a flurry of global headlines citing the *Herald*, Levy's whereabouts turned out to be in Spain, not Brazil, and the *Herald*'s firecracker of an exclusive turned out to be a dud.[16]

A potential *Herald* blockbuster was the December 9, 1974, murder of retired Pan Am executive Humphrey Wallace Toomey, found slumped in a Queen Anne's chair in his daughter's seventh-floor Copacabana apartment with a .38-caliber bullet lodged in his stomach.[17] The Montana-born Toomey had been the manager of Pan Am's Latin American division since 1945. He first arrived in Brazil in 1929, flying a Pan Am amphibian plane from New York to Rio to scout passenger routes between the two cities.[18]

Toomey was quoted and photographed in the *Herald* almost as often as was publisher Montgomery.[19] So, when the seventy-four-year-old aviation pioneer was murdered, it made for headlines in the *Herald*, as well as in newspapers around the world. Toomey had just arrived in Rio on the inaugural, nonstop Miami-Rio Pan Am 747 flight. He came with four heavy suitcases, three of which mysteriously disappeared from his daughter's apartment just prior to the arrival of police following the report of his murder.

Toomey was a man of pedigree and influence. In 1950, he had been the target of an extortion attempt when a man threatened to kill him and his family, as well as blow up a Pan Am plane at Miami International Airport unless Toomey's family paid a demand of $500,000. Two years later, Toomey led an expedition into the Amazon jungle near the Araguaia River in search of the wreckage of a Pan Am Boeing Strato Cruiser that had left Rio with forty-one passengers aboard.[20]

Toomey's second wife, the former Grace Cecilia Strelow, was fifteen years his junior; they had met at a tea dance at the Biltmore Hotel in Coral Gables, Florida. In 1954, the thirty-eight-year-old socialite died suddenly of acute viral encephalitis, leaving Toomey a well-to-do widower with three young daughters.[21] Toomey was to meet his third wife through *Herald* columnist André Fodor and his dubious Miss Estrangeira pageant.

In one of Fodor's come-on columns about the year's phantom pageant, the *Herald* ran a photo of a sultry brunette in a V-neck dress with this description:

This week's Miss Estrangeira Miss Rotraud Schroeder, German, blonde, elegant. Rio's Top Photo model. You can see her in almost all magazines and many commercial films. She also models the dresses, at the best fashion shows with her natural elegance, youthful charm and talented acting. This, she learned back home in Germany in student theatre. . . . She spends her free time in painting and modeling in a little art studio. You can see in her talented works the urge to express her artistic personality. You

Rio By Day And Night

ANDRÉ

Today we have a special edition of this weekly column. First because there are so many events this week, that my Sunday page would have overflowed. The second good reason is that we have first-hand news for the American Colony in Rio, which can't wait till Sunday. Yesterday I received a cable from a friend of mine, PAA's South American Vice President, Humphrey W. Toomey, now in New York saying that he had married there Sunday, the 9th of September, Miss Rotraud Schroeder of Bremen (Germany).

Attractive Rotraud was a Rio resident for the last two years and worked as a top photo and film model and mannequin with different advertising agencies. She is also a talented painter and designer. Her lovely face has appeared in Brazil Herald and different Brazilian publications newspapers and magazines.

It's an interesting fact, that her picture, published in my column last year as one of the favorites of the still postponed "Miss Foreigner" contest, was the first to arouse attention of her future husband. Later Pan-American chose her to act in a short travel promotion film. About a month ago she left Rio, to work in New York. It seems,

that there they met again, after he left Rio too, two weeks ago. They will leave the USA this week, for a honeymoon in Europe. They plan to return, at the end of October. Congratulations to the happy couple!

This week again is full of international happenings. Some of them: Monday night was KLM's dinner-party at Sacha's, hono-

Mrs. Humphrey W. Toomey, née Rotraud Schroeder, the young, charming happy wife of PAA's Vice President, sends her warmest greetings to her Rio friends.

Humphrey W. Toomey, Vice President of Pan American World Airways in charge of operations in Brazil, Urugual & Argentina, married last Sunday in New York.

Fig. 14.3 André Fodor's *Brazil Herald* column, featuring Rotraud Schroeder and Humphrey Wallace Toomey. Courtesy of the *Brazil Herald*.

wouldn't believe when you see her, but she also works as an agent, speaks at least 4 languages and likes books about psychology.[22]

Fodor was so struck by Schroeder that he hired her as his personal assistant. When Toomey cast his eyes on the photo of her in the *Herald*, he too was smitten. Fodor arranged a meeting for the two, and nine months later, the couple was married in New York City, with Fodor breaking the news of the nuptials in his *Herald* column.[23]

By 1960, Toomey had retired from Pan Am and along with Schroeder and the couple's two daughters moved to a villa in Florence. The family returned to Coral Gables and Rio, where Toomey turned his attention to real estate. Among his holdings was property in Barra, a beachside district south of Rio, a hundred-acre estate outside of Brasília, which he had purchased just prior to the opening of the new capital, and parcels of land in the Brazilian states of Goiás and Mato Grosso. By this time, wife Rotraud had become an accomplished jewelry designer whose baubles were must-have trinkets among the rich and famous in the Miami-Rio axis.

There were no signs of forced entry to the seventh-floor beachside apartment where Toomey's body had been found, indicating that Toomey likely knew his killer. Police found two half-filled glasses of whiskey. Nothing had been stolen, with the exception of his daughter's Yorkshire terrier. Among the murder suspects was *Herald* columnist Fodor, who told police that he and Toomey were best friends, had known each other for twenty-five years, and that Toomey had given him a key to the apartment.

Another suspect was Richard L. Fish, a crime novelist who had written the book upon which *Bullitt*, the 1968 movie starring Steve McQueen and Jacqueline Bisset, had been based. Toomey, Fodor, the prominent Rio jeweler Roger Sauer, and a half dozen others had backed the development of a movie, Missão: Matar (Mission: To Kill), based on Fish's 1967 thriller *Always Kill a Stranger*. Fodor was listed in the film's credits as executive producer and Toomey had a walk-on cameo role in the film, playing a diplomat.[24]

Other suspects included Toomey's former son-in-law, Russian precious-stones dealer Paul Lojnikov, of whose business Toomey owned a percentage; Bill Huber, whose family had made a fortune publishing the local Yellow Pages; and wife Rotraud Toomey, whom police conjectured might have hired a hitman while she remained at the family estate in South Florida. Ultimately, a local woman and her boyfriend confessed to the crime, which police characterized as a robbery gone bad.[25]

Perhaps the biggest story the *Herald* ran during this relatively fertile period of tabloid wood derived from a series of interviews with Ronald Biggs, one of fifteen principals in the 1963 Great Train

Robbery, which netted 2.6 million pounds (today, the equivalent of $75 million). Police caught Biggs in the wake of the Glasgow-London Royal Mail heist, but he escaped from Wandsworth Prison by scaling the wall with a rope ladder, fleeing to Brussels, then Paris (where he underwent plastic surgery), Australia, and finally Rio, where he would live for three decades. In Brazil Biggs used the alias Mike Haynes and worked as a carpenter for members of the English-speaking expat community, including Bill and Vânia Williamson. After Biggs had a child with a Brazilian woman, which made extradition back to England next to impossible, every August 8 the irrepressible Biggs would host a steak-roast free-for-all at his Santa Teresa home (not far from where the *Herald*'s Rita Davy lived) to celebrate his birthday and the anniversary of the train robbery. These blowouts were the kinds of parties that Hugh Hefner might have thrown had he lived in Rio, with a bevy of bikini-clad women gyrating to Brazilian samba. Biggs took pride in his dubious fame and used it to his advantage. He starred in multiple Brazilian TV commercials and magazine advertisements, including one to promote a brand of athletic shoes with the slogan, "When you're on the run as I am, you need the best running shoes!"[26] Davy, who covered for the *Herald* all things pertaining to the Commonwealth, loathed fellow Brit Biggs and made it a point never to mention him in her column. In conversation, she always used the word "thug" whenever she referred to him.

Among the staffers employed at the *Herald* at the tail end of this period of journalistic bonanzas was Jean Etsinger, a young and enthusiastic journalist who arrived at the newspaper with both talent and Portuguese-language skills. Etsinger, originally from Bucyrus, Ohio, first got to Brazil as an exchange student from the University of Texas. Upon her return to the United States, she worked for the *Chicago Tribune*, but soon found her way back to Brazil as the *Herald*'s managing editor.

Etsinger had an uneasy relationship with Herb Zschech, whose desk was in the rear of the newsroom, while was Etsinger's up front. In keeping with the era, she would recall that there was no small amount

Fig. 14.4 Bill Williamson (*left*) and Ronald Biggs. Courtesy of the Bill Williamson Collection.

of sexism at the newspaper. Etsinger, hardly a wallflower, recalled that Zschech "resented having a young female attempting to tell him what to do. By unspoken agreement from early on, we pretty much stayed out of each other's way."[27]

Etsinger worked at the *Herald* during the height of the Vietnam War, and one day she and another staffer, Cricket Appel, joined a small antiwar protest amassing across the street from the US Embassy on Avenida Wilson, and collected signatures for a petition of those opposed to the war. Most of the embassy staff walked by without stopping, sniffing at the two young activists dressed in jeans and T-shirts. Appel remembered that a man she suspected of being a CIA agent planted himself in an adjacent park and kept an eye on both her and Etsinger. Back at the *Herald*, the pair's activities prompted complaints from embassy officials, but Williamson said nothing to Etsinger and Appel because, he said, he agreed with their political stance.[28]

Although privately he found such political expression laudable, under Williamson's direction the *Herald* steered clear of any stories that might raise the eyebrows of the newspaper's conservative reader base. This wasn't the result of any planned strategy, but largely because there were so few editorial staffers to produce any such work. Occasionally Williamson spiked copy that he thought might potentially cost the newspaper advertisers or subscribers.

Walter Colton, a *Herald* managing editor in the mid-1970s, remembered that after several Brazilian newspapers had published exposés of a Brazilian manufacturer of macaroni that had given diners food poisoning, Colton gave the go-ahead to publish a story in the *Herald* on the tainted pasta. When Williamson found out about the forthcoming article, he "came into the newsroom and said the company was an advertiser and that we should back off from the story," recalled Colton. "I protested and said people were being poisoned. Williamson just grinned and said Brazilians have eaten poisoned macaroni for a long time and the newspaper needed the advertising." The story was never published.

At times, Williamson would hand Colton a press release of a non-story from a local business or expat association and instruct him to "stick it in," which Colton usually did.[29]

Breaking local news wasn't the reason readers picked up the *Herald*, and on most days, the newspaper showcased its bread and butter: society news of the expat community, financial coverage, syndicated features, world news of particular interest to Yanks and Brits, and favorable reviews of restaurants and nightlife. The editorial menu wasn't too different from what husband and wife Stu and Margaret Morrison had printed when they ran the newspaper two decades earlier.

In addition to columnists Rita Davy and André Fodor, another social butterfly who flitted from party to restaurant to nightclub to museum benefit for the *Herald* was Mary Wynne, originally from Tenaha, Texas. Wynne was the *Herald*'s local equivalent of New York showbiz columnist Ed Sullivan or Earl Wilson of the same era. She started with the *Herald* in 1955 and wrote a name-dropping column that grew so popular that the establishment Brazilian newspaper, *O Estado de São Paulo*, ran her about-town dispatches translated under the Portuguese-English hybrid title "Carrossel-'Mary'-Go-Round.

One of Wynne's early claims to fame was happening onto a wacky nightclub act in the Brazilian city of Campinas, featuring a flirty singer who went by the name Carmen Miranda. Ultimately, through her columns in Estadão, as the newspaper is known, and to a lesser degree in the *Herald*, Wynne could make or break an entertainer or venue with a single mention.

Other *Herald* reporters and reviewers developed their own niches, particularly when it came to the arts, music, and fashion. Millie Norman covered the coming-of-age music scene in Rio during the era of *Bossa Nova* (New Wave), with composers-performers Tom Jobim and Vinícius de Moraes, the political music of Chico Buarque, and the birth of what became known as *tropicalismo*. Other *Herald* columnists included fashion writer Adelina Capper; J. C. Garritano, who wrote a wild *Herald* account of his own LSD trip; film critic Alex Kennard; and theater reviewer John Proctor. By the mid-1970s, Mark Gruberg had been hired as a feature writer who covered everything from fashion at the local racetrack to a bizarro imposter, Johann Schmidt, who appeared one day in the *Herald* newsroom, claiming he was a leading candidate for the Nobel Prize, the holder of four doctorates, an award-winning concert organist, and heir to one of Brazil's largest fortunes. Gruberg would spend days hanging out at Rio's colonial plazas along with photographer Robin Lai to produce stories on the distinctive personalities of each. He wrote a sublime account of a soccer match, pitting rivals Flamengo and Fluminense at Rio's colossal Maracanã Stadium, in which he waited until the penultimate paragraph to reveal the match's victor.[30]

For the moment, it seemed that despite its financial and political bumpers, the little expat newspaper might be picking up speed. It would take nothing short of a national crisis to sidetrack the *Herald*. But that's what happened.

CHAPTER 15

Censors and Spooks

ON APRIL 1, 1964, Brazilian President João Belchior Marques Goulart was overthrown and replaced with what turned out to be successive regimes of right-wing generals. "Restoration of order," an oft-quoted slogan during the time, seemed to follow "Order and Progress," the motto that girds the globe on Brazil's starry green, yellow, and blue flag. During the remainder of the 1960s, increasingly hardline military technocrats consolidated control of the Palácio do Planalto, the presidential office in Brasília, suspending civil rights and imposing across-the-board press censorship. Thousands of Brazilians opposed to the dictatorship were imprisoned, tortured, and a still-undetermined number were killed. Goulart was granted political asylum in neighboring Uruguay, and later moved to Argentina, where he was to die in 1976 of a heart attack. Subsequent press and government investigations revealed that Goulart was in fact poisoned as part of Operation Condor, a covert operation organized by intelligence officers in right-wing regimes in South America, with US support.[1]

Both the Kennedy and Johnson administrations actively opposed Goulart (referred to by friends and foes alike as Jango) through a variety of measures. Some operations were overt, but many were black-bag operations funded by the CIA and carried out by CIA operatives. In declassified State Department cables, US Ambassador Lincoln Gordon acknowledged "covert support for pro-democracy street rallies . . . and encouragement [of] democratic and anti-communist sentiment in Congress, armed forces, friendly labor, and student groups, church, and business."[2] Those were the conventional activities that Gordon admitted the US government fostered and financed.

Apart from covering the news of the coup, the *Brazil Herald* seemed to relish the ouster of Goulart. It wasn't so much individual headlines or stories that suggested this, but an overall gleeful tone, reflecting the relief that a majority of *Herald* expat readers shared. The day before the coup, the *Herald* bannered, "Anti-Goulart Revolt Erupts in Minas Gerais," with seven allied stories on page one, including a piece in which an army commander was quoted as saying his troops were advancing towards Rio de Janeiro "to save the Fatherland." The next day, the *Herald*'s headline on page one shouted, "Rebels Oust Jango!" in one-hundred-and-six-point type, with this jubilant unbylined lede under it: "A tempest of patriotic exultation erupted yesterday in the late afternoon almost simultaneously in all cities in Brazil at news that a victorious and almost bloodless military revolution liberated Brazil from a political nightmare of several years during which the nation's plunge into Communist tyranny seemed imminent." The newspaper's second story that day was an account of a speech by Rio Governor Carlos Lacerda with the screaming headline, "End of Brazil's Inferno." That wasn't a quote from Lacerda's fiery address but the newspaper's own editorial voice. On April 3, the *Herald* ran a five-column page one photograph with the boldfaced cutline, "Viva Victoria," along with the headline, "Rio's Population at Monster Gathering Hails Freedom from Communism," and under it: "The people of Rio de Janeiro in a climate of undescribable [*sic*] civic enthusiasm yesterday paraded downtown in a Family with God for Freedom procession." The next day, the *Herald* published a story of the governor of the state of São Paulo calling for the immediate purging of anyone suspected of being a communist and proclaiming the new provisional government was a "halt to Bolshevizing." These were important news accounts, among the most urgent and newsworthy in decades in Brazil, but the euphoric manner in which the *Herald* presented them underscored a frenzied endorsement.

The empowered military police now in charge went on a lawless rampage, one backed by the US government, the *Herald,* and other establishment media, rounding up students, trade unionists, journalists, Goulart supporters, and anyone vaguely considered an enemy of the new regime.

A day after the insurrection, the *Herald* printed an unusual house editorial extolling the coup and the generals behind it.

The people of Brazil have once again shown the world their fibre. They have demonstrated the uniqueness of this wonderful country. Further, they have again proved that the sometimes tortuous path down which their homeland travels leads inevitably towards greatness—in its largest sense.

Events of the last few days could only happen in Brazil. Not the crisis—what country has not gone through serious crises?— but the quick, humane solution. No great country in history, and perhaps no lesser one, has solved its critical problems with as little damage and bloodshed as has Brazil. Even the United States has in the past registered more deaths in small towns over union troubles than occurred in all Brazil during this country-wide revolution.

But the real fight in Brazil still lies ahead. It consists of the battle against financial chaos, inflation, business stagnation, political rancor, poverty, ignorance. It consists of satisfying the unfulfilled hopes of the under-privileged masses whose appetites have been sharpened by the professed reforms of the late administration for a better deal. It consists of bringing the masses on the fringe of society into the producing, consuming, thinking, political markets, to guarantee progress and growth for Brazil, all Brazilians, and the entire free world.

The opportunity is now at hand to tackle this difficult challenge. It is hoped that just and well-planned reforms will shortly be forthcoming to provide the better life deserved for the great majority of Brazil's democratic people.

And successful application of the necessary reforms will more than compensate their trials and tribulations suffered during the last few years.[3]

That the *Herald* blithely labeled a century of violent union-busting tactics directed at American workers as "union troubles" in "small towns" said volumes about the newspaper's editorial voice and the pro-business sentiments behind it.

By the time the Goulart administration had been toppled, vast amounts of foreign and domestic capital had left Brazil. General strikes, food shortages, and endless queues, stretching for blocks, to buy limited amounts of staples such as rice, beans, and bread, had paralyzed the country. American business titans and politicians, such as those Hunter S. Thompson lampooned at the Hotel Glória two years earlier, feared that Brazil would follow Cuba's path under Castro, an ignominious rebuke to US hegemony in the region. Georgia Senator Herman Talmadge's prophesy was about to come true.

Brazil is seventy-seven times as large as Cuba, half the size of all of South America, and larger than the continental United States. Its population in 1964 was eighty-two million, the seventh largest in the world. Brazil's medium age was seventeen, compared to twenty-eight in the United States at the time.[4] The specter of a geopolitical nation as significant as Brazil falling out of the US sphere was anathema to American commercial and political interests, a panic reflected in the *Herald*'s overwrought coverage.

US mainstream media at home took a similar partisan editorial stance. *The New York Times* published an exultant editorial titled "Finis for Goulart" that read, "No lamentation should be wasted on a leader who showed himself to be so incompetent and irresponsible." The largest-circulation newspaper in the US at the time, the New York *Daily News*, ran a pull-no-punches editorial headlined "Kremlin vs.

Brazil" that read, "all hemisphere people would realize the achievement of Brazil's efforts in favor of democracy."[5]

US correspondents in Brazil celebrated the Goulart administration's overthrow as free-market capitalism triumphing over the tyranny of faceless communism. The so-called dean of the foreign press corps in Latin America at the time was *Chicago Tribune* correspondent Jules Dubois, the longstanding chairman of the Freedom of the Press Committee of the IAPA, the clubby group *Herald* publisher Montgomery and local manager Williamson so venerated. Dubois was joined by Edward C. Burks, who covered the coup for *The New York Times*, Hal Hendrix of the *Miami News* and Scripps Howard, Edward Cony of the *Wall Street Journal*, and George Daniels of *Time*. The recurring message from all these journalists was that the overthrow of the Goulart government was a salvo for democracy and "free people" everywhere.

Fig. 15.1 Bill Williamson (*left*) and AP correspondent Ed Miller. Courtesy of the Bill Williamson Collection.

At the time, Ed Miller, the AP correspondent who had such an aversion to Thompson when the gonzo journalist had showed up at the Rio wire-service office, was a staffer under bureau chief Frank Brutto and correspondent Ewaldo Castro. Miller's dispatches occasionally appeared in the *Brazil Herald*. Later, when he became bureau chief, he poached the best and brightest from the *Herald* to work in the Rio AP office as local hires.

Miller would turn into one of the best wire-service correspondents in Latin America. Like Williamson, he was married to a Brazilian, and also like Williamson, he was young, eager, and indefatigable. Miller's boss, Brutto, was new to Brazil, having come directly from AP's Vatican bureau. He couldn't speak more than a handful of words in Portuguese. Miller would charitably describe Brutto as a "lost dog in the weeds." This, though, played nicely to rookie Miller, who had written daily walkups to the coup, as well as dramatic accounts of the incipient collapse of the Goulart administration, distributed worldwide by AP.

Miller remembered covering a last-stand Goulart rally in Rio during which the president appeared, his back politically and physically against a wall. Goulart had just signed a declaration expropriating land for *camponeses* along national highways and had advocated for rent-stabilization measures—steps seen by the agitated military and US government as moving perilously close to an out-and-out communist takeover. "Goulart had chosen the spot for his massive rally next to the War Ministry, perhaps hoping to show his military opponents his popular strength. As it turned out, it was like rubbing salt in an already festering wound," wrote Miller in an unpublished account of his career as a newsman. At the time, Brazil's Catholic Church was stoking opposition flames, warning parishioners that Goulart was driving the country toward Godless anarchy, while hundreds of thousands of mothers, largely middle- and upper-class, had organized themselves into protest units throughout the country. The nation was headed to an inevitable showdown.

On the Sunday after the coup, just as Miller was filing his wire-service write-through to be distributed worldwide, soldiers representing the new regime stormed the AP bureau, rifling through cabinets and tossing files. Miller assumed the battalion had confused the AP office with Gosteleradio down the hall, an overseas news service beamed to Russian-bloc nations. Miller and the military phalanx's captain got into a scuffle, and Miller found himself under arrest, thrown in the back of a paddy wagon that stunk of vomit and urine.

Miller secured his release through his own back channels, but after US Ambassador Gordon was told of the correspondent's arrest, he castigated Miller, saying, "It could have caused considerable embarrassment to the United States," as the newsman recalled. Normally unruffled, Miller angrily replied to Gordon, "Piss off!"

Miller surmised that the ambassador had been smarting over the AP correspondent's dogged reporting during the previous three months, as well as his insistent questions at daily embassy briefings, which had needled Gordon.[6] Miller had been so busy day and night in the throes of covering history in the making that when his father died suddenly a month prior to the coup, the young correspondent wasn't able to attend the funeral. Ambassador Gordon's outburst was a replay of the earful *Rio News* editor A. J. Lamoureux heard when he had clashed with US Envoy Charles Page Bryan more than half a century earlier. It was the same reaction that *Brazil Herald* editor and co-owner Lee Langley had gotten when he angered Ambassador Pawley by publishing editorial content that displeased him, leading to his ouster.

To Miller, the adversarial role between the press and the government was healthy, normal, to be expected. Ambassador Gordon had other ideas about the press's role—which lamentably coincided with how a number of longtime US correspondents based in South America viewed the exigencies of their jobs, as well as the expectations of their employers, and perhaps their customers, back home.

In fact, several of those journalists stationed in Brazil turned out to be paid CIA informants. Among the most shocking US intelligence assets at the time of the Brazilian coup was none other than *Chicago Tribune* correspondent Dubois, described by *The New York Times* in his 1966 obituary as "the world's most widely known and most decorated reporter of Latin American affairs."[7] Other journalists who covered Latin America, also paid intelligence assets at the time, included Hal Hendrix, who received travel funds and payments from the CIA.[8] Hendrix, perhaps coincidently, perhaps not, had written a valentine about the *Brazil Herald* and publisher John Montgomery in 1954 that ran worldwide on the Scripps Howard news wire in which he noted without foundation that the newspaper was "doing very well. It never mixes in Brazilian politics. That in itself is relief to all of its readers."[9]

Another CIA asset at the time of the coup was Bob Berrellez, a Latin America AP correspondent who would spend twenty-eight days in a Cuban prison supposedly because of his virulent anti-Castro reporting. Many of Berrellez's wire accounts, run in hundreds of newspapers, amounted to rabid propaganda of creeping communist "terror" south of the border.[10] *Time* magazine was also alleged to have a Brazil correspondent at the time who provided intelligence to the CIA.[11]

Even if correspondents weren't directly paid by the CIA, all of them routinely traded information with US embassy officials who had access to details about covert intelligence operations coordinated by the American government. Embassy officials often leaked rumors and floated self-serving innuendos to US correspondents to further the US government's agenda. Each side used the other to its advantage.

That cozy, quid-pro-quo relationship extended to the *Brazil Herald*. At least one top editor at the *Brazil Herald* was a paid informant for the CIA during the same general time period. Joseph Stanley Sims, who covered the 1964 coup in Brazil for UPI and a year later left the wire service to become managing editor of the *Brazil Herald*, it turned out, had worked for the CIA for years. Sims quit the *Herald* in 1966 to pursue a career in public relations for Pan Am in Brazil during which he was a CIA paid asset. As Sims would explain it, "A short time after joining Pan Am, I got a phone call from a gentleman in the US Embassy inviting me to lunch. At lunch I learned he was with the

Fig. 15.2 Joe
Sims's identity
card.

Agency and they had been keeping their eyes on me while I was making all my career changes and they thought I might be an asset. He
offered me a job—with more dollars for my pocket—and I accepted
it on the spot."[12]

Sims said he used the connections he had established as a newsman with UPI and the *Herald* to feed information on Brazil to the
intelligence agency. Once he was transferred to Pan Am's US offices,
Sims said, his relationship with the CIA ended. Square-jawed, long-
faced Sims, the son of a Paris, Illinois, police officer and a graduate
of Indiana State University, would eventually work as a public affairs
officer for the Federal Reserve Board in Washington, DC under Fed
chair Paul Volcker, during which he accompanied Volcker on a fact-
finding trip back to Brazil.

In 2011, in an email Sims sent to a circle of journalist friends, he
explained what motivated him to work as a CIA asset:

Dear folks and gentle people:
This is the toughest and scariest email I have written in a
while. . . . It gives me a chance to get something off my chest
that has weighed on me for 50+ years. [Former Associated Press
Brazil Bureau Chief] Ed [Miller], you can add my name to those
of Hal Hendrix and Bob Berrellez. However, I want to assure you
and others on this list that my job had absolutely nothing to do

with reporting on what my fellow journalists were up to. Their names were never in any of my reports. Rather, I was keeping tabs on Jango and his crowd both before and after the '64 coup with the help of a couple of his folks who kept me very well informed. I did nothing in those years that I was or am ashamed of. Actually, there were a couple of times when I was pretty proud of myself. Anyway, I've felt for many years that I should inform the journalists who were down there with me that although a "spook" I was not interested in their comings and goings. Just about everyone I worked with or reported to are now deceased but there are at least a couple of guys out there who may decide to write a book someday. I would rather the press corps hear it from me instead of some other source who might paint an inaccurate picture and plant suspicion that I was snooping on my fourth estate friends, rather than on Jango, [left-wing Brazilian politician, two-time governor of Rio de Janeiro, Leonel] Brizola and the PTB [Partido Trabalhista Brasileiro, Brazil's Worker Party]. There have been a couple of times when I thought that Ed [Miller] suspected my ties with the Agency, and I hope he's not now going to dedicate a chapter to me in his memoirs. As far as I know, there were no other American journalists who were on the payroll while I was there, and at one point the Agency decided that they would steer clear of the press corps. There was one Latino guy, but I don't remember his name or his organization.

Wow! Feels good to get this outta my system! . . . I was with the Agency for more than 10 years and no one seemed to be suspicious of me— not even my family. I almost blew my cover once in a conversation with another old buddy, Baltimore Sun's Nate Miller [correspondent based in Rio de Janeiro, 1962 -1966] but I think whatever I said went unnoticed and over his head.

Joe[13]

At the time Sims said he severed his relationship with the CIA, he said he signed a nondisclosure agreement, which made it a felony to disclose further details about his undercover work with the agency.[14] Sims died January 1, 2021.

In addition to Sims, another alleged connection between the *Brazil Herald* and US intelligence agencies was John Franklin Thrall, a convicted federal felon who had worked as an editor at the *Herald* in the mid-1970s. When I first arrived in São Paulo in 1979, *Latin America Daily Post* executive editor Steve Yolen put me onto Thrall, who at the time was an editor at the start-up publication *Data News*, and who threw freelance work my way. The freewheeling Thrall struck me as pleasant though unconventional. He looked more like a roadie for a band than an editor for an up-and-coming personal-computing journal.

Unbeknownst to me at the time, Thrall would later claim that he had worked as a paid asset for the CIA. "In Brazil I had only one contact who passed orders, info or money," Thrall would write in an email in 2012. "As a journalist I was seldom under scrutiny, and I acted erratically, so when suspicion occurred, my actions and life appeared too crazy for me to be any kind of agent. The cover was basically so crazy, it allowed me to move with zero suspicion. I never went to the embassy, and I assumed they knew nothing about me or the orders I followed."[15]

Thrall's former wife, Susan Lightcap, who for a while also worked as an editor at the *Herald*, discounted any such affiliation Thrall may have had with the CIA, describing him as a "fabulist." Lightcap said Thrall "found great satisfaction in developing theories and situations, and was a teller of tall tales."[16] He died in Brazil on August 19, 2020.

Other alleged nexuses between US intelligence agencies and the *Brazil Herald* long predated Sims and Thrall. *Herald* founders Joe Brown and Frank Garcia maintained longstanding connections to American embassy and Western intelligence officers. That US Ambassador William Pawley had given an infusion of funds to Brown and Garcia to keep the *Herald* going, as well as act as a go-between for John Montgomery to purchase the *Herald*, seems telling, especially considering that after his term as ambassador concluded,

Pawley kept in close contact with CIA Director Allen Dulles, was appointed to a secret committee to examine inefficiencies in the agency, and made it his practice to suggest names of potential CIA assets in Latin America to Dulles.[17] When I petitioned the CIA with a Freedom of Information Act request to uncover any historical ties between the *Brazil Herald* and the CIA, the agency assigned an agent to the task, but as is its routine, ignored repeated correspondence and phone calls from me.[18]

For his part, Bill Williamson maintained that "absolutely, there was no connection, or at least none that I knew of," between the CIA and the *Herald*, dismissing all such allegations as "the stuff of conspiracy nuts." Even after Joe Sims, whom Williamson had hired at the *Herald*, acknowledged that he had been on the CIA payroll, Williamson doubted Sims's account. "I'm not convinced of it. If you knew Sims, you wouldn't be, either," he told me, shrugging his shoulder when I pressed him to elaborate." Williamson added that he didn't believe that Thrall had worked for the CIA or any other intelligence-gathering organization.[19]

To me, Williamson too readily denied any possible CIA links between the newspaper he managed for two decades and the hundreds of employees he hired over the same period. Perhaps to maintain his own legacy, Williamson flatly ruled there had been no collusion, official or informal, between the *Herald* and CIA, or US intelligence agencies. A more sinister view might hold that Williamson's hobnobbing with so many expat business executives and US officials with or without cover for so long had made him a de facto intelligence asset agent, if not in name, in spirit.

Williamson acknowledged that on occasion he talked to intelligence operatives posted to the US embassy, and later, the US consulate, in Rio, alerting them of items of interest as a matter of reciprocal courtesy. "There was a guy registered in the commercial department. He'd quiz me on situations, and I'd answer to the best of my knowledge. The FBI was everywhere at the time, during the 1960s. I think almost every embassy had an FBI agent in some capacity." Williamson said he occasionally met with CIA agents, but such affiliations were based on collegiality, not as a conduit for intelligence.[20] Among his friends employed by the CIA was Lee G. Mestres, who worked in Northeast Brazil and São Paulo for the agency.[21] Mestres' father had been financial vice president of Princeton; his brother was chairman of the New York law firm, Sullivan & Cromwell. Another Williamson crony at the time was naturalized citizen Peter Rodenbeck, who brought McDonalds, Outback, and Starbucks to Brazil. The three men—Williamson, Mestres, and Rodenbeck—collaborated on a political thriller based on the kidnaping of an American official in Latin America, but that project never got off the ground.[22]

Herald journalists certainly didn't need to be on the US government payroll to write glowing accounts of US interests in Brazil. One hire Williamson made prior to the buildup to the 1964 coup was Paul Vanorden Shaw, who wrote a political column several times a week for the *Herald* that was business-centric and politically conservative, a reflection of the majority of the newspaper's readers. Shaw's column ran alongside those of syndicated columnists Walter Lippmann and humorist Art Buchwald. But there was no confusing the three journalists. Shaw was a shrill booster of US interests in Brazil. If the generals in charge in Brasília after the 1964 coup ever needed reassurance that the *Herald* was on their side, they got it from Shaw and his right-wing rants. [23]

Shortly after the 1964 coup, Shaw wrote:

There is no doubt whatsoever that the great majority of the people of this country and almost 90 percent of its Armed Forces believes strongly enough in the Christian and democratic institutions of their land to fight for them, and that they repudiated totalitarianism and corruption in government strongly enough to force them out of the land. The lightning victory achieved in less than 48 hours or so, disproved the myth that Brazil's Armed Forces were too divided to decide any issues without a long civil war and it proved that Sr. Goulart's student-labor military 'dispositivo' was no stronger than an empty shell which a bare-foot boy could have crushed easily in his sleep.

As opposed to AP correspondent Ed Miller's critical assessment of US Ambassador Gordon, Shaw lavished praise on Gordon. Shaw wrote that Gordon "and his pipe are inseparable companions and adjuncts of his personality and success as a diplomat. The informality of his attire, the simplicity of his manner and the sincerity of his approach to people and problems, ever since his arrival last year, have more than compensated for his inexperience as a career diplomat and explain, in part, his acceptance by the VIPs of Brazil."[24]

Even with shills like Shaw using the *Herald* as a megaphone, across-the-board press censorship flourished as a byproduct of the 1964 coup, at times even directed at the *Herald*, as pro-military as any newspaper in the nation. David Hume, the young editor and reporter hired while still in high school by Herb Zschech, recalled, "[T]he military government censors would not allow us to do any original reporting [not that there had been much at the *Herald*], so we had to rely on wire copy and translations from censored Portuguese-language papers. I remember asking Mr. Zschech what kind of reporting I'd be doing and he said none."[25]

Every day, two copies of the *Herald* were delivered by courier to the military police's headquarters less than a mile away. Any review of what the *Herald* printed turned out to be more a formality than anything else. The *Herald* was not on the radar of government censors. The newspaper's circulation was tiny in comparison to that of Brazilian dailies, and the *Herald*'s audience was well-to-do expats, American and British businessmen and their families, not the types of subversives the military was worried about. And even if government minders had been concerned about what the *Herald* was reporting, few had any degree of English proficiency to know what to censor.

What most concerned the overseers were the Portuguese-language media in Brazil, including the proliferation of both populist and intellectual newspapers throughout the nation. Perhaps paradoxically for a Third World country with an illiteracy rate at the time approaching fifty percent, there was an abundance of all kinds of print media in Brazil.[26] Government censors were physically installed in newspaper offices, requiring editors to submit copy directly to them before it could proceed to typesetting and printing. This multi-stop process made the ability to publish unfettered ideas and news coverage virtually impossible for the better part of a decade. Much investigative and interpretive journalism was to collapse in Brazil. Almost all newspaper, radio, and television news had effectively been rendered propaganda of the state.

To be sure, press censorship in Brazil after the coup was far from a novelty. Dating back to before the Vargas administration, even before Andrew Jackson Lamoureux's tenure at *The Rio News*, military regimes had imposed periodic bouts of censorship of varying degrees of severity. In 1962, when CBS correspondent Charles Kuralt had assayed newspapers in Rio, President Jânio Quadros had just resigned and the military, amassing increasing authority over the civilian government, had tried to impose a regimen of censorship with mixed success.

"The reaction was something to see," Kuralt said in his CBS radio dispatch. "Some newspapers slammed their doors and kept their presses running in defiance of the censors, made the soldiers confiscate every edition off the streets. Other newspapers closed down in anger. One—*Diário de Notícias*—let the censors do their worst and hit the streets for three days running with great blank spaces where the censored stories would have gone. There was great eloquence in those yawning blank columns—the silence, as they say, was deafening, and Rio's press censorship lasted 72 hours."[27]

After the coup, to get around the renewed efforts of federal censors, many in the Brazilian press used innovative ways to alert readers of the government oversight and intrusion. Some methods were overt, others more subtle. In the place of censored news, several Rio newspapers took to printing poetry, occasionally of Luís de Camões, a canonical sixteenth-century Portuguese poet, or of contemporary Vinícius de Moraes, Brazil's beloved poet and lyricist of the twentieth century. Several newspapers published satirical news, lampooning the government with sly accounts that slid past censors.

Brazil Herald editors went about their tasks, putting out the newspaper as they ordinarily would, but they were mindful not to agitate government minders, even though military censors were not focused on an also-ran English-language newspaper read by expats, which seldom printed anything that might rile the government. Still, Bob Nadkarni, a British proofreader at the *Herald*, remembered that almost everyone at the newspaper "knew that there was a government plant working in the print room at the BH," although Nadkarni could provide no hard facts to corroborate such an assertion.[28]

Paranoia descended upon the *Herald* and other media throughout the country. "No one talked politics where you could be overheard," remembered *Herald* reporter Liza Fourré, a young journalist with a recent degree in political science from the University of Minnesota. "You could get disappeared or killed."[29] It's doubtful whether such off-handed musings resulted in such outcomes, but still an Orwellian specter of intimidation muted public and even private conversation for a decade after the coup.

Out of caution, cartoons and news items in the *Herald* that might be interpreted as even mildly critical of the government were eliminated in preemptive editorial self-censorship. Any local news was largely limited to AP and UPI wire stories, also subject to censorship. If those accounts proved to be too much for the censors once published, blame could handily be assigned to the international news agencies, not the *Herald*.

Herald managing editor Jean Etsinger remembered that in late 1968 Rio's journalistic mainstay, the *Jornal do Brasil*, one of South America's most prominent dailies, ran discreet editorial nods, noticeable in the newspaper's "ears" on either side of the page one mast, such as this weather forecast: "Black. Temperature suffocating. The air unbreathable. The nation is being swept by strong winds."[30]

Etsinger recalled an incident when she was summoned to military police headquarters to answer vague questions about the *Herald's* next-day content. "Around 1 a.m., after the Linotype machines had been shut off, the hot metal had cooled and the typesetters had left, I was told that a couple of articles on the next morning's paste-up pages had to be removed before we could print. I explained that we had no way to set more type that night and that readers would easily see that we had been censored if we ran the pages with large blank spaces. I proposed a plan that was acceptable: We stripped stories off previous days' pages and pasted them into the spaces, chopping them to fit. Probably not all of our readers got the message, but certainly many did."[31]

When Ramez Maluf started as the *Herald*'s managing editor in 1970, his recollection of censorship at the newspaper was similar. "You could not say anything negative about a friendly country or anything positive about a country not on friendly terms with Brazil," he said. "The rules were ridiculous."[32]

One of the underlying effects of press censorship is that it seldom ends with the government's attempt to eliminate contrary political views. After the coup, newspaper and magazine photographs deemed remotely sexually suggestive or salacious were also censored. Non-political general news perceived as negative to "family values" and the supposed social wellbeing of the nation was also considered suspect and often excised by censors.

Censors' roles eased by the mid-1970s, but their behind-the-scenes influence persisted and spread to private industry, where managing the press has always been commonplace. The government mandate of controlling the media, though, seemed to give carte blanche to the private sector also seeking to restrict publication of any news perceived as inconsistent or contrary with its interests.

An example of this happened when *Herald* reporter Paulo Paladino, one of the editorial staff's few Brazilians, was sent to cover a feel-good press conference on the occasion of the visit to Brazil by the international head of Coca-Cola. Not incidental to the visit had been leaked news that two workers in a Brazilian Coke plant had fallen into a vat of Coca-Cola syrup and had drowned. At the press conference, Paladino asked the visiting Coke dignitary about the accident. Immediately, Paladino was grabbed by security guards and strong-armed from the press conference.[33]

In 1975, Bill Williamson was called to military police headquarters just as the *Herald* was about to run a favorable piece on Brazil's globally known liberation theologian, Archbishop Dom Hélder Pessoa Câmara, of the Northeastern cities of Olinda and Recife. Câmara was a genuine newsmaker. He also was a vocal, popular, and powerful critic of the government; a protected resister because of his cleric's collar and title; and a favorite among journalists. All of these virtues made him a perceived threat to military leaders in Brasília. Williamson said he had no choice but to kill the story.[34]

On another occasion, government agents seized copies, as well as page negatives, of *Cadernos de Opinião*, the weekly political tabloid the *Herald* printed on its presses. *Opinião*, as it was known, was a serious tabloid that sought to publish groundbreaking journalism, as well as occasional satirical swipes at the government when it could get away with it. The news magazine's offices were in the same building down the hall from the *Herald* on Rua do Resende. Maggie Locke, a *Herald* editor and reporter at the time, recalled that a writer for *Opinião* had been interrogated by the military police and returned to the *Herald* building with a profusion of bruises.[35] Government censors had been installed in the offices where *Opinião* was edited, although rarely did they interfere with the *Herald*'s copy or its staff.[36]

Managing Editor Walter Colton remembered in 1975 when *Opinião* sought to publish an exposé about Swiss multinational Nestlé's advertising campaign to convince Brazilian mothers to give up breastfeeding in favor of the company's baby formula. *Opinião*'s cover featured the Nestlé logo overlaid with a skull and crossbones. The story attracted immediate scrutiny from censors since, among other allegations, it detailed government collusion with the roll-out of the Nestlé product. A delegation of military censors made an impromptu appearance at the *Herald* building and seized copies of *Opinião* as the news magazine rolled off the basement presses.

As former business editor Don Best recalled, "The federal police burst into the newsroom with their automatic weapons drawn. The police confiscated the entire issue, took the plates off the press, and scared the living daylights out of us."[37]

On the scene, Williamson attempted to tuck a copy of the offending issue of the news magazine into his briefcase as he exited the *Herald* building. But at the front door, an officer holstered with a sidearm blocked him and demanded that Williamson surrender the magazine.

"I am the owner of Editôra Mory!" Williamson remonstrated, overstating his title. The officer demanded that Williamson open his attaché case and snatched the issue.[38]

A sidenote to the confrontation is that Nestlé was a longtime *Herald* advertiser. The Brazilian subsidiary of the global company provided the newspaper with spring gift baskets filled with products to be given away as prizes to readers who answered a poll about what they liked most about the *Herald*'s women's pages, under the headline, "Our Easter Present."[39]

Outside the *Herald* newsroom, perplexed Brazilians got accustomed to Americans who through the strangest of circumstances often materialized in their country. Such was the case when in the spring of 1962 a self-styled American evangelist from Crete, Indiana, and his family took up residence in the interior city of Belo Horizonte before moving to Rio de Janeiro, where the preacher lived till December 1963, five months before the coup. Thirty-two-year-old James Warren Jones was in search of a flock and in his spare time worked for Brazilian investment firm, Invesco, as a mutual-funds salesman. Jim Jones, as he was known, was employed on a commission basis, but after three months of not reeling in a single account, he left Invesco and thereafter Brazil. Some journalists have conjectured that Jones was working for the CIA under the cover of an itinerant evangelist-turned-equities salesman who didn't speak the language of the country in which he was supposed to sell locals first on Jesus, then on commodities.[40]

A fellow Indiana resident from the city of Richmond was another curious case of an American who also happened to drop into Brazil.

Dan Mitrione had quit his job as Richmond police chief and, under the auspices of the US Agency for International Development's Office of Public Safety, moved to Brazil to train local police officers, first in Belo Horizonte, then in Rio in 1962. Mitrione and his wife, Henrietta, had nine children, and like the AP's Ed Miller, were members of Our Lady of Mercy Catholic Church in Rio. Mitrione was captain of the American Society softball team in Rio, awarded a *Brazil Herald* trophy upon winning the most games during the 1966 season.[41]

After his initial tour, Mitrione returned to the States, but returned to South America in 1969, this time to Montevideo, Uruguay, where he was alleged to have taught local military-police officers interrogation techniques, including the use of a device labeled by left-wing guerrillas "the Mitrione vest," described as "an inflatable vest which can be used to increase pressure on the chest during interrogation, sometimes crushing the rib cage."[42] In 1970, Mitrione was kidnapped by Tupamaro extremists who demanded the release of political prisoners in exchange for the return of the former Indiana police chief. The demands were not met, and Mitrione, shot twice in the head, was found in the trunk of a car eleven days later. The events surrounding the kidnapping and murder were made into the 1973 film *State of Siege*, directed by Greek-French filmmaker Costa-Gavras.[43]

During the same period, a proofreader and part-time reporter for the *Brazil Herald* was Bob Beadle, who, having tired of working as an airline employee behind the Pan Am counter at the Honolulu Airport, took off for Rio de Janeiro. One draw had been the 1959 Brazilian film *Black Orpheus*, but it also had been the prospect of surfing at Apoador Beach, between Copacabana and Ipanema, then considered the mecca of the sport, which had attracted Beadle to Rio.[44] Beadle rented a room in a party house in the city's Santa Teresa district on Rua Dr. Júlio Otoni. For the *Herald*, Beadle wrote several music reviews, but when asked by managing editor Jean Etsinger to write about Brazilian soccer, he demurred, "because the only thing I was interested in at the time was surfing," Beadle would recall.

"Everyone thought we were hippies because we had long hair and partied every night," Beadle said. One evening in 1969 he was scooped up in a raid that resulted in the arrest of fifteen people after military police found marijuana and other drugs, including LSD, in the basement. Beadle and another American, Peter Jarvis, pleaded guilty and served time in three Brazilian prisons for eight months. Both men were jailed with political activists who talked theory and strategy into the night, but who refused to associate with the two Americans because the pair was viewed as "decadent American drug users," Beadle recalled.[45] Among the inmates incarcerated were Alípio Cristiano de Freitas, a priest from Northeast Brazil, and Cláudio Torres da Silva, a Rio Grande do Sul academic who had tried to organize Rio's *favelas* into political resistance groups.[46]

At the time, several journalists in the *Herald* newsroom, including editor Ramez Maluf, were incentivized to move to the left politically. One day, a staffer at the *Herald* pulled Maluf aside and asked sotto voce whether he wanted to meet dissidents active in an underground cell. Muluf remembered it this way:

I said yes, I'd love to do that. So, she arranged a meeting for me. She instructed me to go to a downtown café near the Municipal Theater, and while standing drink a cup of coffee at the corner. So I went, and this guy comes by and says, 'Follow me.' We walked to the Santa Teresa train station. And we got on the train and then walked to the next car to make sure no one was following us. I was interested in the theory of Marxism, so I began meeting with these guys. Until then, I hadn't been involved in Brazilian politics. After a couple of months, it got to be a little hairier. I was being asked to do things that I really didn't want to do to show my commitment. Like go to a meeting where guns were placed on the tables. By then, I was afraid to tell the guy I wouldn't do it. I was intellectually interested, but I thought there might be a government agent involved. At the same time, I was also afraid to say no, now that I knew all of them. I realized one day I just couldn't continue.[47]

By the mid-1970s, the oppressive aftermath of the 1964 coup had given way to a hardened and widespread dissidence in the nation. For many, particularly young people, this was due to a sweeping dissatisfaction with the woefully out-of-touch military regime, as well as the emergence of a pervasive counterculture, driven by politics, sexuality, drugs, and music surging through Brazil and rest of the world. The *Herald* newsroom would become an incubator for such spirited rebellion.

CHAPTER 16

Merry Pranksters

THE *BRAZIL HERALD* operated as a daily improvisation based on the personnel that happened to be putting out the newspaper on any given day, month, or year. The newspaper's eclectic, whoever-entered-the-front-door-and-made-it-to-the-top-of-the-worn-marble-staircase-to-the-third-floor newsroom led to a zany and madcap place to work. Not taking anything away from the assorted English-language newspapers published in other countries around the globe at the time, it would be difficult to conceive of a newspaper more eccentric and wackier than the *Brazil Herald* whose newsroom by the mid-1970s had turned into a steamy version of writer and troubadour Ken Kesey's Merry Pranksters.

Canadian Garry Marchant, a gifted writer who became the *Herald*'s managing editor in 1973, recounted a typical day:

> John, the assistant editor, a mad mystic recently released from the Georgia state prison after serving two years on a drug conviction, is hiding somewhere, smoking a joint. The social editor, Laura, is drunk again, gleefully cursing me from across the desk, rejoicing in her bilingual command of the invective. The Latin American editor, a tall, pale bland Canadian girl, appropriately named Pamela, is in a tearful tizzy because she had lost all of her wire stories. Walter, our sports editor, a large shaggy American college student, is, as usual, brooding about the true spiritual meaning of life ("I mean, what does it all boil down to?") instead

of writing headlines. And business editor Betty, an executive-wife newspaper groupie, is urging the meagre staff to 'Screw the paper. Let's go downstairs and get drunk.'"[1]

For a newspaper whose demographics were strait-laced business-men and their sheltered families whisked away to a pampered Third World cocoon, the *Herald's* personnel were a total mismatch with its core readers. Marchant charitably described the staff as "a mixture of European refugees, semi-literate North American hitchhikers, drifters, criminals, dope-smoking misfits, boozers, and a few out-of-place college students taking a year off school traveling around South America."

The "mad mystic" Marchant referred to above was, in fact, John Franklin Thrall, the former Navy technician and supposed CIA asset I would work for as a freelancer when I first arrived in Brazil. Born in the southern Wisconsin town of Merrill, beaten as a child by an alcoholic father who managed the local tavern, the gangling Thrall had been a sailor on the nuclear submarine the USS *Patrick Henry* directly out of high school. While in the Navy, Thrall said, he had unwittingly been dosed with LSD, although he never allowed how or why this happened or who did it.[2]

Upon his discharge, Thrall cut loose and got involved in experimental theater in New York and Atlanta working as a projectionist and stage manager for *Oh, Calcutta!*, the avant-garde nude theatrical revue. When Thrall was twenty-six, he and an associate were arrested at the Atlanta International Airport after returning from Los Angeles, charged with transporting fifty pounds of marijuana, eight ounces of hashish, and fifty tabs of LSD. Thrall, who at the time was working as a photographer for an Atlanta underground newspaper, *The Great Speckled Bird*, was sentenced to five years in prison, where he worked in the correctional facility's library.[3] For a while, Thrall was housed in solitary confinement, and in a lawsuit he charged that his sanity was being undermined by the prison's lack of ventilation, shampoo, deodorant, dental floss, and exercise facilities. He petitioned authorities for copies of *The Great Speckled Bird* and *The Communist Manifesto*, and for an immediate halt to fundamentalist sermons he said were being beamed into his cell.[4] Thrall was released from prison after serving almost two years. His accomplice, Stephen Jeffrey Lee, a music producer later turned police informant, would be found dead, shot twice in the head, with his penis stuffed in his mouth.[5]

Meanwhile, in a bust-'em-out celebration, Thrall and a friend, Bill Hall, cooked up a crackpot scheme that would take the pair to Brazil. Their hair cut, beards shaved, and dressed in business suits, the two flew to Brasília, where they met with government bureaucrats to pitch a series of fantastical plans to buy land, grow food, and open a canning factory in the undeveloped state of Goiás along the Novo River, to be financed by Brazilian government subsidies. At the new capital's five-star Palace Hotel, where Thrall and Hall were staying, the pair dropped acid, put on pirate costumes (for some reason), and acted out theatrical riffs while taking videos and photographs as performance art for a sound-and-light show that Thrall intended to debut once he got back to the States.[6]

In 1972, Thrall got work as a "Baby, you can drive my car?" chauffeur for a wealthy American woman who was an itinerant coke dealer in South America. The two parted ways in Colombia, and from Leticia, Thrall got himself to the Brazilian border town of Benjamin Constant, where he bought a canoe, stocked up on canned sardines, and started paddling down the Amazon River, slathering himself with mud in a futile attempt to keep ravenous mosquitos at bay. One evening, he spied a campfire and paddled ashore to find six Indians sitting in a circle. They invited him to share charred piraiba, mandioca, and a cigar-sized marijuana torpedo, which Thrall recalled "was so strong I was soon flying."[7] By morning, the Indians had vanished and Thrall made his way back to his canoe, paddled four days upstream to Manaus, got himself to Belem on the mouth of the Atlantic, abandoned his canoe, and hitchhiked south to Rio, where friend Bill Hall was now living. The two found their way to the *Herald* newsroom, met with Bill Williamson and got hired. There they joined a spacey crew of journalists, few of whom knew what they were doing.

Don Best, a *Herald* editor in 1975, recalled, "I can tell you with full confidence that the proofreader at the time (from Australia, I think) couldn't spell his own name and would wander around the newsroom in a marijuana fog."[8] Bob Nadkarni recalled that another *Herald* proofreader at the time "had fled from prosecution for negligently exploding his drug laboratory back in New Zealand."[9]

Multiple relationships in the newsroom went hand in hand with the tropical heat and humidity, buffered by alcohol, drugs, and the Rio beach vibe.

Thrall's wife at the time, Susan Lightcap, joined him at the *Herald*, along with French-born managing editor Eric Hippeau and Glasgow-born social editor Laura Reid. They lived in an Ipanema apartment, where other staffers, including sports editor American Walter Colton and Brazil-reared reporter Janet Huseby would drop by to unwind, smoke dope, and drink beer while sitting on parquet floors, gazing out the window at the Christ the Redeemer statue.[10]

Lightcap remembered getting into trouble for writing headlines that were either "too political" or "sarcastic." She quit, worked at the British School in Rio, and then got into a relationship with an expat American physicist and mathematician. The couple had a daughter and moved to Barra da Tijuca in the south of Rio, where they "had some bang-up parties, our friends and neighbors happy to come out on Sundays to what we called the Barra Breakfast Club (eat good food, smoke good weed, go to the beach)."[11]

Laura Reid and Rita Davy split coverage of the expat British social scene. Editor Marchant recalled that Reid "after a morning of smoking grass at home would wander into the office with a double Cuba Libre in hand from the bar downstairs, and drink her way through the night."[12]

Betty, the executive-wife newspaper groupie Marchant wrote about, was Betty Sausser, who showed up for her shift in a chauffeur-driven car, which returned for her in the evening, often with the driver waiting in front on Rua do Resende on overtime.[13] In the newsroom, Sausser had the habit of smoking cigarettes in long cigarette holders.

Rio's adoration of youth and beauty had seized her middle-age psyche, and Sausser developed a fascination with plastic surgery, which she volubly shared with the staff as she was about to go under a surgeon's knife for an assortment of cosmetic procedures.[14]

Sausser wrote a recurring feature in the *Herald* called Potpourri, a knockoff of journalist and homemaker Erma Bombeck and chef Julia Child, probably more the former since Sausser had five children and a chaotic household of feral animals, which even with the service of several maids, seemed on the verge of daily detonation.

Now, ordinarily I love dear Henry, the Super Cat, and even Chico the parrot wouldn't be so bad, if he would just learn to do something except try to bite the hands that feed him, but today I would gladly throw them out, bag and baggage. Between them, they've managed to knock down two boxes of chalk, one of them being colored chalk naturally, and the floor in the service area looks as though an "escola de samba" had marched through. I am telling you definitely, my house is an uncontrolled disaster area. Now you know the secret of why I go out to work every day!

In the same column, Sausser shared recipes for an assortment of house specialties: chopped chicken liver, beer-sour cream-curried potatoes, and beer-braised shrimp.[15]

As long as the newspaper came out every day, didn't have too many typos, published a reasonable assortment of wire and local copy, made it to news bancas and subscribers on a relatively timely basis, and ran enough advertising to meet its monthly payroll, the unflappable Williamson didn't have much to complain about. He had become a Brazilian, if not a legal citizen, surely one in spirit. Williamson had learned that resisting the way many businesses operated in tropical Rio had little payoff. He had left any notion of punctuality and efficiency back in the States. Which seemed to suit the *Herald*'s whatever staff fine.

Mary A. Lenz, who worked for the *Herald* in 1975 when she was twenty-three before moving on to the local AP bureau, remembered while hiking a nature trail in Rio she met an Irishman who had a part-time job teaching English, a fallback for just about anyone living in Brazil who could speak English passingly well. "He kinda gagged at the idea of working for the *Brazil Herald*. 'Jaysus,' he said, 'when you've gone through everything else in your life, you either drive a taxi or work for the *Brazil Herald*,'" Lenz wrote her parents at the time.[16]

Still, the *Herald* was a newspaper and for anyone willing to work for next to nothing, there was a surfeit of benefits, especially for an American woman in her twenties who wanted to live in South America and launch a career as a journalist, just as Teddy Hecht, Betty Dyer, Dawn Addams, Jean Etsinger, and scores of other women had done.

Before Rio, Lenz had lived in Buenos Aires and recalled being harassed by random men on street corners who took to pursing their lips and dispatching kissing sounds or crude comments her way. It seemed an everyday occurrence that had nothing to do with where she was going, what time of the day or night it was, what she was wearing, or whatever disposition she seemed to be displaying at the moment. It happened when she was walking alone, with another woman or in a group of women; if she were accompanied by a man, the come-ons disappeared. Lenz's complaint wasn't uncommon from women who were foreigners or locals, and not just in Argentina but throughout much of the continent, as well as other parts of the world. Lenz found Rio, though, to be far more welcoming to women. In a letter to her parents, she wrote, "Brazilians are so much nicer than Argentines. They are Latin and therefore required to flirt, but they're really nice and pleasant about it, so you can flirt back if you want or just ignore them if you want and nobody hassles you.... You'd just get in a horrible mood walking down the street down there (in Buenos Aires) because everybody was making smart remarks and following you and behaving like boors and creeps. Here, everyone is so relaxed . . . . You cannot believe how happy I am. . . . The whole town looks like an expensive photo layout advertising vacations to tropical isles."[17]

Without suit-wearing Herb Zschech as editor any longer (he had retreated, once again, to writing his political column and plumbing his fascination with macabre crime, showing up at the newspaper offices only to deliver his copy and then disappearing), the chaotic and disorganized environment at the *Herald* now was leavened by a newer and younger cast, mostly short-termers of a year or two, not the entrenched expats of the previous generation. This made for opportunities that likely would not have existed at more conventional newspapers with established levels of hierarchy.

"The editors are willing to let me do just about anything I want, so I'm going to do a feature, maybe a series on women's changing role in Brasil," Liza Fourré, who joined the *Herald* in 1976, wrote her father in Minnesota. "Women's lib has not really gotten to Brasil yet and there are a lot of really frustrated, educated young women who cannot get jobs. Also there are a lot of American women who cannot get jobs in business and end up teaching and many Brazilian women who like it that way and just want to be *donas da casa* [housewives]. That's got to be boring because they don't even do anything, they just tell the maids and nanny's [*sic*] what to do."[18]

For managing editor Jean Etsinger, the variety of big names she got to cover made for a bulging portfolio of impressive clips, particularly for a journalist not yet twenty-five. Etsinger's assignments ranged from a breakfast interview with American civil rights leader Ralph Abernathy to press conferences with Indian Prime Minister Indira Gandhi and heart transplant pioneer Christiaan Barnard. Covering Carnival in 1970 in Rio, Etsinger happened onto hard-driving blues belter Janis Joplin wandering an empty Zona Sul street in the wee hours of the morning. Joplin and a friend had been kicked out of the Copacabana Palace after they'd jumped into the pool nude. The Copa had been the hotel where *Herald* publisher John Montgomery lived as a young newsman; it also was where Hollywood director Orson Welles had pushed the furniture out his window and into the hotel pool after Dolores del Rio had broken up with him in 1942. Etsinger found temporary lodging for Joplin and her gal pal.[19]

Diana Page, a *Herald* night editor and former Peace Corps volunteer, interviewed French playwright Eugène Ionesco and world-famous Brazilian landscape architect Roberto Burle Marx. She also got to meet soccer star Edson Arantes do Nascimento, better known as Pelé.[20] Just about any story idea found some degree of currency at the *Herald*. The enterprising Page entertained the idea of committing a minor crime so that she could report firsthand inside a Rio jail, but got talked out of the experiment by friends concerned about her safety.[21]

Williamson's default hiring plan was to employ a pick-up assortment of fifteen or so editors, reporters, and proofreaders who ran the newspaper largely on their own. He was a benign authority figure, a hang-loose R.A. to a floor of post-college-age students. Page's assessment was that Williamson was "elegant, apparently bored, and somewhat inconsequential." She wrote that he "spent a minimum amount of time at the paper, mostly checking in with the social page editor to ensure that his friends got flattering coverage of their events."[22] But it was precisely Williamson's lack of direction that often played to the fledgling staff's strengths.

The backdrop to such laissez-faire management was the newspaper's continuing financial woes. Publisher Montgomery increasingly appeared to be getting impatient with his Brazilian loss leader. On May 4, 1970, he wrote Williamson a letter in which he stressed, "I don't want to go back to the way things were running three and four years ago, and I am proud of the present setup, but unhappy that the loss continues. You must have a good explanation. . . . I know you are tired of hearing it, Bill, but the object of being in business is to return a profit to the people who put up the money and who do the kind of work that you have been slaving on. Unless you convince yourself of that fact, a year from now you may be writing me as you did in your letter No. 36, that 1970 was lost just like 1969 was."[23]

On another occasion when Montgomery complained about excessive numbers of employees at the newspaper, Williamson shot back: "I don't have an answer—except if you want a real shock, you might compare [the] number of employees at a Brazilian bank with one of the size of First National there."[24] That was as tart as Williamson ever got with Montgomery. Three days later, a contrite Williamson added in another letter to his boss, "I realize that from where you sit you are perfectly justified in writing critical letters. Which just makes me feel worse. . . . Seems every time things start looking up and I see us about to round a corner, something slaps me down. And with you at such a distance, it has been wrong of me to pass on those occasional moments of optimistic feeling only to disillusion you a letter or two later."[25]

Some of the *Herald's* disorder diminished when Williamson hired a twenty-year-old editor, Eric Jean Charles Hippeau, who would go on to launch himself into the stratosphere of American journalism. Hippeau had lived in Switzerland until he was ten, when his father, Claude, a UPI journalist and bureau chief, was transferred to London, where Eric attended the Lycée Français and learned to speak and write English. He enrolled at the Sorbonne, dropped out, and found himself in Rio when UPI had transferred his father there.

Here's how Bob Nadkarni described first meeting Hippeau and *Herald* junior social editor Laura Reid at a Rio restaurant on a Sunday morning in 1970.

A couple plonked themselves at the next table with nothing but their belongings in a few plastic bags. With one last cigarette between them, the girl asked me for a light. It became obvious that her boyfriend thought she was chatting me up and turned his back on us. She told me how they had been thrown out of what remained of their apartment because they had constant, through-the-night parties and eventually their floor had collapsed. They had three weeks to payday, no money and nowhere to stay.

My reaction was, 'Party people? You can move in with me!'

At which, the guy turned around, hand outstretched and said, "Nice to meet you. I'm Eric."

265

Hippeau (whose first name was pronounced in Portuguese Air-ick-KEE, seemingly always with an exclamation mark; his surname in French was pronounced Hip-POE, but in Brazil it came out Hippo) and Reid hauled their trash bags of clothes over to Nadkarni's Copacabana apartment, where the three became instant roommates. Hippeau and Reid told Nadkarni they worked at a laid-back English-language newspaper, and the next week Nadkarni figured he'd join them, so he showed up at the *Herald* and began proofreading for free. Alan Patureau was the *Herald*'s managing editor at the moment, but as Nadkarni recalled, "after a week he disappeared. I saw him a couple of times and he never asked me what I was doing there. It must have been a month before we found out that he had landed in a mental institution and wasn't coming back."[26]

Nadkarni himself had an exotic pedigree, in tune with others at the *Herald*. Born in Swindon, England, he was the son of a London vicar, worked as a sculptor on the set of Stanley Kubrick's *2001: A Space Odyssey*, followed by a series of jobs as a television-globetrotting cameraman before settling in Rio, where he would start a popular jazz club in a notorious favela.

With Patureau gone, Hippeau, who had started as sports editor at the *Herald*, got promoted to editor, more out of default than anything else. While Hippeau was no doubt talented and had a plethora pocketful of innovative ideas that he would implement, to at least one staffer, he was "a spoiled brat par excellence. He thought he was God's gift to mankind." Fifty years after the staffer worked at the *Herald*, the staffer refused to allow me to use a name alongside the assessment of Hippeau. "Eric was the stereotype of the immature rich white European who espoused disdainful views of other religions, ethnicities, or races. [He] would engage in racist, anti-Semitic, and a disturbing disdain for the poor in Brazil."[27] Hippeau boasted to anyone in earshot that he was "the youngest daily newspaper editor in the world," as well as the scion of four generations of journalists.[28] To Harold Emert, who would become one of the *Herald*'s most beloved columnists, Hippeau was a dismissive, "nasty SOB."[29] To others, he was organized and methodical, just what the ailing newspaper need-ed. As another managing editor, Walter Colton, put it: "Eric was very creative and assembled a good editorial staff. He was cocky but he also very capable."[30] To Don Best, Hippeau "was smart, ambitious, and well-connected."[31]

During his watch, Hippeau hired Maggie Locke, who had moved to Rio with a long-distance promise from Marvine Howe, *The New York Times* Brazil correspondent at the time, that she would mentor young Locke. Born in Ireland and having lived in Africa and Europe as a military brat, Locke was accustomed to the pleasures and demands of living abroad, and hoped to use her Brazil experiences to launch a stateside newspaper career. "I wasn't in Rio more than a couple of weeks when I saw a copy of the BH at a local café," she would recall. "I immediately contacted the paper and got an interview." When Locke arrived at 65 Rua do Resende, she walked into a 1930s newsroom of languidly swirling ceiling fans and wooden desks cluttered with pa-pers anchored by cigarette-butt-filled ashtrays, coffee cups and beer bottles with varying quantities of liquid inside.

"How's your Portuguese?" Hippeau asked Locke, to which she re-sponded, "Nada."[32]

Locke, who had been a reporter at a newspaper in Virginia's Shenandoah Valley, became proficient enough to turn into an accom-plished reporter at the *Herald* over the next two years. She would leave to work at the AP, followed by a three-year stint at the *Washington Post*, and later at the *Los Angeles Times*.

Another Hippeau hire was Best, who began by editing the business pages. "Can you imagine how many years it would take an aspiring young journalist in the United States to become an actual editor? The *Brazil Herald*, despite its checkered history and flaws, put a lot of young writers—myself included—on a fast track in the world of journalism and publishing."[33]

As managing editor, Hippeau instituted a series of innovations, one of which was to eliminate "jump pages," i.e., stories that start on one page and continue inside. While this made for shorter stories, it also streamlined the look of the newspaper and made for a more effortless reading experience. At the same time, Hippeau increased the news hole for Latin America coverage.[34] "Day by day, Eric worked to get rid of the deadbeats, hire better people, and improve the overall quality of the paper," remembered Best. "During my tenure at the *Herald*—less than two years—I saw an extraordinary transformation."[35]

Even with Hippeau's tighter management and portfolio of ideas, technical glitches continued to abound. The odds of one in a series of Rube Goldberg interlocking pieces not fitting quite right on any given afternoon or evening were considerable. In addition to the heat in the newsroom, the composing equipment and heavy presses in the basement broke down with maddening and unpredictable regularity. There also were frequent power outages, commonly referred to as *faltas,* which included scheduled outages to ration electricity during the hot summer months. Such brownouts meant that everything would grind to a halt, including the *Herald*'s wire machines, the paper's lifelines for news, with no one having a clue when power might be restored, which could be in minutes, hours, or days.

"Last night our computer broke and we had to gather up all the teletype tape and take it over to *O Globo* [a Rio newspaper] to run it through their machines, which meant we were up till four a.m.," Mary Lenz wrote her parents. "I felt like a band of raggedy Chinamen bringing their stories up to the *San Francisco Examiner* because the abacus broke. I think that's kind of the way the *O Globo* staff looked at us. Standard dress for the *Herald* is your very oldest pair of blue jeans and some kind of shirt you had left over from college...and your hair kind of combed, and tennis shoes. You can always spot us at press conferences."[36]

For Lenz and other young expats at the newspaper, the *Herald* turned into a second home. "The staff ranges in age from 21 to 24," Lenz scribbled to her parents. "Everybody is nice and I happen to think that even if the BH is pretty humble, it takes some pretty sharp kids to go knocking around the world at that age. Saturday the whole office was blaring with Beatles music from the local radio, the Brazilian composition staff was samba-ing and the rest of us were frugging or whatever we do and some of us seemed to be floating about a little. I'm surprised the paper didn't get printed upside down. I love it! I love it!"³⁷

An essential part of the daily improv was that whenever there was a soccer match, pretty much every afternoon and evening, the Brazilian paste-up crew would stop working, leave their posts, hushed and huddled around a tinny transistor radio, listening to the screaming static of a crazed partisan announcer and the cacophonous, rolling roar of riotous fans in the background. When a player for the home team scored, the announcer would scream as though he had been stabbed— "GOOOOOOOOOAAALLLLLLLLLLLLLLLLLLLLL!"—elongating the shriek to a full ten or fifteen seconds, while two dozen *Herald* staffers would erupt, jumping and whooping, high fives sweeping the newsroom. While the newspaper might have been experiencing an electrical outage at the moment, a power surge of emotion and joy overtook everyone.

A less felicitous facet of the daily tumult in the newsroom was the erratic phone system. This was not a problem at just the *Herald*, but throughout Brazil. In addition to crossed lines that produced parallel conversations and an auxiliary phone book that consisted of not names but phone numbers that had been updated to *other* phone numbers, phone calls would regularly disconnect. A call that lasted more than ten minutes without disconnecting several times was unusual.

"Once while doing an interview, the connection went in and out until it finally died," recalled Mark Gruberg, a former New York taxicab driver with a degree from Brooklyn Law College who had presented himself at the *Herald* after a canoe trip down the Amazon with just a few damp cruzeiros in his pocket. "This wasn't the first time that it had happened to me, and in the heat and frustration of the moment, I yanked the phone cord from the wall. The office manager was not pleased."³⁸

While Gruberg's reaction was extreme, the high-decibel Portuguese exclamation "*a linha caiu!*" ("the line dropped!") was an often-heard refrain in the newsroom, followed by "*merda!*" ("shit!") or "*porra!*" (a variation of "fuck!").

An allied telephonic complaint was the dial tone, or lack thereof. The wait to dial a call could range from several seconds to several hours to all day. With a phone receiver cradled between their shoulders and ears, Williamson's retinue of secretaries completed crossword puzzles, polished their nails, and applied make-up while holding compact mirrors as they waited for a dial tone. When they finally got one, they'd frantically call out, "Tem linha, tem linha! Senhor Bill, vem, vem!" ("I have a dial tone! Senhor Bill, come quickly!") and try to locate Williamson, who by then could be anywhere in the three-story news building. Invariably, Williamson would rush back to his office, hurriedly take the phone handoff from the secretary, dial a number, shout "*Alô! Alô!*" and then, as though on cue, the line would drop, thereby requiring a replay of the entire Sisyphean process.

Staffers had only so much patience. In 1972 when Janet Huseby was working at the *Herald*, one of her tasks was proofing the stock market pages—one person reading share prices off the wire, another person double-checking them on the proofs. It was the last job of the night. "Every now and then we were just not interested, or they came up late, or who knows why, but we'd send the stock papers down without checking—chuckling at the thought of people jumping out of windows after recalculating their worth. After the stocks, we'd go out drinking and dancing."[39]

Williamson had hired Huseby, who had grown up with the *Herald* delivered to her family's apartment in Copacabana. Williamson and her father, Bill Huseby, who worked for the Toronto-based electric company Light S.A., which serviced Rio's grid system, were members of the Rio Yacht Club and often raced their wooden ketches out of Guanabara Bay into the open ocean, followed by toasting each other in the clubhouse bar.

After Huseby quit the newspaper, like many ex-*Herald* employees, she got hired at the Rio bureau of the Associated Press, where correspondent Bruce Handler taught her to write in terse, succinct AP style. "But I'd still go back to the *Herald* almost every evening after my shift at the AP was over," Huseby said. "It continued to be the biggest party in town."[40]

Even though she had grown up in Brazil, Huseby was still enchanted by the annual spectacle of Carnival in Rio. The four-day extravaganza of glitter and debauchery is a multi-sensory experience not easily forgotten. By the time Carnival comes around (in Portuguese, the word is spelled *carnaval* and literally means "farewell to flesh"), the oppressive summer heat and humidity gives way to a sanctioned week of nonstop revelry. "The air's been used by a thousand lungs," Huseby wrote in an impressionistic account for the *Herald*. "Slippery elbows slide against elbows and thighs and bellies and backs. And the blood pounding drums. Jostling *xu xu belleza* samba. And no one's tired until the music stops and then they push for another Brahma [beer] or another Guaraná [a soft drink packed with caffeine]."[41]

While Huseby was at the *Herald*, another reporter, Alison Raphael, wrote an assortment of fascinating take-outs on Brazilian culture, including a masterful four-part series on the historic origins of samba schools, *escolas da samba*, the clubs scattered throughout Brazil that vie to compete in street parades during Carnival.[42] Raphael's articles were, in reality, immersive, reader-friendly dissertations. She ultimately would receive a Ph.D. in the history of Latin America from Columbia University and become a UNICEF consultant.

As they had been for Teddy Hecht thirty years earlier, the Rio beaches were a draw for *Herald* staffers. Such was the case for Minnesota-born Liza Fourré, who recalled, "I became an absolute beach goddess. I went almost daily. I generally lived just a block or two away. I was as dark as many blacks."[43]

Fourré kept a diary of her activities while working at the *Herald*— her assignments, outings, joys, frustrations. Poring through her entries, as I was able to do, was akin to opening a time capsule. Here are some (with "——" to indicate names of anonymous *Herald* staffers):

Monday—Nice day, so went to the beach, then my first day at work. Of course, fucked up the bus connection. Worked with —— all day on layout. Nice guy!

Tuesday—Second day at work, and —— put me on coffee story. I don't believe it. I'm already supposed to be interviewing in Port[uguese]? The phones and noise are terrible. Worked again on layouts and heads. At least in English!

Wednesday—Worked at home on the coffee story. At least I can hear the phone at home! And then they gave me the drought story to do. I admire their confidence in me! Went to Ray Armando's Sextet concert with —— Party at ——. Brazilian men can be such babies. Took taxi home @ 3 a.m.

Thursday—Press conference with [Israeli physic] Uri Geller at 11. Went to the beach before work, didn't get in till 6:30. Finally got Concorde story done. Finished Doris Lessing's *The Summer After The Dark*. Rain like you wouldn't believe. Then floods. Traffic totally bottled up. Took 3 hours to get home!

Friday—Today was the big day to cover something in English. The Ambassador talked, but I sure still needed my Port[uguese]. What would I have done without [social editor] Rita [Davy]? Too bad he didn't say much worth writing about. We had a staff meeting about direction of the paper. Got 3 letters from home!

Saturday—Went to the beach all day with ——, —— , and ——. Played volleyball and played in the ocean really for the first time. The chicklets scene. Saw *Midnight Cowboy* with ——, then went to dinner at Esquilos in the forest—gorgeous! Started reading *Alive*. Good book!

Sunday—Made waffles. Maracaná! Super Flu-Fla game.[44] Went for pizza with ——, ——, and ——. Talked with ——, ——, and —— about the ERA.[45] Didn't get home till 6 a.m. What a week![46]

Fig. 16.1 Liza Fourré
at the beach in Rio de
Janeiro, 1978. Courtesy
of Liza Fourré.

Joining Fourré and Huseby at the *Herald* were Robin Lai and Elly
McGilly. Lai was a photographer; his girlfriend McGilly, a writer.
Born in Guyana of Chinese parents, Lai's father sold Linotype machines and relocated his family to Jamaica to sell printing equipment
to newspapers in the Caribbean. After high school, Lai moved to
Toronto, but hated the cold, so he and McGilly on a whim flew to
Rio. "I thought it was the most beautiful place in the world. We took
a bus to Copacabana, and I thought the wavy mosaic sidewalks were
amazing. We saw an old couple making out, really going at it, and I
kept on thinking, 'Wow, this is the place!'"[47]

One of McGilly's first assignments for the *Herald* was covering a
ballet at the Municipal Theater, and Lai came with her, toting a camera. Midway through the performance, McGilly nudged Lai to take
photographs. "I didn't have any press credentials, but that didn't make

any difference. I went up to the stage and started snapping away, and no one stopped me! That's how I started." Lai's photographs ran with McGilly's story in the *Herald*'s weekend edition. Soon, Lai had taken over the second-floor bathroom in the *Herald* newsroom and had converted it into his personal darkroom even though he never was on the newspaper's staff, and no one ever told him to vacate.[48]

By January 1973, the modern computer age of newspaper production began at the *Herald*. A refrigerator-sized typesetting compositor from Chicago had arrived at 65 Rua do Resende, heralding the newspaper's transition from hot-lead Linotype machines to cold type, which created paper strips of words to be photographed and then printed. Eric Hippeau and Janet Huseby breathlessly wrote about the transformation: "The plant foreman got himself a cleaner job, the proofreader had a clearer view of mistakes, the managing partner was rubbing his hands in expectation, the production manager had never worked so much in his life, the editor suddenly seemed very professional, the readers could actually decipher what they were reading, and the staffers stood in awe."[49]

With cold type came three keyboards, a six-foot-tall computer console, and spools of half-inch-wide yellow perforated tape that inched out of a slot. The Compugraphic program was bilingual, so for the first time, the *Herald* could be programmed to identify English words and break them into syllables that made sense. As Hippeau and Huseby noted, "This is of great relief to the faithful BH reader, who has long been annoyed by such sights as 'everythi – ng' or 't – hrough.'"[50]

With newspaper technology he could brag about, Bill Williamson had an extra bounce in his step as he made the rounds of advertisers, promoting the *Herald*'s sparkling innovation. Meanwhile, in an effort to monitor expenses more closely and improve the bottom line, publisher John Montgomery began giving more control of the family business to his only child, John Grey Montgomery. On occasion, the publisher's son would travel to Rio for a walkthrough at the *Herald*, a glance at the company's scrambled books, and a stop-off at the family's coffee plantation in Paraguay.

The younger Montgomery had gone to elite Andover for high school, followed by Yale, and an MBA from Stanford. He had worked for the San Francisco Newspaper Agency, the business entity that operated the joint operating agreement between the *San Francisco Chronicle* and the *San Francisco Examiner*. By 1973, he had returned to Junction City, Kansas, to manage the family business, which included the distant *Brazil Herald*. John Grey's name began appearing on the newspaper's masthead. To rein in the *Herald's* still-ballooning finances, the global accounting firm of Arthur Young, Clarkson, Gordon & Co. was hired in to produce annual audits of Editôra Mory.[51]

Bill Williamson and the younger Montgomery did not enjoy the same relationship that Williamson shared with the senior Montgomery. Williamson and John D. Montgomery were of the same age and cultural vintage. Both were natural raconteurs who thrived in the spotlight. John Grey, who was adopted, didn't seem to share the same exuberance that his father amply demonstrated. Once, when John Grey was scheduled to go to Rio, Williamson recalled that the senior Montgomery suggested with a chuckle that Williamson show John Grey a "good time."

On a previous trip, the senior Montgomery had traveled to Brazil with a Kansas trade delegation, and Williamson had arranged a catered event at the Copacabana Palace for ambassadors, consular officials, bankers, businessmen and anyone else interested in meeting the visiting Americans. Williamson mentioned the upcoming soiree to the *Herald*'s all-purpose man-about-town, nightlife editor André Fodor, the originator of the phantom Miss Estrangeira pageants, "who produced a few comely Brazilian gals," remembered Williamson.

As Williamson recalled, one of the politicians "disappeared with one of the girls upstairs and came back very impressed." On a subsequent trip by the junior Montgomery to Rio, John D. suggested to Williamson that he set up a similar liaison with the same woman for his son. Ever Montgomery's loyal man, Williamson leaned on Fodor to engage the woman's services.[52]

Fig. 16.2 John D. Montgomery celebrates the twentieth birthday of the *Brazil Herald* with Bill Williamson (*center*) and John Grey Montgomery (*right*). *Brazil Herald* arts critic Marc Berkowitz stands in the background to the *left* of John D. Montgomery. Courtesy of the Bill Williamson Collection.

On trips to Rio, John Grey Montgomery seldom met any of the *Herald* staff. He would recall meeting Herb Zschech once or twice, but as for other staffers he has no recollection. "My interest was always on the financial end, then sales, not editorial," the younger Montgomery would say. "While in Brazil, I probably spent too much time looking at the books and getting schmoozed by Bill [Williamson]."[53]

On the trips, the younger Montgomery took to sneaking into the nation suitcases filled with pieces of type or spare parts for press equipment. "Everything was greased with customs," he would remember. "Brazil had a high duty tax for such things, so I essentially was smuggling these things in. I was very uncomfortable with that. But that's how Brazil works. I used to deliver cases of scotch to customs personnel. It's the world of the *jeitinho*, [a social concept ingrained in Brazilian culture; literally "little way" in Portuguese, it means finding a solution by bending or circumventing rules using creativity or personal connections]."[54]

At the newspaper, after editor Eric Hippeau, who was a French citizen, got conscripted into the French Army, sent to Devil's Island in French Guyana and would within two years return to the Rio and the *Herald*, he came up with the visionary idea of a supplement focused on the then-dawning-age of personal computers. But with the younger Montgomery determined to stanch expenses, Williamson nixed Hippeau's idea as impractical and too costly. Williamson knew such an editorial foray would require an infusion of funds and would be an impossible sell to the Montgomerys in Kansas. Not to be rebuffed, Hippeau was sold enough on the concept to create the publication in Portuguese he called *Data News*. He quit the *Herald* and teamed up with staffers Don Best, Elizabeth Kussmaul, and John Thrall to launch the magazine themselves. For the first six issues, *Gazeta Mercantil*, Brazil's leading financial newspaper, printed *Data News*, and after that and a modicum of success, the four partners would sell their start-up to the US-based magazine *Computerworld*.

With Hippeau out as editor, Williamson hired former sports editor Walter Colton, who in turn hired Thrall's running partner, Bill Hall, as his second in command. When Colton left to work at the local AP bureau under correspondent Ed Miller, Hall took over as the *Herald*'s managing editor.

By the fall of 1977, former *Herald* staffer Liza Fourré wrote Hall, inquiring about returning to the newspaper from Minnesota. Fourré received this chill reply in all caps:

It was good to get your letter and even better to be able to write back and say that I can hire you. I will be able to pay you cr$4,000.00 [about $300] a month. What you will be responsible for it still kind of vague (another Cuba Libre will help clarify matters somewhat). But never fear, I will work your tail off. Basically I need you to do "By nights" and "Brasilia" as a daily chore and staff writer on the side. (You pick the side). I have told

Willy [presumably Bill Williamson] you will arrive here around Nov. 1 and he says OK. The staff at the moment is almost non-existant [sic], with myself as editor, Laura [Reid] as assistant, a guy named Tom Murphy on Page 5. . . .The proofreaders are two and a half—two full timers plus what ever I can get out of Chris Phillips and that's it. I do the paper and the rest cheer. Anyway when you get here things will be much clearer than this letter. (I hope.). . . .

One thing I must be clear before you come. I will pay you the above mentioned amount but I have no idea when or if you will get more. I don't wish to sound as if I'm some kind of Scrooge but I don't make the pay policies around here.

So, if this letter hasn't turned you off completely, come a run-nin'. . . . I'll put your nose to the grindstone. If you like (or at least accept) the deal let me know so I can make plans for you. (Have another beer, Hall)"[55]

In the letter, Hall asked Fourré to buy for him a Mickey Mouse wristwatch and bring it with her to Brazil. She did, and when I would work at the combined *Herald* and *Daily Post* four years later, Hall proudly wore it, a symbol, it seemed, of how he viewed the newspaper.

Meanwhile, Hippeau's success at launching *Data News* had convinced several *Herald* staffers to consider starting their own English-language newspaper that would compete with the *Herald*. "Professionally this could be where there is a good future," Fourré wrote to her parents. "Or damn good experience that I'd never get at home. Right now I would say that a lot depends on this business of starting a paper. 4 of us have had one meeting and decided it would be feasible, and are doing a little more practical research—how much capital do we need and is it available. We are talking on the scale of something like the European Herald Tribune here in Brazil. If Brazil could support such a venture I sure as hell would like to be one of the founding fathers. How exciting. . . .We are checking it out. . . . We just need people with lots of capital."[56]

That dream enterprise never went anywhere, but was identical to John D. Montgomery's vision back in the late-1940s when he bought the *Herald*, as well as to Mauro Salles's and Steve Yolen's intention when the pair would launch the *Latin America Daily Post* and I would join the newspaper.

Laid-back Bill Hall's hands-off style had erased much of uber-editor Hippeau's innovations at the *Herald*. Cowboy-boot, western-shirt-open-to-mid-chest-wearing Hall and his now-girlfriend Laura Reid were running the newspaper more as a personal sideshow than as anything close to a comprehensive chronicle serving Brazil's expat community. "One day they arrived a little late with Bill explaining loudly that the delay was due to the number of times they had had sex that morning," Brian Nicholson, another expat at the *Herald*, would recall. A second bragging right for Hall seemed to be the number of bar fights he'd been in and the quantity of alcohol he had consumed before and after each. Reporter Jim Bruce recalled that Hall "left his calling card in the form of fist-smashed restroom doors in Rio's honky-tonks and bars if they somehow roused his displeasure."[57]

The *Herald* slid back into a rote operation rather than one of fanciful aspiration that Hippeau, Marchant, and Colton had tried to create. The newspaper had turned into a print variation of radio and television rip-and-read news.

"The *Herald*'s editorial priorities were simple, and depressingly transparent: just fill in the space between the ads with UPI and AP wire copy, and go for a beer," recalled Nicholson. The newspaper's daily menu showcased little variety: "U.S. politics, business and overseas warmongering were top priority, with U.S. sports a close second," followed by a dose of society news, complemented by an excess of photographs of stuffed-shirted ambassadors and their evening gown-clad wives frequenting the local party circuit.[58]

Nicholson was made a news editor/reporter/page designer. Among the Brit's duties was deleting the British "u," transposing "e" and "r" from words in news stories originating from the UK, as well as inserting "c" for "s," adding the period from Mr. and Mrs., flipping ". with

.", and substituting while for whilst and program for programme to follow the newspaper's American convention.

Motivated by the opportunity that anything he wrote would get published, Nicholson came up with the idea of a Sunday column reviewing US and British vinyl. He titled the feature "Bend Down Low" from a track on Bob Marley's 1974 album, *Natty Dread*, and gave the column the equally obscure byline of Felix Krull, expropriated from an unfinished 1954 Thomas Mann novel.[59] As word circulated to local record distributors of the *Herald*'s new column, vinyl came pouring into the newspaper office and Nicholson was able to build what would become one of the largest record collections in Rio. He also got to interview dozens of musicians riffing through Rio, including the Beatles' George Harrison.

Armed with a master's degree in economics from Scotland's Dundee University, Nicholson had arrived in Brazil in 1976 and rented a room at a former coffee plantation on the outskirts of Rio. Aided by some killer weed, at midnight on his thirtieth birthday, under a canopy of lucent Southern Hemispheric stars while frogs croaked and fireflies flickered with two stray dogs leading the way, Nicholson in a Carlos Castaneda-Don Juan epiphany realized it was a propitious time to figure out what he wanted to do with the rest his life, so why not journalism? Nicholson's only connection with the profession had been reading the British satirical magazine *Private Eye* and hanging out at a Fleet Street bar in London called El Vino. Journalists were cool and rakish and always got the girl in the end. He could do worse, Nicholson mused.[60]

The next week, he walked into the *Herald* offices, met editor Bill Hall, and got hired as a proofreader. The meager salary that came with the job didn't bother Nicholson. Actually, it was part of the attraction.

Nicholson lived a couple of blocks from the newspaper. He survived on one meal a day. "I was working in a real newsroom straight out of a Hitchcock set, with grubby dark-wood tables and decrepit typewriters under high-slung ceiling fans. And there were real tele-type machines! Hot and noisy, shaking and shuddering and smelling of sewing-machine oil, they hammered out a non-stop stream of distant earthquakes, sports results, plane crashes, coup d'états and election results at sixty words per minute, day and night, printing all caps onto jumbo rolls of eight-inch-wide telex paper."[61]

While many at the *Herald* may have been driftless, the expat newspaper still was the same draw it always had been for journalists hellbent on making a name for themselves far away from home. Among the reporters who joined the staff during this era was Jim Brooke, who had graduated from Yale, worked as a desk assistant for famed *New York Times* Washington columnist James "Scotty" Reston, and would go on to work in Rio for the *Miami Herald*, then as a correspondent for the *Times*, a role he had coveted since childhood. Curly-haired Brooke always was angling, whether for a better desk, assignment, or girlfriend, ultimately becoming a *Times*, then Bloomberg, correspondent in Africa, Canada, Tokyo, and Moscow.

Another editor who joined the *Herald* during one of Bill Williamson's periodic efforts at taming the newspaper was Ramez Maluf, the staffer who had joined and quit the cell of would-be urban guerrillas. Maluf hadn't been a journalist but was literate and smart. Like *Herald* editors before him, he was an adept multi-linguist. Born in a São Paulo suburb near Guarulhos airport, Maluf attended elementary school in Brazil, but when he was twelve his parents moved to Lebanon, where Maluf picked up enough English at an international school to get accepted at Duke University as an undergraduate. Back in São Paulo at a snoozer of a job in a travel agency, Maluf read a seemingly urgent ad Williamson had placed in the *Herald* to find a new managing editor. Maluf knew next to nothing about journalism, with the exception of having written several letters to the editor at the Duke student newspaper.

Maluf called Williamson, who, after a quick phone interview, offered him the top job with one proviso: Maluf would have to get to

Fig. 16.3 *Brazil Herald*'s Ramez Maluf (*left*) and Bill Williamson. Courtesy of the Bill Williamson Collection.

Rio and the *Herald* offices within twenty-four hours to put out the next day's paper.

Maluf had two stints as managing editor, one in 1971–72 and the other in 1973–74. It was during the second round that he made a particularly noteworthy hire: Harold Emert, a nerdy oboe player who would turn out to be as trademark a *Herald* columnist as now-septuagenarian Herb Zschech. Emert, the oldest of five sons of a Jewish New York City police detective, was a winsome but neurotic combination of Rodney Dangerfield, Peter Sellers, and Woody Allen. With Emert on the staff, the *Herald* would never be quite the same.

CHAPTER 17

"Just Put Your Lips Together and Blow"

ONE RARE SUNDAY afternoon when Ramez Maluf wasn't on deadline, (the *Herald* published a combined Sunday–Monday issue on Saturdays, which left the newsroom idle on Sundays), he took in a matinee at the Roxie Theater in Copacabana. Maluf was frazzled from the top editorial job at the *Herald*. Even though this was his second go-around as managing editor, he was exhausted from the sixteen-hour days he was putting in for next to nothing. The editorial staff he had inherited was more interested in drinking Cuba Libres than in writing headlines (actually, they did both simultaneously but were better at the former than the latter). Putting out any newspaper, but especially this one, required a prestidigitator's sleight of hand to pull a rabbit out of a hat daily. One day, it could be two or three typesetters showing up inebriated, or not at all; another day, a customs official holding up a shipload of newsprint because no one had remembered that tomorrow was his "birthday." It also could be the clacking wire machine, the *Herald*'s only sure-fire supplier of copy, suddenly silenced by an electrical outage planned or unplanned, which handyman Igor Tsvik could not coax back to life. Maluf had the same nightmare all newspaper editors have: What happens if one day there is no news to print?

Also waiting in the Roxie lobby to go into the darkened movie theater that Sunday happened to be a thirty-one-year-old American. The two men struck up a conversation. The American, Harold Emert, seemed overjoyed at meeting a fellow English speaker. Emert had been in Brazil for just three months and harbored crushing doubts about his decision to launch a full-time musical career there. On top of whether he'd made the right move, there was the daunting issue of Portuguese: *No one* seemed to speak English in Rio. Emert was lost. No matter how much he studied and practiced, whenever he opened his mouth, locals either stared wide-eyed or dismissed him outright, often both. How was he ever going to succeed as even a mediocre speaker of the local tongue?

The first thing Maluf noticed about slight, dark-haired Emert was his impenetrable accent. Emert spoke English, yes, but an English Maluf had never heard before. Emert's New York accent was so thick that to Maluf it seemed a put-on, as though Emert was using it as both armor and armament to proclaim where he was from and that you "bettah not forget it cuz New Yourk's da greatest city in da whole world!" Maluf, who spoke elegant, precise, and flawless English, had a difficult time understanding Emert. He leaned closer, several times asking Emert to repeat himself.

Fig. 17.1 *Brazil Herald* columnist Harold Emert (2007 painting of Emert circa 1974, by Ana Maria Emert). Used with permission from Ana Maria Emert.

From what Maluf could piece together, Emert played oboe with the Brazilian Symphony Orchestra. That intrigued Maluf; he'd never met a professional oboe player before. But what Emert said next made Maluf do a doubletake: Emert's first love wasn't music but newspapers.

Emert had grown up in a brick-tower rent-controlled housing project in Lower Manhattan in a postwar, Jewish-American household: mezuzah on the doorjamb; Shabbos candles and challah Friday nights; racing his four brothers to find the afikomen on Passover; Sunday dinners of Chinese food after visiting grandparents who owned a penny candy store around the corner on Hester Street.[1] The son of a New York City cop who liked to sing Broadway show tunes and Yiddish melodies, Emert had played saxophone for the Henry Street Settlement Music School as a youngster. A Jewish police officer was unusual among the city's army of tough Irish cops, and as a way to show his mettle, Harold's father, Fred, took up boxing. He played tennis, baseball and swam as often as he could; he also would become president of the local synagogue. Emert's mother, Edith, a housewife and mother pulled in all directions by five headstrong sons, was the family's Shabbos queen and hard-knocks referee. Fred and Eadie, as she was called, met as students at Seward Park High School on New York's Lower East Side.

Fred Emert used his far-flung police-department connections to get Harold a summer job as a copyboy at the Hearst tabloid, the *New York Daily Mirror*, during its final heydays. Through cigarette and cigar haze, banging typewriter carriages, and insistent shouts of "Copy!" young Emert sprinted around the legendary newsroom delivering the latest dispatches from labor writer Victor Riesel (who'd been blinded when a mobster threw acid in his face; subsequently, Emert's police officer father had been assigned to protect Riesel), Walter Winchell (whose radio sign-on was, "Good evening, Mr. and Mrs. America, and all the ships at sea!"), columnist Nick Kenny (who had a piano in his office), and Bill Slocum (who knew everyone and everything; his column was titled "Bill Slocum Everywhere"). Another scribe at the newspaper was Ring Lardner Jr., son of the sports writer and short-story writer, and a member of the "Hollywood Ten," screenwriters blacklisted by motion picture studios. An up-and-coming reporter at the *Mirror* was Larry Van Gelder, who went onto a storied career at *The New York Times.*

Emert's pugilist father wanted his eldest son to attend law school and become a Manhattan district attorney. Harold had other ideas. He liked music and was good at it. Fred assented, as long as the instrument Harold played wasn't the drums or the tuba. Too noisy in the crowded apartment shared by seven family members with each of the Emert boys playing musical instruments. In addition to the saxophone, Emert played the clarinet, but ultimately chose the double-reed oboe as a way to get away from the apartment's unremitting commotion, but also as a singular way to draw attention to himself.

Emert graduated from New York's famed High School of Music and Art, known as the "Castle on the Hill" in the Hamilton Heights section of Harlem, then earned a degree in music from Queens College. While a graduate student at the Manhattan School of Music, he returned to the world of newspapers with another job as a night copyboy, this time at the *Herald Tribune,* just before reporters and editors would go out on a crippling four-month-long strike. Stars at the *Herald Tribune* included writer-extraordinaire Gay Talese, drama critic Walter Kerr, music reviewer Alan Rich, and the generation's defining magazine editor, Clay Felker.

One weekend Emert happened onto performance artist Louis Abolafia on a hunger strike (Abolafia would become a perennial presidential candidate for the Nudist Party and become involved in a publicized romance with Canada's former first lady, Margaret Trudeau). Emert interviewed Abolafia, and, back at the *Herald Tribune* newsroom, two-finger typed a story, dropped it into the city editor's wire basket, and the next day, read his feature in the newspaper.

Transfixed by the euphoria of getting published, Emert applied to the graduate school of journalism school at Columbia University, but when he was put on the waiting list, he took a reporting gig at the *Ithaca Journal,* a job Van Gelder helped him get.[2]

Emert lasted six months. If your idols were Manhattan word slingers Jimmy Breslin and Pete Hamill, it wasn't easy transforming mundane happenings along Ithaca's Tioga Street into Broadway drama. Emert wrote a whimsical piece in the form of a memo to his editor about tailing Cornell students painting everything green for an annual celebration called Dragon Day. He warned motorists about the coming perils of newly installed traffic radar. He traveled with the Ithaca College choir to write a month-long diary about the club's tour in Europe. He covered the Kiwanis Club, a Vietnam War protest, and the demolition of a century-old fire station.[3] Like another newsman before him, A. J. Lamoureux, Emert's reasoned conclusion was that it would take him a very long time, if ever, to make the life he envisioned for himself as a journalist in quaint upstate Ithaca.

Emert's life was to pivot when a rabbi from Flushing, New York, told him it would be a sin not to fully develop his natural talent, and Emert thereafter decided to go into music full time, focusing on the impossible-to-master woodwind instrument, the oboe, even though his dream job had always been to become music critic for *The New York Times* or *New York Herald Tribune*, "and go to concerts every night for free."[4] He would go on to playing for orchestras in Johannesburg, South Africa, and Saarbrücken, Germany, as well as with Zubin Mehta for the Israel Philharmonic Orchestra on a tour of Europe. He studied under the Swiss virtuoso Heinz Holliger, among the world's most prominent oboists. In 1973, Emert accepted an offer to become the first oboist for the Brazilian Symphony Orchestra in Rio de Janeiro.

At the Roxie that Sunday, talking with *Herald* editor Maluf, Emert felt his heart sing while waxing about his glory days as an aspiring New York City journalist. Maluf offered Emert a job on the spot.

Emert showed up at the *Herald* the next day for his first assignment: covering the Royal Winnipeg Ballet Company's weekend performance at the Municipal Theater. That started two decades of writing thousands of columns for the *Herald* and later for the *Latin America Daily Post*, where I would meet him, about music, films, food, politics, theater, art, really anything, in a column that carried the headline "Inside Cidade Maravilhosa."[5]

"Once Emert took the job, he was all in. Completely. One-hundred percent," recalled editor Maluf.[6]

In a touch of irony, finally realizing his dream job as a newspaper music critic made Emert discover that he hated reviewing fellow musicians' performances. Years of practice, sleepless nights, untamable butterflies, endless tryouts, bitter disappointments—all of it savaged by the keystroke of capricious reviewer, who may have become a critic because he or she hadn't made it as a musician.

Emert's columns, usually written in the first person, gave the expat New Yorker an opportunity to share his multiple idiosyncrasies with readers, delighted to go along for the ride, even if it meant a series of wrong turns and near head-on collisions. Emert had a disjointed, haphazard way of walking, talking, and writing. Fortunately, the Manhattan native had never learned to drive an automobile. His raw copy was full of typos; Emert defended himself by saying he didn't have the patience to proofread his articles (he also could blame the Brazilian typesetters for errors that made it into the newspaper).

Emert's physical affect was the opposite of that of *Herald* managing partner, square-shouldered, stalwart Bill Williamson, who resembled the classic *Esquire* man. High-strung Emert had fine-boned musician's hands, his glasses were seemingly always crooked.

In 1977, Emert shared with *Herald* readers that he was about to get married to a Brazilian woman who was working at the American Consulate (in a similar manner to how Williamson met his wife, Vânia). In the column, Emert described their courtship:

The love affair got off to a typical Carioca start: he asked her out, she said yes and never showed up. Afterward she explained that following the native manner she was trying to be *simpática* when she said *sim*. A good Carioca girl supposedly doesn't *sair* [go out] with just anyone without knowing him well!

The next time he saw her, she tried to hide behind her secretarial desk, but it was too late to escape destiny. . . .

In the world from which he came, the family of the girl one was courting was to be avoided at all costs until the *último momento*. But this was Cidade Maravilhosa and the family was, or seemed to be, everywhere. In fact, after a while, he had the strangest sensation of even liking them. The jazz musician, the filmmaker-lawyer, the industrialist, the psychiatrist, the contact with this tight-knit bunch was somehow adding a new dimension to his life. . . .

What he really wanted was to keep the spirit, the *alegria* of CM [Cidade Maravilhosa] with him at all times. And that meant the *garota* [young girl] *de Copacabana* always near his side.[7]

In Yiddish, there's an oft-told and beloved distinction, sometimes subtle and incalculable, between two classic characters: the *schlemiel* and the *schlimazel*: A schlemiel is the guy who spills soup; a schlimazel is the guy he spills it on.[8] In almost every one of Emert's columns, he was to confront and confound both descriptions. His unabashed love for Rio turned the city into a *shidduch*, or matchmaker, for Emert's seemingly never-ending trials and tribulations. You couldn't help but like the writer after finishing one of his "am I really reading this?" columns.

Some examples:

While attending an art auction, Emert unwittingly raised his hand, the auctioneer's gavel came down, and Emert found himself the owner of a provocative painting of a nude Pelé, the world's late preeminent soccer star. This led to a series of interviews on Brazilian television, including the nation's version of *The Tonight Show*, with everyone asking Emert the same question: Why would anyone want a nude drawing of Pelé? Local paparazzi stalked Emert for weeks.[9]

In another column, sultry Brazilian movie star Sônia Braga, rumored at the time to be in a relationship with actor Robert Redford, was to be cast in a TV soap opera that called for her to play a musical instrument, initially the flute. Emert wrote the screenwriter, Carlos Eduardo Novaes, and recommended that Braga's instrument be changed to an oboe. During intermission at the Brazilian Symphony Orchestra, Braga and Novaes showed up and introduced themselves to Emert, who didn't waste any time and started Braga on her first lesson, showing her how she ought to hold the instrument and position her mouth around the mouthpiece. It was a replay of Lauren Bacall's directive to Humphrey Bogart in *To Have and Have Not*: "Just put your lips together and blow." Emert did all he could to tutor the actress in the nuances of the beloved mistress that had brought him to Brazil. That would have been the end of the story, except for a vintage Emert twist. When Braga's novela *Chega Mais* (Come Closer) aired in 1980, Emert was to discover that despite his instruction, the soundtrack of her oboe-playing was performed not by Emert but by another musician.[10]

A third *Herald* column Emert wrote libeled Frank Sinatra. At least, that's what Sinatra's longtime press agent Lee Solters charged. The Chairman of the Board had been scheduled to give a concert at Rio's colossal Maracanã stadium on January 26, 1980, and Emert tried the impossible: to get an interview with Sinatra. Emert was rebuffed at every turn. In a column that chronicled his multiple failed entreaties, which could have been headlined "My Way" or "I'm a Fool to Want You," Emert cast a snarky aside about what appeared to be a toupée that Sinatra had worn at the concert, which 175,000 people attended.[11] Sinatra flack Solters exploded at the accusation, telling Emert, "You'll never work again in this town!"[12] It made no difference whether or not Sinatra wore a rug. It was the back-and-forth contretemps over a thatch of hair atop the world's most famous singer's head that made Emert's column classic.[13]

Another column detailed how after several years in Rio happily married, Emert received a letter from a reader who confessed a wild crush on him. The married admirer revealed that she took to reading Emert's column while soaking in a bubble bath with a glass of wine.

Emert scheduled a lunch date at Café Lamas in the Flamengo section of Rio with the fan, whom he described as a blonde resembling "a cross between two Janes: Fonda and Mansfield." After their flirtatious meal concluded, the woman offered to give Emert a ride back to his apartment in Copacabana. Emert claimed loyalty to his wife, but simultaneously expressed wistful regret.[14]

In a third-person Walter Mittyesque column, Emert wrote about an oboe player who had handcrafted perfect reeds for the much-anticipated opening night of the symphony. The musician berated himself for not playing his solo performance during the second movement better. But all in all, it had been a triumphant, gratifying first-night showing—until an audience member approached him later in the evening.

"It was a wonderful concert tonight. Did you play?" she asked.[15]

Once in a while, Emert wrote a pointed political column, mimicking the stodgy journalism convention, "in this reporter's opinion," "your correspondent," "this observer," or "in my humble opinion" used by trailblazers of a previous generation such as Edward R. Murrow, David Brinkley, and Howard K. Smith. Outside the *Herald*, he would continue playing oboe, whittling the double reeds particular to the black instrument with silver keys, and composing musical scores, which would include the first act of an opera about British Train Robber Ronald Biggs called *Crime Doesn't Pay*, "Pesach Variations," "Love Song – Twice with Helena," "Diary of a Day," "Unemployed . . . but Overjoyed," and "I Live with a Cat." Emert was a creative genius, another talented expat wanderer who happened onto the *Herald*'s theatrical set to play a leading role in a host of ensuing dramas.

Williamson was alternately bemused or put off by Emert and yet another international trip the musician would finagle to combine oboe playing and column writing. Only to himself would Williamson admit to enjoying the neurotic fanfare that Emert had created in the pages of the *Herald*.

Going on two decades in Brazil, Williamson continued as managing partner at the *Herald* still with glee, mingling with prominent expats and locals alike, now more for his own pleasure than for the paper's bottom line, which seemed more often flat than upwards-diagonal no matter what gimmicks he came up with. By now, Williamson was thoroughly acclimated to Brazilian life. The Williamsons had two daughters and a son enrolled in Rio's private American School; they enjoyed hobnobbing with other expat parents at the school's Fourth of July picnics and opening-night student theater productions. Nearly every weekend Bill and Vânia sailed around Rio's Guanabara Bay and to the islands to the south, often inviting friends and select *Herald* staffers to join them.

Through the circuit of parties, cocktails hours (*coquetels*, pronounced cock-ee-tails in Portuguese), and celebratory dinners, Williamson stayed connected with whoever shared his sunny outlook. From Harold Emert's perch, the columnist-cum-musician would remember, "I can't recall one gruff, loud, or unkind word from Bill Williamson ever."[16] Williamson kept framed photographs of himself and an array of Brazilian presidents in his office. In 1975, he was named an honorary citizen of Guanabara, the federal state where Rio is located. In bestowing the award, which took place in the *Herald* newsroom when publisher John Montgomery and his wife were in town, along with eye-rolling members of the newspaper staff, deputy Darcey Rangle, first secretary of the legislative assembly, announced, "It is appropriate that Sr. Bill receive this title of citizen of the State of Guanabara today on the day the *Brazil Herald* completes its 29th year and prepares to enter its 30th serving this land." To no one's surprise, the event was amply covered in the *Herald* with photos of Williamson and Montgomery, alongside a birthday cake celebrating the newspaper's anniversary.[17]

Such back-slapping commendations went only so far. The financial and editorial limitations of the newspaper as set forth by the Montgomerys—along with the capped audience of readers and advertisers—were unlikely to change. Williamson's job, though, carried a low threshold. It was to make sure everything worked as well as it could. "Williamson exemplified the Southern gentleman, even though I knew he was from Iowa," former managing editor Ramez Maluf would recall. "He seemed to me to be a character out of *Gone with the Wind*. Always sharply dressed, always pleasant. But his lack of attention and direction was unfortunate. He found himself with not an awful lot to do."[18]

Outside of going from hot to cold type, Williamson did make one major innovation, and that was to transform the *Herald*'s revised tabloid format back to its original broadsheet origins to give the paper a more respectable presence, in keeping with serious US and Brazilian newspapers. The move was prompted by economics. As Williamson would recall, the transition to a larger format "increased the print area by using the blank tabloid gutters, as well as increasing ad space to advertisers who wanted larger areas on pages with news copy but not full pages. At the same time, we were able to increase editorial acreage."[19] Once again, Williamson was tooting the *Herald*'s horn even though the paper wasn't printing much that merited increasing its news hole.

For the moment, Williamson and the Montgomerys shrugged, accepting the *Herald* for what it was. The newspaper had a loyal-but-contained following, its circulation rarely going beyond ten thousand a day. The *Herald* had proven that it could maintain a niche in the local marketplace, even though it never realized much of a profit or sustained editorial competence beyond an offbeat columnist or two and an occasional exclusive that came its way through its front or back door. The newspaper seemed to maintain itself, and that seemed to satisfy (and at the same time, dissatisfy) just about everyone who picked up a copy, with the rejoinder, "Didja see what the *Herald* printed today?"

To no one's surprise, Montgomery was quietly on the lookout for a buyer. His son was more than ready to jettison the outlying newspaper property. Buttoned-down, efficiency-minded John Grey, increasingly skeptical about his father's fanciful Brazil investment, had little interest in maintaining the loss leader. He shared none of the Latin American brio that had seized his father when Ambassador William Pawley three decades earlier had dangled before the publishing hotshot from

Kansas and Miami the idea of taking over an ailing English-language newspaper tailored to expats.

By this time, Williamson has accumulated a third of the *Brazil Herald's* total shares, but as a minority shareholder in a private company, he would have to go along with whatever deal the Montgomerys would negotiate with a potential buyer.[20]

When faced with the possibility that his long-term sinecure may be taken away, in a September 13, 1976, letter to the senior Montgomery, Williamson suggested that "if an interesting offer materializes and you are seriously considering selling, I will of course sound some possible prospects at IAPA but I need to have some idea of what type of offer might be one you just 'couldn't refuse.'" As the Montgomerys' emissary, Williamson approached executives at Knight-Ridder Corporation, owners of the *Miami Herald*, logical prospective suitors, but they expressed no interest in buying the newspaper.[21]

On at least two occasions, local Brazilian executives contacted Williamson about purchasing the *Herald*. The first was in the mid-1970s, when Gilberto Huber Jr, a man who had made his fortune by printing Brazil's phone books and whose family had been involved as a vendor to the CIA-funded Brazilian Institute for Democratic Action in the early 1960s, got an audience with Williamson and Montgomery when the latter was in town.[22] Huber, an ex-marine like Williamson, had been born in Brazil to American parents. His father, Gilbert Jacob Huber Sr., had worked for the R. H. Donnelley Co. which published the Yellow Pages directories in the United States and other countries. Williamson recalled that Montgomery didn't like anything about the boastful, swaggering Huber and asked him to leave almost as soon as the meeting had begun. Williamson couldn't recall what it was that Huber had said or done. It was more a sense of chemistry. None existed between the two men.[23]

The second time was when a Brazilian advertising executive, who had once been a journalist for Rio's *O Globo* newspaper, invited Williamson and his wife to his São Paulo home for dinner. Little business was discussed, as is normal for such initial encounters.

Williamson transmitted Mauro Salles's interest to Montgomery back in Kansas, but it quickly seemed to have been forgotten.[24]

CHAPTER 18

Manic

MAURO SALLES, THE advertising and public relations executive who had sounded out Bill Williamson about buying (or buying into it) the *Brazil Herald*, came from a politically well-connected family. Salles's father had been agricultural minister under Brazilian dictator Getúlio Vargas, and Salles himself was a close associate of Tancredo Neves, a moderate Brazilian senator with presidential aspirations. Salles had ego and determination, two requisites for either a politician or publisher. He also had deep pockets. At least, that's what he led people to believe.

One of four sons born in the northeastern city of Recife, Salles graduated from Pontificate Catholic University of Rio de Janeiro and then got a job working in the Time-Life bureau in Rio as a photo assistant. That meant whenever *Life*'s world-famous photographers came to town, he had the enviable assignment of accompanying them on photo shoots. This included such legends as Philippe Halsman, Alfred Eisenstaedt, and Margaret Bourke-White. The Time-Life job led Salles to be named editor of a Brazilian version of *Life*, *O Mundo Illustrado* (the Illustrated World). Salles then moved to Rio's *Globo* newspaper, where he was a photographer, reporter, and editor. For a time, he was the newspaper's automotive editor, which allowed him to tool around town behind the wheel of the year's swankiest models. In 1965, Salles was named director of programming at what would become Brazil's largest television network, TV Globo, once a sleepy local network owned by Time Inc., which by the time I arrived in Brazil had turned into the fourth largest commercial television network in the world.

Salles left the TV network to start his own eponymous PR company, Mauro Salles Publicidade, and after merging with another firm, the business became known as Salles/Inter-Americana de Publicidade S.A., Brazil's third-largest advertising agency and thus one of the leading ad agencies in Latin America.

Slight and impish, brainy and manic, Salles never stopped hustling. He was impulsive and unpredictable, seemingly unable to focus for any sustained period of time. He hopped from project to project with childlike delight. He had a textbook case of attention-deficit disorder.

At forty-six, Salles got an opportunity that played to his wired personality. Executives at an ailing chain of Brazilian newspapers, magazines, and TV stations, Diários e Emissoras Associadas, hired him as a vice president to come up with creative ideas to save the multimedia company from going bankrupt. One of several ideas was to start an English-language newspaper in Brazil.

By creating a new publication printed in English, Diários Associadas, as it was known, would not only be able to utilize the company's existing infrastructure (newsprint, printing presses, Linotype machines, advertisers, subscribers, skilled employees, newsstand and home-distribution channels), but it also might be able to create a new revenue stream from a high-end demographic the Brazilian media company had never specifically courted. On paper, it seemed like a smart business model that might deliver an infusion of revenue.

Salles's idea was to establish a brand-new publication under the umbrella of a well-regarded media company and use it as an add-on to Diários's array of multimedia offerings. The *Brazil Herald*, the nation's only regularly published, non-specialty English-language newspaper, was not seen as competition to the imaged publication. It was viewed as an also-ran beneath the dignity of one-time powerhouse Diários Associadas.

To jumpstart his newspaper idea, Salles hired American-born advertising executive John Hills Garner, who had worked in Brazil for Kaiser Industries and Willys Overland (later acquired by Jeep, then Ford). Garner had grown up in Ashtabula, Ohio, midway between

Cleveland and Erie, Pennsylvania, and after studying journalism at Ohio State, had moved to Brazil to work in publicity for a succession of automotive manufacturers. Like Teddy Hecht, he was an avid equestrian, active in the São Paulo Sociedade Hípica Paulista.[1] Garner was to be Salles's point man on the prospective English-language newspaper project.

Along with Garner, Salles brought on another consultant, Brazilian public-relations executive Francisco Crespa. Because neither Garner nor Crespa knew much about the newspaper business, Salles approached Ed Miller, the AP bureau chief for Brazil who had tangled with former US Ambassador Lincoln Gordon (and with Hunter S. Thompson on an earlier occasion), about the possibility of launching the yet-to-be-named English-language newspaper as its executive editor.

Miller rejected the idea as impractical and overly ambitious. "The distribution problems of a paper published daily in Brazil for all of Latin America would be huge, unlike Europe where the distances were not as great and the flights and train schedules more frequent," Miller would remember. "Salles didn't think that would be much of an obstacle. We talked about a lot of things, including editorial content and advertising (definitely not my expertise). But it just wasn't in the cards for me, and I told him so."[2]

Bowing out, Miller recommended Steve Yolen, a former UPI reporter with more than a decade-and-a-half of news experience in the Caribbean and Latin America. Yolen had covered the 1965 Dominican Republic's civil war, worked for UPI in Buenos Aires and in São Paulo, and had reported Chilean President Salvador Allende's overthrow in September 1973 while dodging bullets flying through the windows of UPI's office in Santiago.[3] Yolen was a genuine newsman; he knew practically everything there was to know about journalism—except how to start a publication from scratch.

Yolen had left UPI and, more recently, Fairchild Publications in São Paulo, a New York-based company of industry magazines and newsletters. Yolen met Salles emissaries Garner and Crespa in late 1977 and accepted their offer to become the project's third consultant, even though he had yet to meet Salles. "Garner became executive director of the project, responsible for administrative and commercial details and as the primary contact with Salles; Crespa was to produce the sales and marketing plan; and Yolen would oversee the newspaper's editorial side.

Yolen's first item of business was to come up with a prototype of the newspaper, which he did and presented it to the board of Diários Associadas. "The executives adored the idea," Yolen would recall. "The green light was given on the spot. We had low-cost access to in-house printing, layout, paste-up, typesetting, circulation, technological and physical facilities that would allow us to bring the project on-stream quickly. Nothing could go wrong," was how ever-optimistic Yolen saw it.[4]

Four months into the job, Salles and executives at Diarios Associados had a falling out and Salles abruptly quit. That left Garner and Yolen (Crespa had left as quickly as he'd been hired) with just an idea, sketches, and page dummies for a newspaper. Both men were still intrigued by the prospect of a pan-Latin America English-language newspaper, but neither had the connections or financial resources to see to fruition such a bold undertaking.

Not ready to throw in their cards, Garner and Yolen hatched a plan. They'd play to Salles's ego. They'd try to convince him to pull off the concept of the English-language newspaper independent of Diarios Associados. If Salles didn't have the financial wherewithal on his own, he surely had access to it, they figured. "He was a politically connected and deep-pocketed individual, owner of a very prosperous advertising agency in the largest advertising market in the Western Hemisphere after the U.S. He could do it if he wanted to," Yolen recalled.

The more Garner and Yolen thought about Salles alone heading up the project, the more they liked the idea. The two Americans wouldn't be putting any of their own money into the prototype, and working outside the limitations of an ailing media company controlled by a board of directors appealed to them. Garner and Yolen would only have to sell Salles, not the board of a tanking communications conglomerate. Diarios Associados had already vetted the newspaper proposal and had endorsed it. Salles could rest assured that the project made sense.

Salles was a cagey, irrepressible, 24/7 salesman. He liked to keep potential suitors guessing. He enjoyed a reputation as unpredictable and slightly off-kilter, an original thinker. "It was very hard to pin Salles down, mainly because he was never in his office for more than a few minutes a week," remembered Yolen. "He was in constant motion." Salles also was notedly absent-minded. "His secretary Juliana was brilliant in juggling his schedules and there was no telling where he might be at any given hour. Actually, one of her main duties was to discreetly tell Mauro that his fly was unzipped. He habitually forgot to zip up his pants when in public places, like walking around his agency or at meetings and events. Everyone in the agency was alerted to warn him. He was a brilliant ad man and could pitch any product. He was short and pixie-like, a captivating storyteller, always flitting around when working a room, and he was a real closer."

As Yolen would recall, "Salles had to convince Mauro's brother, Luiz Sales, who was the administrative and financial director of the family ad agency, to go along with the idea and co-authorize funding the newspaper.[5] It seemed to us that Luiz Sales's main function was to keep Mauro's grandiose schemes within the realm of reality, playing bad cop to his brother's open-handed nature and rapid-fire ability to dream up outsized and costly projects that had little to do with the advertising business. Luiz was lukewarm about the idea but at least he didn't kill it." As a first step, the Salleses opened their advertising agency's boardroom to Garner and Yolen so the pair could work on the newspaper prototype. That worked until anyone at the agency needed to use the boardroom, and Garner and Yolen had to pack up page dummies and mock-up newspapers and vacate at a moment's notice.

As the project inched forward, the imagined newspaper under Salles's titular direction wasn't perceived as competing against the *Brazil Herald*. That the still-unnamed publication would also be an

English-language newspaper didn't seem to worry Salles, Yolen, or Garner. The two newspapers would occupy very different niches. Even though the *Herald* proclaimed that it was distributed daily throughout Brazil, its availability was limited. The *Herald* reliably circulated on a same-day basis only in Rio, and occasionally in São Paulo. There also was the matter of the *Herald*'s Rio-centric focus. By the mid-1960s, the business locus of not just Brazil but all of South America had decisively shifted to São Paulo, where the Salles newspaper would be based. With government functions having moved to the capital of Brasília, Rio no longer was the seat of the federal government's infrastructure or bureaucracy. While Rio still retained much of its glitter, it increasingly seemed to showcase the past, not the future. Rampant crime began to taint Rio's image as a vaunted destination for tourists, as well as for international investment.

The new publication would be business-centric, offering same-day delivery and circulation in every South American capital city. It would also carry its own editorials, a feature the *Herald* generally avoided. The Salles-Garner-Yolen newspaper would hire staff correspondents in the capitals of Latin American countries, as well as in Washington, DC. It would be a serious, comprehensive, and influential newspaper that would rival the Paris-based *International Herald Tribune*.

For Yolen, who had spent his entire career in Latin America chasing earthquakes, coups, currency devaluations, and title soccer matches—and didn't foresee returning to the States—grand journalism opportunities like this didn't come by often. When it came to choosing a name for the pilot newspaper, Yolen researched dozens of titles before settling on the *Latin America Daily Post*, "which seemed to contain all of the elements we needed," he reflected. Yolen and Garner, both detail-obsessed, spent weeks debating whether the title should be "Latin American" or "Latin America," ultimately deciding that "America" had a subtler and more elegant ring to it.[6]

A graphic artist at Salles Interamericana came up with the *Latin America Daily Post*'s page design, modeled unabashedly on the *International Herald Tribune*, at the time owned by The New York

Times Co. The *Daily Post*'s nameplate, or mast, would be a variation of the classic gothic type that the *International Herald Tribune* used, with lighter shades of Cheltenham font to make the title seem more modern. The words "Latin America" would be uppercase in a sans-serif typeface, above a small, circular graphic of the iconic statue at the entrance to São Paulo's central Ibirapuera Park, the *Monumento às Bandeiras*, a 1954 memorial of settlers on horseback.[7] "Daily Post" would be in a larger point-size on a second line, each word on either side of the monument's rendering. The reasoning behind using the recognizable statue as part of the newspaper mast was Salles's idea—to identify the *Daily Post* as a São Paulo-based newspaper. Centered under the newspaper's nameplate was the slogan, "Latin America's Only Multi-National Newspaper," an epithet Yolen came up with. Whether or not the team had considered the *Brazil Herald* its competition, the slogan anchoring the new newspaper would triumphantly go beyond the motto that had underscored the *Herald* since its first issue, "Brazil's Only English Language Daily."[8]

Some saw the *Daily Post*'s mast and layout as too derivative, neither sufficiently original nor distinctive. But to Yolen's way of thinking, why not follow the examplar of the respected and well-known *International Herald Tribune*? If readers were ever to confuse the two, that wouldn't be so bad.

The *Daily Post* would be a serious, professional, *newsy* newspaper, whereas to Yolen the *Brazil Herald* was amateur hour. Yolen had no connection with the *Brazil Herald* and had no allegiance to Williamson, anyone on the staff, or majority-owner Montgomery and his son. He rarely read the paper and when he did he digested it in minutes.

Word circulated quickly, as it always does in journalism circles, of the potential arrival of a new newspaper. In a letter *Herald* journalist Mark Gruberg wrote to fellow reporter Liza Fourré about slipping ad revenue. Gruberg wrote, "I'm wondering if that's not an omen. With the [Daily] *Post* to start up, the *Herald*'s prospects never seemed so dim. Williamson seems determined to try to stick it out—as determined as he gets, anyway."[9]

Beyond any commercial or editorial advantage Salles, Garner, and Yolen believed the *Daily Post* would have over the ailing *Herald*, what lurked in the background of their brainstorming sessions was something the trio never discussed, as Yolen would remember. It would be a card that Salles could play at any moment.

The team's ace in the hole was that the *Brazil Herald* was majority-owned by a non-Brazilian, John Montgomery, and managed locally by his manager, Bill Williamson, also an American, although Williamson was to become a naturalized Brazilian in the fall of 1979.[10] The name George H. Newman on the *Herald*'s masthead for three decades was a figurehead to ostensibly show that the newspaper was under the direction of a Brazilian citizen, even though Newman had no actual connection to the *Herald* except for a tiny financial interest. In two decades, Bill Williamson had never met Newman.

These irrefutable facts could box the *Herald* into a fatal corner, both politically and legally. Under Brazilian law, a newspaper published in Brazil had to be owned by a Brazilian or group of Brazilians; no foreigners were permitted to head any Brazilian media firm. This was a technicality that somehow Montgomery and Williamson had successfully evaded. If there ever were a showdown between the two newspapers, Salles could raise the *Herald*'s de facto foreign ownership to his advantage.

The *Latin America Daily Post* would be one-hundred-precent Brazilian-owned. Yolen's name wouldn't appear on the masthead, and he would have no financial interest in the newspaper. Salles would call his new publishing company, São Marcelo de Publicações, which, while sounding thoroughly Brazilian, came out of whole cloth with no real meaning or attachment. The point was to make sure the new *Latin America Daily Post*, while published in English, would resonate as a wholly Brazilian-owned enterprise.[11]

Soon, Garner and Yolen and their burgeoning newspaper project needed an office outside of Salles's otherwise occupied boardroom. Their idea was to locate the physical presence of the still-unpublished daily inside a São Paulo newspaper building, to rent press time from that newspaper to publish the new broadsheet, and to piggyback the *Latin America Daily Post* on the local newspaper's printing and circulation infrastructure. They did all that at the *Folha de São Paulo*, a well-regarded São Paulo daily, second in prestige and circulation to *O Estado de São Paulo*.[12] Yolen had stationery and business cards printed with the *Daily Post*'s logo and address on them, and he hired a secretary.

Next, Yolen began assembling an editorial staff, first poaching newsman Stan Lehman from the local UPI bureau. Born in New York but raised in Venezuela, Lehman had been a Peace Corps volunteer, worked for the English-language *Daily Journal* in Caracas, and had covered Rio and Buenos Aires for UPI. Like Mark Gruberg, he had also been a cabbie in Manhattan. Lehman was married to a Brazilian, had a child on the way, and was a permanent resident of Brazil. Like Yolen, he wanted in on what might turn into a once-in-a-lifetime opportunity.[13] It would be Lehman and Yolen working together who would produce the newspaper's pilot issue, using UPI copy as placeholder-news items. Once just a dream, the new newspaper was turning into a reality.

Garner hired a designer, Constantino K. Korovaeff, along with an ad salesman, Diki Schertel, and on September 21, 1978, the first promotional edition of the *Latin America Daily Post* rolled off the presses of *Folha de São Paulo*. Mid-December was set as the newspaper's launch. In the meantime, with hundreds of copies of the pilot issue in his suitcases, Mauro Salles flew to New York, Washington, DC, and Miami to introduce the *Latin America Daily Post* to assorted big-name global influencers.

If there was one thing Salles knew how to do, it was generating enthusiasm. Salles appeared before a curious audience at the National Press Club in Washington, DC, as well as at any assembly of newspaper or financial elites whose meetings he could wiggle his way into. He'd thrust a copy of the prototype into the hands of an unsuspecting bigwig and at that instant have the recipient's picture snapped by a trailing photographer on Salles's payroll. Salles convened meetings at the United Nations and International Monetary Fund. He crashed boardrooms, luncheons, and cocktail hours to sell anyone remotely or potentially interested in his new venture.

Back in Brazil with scores of photographs taken on Salles's northern sales excursion, Yolen and Lehman published a series of brochures and advertisements touting the coming of the new newspaper. One such mockup carried the banner headline, "Look Who's Reading the Latin America Daily Post" with, "Tycoons, Bankers, Presidents, Ministers, Diplomats, Magnates, Company Directors, Financiers" as a subhead. Pictured on the promotional front page was former US Secretary of State, Henry Kissinger, ogling the prototype, quoted as saying, "Why, this really looks like a very fine newspaper. It should do a great service to the Latin American cause." Others photographed in the mockup included Brazil's minister of finance, Mário Henrique Simonsen; Alejandro Orfila, the Argentine secretary general of the Organization of American States; Brasilinvest President Mário Garnero; Banco do Brasil President Karlos Rischbieter; US Treasury Secretary William Simon; and Sir Yue-Kong Pao, described in the broadsheet as "the world's leading shipbuilder.[14]

No longer able to ignore what was happening two-hundred-and-seventy miles away, down BR-116, the highway that connects Rio to São Paulo, Bill Williamson pounded out an unusual editorial, cagily welcoming the new newspaper. It was both congratulatory and cautionary. Reading between the lines, the imminent appearance of the Latin America Daily Post scared the bejesus out of Williamson, and by extension, Montgomery.

A new newspaper in English was reported to have a pilot edition circulating in São Paulo yesterday, with the announced intention of being Latin America's 'multi-regional' newspaper and beginning five-day-a-week circulation sometime within a couple of months. We extend it a warm welcome.

It is a most encouraging sign to know that Brazilian capital and local advertising executives—not always easy to convince of the importance of the English-language market—are taking increasing note of the community which the Brazil Herald has been serving faithfully here for nearly 33 years.

Many would-be competitors have come and gone since this newspaper began its continuous daily publication in early 1946 —the first in a foreign language to be founded in Brazil after World War II, when all non-Portuguese periodicals were prohibited. During some of the early years, times were not easy and the paper was kept alive only thanks to a few far-sighted and patriotic businesses and individuals, who saw a need to serve their community and their native and adopted countries.

But in its more than three decades, the Brazil Herald has steadily grown, to some extent accompanying this great country's development, on which it has always reported with enthusiasm. It has consistently tried to inform the English-language public both here and abroad [of] the positive results stemming from the industriousness of the nation's people, the vision of its many of its leaders and the contributions made by foreign capital and technology to Brazil's development. The spectacular advances of the country have been accompanied by a growth of the foreign community, both resident and transient. Another newspaper published here in today's 'World language' is one more proof of our own importance.

So we are the first to wish every success to any new colleague.[15]

At the same time, Williamson directed *Herald* staffer Brian Nicholson to write a financial-and-content analysis of the competition's pilot issue. The economics-trained vinyl-record music reviewer produced a thoughtful and detailed internal report titled "The Latin America Daily Post and the Brazil Herald—A comparison, some thoughts, and a statistical analysis." In his assessment, Nicholson noted, "The POST pilot was a very news-oriented paper, in that it carried virtually none of the 'human interest' and social materials which occupies a large amount of space in the HERALD." Under a section titled, "Reporters," Nicholson wrote, "This I think could be a serious problem, in that it could give the POST a real and important source that the HERALD does not have. . . . If the POST puts a full-time reporter, for example, just working among the foreign companies based in São Paulo providing features and company gossip then I think that could become a real threat."

In terms of advertising, Nicholson wrote:

I have heard rumors that the POST has already sold enough advertising to show a profit for the first six months, irrespective of sales.

It could well be true, but I would prefer to be optimistic and take it with a pinch of salt. I would guess that the true figures of the POST's financial situation are going to be a very closely-guarded secret and any noises coming out of São Paulo are obviously going to exude confidence. But Salles must have settled on some kind of break-even target. He could well have set a time limit for profitability—I have heard one year suggested. Whatever the situation, it is a fair bet that he is prepared to run at a loss for a good few months to establish his new paper. The implication here is that the HERALD may have to run at a loss to win against the POST. [16]

Meanwhile, news of the *Latin America Daily Post*'s debut was heralded through a series of well-timed press releases, as well as through any connections Salles, Yolen, Garner, and Lehman could muster. Syndicated *Chicago Tribune* business columnists Myron Kandel and Philip Greer hyperbolically wrote that the planned newspaper was "one of the most ambitious publishing projects outside the United States in recent years."[17] David F. Belnap, the Brazil correspondent for the *Los Angeles Times*, wrote a puff piece, wholly speculative. "The pilot issue admittedly resembled the *Herald Tribune* with its standard-size, eight-column format. To a lesser extent the *Post* hopes to occupy the kind of position in Latin America that the *Asian Wall Street Journal*, published in Hong Kong, seeks to hold in the Far East."[18]

Belnap's *Los Angeles Times* article was the one I came across in the upstairs breakroom while working as a waiter at Giovanni, which prompted me to write Steve Yolen and apply for a job.

With momentum mounting, Yolen hired Ed Taylor, a former Peace Corps volunteer and reporter for the *Miami News*, as the *Daily Post*'s full-time correspondent in Brasília. When that post was eliminated in a preemptive cost-cutting measure, Yolen appointed Taylor managing editor. To round out the staff, Yolen would poach Brian Nicholson from the *Herald*, the reporter who had written the assessment of both newspapers going head to head, as business editor; Margaret Grammer, a talented reporter who had worked in Buenos Aires; Karen Lowe, a deft writer from Virginia, married to Digby Solomon, the UPI correspondent in São Paulo who had taken Lehman's old slot; and Frank Braun, a Brazilian-born UCLA graduate. In Rio, Yolen would hire Tom Murphy and Richard Cole, two energetic reporters who'd been working for the *Herald*, along with a young Princeton graduate, Eduardo Gentil, from a prominent Brazilian-American family in São Paulo.[19]

Fig. 18.1 Tom Murphy in the *Brazil Herald* newsroom, 1978. Photograph by Liza Fourré.

News of the prospective competition made its way back to John D. Montgomery and his son in Kansas. On trips to oversee the *Herald*, John Grey Montgomery had come back appalled. He was a businessman, and as far as he was concerned, the reason to own a newspaper was to make money, a goal the *Herald* had fallen short of month after month. As the younger Montgomery recalled, "My dad was a PR guy. I took a more cynical look at how the business was run. I started looking at these numbers at the BH and they didn't make sense. I couldn't explain them. What I found was the automobile and the chauffeur that Bill Williamson used were trade-outs; in essence, they were being paid for by the newspaper. The furniture at his apartment was a trade-out from a department store advertiser. That was the same with the school he sent his children to. And even with the maids he used, they came from an agency that advertised in the *Herald*. A lot of Bill's perks were coming out of the business."

When John Grey told his father about these side deals, John D. expressed surprise, although he surely had known about all or some of them. "I started talking to my dad, and I said to him, 'Whenever you are ready to sell the paper, I'm ready.' He said, 'Fine, I'm ready.'"[20]

One prospective offer came from a Brazilian businessman who wanted to purchase the newspaper illegally in Swiss francs, a deal the Montgomerys outright refused.[21] A more successful transaction occurred when they negotiated a deal through John Garner to sell the *Herald* to Salles. The transaction amounted to 23,218,118 cruzeiros, a little over one million American dollars at the time.[22]

It was a reasonable offer, considering the *Herald*'s real-figures circulation, that the sale came years before the onset of the internet, and that at the time newspapers were still physical products made from expensive rolls of newsprint processed through large labor-intensive machinery whose final product had to be physically delivered to customers. The transaction came with the *Herald*'s rented physical building, its presses, staff, typesetting equipment, a host of contracts to print other publications, as well as a roster of advertisers and subscribers.

But Williamson was blindsided by the sale. The Montgomerys never mentioned they had been talking to Salles's lieutenants. When informed of the deal to which the Montgomerys had already agreed, Williamson, a minority owner of shares, had no choice but to agree. Ever optimistic, Williamson initially was enthusiastic about the change of ownership, saying, "Salles had one foot in the Brazilian advertising world and the *Herald* had another foot in the newspaper world. I thought it could turn into a terrific partnership." Such a synergistic axis might benefit both men, as well as the combined newspapers' bottom line, Williamson optimistically imagined.

Fig. 18.2 Bill Williamson (*left*) and Mauro Salles. Courtesy of the Bill Williamson Collection.

On the day before the deal was announced publicly, Williamson, in a classic old-school move, chose to write the news story and headline about the sale of the newspaper to which he had devoted twenty years of his life. Williamson typed the story himself on his office Underwood, wrote a headline, and gave the copy to the *Herald* night desk with explicit orders not to make any edits. Williamson wanted the story and headline to read exactly as he had written them.

Williamson's copy landed on the desk of Richard Cole, at the time working as the *Herald*'s night editor. Cole glanced at the story, but didn't read it till later that evening since he'd been instructed not to make changes. That's when he discovered a problem.

"Bill wrote that the *Herald* had been 'nationalized,' meaning it the way Brazilians mean it, which is that it had been sold to Brazilians," recalled Cole. "But, of course, to 'nationalize' something in the English-speaking world means a government takeover, which would alarm many of our readers. I suppose Bill had been in Brazil too long to realize this."[23]

Brian Nicholson agreed with Cole. "The front-page headline was wrong," Nicholson would remember. In British and American English, the primary meaning of 'nationalize' is to pass from private to state ownership, something that for the *Herald*'s conservative readership would normally raise specters of the Red Peril, but in the Brazil of 1979 could also hint at military government control. It was exactly the kind of mistake that an expat far too long away from his native language might make, and quite forgivable. This blooper we noticed late in the evening, as the front page was due to print. So after much agonizing, we changed it."[24]

Another reading of the alleged miscue was that it wasn't a miscue at all. Perhaps Williamson was sounding a coded alarm, warning *Brazil Herald* readers that Salles's purchase amounted to a government takeover over of the newspaper. As former *Herald* reporter Mark Gruberg would later muse, "Bill's insistence makes me wonder. Might Salles have had ties to the dictatorship, and if so, was Williamson aware of

Manic

it? If that was the case, Williamson might have used the word 'nation-alize' deliberately, playing upon its dual meanings."[25]

The next morning when Williamson saw his story edited and the headline changed, he was furious. Even though Cole had made the right call when it came to the language used, Williamson collared him and fired him on the spot.[26]

It was an uncharacteristic move by the Williamson, and the flap left Cole shaken. The young American who had grown up in Stoneham, Massachusetts, didn't have any savings, was in a foreign country, and had just lost his sole means of support. Cole sat in the middle of a newsroom suddenly gone silent. So much for worker solidarity.

Just as Cole was putting the last of his belongings in a cardboard box, the *Herald*'s new owner, Mauro Salles, strolled into the Rio news-room in a whirlwind, introducing himself, going from desk to desk, effusively shaking everyone's hand. When Salles spotted Cole deject-edly filling up the carton and learned that Williamson had canned him, the new owner intervened. Calling for everyone's attention, Salles made an announcement: Under his ownership no one would be fired. That prompted a round of applause and cheers in an otherwise-glum newsroom, as though to say, "Maybe this Salles might not be as bad as we had feared."

To be sure, Salles's action was a transparent attempt to win support from a roomful of cynical journalists, led by bruiser Bill Hall, who, for one, viewed the São Paulo ad man with apprehension and mis-trust. Salles's move was a thumb-in-the-eye put-down of Williamson, a rejoinder that said, "*I'm* in charge from now on." But from Cole's point of view, Salles's intervention was a magnanimous gesture. "I was always grateful to Salles for what he did," Cole would say.[27]

By February 1979, Salles had installed his younger brother, Cláudio, trained as a civil engineer, to oversee integration of the *Brazil Herald* into the planned *Latin America Daily Post*, effectively eliminating Williamson's role. Senhor Bill could stay on at the new *Daily Post* for as long as Brazil's labor laws would allow, but in reality he had been shown the door. With the *Herald* sale, he was to receive a structured payout of the one-third equity he owned, paid out in six installments over three years.[28]

The inaugural issue of the *Daily Post* came out on May 14, 1979, with a six-column headline ("Rocket Attacks, Fighting Threaten Mid-East Talks") over a UPI wire story from Tel Aviv. Six stories showcased the newspaper's front page, three of which carried Latin American datelines, alongside a boxed editorial titled, "What We Believe" in the lower righthand corner, which sounded all the pomp and circumstance of a new newspaper.[29]

For Steve Yolen and his newly assembled editorial team, exhilaration turned into frustration and anger when ten days into the *Daily Post* launch, the São Paulo journalists union called for a general strike. The work stoppage was confined to São Paulo's print journalists, who had encircled the *Folha de São Paulo* building, where the *Daily Post's* main offices were located. Under Brazilian law, editorial workers at the *Daily Post* weren't classified as journalists. Only those with diplomas from accredited Brazilian university journalism schools could "exercise the profession," as it is called. That, though, had little bearing on whether editorial employees at the *Daily Post* would honor the strike. Almost everyone did.

Yolen and Taylor stayed on, putting out the new newspaper, but Lehman and the other editorial staff in São Paulo joined the Brazilian journalists in the walkout. Lehman, Yolen's first hire, recalled, "I felt I couldn't cross the picket line at the *Folha de São Paulo* newspaper, where I was friendly with many of the journalists. Many had helped me with tips and names of sources for stories I did for UPI. I explained my feelings to Yolen and Taylor. There were no ramifications other than an angry outburst from Taylor."[30]

From the perspective of Brian Nicholson, who had been hired from the *Brazil Herald* as the *Daily Post's* business editor after assessing the new newspaper for Editôra Mory, the strike had more to do with labor equality, solidarity, and justice than petitioning for overdue raises for chronically underpaid Brazilian journalists. To the Scotsman, the strike resonated with Brazil's post-1964 history and helped foster a sense of unity with workers of all stripes. "Demands were a twenty-five percent wage hike and immunity for union reps in the newsroom. But it was not just a wage and conditions stoppage. It went further, mixed with a desire to at last stand up to the stultifying military regime and its supporters in the Brazilian establishment." The strike was also an opportunity to debut a charismatic and young trade unionist, Luiz Inácio "Lula" da Silva, who started out as an autoworker in what came to be known as the ABCD manufacturing sector of São Paulo, would enter Brazil's political world, and eventually would get elected president of the nation twice, in 2003 and in 2023, as the leader of the national Worker's Party.

In that context, Nicholson saw the local journalists' strike as a nascent point for a nation struggling to move from a government of strongmen to a democracy.

Brazil's economic miracle of the early seventies was fading. Most people were increasingly fed up with generals who no longer seemed to have answers to the country's vast problems—the unresolved legacy of slavery, shameful inequality, endless *favela* slums that had spread around many cities during years of rapid industrialization and urbanization, mounting foreign debts, signs of an economic slowdown.

The generals had promised a snail's-pace return to civilian rule, but civil society was already starting to flex its muscles. Lula was surging as a dynamic young labor leader among factory workers in the São Paulo industrial belt, addressing huge strike rallies in football stadiums. He was challenging, not just a slew of multinationals, such as Ford, Volkswagen, Mercedes, Chrysler, Pirelli, Philips, and General Electric that had prospered under the military regime, but also a bureaucratic, corporatist trade union movement that had been largely co-opted by the state.

Lula also inspired a generation of young middle-class Brazilians who might never have seen the inside of a factory, but had come of age listening to the Rolling Stones, the Doors *et al.* [31]

Nicholson and other *Daily Post* staffers had worked twelve-hour days for weeks to ready the newspaper's premiere. They shared pride in what they had hoped would become a landmark editorial product. For most, it was an agonizing decision to walk out and join the striking Brazilian journalists. There was no reason to do so, other than demonstrating symbolic support even though it might mean undercutting the brand new *Daily Post.* "We all knew that it would be a setback for the paper, coming so soon after its launch," Nicholson would reflect. "We picketed our workplace as best we could but the paper still came out, basically stuffed with wire copy by Yolen, Taylor, and I guess a few helpers. In the best traditions of a free press, we staffers stood shoulder to shoulder with our Brazilian colleagues (albeit they never really noticed us) while a couple of editors bust a gut to put out a thin semblance of a paper, and succeeded."[32]

For his part in supporting the striking workers, Nicholson one evening went to the UPI bureau office in São Paulo to try to convince a technician there to pull the wire feed from the news agency to the *Daily Post*, thereby making it even harder to put out the new newspaper. But the UPI technician "just laughed at me," Nicholson would remember.[33]

The *Daily Post* ran two measured editorials during the strike. Both shared the frustration of the work stoppage, but as often is the case with newspaper editorials, both equivocated so much that neither said much.

The strike was marked by scattered incidents of violence. Yolen and Taylor left the newspaper building several evenings escorted by police. Ultimately, the walkout turned out to be an abject failure for the striking journalists. *Daily Post* staffers returned to work several days before the strike's ignominious end. "We met for coffee at a nearby lanchonete, gave a collective sigh, went back to our desks and started working in a frigidly quiet newsroom," Nicholson would recall.

Several days later, Nicholson was summoned by Mauro Salles's son, Paulo, who for the moment had become management's representative at the *Daily Post*, and was fired for his part in the strike.[34]

It was into this tense and agitated setting that I showed up in my stifling and ridiculous worsted wool suit to meet Yolen in São Paulo to start working at the *Latin America Daily Post*.

PART THREE

CHAPTER 19

Sharpened Pencils

THREE MONTHS LATER, when Mauro Salles climbed atop the copy desk of the *Daily Post* in São Paulo and announced that the newspaper would be moving to Rio and consolidating with the *Brazil Herald*, I was ecstatic. São Paulo was inland, gray and gritty; Rio was littoral and full-bloom Technicolor. I couldn't wait.

From a professional standpoint, Rio also was a more recognizable international dateline. Geographically-challenged readers in the States had hardly ever heard of São Paulo. Brazil was a tough-enough sell. Rio conjured up images of bikini-clad girls on Ipanema Beach with Sugarloaf Mountain in the background and a jubilant Pelé bicycle-kicking a goal at Maracanã Stadium. I had fully recovered from my appendectomy, and even though I'd miss the *Daily Post* crew in São Paulo, I was ready to start over in Rio.

In Rio, Bill Williamson once again took to his Underwood to notify readers that the *Brazil Herald* would be folded into the new newspaper, the *Latin America Daily Post*. In an editorial, Williamson sounded the same historic pomp of the dozens of English-language newspapers in Brazil before the *Herald* that had also been shuttered. It was a bittersweet goodbye.

After 34 years of hard work, laughs and cries, good times and bad, it is time for us to say goodbye to our readers. We leave you confident that for more than three decades we have done our best, and that despite our human tendency to make mistakes, our effect on our readers has been positive.

We say goodbye because after tomorrow we will no longer be on the newsstands, at least not in the same form as before. At the same time, however, we give a hearty welcome to our successor, the *Latin America Daily Post*.

We are pleased to welcome a newspaper that believes in Latin America and in our own country. We are gaining a newspaper that believes a continent with 21 independent nations, more than 330 million people and a combined gross national product in excess of $400 million must have a tool to speak up for Latin America to the rest of the world. The *Daily Post* believes in Latin America's rich heritage, its tradition, its history of struggles for liberty and independence and its future as an equal among the great regions of the world in making the decisions which shape history.

By printing the news with impartiality and simultaneously providing an outlet for the views and opinions of the people of Latin America, this region's newest voice will serve as an ambassador to the world. And in that capacity the *Daily Post* will always speak up on behalf of the right of people and nations to self-determination, the dignity of free enterprise and free initiative, the value of international trade, the free dissemination of ideas, and peaceful diplomatic negotiations and arbitrations.

But we also do not want to lose sight of our own community, and we will strive to serve its people even better than we have in the past. To this end the *Brazil Herald* will continue as a supplement to the *Daily Post* to be distributed only in Brasil, giving our readers all the information they need.

So at the same time we say goodbye, we say hello.[1]

Moyra Ashford and Stan Lehman, whom I counted as my closest friends, would stay in São Paulo, continuing to work for the *Daily Post*, as would Jo Ann Hein, the newspaper's ditzy society correspondent.

Rancor stemming from the journalists' strike had lessened, but now that the three-person copydesk and paste-up guys in São Paulo had all been laid off, a renewed sense of resentment swept over the newsroom. The editorial staff still looked askance at managing editor Ed Taylor, who had sided with management during the strike. Steve Yolen was a different story. He was so eternally sunny that it was hard to hold a grudge against him.

The newspaper had survived the launch, strike, and staff shakeup, and although no one seemed to know much about the Salles family's finances and its long-term commitment to supporting an undertaking as potentially expensive as an international newspaper, the remaining staff felt lucky to still be employed. Our meager paychecks, which dropped in value each month due to hyperinflation, had been duly deposited in our bank accounts, and the newspaper was coming out daily. The *Daily Post*, combined with the *Brazil Herald*, seemed to be a solvent and ongoing enterprise. At least for now.

Per Brazilian labor laws, the newspaper was required to pay for any employer-mandated relocation costs, which in my case didn't amount to much. But until I found an apartment in Rio, I was put up at the grand Hotel Glória, where Hunter S. Thompson had heard Richard Fallon, the Chamber of Commerce president and General Electric CEO, make an idiot of himself by talking about the ill-considered mandate to make the Washington Senators' stadium seats wider. My month-long stay at the Glória likely had been made possible by a permutas deal the Salles advertising agency, the *Brazil Herald*, or *Daily Post* had with the hotel. I wasn't sure which and I never asked.

The first day I arrived for work at the newly combined newspaper office in Rio, the remaining *Herald* staff glared at Yolen, Taylor, and me. Hostility hung in the air. The three of us had brought a noxious odor into the still, humid air of a newsroom that had run on its own for three decades. I was part of the Salles cabal that had bought the freewheeling *Herald* and had made it into an insert to the out-of-town newcomer. Even though I had started after the São Paulo journalists' strike had ended, that made no difference. Yolen and Taylor were management who had sided against the striking workers, and I by default was a member of the junta that had swooped in to seize control of the longstanding and largely autonomous *Herald*. We were the enemy.

Consolidating personnel from different organizations is a dicey proposition, and the combination of personalities from these two very different newspapers underscored that. Bill Williamson was as simpatico as could be, even though his head had just been chopped off. Mauro's brother, Cláudio Sales (who, like Luiz, spelled his surname with just one l) had evicted Williamson from his second-floor office, and while no one knew what exactly Williamson's role was any longer, he welcomed us invaders with aplomb. Marlene, Williamson's attentive secretary, was now working for a new boss, rushing after Sales to summon *him* whenever a telephone dial tone became available.

While the machinery of putting out the combined newspaper wasn't yet oiled, the first several weeks went off without any mechanical hiccups. The *Herald*'s all-purpose fix-it man, Igor Tsvik, made sure of that. The consolidated newspaper's editorial content had a little something for everyone. On the best of days, the combined newspaper had a healthy mix of international, US, and Latin American news; a local editorial; staff-produced political columns; a business section compiled from occasional staff-written stories; and an assortment of entertaining and informative features. All of it came with a complement of photos, political cartoons (this was during the last golden era of cartooning, and there was a plethora of sharp-penned stars to choose from: Ranan Lurie, Paul Conrad, Mike Peters, Pat Oliphant, Tony Auth, Jeff MacNelly, David Levine, Jules Feiffer, Don Wright, the *Washington Post*'s Herblock), Dear Abby, and lively stories from great syndicated columnists, including Art Buchwald, Bob Greene, Roger Simon, Nicholas von Hoffman, Mike Royko, Red Smith, William Safire, William F. Buckley, and Ellen Goodman. I had no idea whether publishing any of these luminaries was a violation of copyright laws, but I was elated that the newly combined newspaper had access to the mix. The result was a well-designed broadsheet that, although thin, looked and read like a real newspaper.

The *Daily Post*'s main source of international news was UPI (pronounced "OOO-PAY-EEE!"). The wire machine clicked nonstop as it churned out teletype rolls of copy, unfurling on the rough-hewn third-floor newsroom floor. On rare occasions, a wire story would carry the all-cap advisory BULLETIN or URGENT, signaling significant news such as the death of a US senator, a commercial plane crash, or an indictment of a politician. BULLETINs were accompanied by five bells—ding, ding, ding, ding, ding—to awaken a snoozing editor so that the breaking news might be slammed onto a paper's front page; URGENTs came with three bells—ding, ding, ding—and might be news of the end of a Senate filibuster or a midsized American city's electrical blackout. Only for extraordinary news would the advisory FLASH precede a story, signaling a transcendental event, such as the John Lennon assassination (which happened during my watch). FLASHES prompted a nerve-jangling ten bells in a row—ding, ding, ding, ding, ding, ding, ding, ding, ding, ding.

The official word from Yolen and Taylor was that the *Daily Post* was available throughout Latin America, as well as in Miami and New York, on a same-day basis. Circulation was pegged at twelve to fifteen thousand per day. I doubt any of this was true. You could pick up a copy of the newspaper in Rio and São Paulo, but nowhere else reliably. Circulation might have topped eight thousand on a good day, which was about the same as what the *Brazil Herald* had sold.

Yolen would later recall, "The Salles group almost didn't care about the editorial side of the business, letting me run it merrily along. I had virtually total autonomy over content and staffing. He [Mauro] generally didn't know what was going to be in the paper until he read it the next day. Mauro wanted his own newspaper for future political purposes, unknown to me. Mauro's brother Cláudio was given the unenviable family task of trying to make it financially feasible."[2]

While Salles was busy trying to enlarge his already large circle of political influence, Yolen tried in earnest to make the combined paper's editorial product into his own. He and Taylor demoted *Brazil Herald* managing editor and newsroom tough guy Bill Hall to assistant editor, moving him from the relatively posh third-floor executive editorial suite to the non-air-conditioned main newsroom, where I sat with the rest of the staff. It was a humiliation for Hall, and was meant to be. With few exceptions, Hall had made almost all editorial decisions for the *Brazil Herald*. Scowling Hall looked more like a hod carrier than a journalist, and that's denigrating to anyone in the building-trades profession. Yolen and Taylor tiptoed around him for good reason.

On my first day, I asked Hall where I could find pencils to mark up wire copy. Hall answered by throwing my way a chewed-end pencil nub he had tucked behind his ear as though it were a dart, announcing

Fig. 19.1 The *Brazil Herald*'s Bill Hall, US Ambassador Robert M. Sayre, Tom Murphy, and Brian Nicholson. Courtesy of the Bill Williamson Collection.

that unless the "Salles assholes" supplied him with *sharpened* pencils, he wasn't about to edit a single story.

"I'm not going to do jack for those shits," Hall sneered, flicking a cigarette ash onto the floor, hoisting his cowboy-boot-encased feet onto his desk. "Fuck 'em!"

Hall's bravado worked. Cláudio Sales immediately sent society editor Rita Davy out to buy five dozen round editors' pencils, and when she got back, she sharpened each and passed them around to the staff as though they were licorice sticks on a silver platter.

Hall, who was put in charge of incoming wire news, begrudgingly returned to editing the day's copy. He had a systematic way of going through the multiple rolls that a copyboy had placed on his desk. In front of Hall sat the first drafts of history, at least since the newspaper's last edition. Brian Nicholson described Hall's routine: "Settling into his editor's chair, Bill would grab a roll, drop it between his feet, and pull the stream of paper up and over his desk so that it could fall down into a large waste box on the far side. He would then slide the teletype paper rapidly over his desk, scanning for the nuggets that would merit front or inside pages."[3] Those nuggets might or might not have been newsworthy. Another *Herald* editor, Jim Bruce, recalled that Hall "could have edited the entire Rio de Janeiro telephone book and dummied it forthwith, page by page, into the newspaper."[4]

My job responsibilities varied. Some days it was editing the editorial page or business pages; other days, it was the national-news page. Occasionally, I laid out page one—writing headlines, choosing wire photos, and editing six or seven lead stories. I gladly left the sports pages to Hall. Yolen and Taylor were open to letting me write stories, and they ran everything I ever pitched—hard news, features, opinion pieces. The newspaper's laid-back "what me worry?" default proved to be its strength. At least, for me it was. I knew I'd never have the same degree of freedom at any other newspaper ever again.

As there had been at the *Daily Post* in São Paulo, there was a battalion of paste-up guys in Rio who affixed typeset copy with glue to page blanks to be photographed and then printed on presses downstairs.

The Portuguese pronunciation of my name hadn't changed, and it still echoed through the newsroom, Eh-SCHTEE-vey! Whenever Carlos Augusto, Edgar (pronounced Ed–GEE–gar), or another paste-up guy who went by CE-bo-la (onion), presumably because at one time he had shaved his head, wanted to call my attention to something, they'd shout my name, then motion me by flapping four fingers, all the while hissing "*pssssttt!*" sounding like they'd just opened a vacuum-packed can of peanuts. When we decided that making a change on a page would be too much trouble, Carlos Augusto would hold his hands vertically at chest level and slap his fingertips as though to say "Done!" followed by "*Chefe*," pronounced "CHEF-eh," which means boss. If any of the paste-up guys ever got reamed out by Roberto, the paste-up foreman, Edgar would raise an eyebrow, lift his right hand and vigorously shake it, somehow managing to slow his index finger to make it snap against his middle finger (a mime to this day I have not mastered). An extension of that digital expression was hitting the palm of his hand, held horizontally, with the top of the closed fist of his right hand. That meant, You're totally screwed! When I'd make a suggestion that Carlos Augusto, Edgar, and Cebola disagreed with, they'd shake their heads, click their tongues, and raise an index finger, wagging it horizontally like a metronome.

I also became familiar with a host of Portuguese lingual expressions, none of which had anything to do with journalism. One was the popular use of *o seguinte*, which means "the following." A speaker would list four or five reasons, for instance, why he had disappeared for a week or had arrived five hours late because of "o seguinte." The use of o seguinte was so common in Portuguese that no conversation that lasted for more than five minutes seemed devoid of it.

As had happened in São Paulo, the paste-up guys relentlessly hit up the reporters and editors for loans. Yes, we made more money, but no one was making much. "My mother got hit by a truck last night, and we have no food for me and my nine sisters," Carlos Augusto would start, touching my right elbow for emphasis. "Could you possibly consider lending me fifty cruzeiros till the day after tomorrow?"

We'd be hunched over the angled paste-up tables while I'd be figuring out how to cut three paragraphs from a fourteen-inch wire story, and Cebola would lower his voice to a whisper. "I only ask this of you once, Eh-SCHTEE-vey. My father needs an operation. Unless we get enough money to pay the doctor, my father will be forced to sell one of his kidneys! He could die!" "Bicho, falo com a coraçao nas mãos! Por favor, ajudê-me, o meu amigo! Deus lhe pague!" ("Dude, I speak from the bottom of my heart! Please, help me, my friend! God will reward you!")

Others in the newsroom had warned me. You'll never get paid back, despite all assurances. I had to watch what I spent, or I'd have a hard time covering my own rent, the equivalent of two-hundred-and-fifty dollars a month for my one-bedroom apartment in Laranjeiras.

On the combined newspaper staff, in addition to Bill Hall and Laura Reid, was Laura's brother, Andrew, a fair-skinned, patrician-looking Brit with phosphorescent orange hair. Another holdover from the *Herald*, although employed as a proofreader, mysterious Andrew pretty much came and went on his own schedule.

Laura and Andrew's father, David, had been a career employee for the British news service, Reuters, and had worked in London, Lisbon, Paris, and Rio. In Paris, both Laura and Andrew had been enrolled in the French school Lycée Carnot.[5] Like others who had found a home at the newspaper, Andrew was a polyglot, nimbly switching from English to French to Portuguese to Spanish. He had lived in Bogotá, Cuernavaca, and Mexico City, maybe La Paz, perhaps Buenos Aires. No one knew for sure. In 1977, while living in New York, he had worked as a writer of pornography in a lower Manhattan boiler shop, completing two published novels, *The Porto Rican Call Boy* and *Masturbating Missies* under the pseudonym Sissy Hunter.[6]

Andrew rented a weekend house in Paraty, a colonial village between Rio and São Paulo with cobblestone streets and white-washed buildings. He shared the house with two Italian-Brazilians from the film industry, Bruno Stroppiana and Renato Padovani.[7] Occasionally, newspaper staffers went to Paraty with Reid for a weekend of gastronomy and drink.

As columnist Harold Emert put it, "Andrew when he was drug-free was one of the nicest and most cultivated persons you ever would meet."[8] John Thrall, the ex-con and self-proclaimed CIA asset once employed at the *Herald*, remembered Reid as "wonderfully well-read, arrogant, and sharp tongued. Very troubled. He drank a lot, much more than we did, and had a real weakness for coke."[9]

Andrew dressed as though he were living in the wrong century. Despite Rio's heat and humidity, he often showed up for work unaccountably in a thick red velvet suit. On occasion, he wore a white linen suit along with finely cobbled auburn leather boots. He and sister Laura throughout the day lobbed sarcasm-tipped fuselages at each other in French, their arguments erupting into shouting matches, followed by standoffs that could last for days.

For unexplained reasons, Andrew seemed to take pride in how thick his prodigious orange eyebrows were. He specified to waiters that the *filet* he ordered was to be barely seared, virtually raw. His go-to lunch restaurant was a Copacabana hole-in-the-wall, Café Cervantes, where his standing order was pork and pineapple slices on a panino. While standing on line behind a young woman with long blonde hair, he impulsively took out a pair of scissors from his briefcase and snipped six inches from her mane. "Her hair really annoyed me," Andrew explained to me. "She *never* should have had hair that long. I did her a favor, a free haircut. She didn't seem to mind, either. I'm going to meet her tonight for drinks."[10]

Another carryover from the *Brazil Herald* was proofreader Chris Phillips, a seventyish former US Air Force pilot with a waxed-tipped mustache who dressed in a daily uniform of khaki shirts, pants, and matching desert boots. Phillips had the unnerving habit of rubbing his hands with an assortment of musky oils and lotions at his newsroom desk throughout the day. As a collegiate fencer at the University of California, followed by a job as an extra in Hollywood, Phillips boasted that he had taught Hollywood actor Errol Flynn, known for his cinematic swashbuckling, how to wield a foil. Phillips tried out the story on new staffers, particularly young women, few of whom had ever heard of Flynn. Reporter Maggie Locke recalled that Phillips carried himself like an "ex-B movie actor who at seventy thought he was thirty."[11]

At a newsroom gathering, Phillips peered down on a pale female newcomer from Canada and sniffed, "You reek of virginity," remembered former *Brazil Herald* managing editor Garry Marchant.[12]

On occasion, Phillips contributed first-person columns to the *Herald*, and in one memorable account, he described toiling in a sooty western Pennsylvania coal-mining town during the depths of the Depression. A friend had talked Phillips into hitchhiking to Florida, and on the way, they picked cherries and strawberries.

We were in no hurry so we dawdled along the early spring countryside, along the great Susquehanna River where we camped and enjoyed our freedom in the cool, fresh, open air. It was glorious for me after spending six months in that coal mine. It was lovely to see the green meadows and the trees veiled in that faint green light of budding leaves.

On the trip, Phillips's traveling companion brought a woman back to the room the two men shared.

I was astounded by her attractiveness. She was small and petite, but with a strange look of latent savagery in her face. Ted looked mountainous and impressive standing next to her. A beautiful woman is a gift from heaven but when she started taking some deep pulls straight from the vodka bottle I could see we were probably in for some interesting times.

Ted looked at her as though seeing her for the first time. And it was then that things began to deteriorate. . . .

Late that night I heard them come into the room and get into bed. I fell off into a deep sleep. Suddenly I was awakened by a tremendous crash and a dreadful animal cry—a shattering sound that echoed around the room. It sounded like something you hear in a zoo.

In a state of shock, I jumped out of bed and hit the lightswitch on the wall. I saw something then I'll never forget. There on the floor, in the debris of the wash sink sat a completely naked Mary. And over her left shoulder a jet of water shot straight at Ted Curtis sitting in the bed yelling his head off.

There was a lot of noise and confusion in the hotel for a long time. What we figured out was that Mary, too drunk or too lazy to use the bathroom down the hall, decided to relieve herself in the sink. While squatting on it, the whole thing gave way from the wall, breaking off the water pipe.

Needless to say, we were asked to terminate our residence at that fine hostelry. Anyhow it was time we headed for the south as planned. [13]

Who knew if any of it were true. But did that matter? Chris Phillips had turned into a Henry Miller troubadour.

Phillips's retelling of well-worn yarns grated some in what by late afternoon had turned into an oven of a newsroom. Clip-on, miniature desk fans did nothing to reduce the heat. On particularly hot afternoons, the indoor temperature could climb past ninety degrees, which often resulted in testy exchanges among the wilting staff. One of the very few behaviors absolutely not tolerated in the otherwise anything-goes newsroom was to complain about the heat. Yes, it was stifling and unbearable. A sweatbox unfit for humans. But to whine about it was unacceptable. Complaining made everyone hotter. One word about how thermal the still air was would get dagger eyes from the rest of the staff.

One sweltering afternoon, a New York transplant who had made it onto the staff found himself sitting several desks behind Phillips.

After hearing yet again the same repertoire of tired tales, the newbie announced loudly to Phillips and everyone else, "Hey old man, when are you going to quit boring us with all these make-believe stories?" followed by a loud "Ha, Ha, Ha!"

Without missing a beat, Phillips put down his editing pencil, took off his reading glasses, and walked back two desks.

"Get up, you punk!"

When the young man stood, Phillips punched him squarely in the nose and said, "Don't you *ever* speak to me like that again! You understand?"

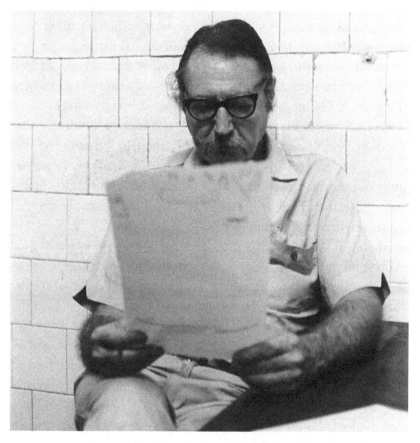

Fig. 19.2 Chris Phillips proofreading news copy in the *Brazil Herald* newsroom, 1978. Photograph by Liza Fourré.

Phillips returned to his desk, doused his hands with his assortment of oils and lotions, rubbed them, picked up his pencil, and resumed proofreading. No one said a word.[14]

Venerable columnist Herb Zschech still worked at the combined newspaper when I arrived. He'd trudge into the newsroom at ten a.m. or so to deliver his daily column. It was my unenviable job to edit Zschech. Perhaps owing to his native German and that English was his seventh or eighth language, Zschech dangled verbs at the end of very long, compounded, and fractured sentences. He confused tenses, often writing about the past as though it were still happening. His prose was a mélange of poorly translated Goethe, Kafka, and Sartre. After several weeks of trying to edit the columns into anything close to a remote version of English, all I could do was fix the spelling errors and let everything else fly. I came to realize that the manner with which Zschech expressed himself was his innate charm, and I learned to appreciate his one-of-a-kind prose. I trusted readers agreed.

Harold Emert was equally charming, although in a different way. While playing oboe for the Brazilian National Orchestra, he was still able to deliver his column more or less on deadline, as well as undertake a career as stringer for a number of British and US publications, further fulfilling his career dream of playing music and doing journalism. In addition to contributing to *The Double Reed*, the International Double Reed Society's quarterly, mandatory reading for all oboe players, Emert knew how to hustle and would turn into the go-to correspondent for gruesome murders and other sensationalist stories whenever they landed in Brazil and there was a tie-in to the UK or US. He was hot on the trail for a host of British and American newspapers when Nazi "Angel of Death" Josef Mengele was reported to have drowned in the Atlantic Ocean near the coastal village of Bertioga in February, 1979, as well as for Mengele's exhumation six years later. After being stiffed numerous times for numerous freelance contributions, Emert would demand payment from overseas newspapers upfront. An expression he used with editors insistent that he follow a breaking story without remuneration first deposited in his bank account was a succinct, "No money, no honey."

After we got all our edited stories to the compositors, signed off on our proof pages, and took one last glance at the rolls of wire copy sprawled on the floor in front of the UPI machine to make sure we hadn't missed a distant revolution or deadly tsunami, we made it to Bar Brasil, the tavern down the block where bow-tied waiters kept count of multiple draft beers they served us *ben gelada* (ice cold) by tossing cardboard Antarctica beer coasters our way. Bill Hall, Laura Reid, Rita Davy, or Chris Phillips never joined us. Nor did Steve Yolen or Ed Taylor, certainly not Cláudio Sales. That probably was for the best. A revolving family of six to ten newspeople happily convened every evening, each of us celebrating the same momentous decision that had brought us to where we were, miles away from wherever "home" had been.

Nothing, though, could have prepared us for the arrival—and abrupt departure—of a reporter by the name of John Sullivan.

CHAPTER 20

Without Spurs

WHEN *LATIN AMERICA DAILY POST* publisher Mauro Salles bought the *Brazil Herald*, executive editor Steve Yolen inherited a tall, burly, and imposing twenty-five-year-old reporter by the name of John Joseph Sullivan III. Sullivan was a carouser from New Jersey who, when not at the center of a bar fight, looked as though he ought to have been. He and Bill Hall vied for the distinction of Most Macho in the newsroom. Any scuffle between the two men would have ended with one clocking the other. Or both knocking the other out cold.

Sullivan was a blustery, two-fisted journalist in a hurry. At this point in his career, he found himself trailing the pack in a profession that pays lip service to comradery but more often than not is driven by intense, often unhinged competition. To succeed in journalism, you need to fly out of the starting gate and stay vigilant of those nipping at your heels. While powering ahead, you must have the concomitant ability to look over your shoulder and bat away anyone closing in. Sharp elbows help. So does raw talent, but not as much as an unrelenting, compulsive obsession to finish before everyone else. Throw out any notion of *esprit de corps*. To be first, you must be talented. But in this business everyone's got talent, be it raw, refined, or extraordinary. You have to have more. You have to be distinctive, driven, ambitious, egomaniacal, relentless, and determined. In all of these professional attributes Sullivan scored high.

Large and physical, Sullivan demanded attention wherever he went and usually got it. He had a loud, rolling laugh that seemed to expand in volume to the size of any room he entered. To listen to Sullivan nonstop namedrop, he knew *everyone* in journalism, at least everyone who had made it. He bragged that he was friends with Malcolm Forbes, the motorcycle-driving publisher of the eponymous business magazine that annually ranked the world's richest people. Without any prompting, Sullivan would regale strangers with how he had talked his way into an interview with Forbes for a story on motorcycling and hot-air ballooning, and, once in Forbes's inner sanctum, how the two had become buddies. They exchanged letters on a regular basis. They went on outings together. To anyone who doubted the bromance, Sullivan had proof: He carried in his wallet a folded letter of introduction from Forbes, which he took to passing around Bar Brasil even though no one ever asked him to.

I had doubts about the authenticity of the Forbes letter. It just isn't how journalists roll. In my circle, at least, no one had ever heard of writing a "letter of introduction" for a reporter. References and phone calls yes, but a letter of introduction? That was out of the 1950s, if at all. And why would Forbes hang out with a nobody like Sullivan? The Forbes letter, and pretty much everything about Sullivan, struck me as over-the-top.

Sullivan crowed that he'd been to Kenya, Nigeria, Hong Kong, Thailand, Japan, Nicaragua, Argentina, Chile, Venezuela, Colombia, and Bolivia. He opened conversations by announcing that he was a stringer for ABC Radio, even though he never got around to saying what stories he had filed, when, or if they ever aired. Most reporters have a quiescent novel banging around in their heads, but Sullivan actually talked about his, set in Afro-centric Brazil, with one chapter titled, "Voo Doo Something to Me." The shoot-em-up plot starred, no surprise, a cocaine-snorting journalist, Conor Ryan, who "falls prey as a pawn in one very large and particular seedy game of international politics," as Sullivan explained it.[1]

That Sullivan was handsome and brawny played against stereotypes. Most print journalists are nerdy, stressed-out, fidgety, and detail-obsessed. Harold Emert was a good example. If you looked like Sullivan, you might be a TV journalist, but not an ink-stained scribe who worked in newspapers. In high school, Sullivan had been named Best-Looking. The high school yearbook described him as "manly, easygoing, athletic."[2] Print journalists *cover* athletes. They *write* about actors and politicians. They don't look like them.

"He reminded me of Kris Kristofferson," Ava Annese, Sullivan's high school journalism teacher, would remember.[3]

Fig. 20.1 John Sullivan. Used with permission from Donna Sullivan Igoe.

Something that dawned on me and others in the Bar Brasil was that perhaps Sullivan wasn't a journalist at all. In the never-ending game of who at the newly combined *Daily Post* was the undercover CIA agent, Sullivan made a good candidate. Too much about him didn't add up. He was a caricature of the hard-driving, hard-drinking reporter galloping over everyone else to get the story. Who had paid for all of his globe-trotting travels? What exactly had he done after parachuting into so many Third World ports of call? Might Sullivan have been a newer-generation Joe Sims, the CIA man who had conned Bill Williamson into hiring him as managing editor of the *Brazil Herald*? Sullivan's oversized personality reminded me of John Thrall, the

Herald editor who had thrown freelance work my way when I first arrived in Brazil and later claimed that he worked for the CIA.

Sullivan's politics—at least what he allowed in print—underscored that suspicion. In a *Daily Post* column he wrote about his celluloid idol, tough guy Clint Eastwood, Sullivan quoted Dirty Harry grumbling that there were two kinds of people in the world: "those who wear the spurs and those who don't."[4] That distillation seemed to suit Sullivan, who was decidedly among the latter. Why wear spurs if you didn't need them to get the job done?

Sullivan followed with a column in which he trashed actor-turned activist Jane Fonda, writing, "Jane my dear, your bust and buns are as lovely as ever, too bad your brains aren't."[5] In the *Daily Post*'s news pages, during the same period of time, he wrote stories on a metalworkers' strike, Brazil's new president João Figueiredo, Iran's oil deals with Brazil, a speech by General Motors' chief operating officer Elliott M. Estes, and Portugal's monarchical colonial architecture in Rio.[6]

Born in the working-class Irish-Italian New Jersey borough of Bogota, six miles west of the George Washington Bridge, Sullivan's mother, Lorraine, was a "lunch lady" at the local high school. The family lived on Summit Avenue in a modest three-bedroom house built in 1925, fronted by a "lemonade porch." After graduating from Bogota High, Sullivan worked as a copyboy for the New York *Daily News*. Like Harold Emert, Sullivan got the job through his father, in Sullivan's case, John Sullivan Sr., who was a foreman at the newspaper's photoengraving shop. Like Emert, Sullivan admired Jimmy Breslin, the *Daily News*'s fight-for-the-little-guy columnist. Sullivan tried to get hired as a reporter at the *Daily News* straight out of high school, but the city editor told him, "Get some clips, then come back."

That's why Sullivan had traveled to Africa, Asia, and Latin America. At least, that's why he said he had gone to those places, although it's unclear whether Sullivan had written anything with such datelines.

Like Bill Hall, Sullivan had a temper and wasn't afraid to show it. There were stories about how Sullivan had gotten even with a drunk who intentionally had spilled beer on a new leather jacket he had recently bought. Sullivan waited three hours outside the bar and when the drunk emerged, Sullivan rammed him in the stomach with a two-by-four.[7]

"We were in a couple of bar fights down there, and we sort of held our own," recalled friend Jon O'Conner, another American expat in Rio. "Wild side? There wasn't any side of John that wasn't wild. John was a very, very gutsy guy. He really didn't know the meaning of fear."[8]

To another friend, Stan Godleswki, Sullivan "always had the windows open and the stereo going. He'd be sitting at this table too small for his typewriter, doing the two-finger typing routine. He said, 'Stan, listen to this,' as though it was a treat or something."[9]

After a year of banging around, giving free English lessons to girls on the beach, playing volleyball on the sand, working on his novel, pitching freelance pieces to British and American newspapers, and writing occasional news stories and columns for the *Daily Post*, Sullivan came to the realization that he'd just been marking time. By the time I met Sullivan in 1980, his journalistic cred had just about run dry. He needed to do *something*. The starting gun had gone off and Sullivan was still running in place behind the starting blocks. He and I had come to Brazil to jumpstart our newspaper careers. I was reasonably happy with where I had banked mine to be headed. Sullivan's hadn't moved fast enough.

As though on a mission, Sullivan approached Yolen and asked him to write another "letter of introduction," this one to be carried into Bolivia, where Sullivan planned to go next—to do exactly what no one knew for sure. Sullivan would snoop around La Paz, the highest capital city in the world, then fan out to the provinces to report. At least, that's what he told Yolen. "He wanted a retainer letter from the LADP identifying him as a freelance writer, to be used in Bolivia and onwards in his travels," Yolen would later recall. "That sounded good to me, since he didn't ask for a stipend and he was happy to receive payments per story accepted. I wrote him up a letter 'To Whom It May Concern' that he was authorized to write stories on our behalf."[10]

It was the same arrangement that Hunter S. Thompson had gotten from Clifford Ridley at the *National Observer*, as well as what the Field News Service had done for me to get me to Brazil.

Bolivia is South America's most primitive, undeveloped, and re-mote country. I had traveled from La Paz to Cochabamba to Santa Cruz via rickety bus before I ran into the Canadian girls in Buenos Aires. I'd been fascinated by the hefty, ruddy-faced Indian women in layers of woolen ponchos and black bowler hats, carrying an infant or two, who'd get off the bus ("Baja, baja," they'd shout) in the middle of nowhere and trek miles to their mountaintop homes. There had to be plenty of stories in those hills for Sullivan to bag—*if* he were a journalist and *if* he were really going to Bolivia.

Sullivan and Richard Cole, the *Herald* night editor Mauro Salles had saved from being fired by Bill Williamson, were drinking buddies. They were regulars at Lord Jim Pub, an expat tavern between Ipanema and Leblon. I'd been to Lord Jim's once, and the only locals there were over-the-hill Brazilian women trying to land a gringo for a night or, if they hit the jackpot, a green card. The whole point of living abroad was to shed your identity, to descend into a foreign cosmos, so that no one could make you as an interloper. My take, at least. Outside of the *Daily Post* newsroom, I avoided places where I would hear English. I heard enough every day in the newsroom.

Cole would recall that Sullivan had held forth at Lord Jim's that when he had worked at the *Daily News* as a fill-in copy editor he had come up with the gotcha headline: REDS CHAMPS! YANKS BENCHED after the Cincinnati Reds, led by MVP catcher Johnny Bench, demolished the New York Yankees in the 1976 World Series in four straight games.[11] Sullivan cried into his beer that he had lost out on a New York headline-writing award because the World Series coincided that year with President Gerald Ford's refusal to authorize federal funds to bail out a broke New York City, and the *Daily News* famously led page one with the classic wood, "Ford to City: Drop Dead."[12]

To any self-respecting journalist, Sullivan's declaration was in the worst form. It was akin to whipping out from your wallet folded clips of your own favorite stories (or letters of introduction). Wasted on the sidewalk after closing the bar with Cole, Sullivan would launch into a mournful jam of The Sugarhill Gang's *Rapper's Delight*, singing to anyone drunk enough to join in or listen.[13]

Brian Nicholson, the Brit who got fired for trying to pull the UPI wire feed to the *Daily Post* during the São Paulo journalists strike, remembered an encounter with Sullivan when the two ran into each other at Gugs, the counter restaurant around the corner from the newspaper's newsroom. Nicholson was leaving and Sullivan was arriving when Nicholson amiably asked Sullivan if he wanted to read the raft of magazines and newspapers Nicholson was carrying under his arm. When Sullivan shook his head, Nicholson came back with, "But what do you look at while you're eating?" To which, Sullivan replied, "Normally my food," before shouldering past Nicholson.[14] It was that kind of bravado we came to expect from Sullivan.

As seemingly eager as he'd been to go to Bolivia, Sullivan pulled an about-face. He was onto another story, this one more urgent. He now wanted to go to El Salvador to write a no-holds-barred account of sexual torture of women held captive by right-wing paramilitary soldiers in the war-torn Central American nation. It was a story that had Sullivan's name written all over it. Such a story *might* exist, but how would Sullivan ever get it?

From his days as a journalist in Santa Cruz, California, drinking buddy Richard Cole knew Kelly Garrett, an enterprising journalist who'd recently been named managing editor at Larry Flynt's new skin-saturated *Hustler* magazine.[15] Maybe Garrett would be interested in an X-rated, descent-into-purgatory yarn, Cole suggested to Sullivan over *chopes* at Lord Jim's. It promised all the trademark ingredients that *Hustler* would become notorious for: wanton violence, sadism, women in bondage. A comin'-at-ya, real-life version of Raquel Welch in *One Million Years B.C.*

Sullivan immediately jumped on Cole's connection at *Hustler*. He pitched the story the next day long-distance to Garrett, who immediately warmed to the idea. Garrett, in turn, pitched the story to *Hustler* editor Richard Warren Lewis.

Back on Rua do Resende, word of Sullivan's journalistic coup traveled instantly. But the reception was decidedly negative. The "women-in-chains" story would be impossible to report, if it existed at all, especially for an outsider with no sources. Sullivan didn't know anyone on either side of the civil war in the war-torn Central American nation. At least, no one thought he did. Sullivan couldn't hold a decent conversation in Spanish. How was he ever going to interview the local Che Guevara? And what could Sullivan come up with that the corps of veteran correspondents in El Salvador hadn't been able to piece together?

These, however, were not Garrett's and Lewis's concerns. A hungry journalist writing a thumbsucker about mayhem, madness, and murder in a forgotten, south-of-the-border nation? When can we get our hands on it?

At Bar Brasil, this was another journalistic conundrum we debated. Was *Hustler* the kind of publication a reporter ought to use to launch a career? That is, *if* Sullivan were a credible reporter and *if* he could return home with the goods. Harold Emert came out in favor. Tom Murphy wasn't so sure."

After several back-and-forths, *Hustler* came through with an assignment for Sullivan, promising to pay his expenses (plane fare and $500 in incidental spending money), along with a writer's fee of $1,800 for a 4,500-word story. The potential influx was more than welcomed. Sullivan's credit cards were maxed out, and as he would tell friend Bob Giman at the time, "I really need the cash. I'm up to my eyeballs" in debt.[16]

As Hunter S. Thompson had done after he had gotten the quasi-*Brazil Herald* job commitment from Bill Williamson, Sullivan leveraged the *Hustler* assignment to query other outlets, Independent News Alliance, a supplementary wire service, and the *National Catholic*

Reporter, a progressive religious press syndicate, for pieces he'd write from El Salvador. The three outlets were decidedly an unholy trinity, but one that nicely suited Sullivan. Without telling editors at the add-on outlets about the *Hustler* assignment, they said they'd be happy to look at whatever Sullivan sent their way.

Sullivan had scored. He had a genuine commission from a glossy, national magazine, even if its reputation wasn't top drawer, along with backup commitments from lesser lights. *Hustler* wasn't *Playboy*, *Esquire*, or *The New Yorker*, the gold standards for freelancers at the time, but getting a story in it would accrue him over-the-counter bragging rights at Bar Brasil, Lord Jim, or any other bar Sullivan would surely frequent to share news of his triumph. What Thompson had done with his 1967 breakthrough book, *Hell's Angels: The Strange and Terrible Saga of the Outlaw Motorcycle Gangs*, Sullivan would also do, exposing the gruesome state of affairs of the Salvadoran military government in a Seventh Circle of Hell. The way Sullivan envisioned his pedal-to-the-metal story would be to showcase it with klieg lights.

Back at the *Daily Post*, maybe what we feared most was that Sullivan would actually pull off the *Hustler* story, come back with a bona fide eye-witness account of harrowing atrocities, win a mantle-full of awards, and leave the rest of us in the sand.

Truth is always the first casualty in the rush to cross the finish line first. Sidney Goldberg, the Independent News Alliance editor who had signed on to take a look at Sullivan's stories from El Salvador, would recall Sullivan's previous accounts INS had published contained "some very bright spots with some very vivid writing, and some places, where, let's say, it was *too* vivid. We just wanted him to calm down a bit."[17] Goldberg had bought three Rio-based freelance stories from Sullivan, one, a perennial favorite among newbies, about the city's squalid hillside favelas.

With the *Hustler* assignment, Sullivan promptly quit his reporting gig with the *Daily Post*. Yolen said there might or might not be a job waiting for him when he returned. But by then, Sullivan was flying so high that writing news and an occasional column for the *Daily Post* amounted to beer change. He'd take his chances. Who knew where the *Hustler* piece might take him?

Sullivan flew home to New Jersey for Christmas, then boarded a plane from Newark to Miami, connecting on a TACA flight to San Salvador. He told his parents and two older sisters not to worry. He'd be back in ten days, when they'd all go out to celebrate. Sullivan took off his gold necklace and gave it to his father for safekeeping. "Wear it till I get back," Sullivan told him.[18] From the airport, he called sister Donna from a pay phone and told her that after he left El Salvador, he planned to go shark fishing in either Belize or Mexico, then return home. She ended the conversation the way she ended all their long-distance calls, "I love you, Johnny."[19]

Sullivan arrived in San Salvador on the afternoon of December 29, 1980. He took a taxi from the airport to the downtown Sheraton, where he checked into Room 526. Staying at the Sheraton was a curious decision; most out-of-town journalists avoided the Sheraton, instead staying at the Hotel Camino Real on Boulevard de los Héroes. The Sheraton had an unsavory reputation as a hangout for gun-packing right-wing extremists; among foreign correspondents, it had earned the mordant sobriquet as "the most secure hotel in town."[20]

Sullivan took a shower, made several calls from the phone in his room. He changed into a blue jogging shirt, gray poplin windbreaker, and tan corduroy slacks, then went downstairs to the bar.

That was the last time anyone said they saw Sullivan alive.

At noon the next day, a hotel maid knocked on Sullivan's door, and when no one answered, she let herself in and discovered tools of a reporter's trade—a Silver Reed portable typewriter, an assortment of pens, a notebook, Pentax camera, and Sanyo tape recorder. Sullivan had brought with him two books, *Horn of Africa* by Philip Caputo, a novel about a journalist recruited to go on a secret CIA mission; and *Cry of the People* by Penny Lernoux, a history of activist clerics in Latin America. Sullivan had two bottles of liquor: J&B Scotch and Wyborowa vodka. The hotel maid noticed a faint outline of a man's body on the unmade bed.[21]

Sullivan seemingly had disappeared into thin air.

If he had been reporting his own disappearance, he surely would have compared himself to Ambrose Bierce or Michael Rockefeller, two previous adventurers who had evaporated into the Latin America jungle, one north of the Tropic of Capricorn, the other south. Antonio Gomez, the Sheraton's resident manager, thought Sullivan might have been a "skipper," a guest who checks out without paying; Gomez didn't report to police the journalist's disappearance for a week.

When word filtered back to Bar Brasil that Sullivan was MIA, no one expressed surprise, but most shared a sense of regret that no one had had the sense to talk fearless Sullivan out of what now seemed like a sure way to die. Sullivan had been in way over his head. He'd been foolhardy to think that he could get a story that no one else could. School children, nuns, priests, physicians, farmers, the elderly had all been hacked to death in the killing fields of El Salvador. What made Sullivan think he could report his over-hyped story and get out alive? Lots of assignments pose risks; this one guaranteed them. Someone should have stopped him.

It hadn't been our role to warn Sullivan, I argued. To call his bluff would have been to assure he'd go. Sullivan had consigned himself to the risks commensurate with the outrageous story when he pitched it to *Hustler*. Once he had gotten the assignment, no way would he have backed down.

Harold Emert was particularly shaken by Sullivan's disappearance. Sullivan had called Emert in Rio three or four times from his parents' home in New Jersey, and the two had talked for hours into the night before Sullivan would leave for San Salvador. Earlier that December, on a trip to New York, Emert had met up with Sullivan for drinks at an Irish bar in Manhattan. In addition to the *Hustler* piece, Sullivan was working on another story, one that involved Emert.

At the tavern, Sullivan convinced Emert to give him a letter that Emert had received, which purportedly confirmed that Frank Sinatra wore a toupée. It was a silly, inconsequential twist that came in the response to Emert's throwaway column on the Sinatra concert at Rio's

Maracanã stadium the previous January, when Emert in an aside had quipped that Sinatra looked like he was wearing a thatched rug. The toupée confirmation was just the kind of story that Emert would make into something. Sullivan was insistent on getting the original toupée-corroborating letter posted to Emert. It was hard to say no to Sullivan. It was the least that Emert could do for a fellow journalist heading into the jungle.

That would be the last Emert ever saw of the letter or of Sullivan.[22]

No one knew exactly what had happened to Sullivan, but because there had been no calls for his ransom and he continued to remain missing, media reports quickly speculated that he'd been killed. No one had a clue how and under what circumstances.

"I swear, it's strange," said Raymond Bonner, a former stringer for the *Daily Post* who'd gotten hired as a correspondent for *The New York Times* and was in El Salvador at the time of Sullivan's disappearance. "He came in and he was gone. That's it. Damn, there's a novel there."[23] That seemed excessive and callous, although what Bonner said was what other reporters at the time were thinking.

In an editorial Richard Cole wrote for the *Brazil Herald* insert in the *Daily Post*, he mourned his missing friend with "that cocky New York Irish air, the half-smile and the glinting eyes of the kind of person you'd trust with your life but not your sister." Cole wrote that Sullivan was his "closest friend during the two years I have lived in Brazil." He made the political connection between Sullivan's disappearance and the thousands of Latin Americans reported missing year after year. "What happened? No one knows. Where did it happen? No one knows. Why? No one knows. And most important of all—is he alive? No one knows."[24]

Many at Bar Brasil didn't buy that Sullivan was dead. Several speculated that Sullivan had pulled off the ultimate disappearing act. He had joined the guerrilla forces and was about to deliver the second greatest story ever told. He'd show up sooner or later, hold court ringed by eye-rolling onlookers, buy everyone beers, then jet off to another global hotspot, bankrolled by another slick magazine.

But that never happened.

Sullivan's family in New Jersey became increasingly bitter about the lack of urgency on the part of the US State Department in digging into his disappearance. The State Department did relatively little to investigate, in part, because of the reputation of *Hustler* and that of its corrosive, renegade publisher. For its part, *Hustler* distanced itself from pursuing Sullivan's whereabouts because of the journalist's freelance status, but also because of potential liability.

Although the State Department said it had fully apprised outgoing Secretary of State Edmund S. Muskie on the case, when Sullivan's family got Muskie on the phone, he volunteered, "Until thirty minutes ago, I did not even know John Sullivan existed." After hearing the family's anguished pleas, Lorraine Sullivan recalled Muskie lecturing her, "Do you think your son is the only one this has happened to?" Muskie, who would be out of a job once the Reagan administration would take over in weeks, promised he'd contact Salvadoran President José Napoleón Duarte, but preemptively told the family, "I know it will do no good."[25]

Sullivan's two sisters vented their frustration on national television. They appeared twice on *Good Morning America*. They were interviewed on National Public Radio. They held press conferences. They contacted reporters in an all-out campaign to drum up interest in writing stories about their younger brother.

Hustler released a routine statement of concern for Sullivan. "We had an arrangement whereby he would call us if there were any problems," said the magazine's editorial director, Bruce David.

A lot of help that would have done in a Third World country with spotty phone connections. David went on to say that Sullivan's fate appeared "very grim." Publisher Larry Flynt added, "It goes without saying that *Hustler* is prepared to do whatever is necessary to locate Mr. Sullivan and relieve the anguish his family is now undergoing."[26] That was the last the Sullivans ever heard from *Hustler*.

The family clung to hopes that if Sullivan weren't dead, he might have been kidnapped and was being held for potential ransom in exchange for imprisoned guerrillas or government soldiers. "Mom and my sister Debbie—I guess they think Johnny's been killed," said Donna Sullivan Igoe at the time. "Dad thought that soon after it happened. But somehow, I can see Johnny coming through the door. I can't think of him any other way."[27] With each passing day, such a scenario seemed unlikely.

Yolen, the *Daily Post*'s executive editor, looked at Sullivan's disappearance with sympathy, but since Sullivan hadn't been employed by the newspaper when he had disappeared and the assignment had been for another publication, Yolen had no standing in pushing to find out what had happened to him.

"No one disappears on the face of the earth," pleaded Sullivan's mother, Lorraine. "Someone knows something."[28]

The CIA in El Salvador had nothing to add. In documents declassified twenty-five years after they were produced, the agency would write in an internal memorandum: "The disappearance of Mr. John Sullivan, a freelance reporter for a U.S. magazine, remains a mystery. Although U.S. Embassy reports indicate the continued awareness of the Salvadoran authorities about U.S. interest in the case, no new leads have developed. We have no independent intelligence information that would shed any light on Mr. Sullivan's disappearance."[29]

Could the CIA have been covering its tracks in placing Sullivan in El Salvador in the first place? Might the agency have attempted, and failed, to extract Sullivan held captive in Salvadoran jungles? Both scenarios seemed far-fetched. From the surface, it appeared that the agency, often clueless in such instances, was just as mystified as everyone else about what had happened to Sullivan.

The US Ambassador to El Salvador, Deane R. Hinton, bristled when told by Sullivan's family that he wasn't doing enough. "We've investigated every single lead," Hinton told Michael Massing, co-founder of the Committee to Protect Journalists. "We are going to continue to chase these leads, but we are paid by taxpayers to do many things. A disproportionate amount of resources of the American embassy has been put on this case."[30]

The Sullivan family resorted to taking out ads in Salvadoran newspapers with photographs of a smiling Sullivan, offering a reward for any information. They circulated petitions. They formed a nationwide John Sullivan Action Committee. They hired a series of private investigators. Donna, John's sister, appeared before the Subcommittee on Inter-American Affairs of the Committee on Foreign Affairs in Washington, DC. The International Council of Lithographers & Photo-Engravers' Union, the newspaper union Sullivan's father belonged to, passed a resolution calling for immediate action to investigate the journalist's whereabouts, proclaiming, the "case may be forgotten or given a low priority because of international political considerations."[31] The Newspaper Guild, Committee To Protect Journalists, Overseas Press Club, National Education Association, and American Society of Journalists and Authors followed with similar proclamations. The US congressman from Sullivan's home district flew to El Salvador to launch a fact-finding mission.

A year after Sullivan had gone missing, the family received four anonymous letters that suggested John had been kidnapped by government security forces, held at an army barracks, tortured with electric prods, then killed and dumped in a shallow roadside grave. The writer, whom analysts believed had written all four letters, wrote that Sullivan had been mistaken for a left-wing Belgian priest who had supported guerrilla forces, the FMLN. Sullivan bore a passing resemblance to the priest, Rev. Rogelio Ponseele, who had worked in Salvadoran refugee camps and had gone into hiding because of death threats. A week after Sullivan had checked into the Sheraton, two attorneys representing the AFL-CIO's American Institute for Free Labor Development had been shot dead in the hotel coffee shop, along with a local activist. Some suggested that Sullivan might also have been confused with one of the lawyers, with whom he also shared some resemblance.

The letter writer seemed to have a degree of credibility because he or she had noted a small scar on Sullivan's left leg. One of the letters suggested that Sullivan's body had been buried in Nuevo Cuscatlán, a town twenty miles south of San Salvador; another included a hand-drawn map of the grave's purported location.[32]

The family's hopes were briefly lifted when three New Jersey men, claiming that they had traveled to El Salvador in search of the missing journalist, said they had met with Sullivan in a café on the outskirts of the capital. Vincent Forgione, Martin Jaksa, and Thomas Zambory told the *Asbury Park* (NJ) *Press* that a man had approached them in the restaurant and volunteered, "I heard you were looking for me—I'm John Sullivan!" The trio, who said they'd been trained in "commando-style tactics," described the man as having sunken eyes, graying hair, and looking like he had "gone through hell."[33]

The supposed sighting and conversation proved to be false. Perhaps the rescue commandos had been deceived by an imposter; perhaps they had invented the encounter for their own advantage, however cruel that may seem.

In July 1982, the Salvadoran government exhumed scattered portions of a man's body in Nuevo Cuscatlán from a soil-covered ditch. All that remained were crushed and splintered pieces of a skeleton that appeared to have been blown apart by explosives either before or after the victim was killed; the authorities were unable to tell which. The bone fragments did not match Sullivan's, the officials said, although a forensic pathologist hired by the Sullivan family, Frederick Zugibe, disagreed after examining the remains.[34]

Several months later, the New Jersey congressman was able to intervene on the Sullivan family's behalf. According to sister Donna, "We eventually learned that John was tortured and killed, probably on the day he arrived."[35] What was left of his body, totaling fourteen pounds, was returned to the Sullivan family on February 20, 1983, in an infant's coffin. Remains of bone fragments examined by Zugibe indicated a positive match of the right kneecap with X-rays of a 1972 baseball injury Sullivan had sustained. No one was ever charged with the slaying.[36]

To his friends, Sullivan was Sully, although to his parents and sisters he was always Johnny, a boy whose favorite dessert was cherry Jell-O and Junket custard pudding. As a high school student, Sullivan had played football in the fall, wrestled in the winter, and played baseball in the spring (as the starting southpaw pitcher, he made school history by throwing a no-hitter). For a while, he had enrolled in William Patterson College, in Wayne, New Jersey, but dropped out because, remembered his journalism teacher, Ava Annese. "he was in a hurry."[37] To commemorate her former student, Annese started a high school scholarship fund in Sullivan's name.

Sullivan's father, John Sr, sixty-one, died on what would have been his son's twenty-seventh birthday. The senior Sullivan's death certificate recorded the cause of death as cancer, but he also died of broken heart. "When Johnny disappeared and the State Department started dragging its heels, it just devastated him," Donna Igoe would say.[38] Every day for a year, Sullivan's father had continued to buy *The New York Times* and keep the issues, as Sullivan had asked him to do, so he'd be able to read them when he got home. Every night, the senior Sullivan went into his son's room, held his sweater, and said goodnight to him.[39]

Mourning her son, Sullivan's mother, Lorraine, reflected, "The name John Sullivan is easy to remember, but the person John Sullivan is hard to forget."[40]

Sullivan's funeral took place at St. Joseph Church, where he had been an altar boy, next to where he'd gone to elementary school. Dave Marash, an ABC reporter active in a national journalist-advocacy group, gave the eulogy, even though he had never met Sullivan. "John Sullivan had a perhaps irrational belief in his own innocence," Marash said. "He believed that his curiosity could carry him to the cutting edge of history. . . . Our presence together here today and our determination to keep struggling tomorrow and tomorrow will mean he did not die in vain."[41]

A dozen Maryknoll nuns drove from their convent in Ossining, New York, to the memorial and sang Bob Dylan's classic song, "Blowin' in the Wind." Everyone joined in, filling the church to its rafters. Few in attendance were not in tears. The Maryknoll order had lost three sisters and one lay missionary earlier that year in El Salvador.

Letters from Malcolm Forbes and actors Jack Lemmon and Ed Asner were read to the five hundred mourners. Lemmon had starred in a recent Costa-Gavras film, *Missing*, about another American journalist, Charles Horman, who had disappeared in Latin America, in Chile during the 1973 coup.[42] Asner was known as quintessential gruff TV newsman Lou Grant; in real life, he was a staunch opponent of American support of the military regime in El Salvador.

Malcolm Forbes's letter contained this passage: "Only John's death could prevent him from becoming a significant journalist. His great heart was filled with courage, determination, and a perceptive good humor and all that was reflected in his face, eyes, and smile."[43]

Upon hearing all this back in Bar Brasil in Rio, several of us nodded to each other, an acknowledgment that Sullivan's one-time braggadocio of knowing Forbes and getting the letter of introduction had turned out to be legit. Then we toasted our dead colleague.

CHAPTER 21

Murmurs

NO ONE TALKED much about John Sullivan, but we thought about him constantly. None of us wanted to believe that larger-than-life Sullivan was dead—or even could be dead. We thought he'd miraculously show up one day and regale us with way too many stories about his *amazing* trip to El Salvador.

Sullivan went to El Salvador for one reason: to make it big. Scoring a story of this magnitude would have been his way to jump the queue to respectable newspaper employment. In retrospect, of course, it was a foolish risk. But everyone at the *Daily Post* understood why he took it.

The gloom that hung over the newsroom in the wake of Sullivan's disappearance was offset by the Daily Post's eclectic cast of walk-ons who didn't walk off: Bad Boy Bill Hall speeding through rolls of wire copy, cigarette dangling from his mouth; siblings Laura and Andrew Reid tossing grenades at each other in French; proofreader Chris Phillips rubbing his hands with an assortment of viscous lotions and oils; suit-wearing Herb Zschech showing up every morning with his garbled columns on politics and lurid crime; oboe-playing columnist Harold Emert cooking up yet another global travel scheme; society editor Rita Davy merrily inviting the staff to join her for afternoon tea with some "absolutely delightful" crumpets and petit fours.

Despite the stratospheric humidity in the newsroom and Bill Hall's profanity-laced mutterings about the new regime running the newspaper, the *Daily* Post, for the moment, was not a bad place to work. The *Herald*'s Mr. Fix-It, back shop press manager Igor Tsvik, the Russian-born immigrant who had arrived in Rio via Manchuria, looked the other way as typesetters, editors, and reporters took breaks, imbibing cachaça, beer, or sneaking drags of *maconha* (marijuana). On the rare occasion when Cláudio Sales brought clients into the newsroom, the staff issued an all-clear "pssssssssssssssssssssssstttt" as a signal to stow incriminating evidence.

In São Paulo, Stan Lehman and Moyra Ashford were now anchoring a two-person *Daily Post* news bureau, along with society writer Jo Ann Hein, who continued to file reams of society copy that was impossible to take seriously. I had a soft spot for Stan and Moyra. Stan had helped me find a place to live when I had first arrived in Brazil; he and his wife had me over for dinner several times while their nine-month-old daughter would entertain us eating banana puree. Stan had lived in Brazil for years and was thoroughly familiar with the nooks and crannies of Brazilian politics. Hearing his views on the prospective process of wresting power from the hardline generals in Brasília—rules of engagement that were new to everyone—was a worthwhile tutorial. He had what seemed like an infinite number of Egyptian-Brazilian brothers-in-law who did everything from selling luggage to buying watches. Moyra had nursed me back to health after my appendix nearly burst. She and I had often spent Saturdays together, watching turgid German films. Her son, Jubi, was a nonstop toddler who made whatever we thought of the world a better place.

The newsroom family I had so craved before I left the United States was alive and well, now spread out over two Brazilian cities. In Rio, I became friends with Tom Murphy and another *Daily Post* reporter, Marilyn Balamaci, who through her persistence had convinced the American jazz magazine *Downbeat* to sponsor her visa so she could work at the newspaper. On weekends, a group from the newsroom often went to Club Elite, a big-band dance hall for an evening of *gafieira* in a rundown section of Lapa, near Praça Tiradentes. Marilyn was involved with a TV anchorman she had met in Chicago, who had dropped everything to meet up with her in Rio. For my part, I started going out with the Rio friend of a classmate who'd been in my Portuguese crash course at Berkeley. She spoke no English, and one of the many benefits of our relationship was that my Portuguese improved dramatically.

To help distinguish the *Daily Post* from the anything-goes *Brazil Herald* after the two newspapers merged, Steve Yolen and Ed Taylor circulated a memo to the staff that asked all editorial employees to run by them any possible ethical conflicts. That didn't mean that *Daily Post* reporters weren't allowed to take freebies, just that Yolen and Taylor wanted to be apprised of them first, then make a determination of what was acceptable. Most in the newsroom welcomed the directive. It said we weren't working for an ad sheet dependent on free meals, ticket giveaways, and out-and-out payoffs. It said that the *Daily Post*, for the record at least circulating daily throughout Latin America, would be a fair, honest, and respectable newspaper.

By mid-1981, though, just about everyone at the newspaper began to notice a shift in the commitment that Yolen had conveyed to the staff when the newspaper had launched three years earlier. While ethical bumpers were now in place, the direction of the editorial product seemed on occasion to wobble. Particularly to Moyra, Yolen and Taylor had started to abandon their commitment to in-depth reporting in exchange for soft features or, worse, editorial valentines. Moyra asserted that many of her assignments were being driven by advertisers, existing or potential, as well as targeted demographics. This wasn't an unusual instance or complaint in the world of newspapers, but Moyra couldn't help but see a squiggly connection between some of the stories she was being assigned to write and publisher Mauro Salles's financial interests. Yolen flatly denied this. When she voiced her concerns to second-in-command Taylor, he shrugged his shoulders. Moyra didn't know whether that meant there was nothing Taylor could do about the alleged tilt in the newspaper's editorial menu or that he doubted such a realignment existed.

The nub of any editorial conflict stemmed from why the AP's correspondent Ed Miller had turned down Salles' initial invitation to become editor of the newspaper: As Miller had foreseen, it was impossible to put out a credible newspaper aimed at covering—and circulating throughout—such an enormous geographical area with such limited newsroom resources. The *Daily Post* didn't have the luxury of time or personnel to generate detail-oriented coverage told with style and verisimilitude. While no one expected the *Daily Post* to be *The New York Times*, there'd been hopes that it would at least become a thinking person's newspaper that on a regular basis would probe without fear or favor the critical issues confounding Latin America. Under Yolen, the *Daily Post* wouldn't be what the *Brazil Herald* had been: a provincial paper pandering to pampered expats living in Rio de Janeiro.

To pull that off, though, would be a colossal undertaking. Brazil alone was the size of the continental United States, and the *Daily Post* had committed itself to covering not just Brazil but all of Latin America, from Mexico and the Caribbean to Argentina and Chile, a geography comprising thirty-three very different nations, some governed by democratically elected officials, others run as personal fiefdoms by narco thugs. Latin America's population was five hundred million people. The mandate of the *Daily Post* was to cover news, politics, business, lifestyle, and sports for an entire continent, plus Central America and scores of islands, with a full-time editorial staff that totaled fewer than twenty and a handful of stringers, all paid from the pockets of a manic Brazilian advertising executive with grandiose political aspirations who had never before owned a newspaper.

There were other factors contributing to the *Daily Post*'s inevitable shortcomings. Distribution throughout Latin America via satellite transmission technology available in the early 1980s, along with the finances needed to access it, proved to be a pie-in-the-sky fantasy. Ed Miller had been right. The continent was too unwieldy and underdeveloped to allow a single newspaper to unify all these nations as a feasible, ongoing business entity. John D. Montgomery had discovered this forty years earlier. Despite the boldfaced motto printed under its mast on page one every day, "Latin America's Only Multi-Regional

Newspaper," the *Daily Post* turned out not to be "multi-regional" at all, but, as the *Brazil Herald* had been, a broadsheet available in one country, which on good days meant readers could pick it up in Rio, São Paulo, and a handful of other Brazilian cities.

The dream of creating an agenda-setting newspaper available on a same-day basis throughout Latin America had collided with financial and geographical realities. Optimism and ambition had outpaced the newspaper's financial means, or at least what the Salles family seemed willing to spend. The prospects of the *Daily Post* returning enough to justify Salles' initial and ongoing investment, whatever that was, did not appear promising. Everyone on the editorial staff was all in, but from what little we could determine, week by week we began to see that the newspaper's owner might not share that enthusiasm. Perhaps Salles had moved on to something else.

Stan Lehman looked at his job as just that, a job. He was very good at it, but he also had a full life as a husband, father, brother-in-law, and resident of hectic, energy-draining São Paulo. Moyra Ashford had situated herself more in the Hunter S. Thompson/John Sullivan school of journalism. Journalism was a calling to her, and as such, she found herself increasingly upended by what she perceived as a marked change in the *Daily Post's* aspirational goals.

Moyra, whose British journalism background included writing for elite London newspapers, took to believing that publisher Salles was not beyond using the *Daily Post* for his own political and business agenda. It was hardly a surprising deduction. When John D. Montgomery threw his hat into the race for US Congress back home in Kansas, the *Brazil Herald* dutifully followed with a photo and story on page one. Such coverage was one of the perks of owning the newspaper. Moyra had hoped the *Daily Post* and Salles would be different.

Yolen insisted that Salles never managed the *Daily Post's* editorial content. If he ever even looked at the newspaper, it was to scan the front page and nothing more. Salles had too many other pots bubbling over, or so Yolen maintained.

Moyra remained unconvinced and came up with her own plan of resistance. She wouldn't announce her stealth strategy to anyone. Hers would be a personal, covert protest she'd carry out on her own. Moyra started by fabricating some of the people she wrote about. She knew this was wrong but did it anyway. She turned this professional ruse into a game, the only time in her career she said she had ever allowed fiction to creep into her journalism. By violating the most sacred rule in journalism—thou shall not make up anything—she'd be poking fun at the top-down influence she believed was undermining the *Daily Post*'s news coverage. It might seem like a counterintuitive way to protest an absentee publisher's suspected motives, but to Moyra it was the only way, short of quitting, which was out of the question because she was sole provider of support for her son.

Here's how her resistance played out:

"I became a 'Finnish statistician,' recounting how strangely addictive black beans and salted pork were," Moyra reported for a story she wrote on feijoada, Brazil's national dish, for which she "interviewed" a wholly invented source whose quotes nicely complemented the story's angle of the meal's "soaring" popularity among expats. Another invention was a "banker's wife" from Leblon (an affluent Rio neighborhood adjacent to Ipanema) who flew to São Paulo for "shopping sprees and found the city's sophisticated retail shops and restaurants had grown on her." Moyra's story was an examination of the perennial question Cariocas and Paulistanos fiercely debate: Which is the better city, Rio or São Paulo? A Southern Hemisphere rejoinder to San Francisco versus Los Angeles.[1]

These two instances of fabrication in otherwise routine feature stories were triggered, Moyra would say, by publisher Salles having expressed an interest that the *Daily Post* publish a glowing piece about then-São Paulo Governor Paulo Salim Maluf, a local politician with a reputation for sleaze. Moyra would recall that she was given the assignment to interview Maluf with implicit instructions that her piece would be favorable. She was able to delay writing the valentine for only so long. Salles came back through Yolen and Taylor with another more insistent rocket for Moyra to produce the piece. At least, that was Moyra's take. That Maluf could be a powerful political ally for Salles was what she believed triggered the assignment.

In an attempt to appease Taylor and Yolen, Moyra included an extended item in a social column from São Paulo about Maluf. But that wasn't enough. And at this point, the publisher's phantom or real intrusion into Moyra's supposed editorial freedom fully stuck in her craw.

Moyra soon received an assignment to write a story about the Brazilian state-owned aeronautics firm Embraer. At least, that's how she envisioned the piece she had been asked to write. Moyra chalked up the reason: colluding business and political interests with Salles and his publicity and advertising firm. It made no difference that a probing analysis of up-and-coming Embraer, one of the world's top half-dozen aviation manufacturing firms, was a significant story. To Moyra, Salles was just as guilty of using the newspaper for his personal gain as former *Brazil Herald* procurer-in-chief André Fodor, now retired, had been.

While I would be unnerved with her actions, I wasn't exactly surprised. Many of the quotes she used were too good to be true. People don't talk that way; they aren't as witty, succinct, or clever as Moyra made them out to be. Anyone in journalism will recognize what I'm talking about. I had a sinking suspicion that Moyra had "helped" these people articulate their thoughts. But I never thought that she had invented the characters to utter such pearls.

I never mentioned my suspicions to Moyra. Nor did I ever talk to anyone about them. It wasn't my business to air my doubts. These are issues that journalists seldom talk about, publicly or privately. My reticence in addressing what might or might not have been Moyra's transgression had more to do with my not *wanting* to believe what might have been true.

To be sure, not all of Moyra's stories were manufactured or supposedly mandated for potential gain of the Salles family. She wrote a host of well-crafted profiles of bona fide newsmakers who made stops in

São Paulo, including novelist Doris Lessing, scientist and peace activist Linus Pauling, and Harvard economist and former ambassador John Kenneth Galbraith. She produced an incisive and amusing profile of Ivo Pitanguy, the Brazilian plastic surgeon whose response to whether he had performed procedures on celebrities Elizabeth Taylor and Michael Jackson was a sly smile. To Moyra, these were genuine news profiles, not hopeful political or financial payoffs mandated by Salles through his lieutenants. Maybe Moyra had just been too busy or unmotivated to go out and find actual people who'd say the things that she had so indecorously put in their mouths. Perhaps she was exercising her abilities as a budding fiction writer. Fabricating bits and pieces of stories had become a diversion more compelling than the practice of producing journalism. Moyra was never confronted about any of her editorial improvisations, as much an indication of the editors' rush to fill the newspaper's pages as it was of her skillful journalistic deceit.[2]

While Moyra continued her under-the-radar revolt, Daily Post editors and reporters came and went. Despite her gloomy assessment of the newspaper's altered direction, most of the journalists who continued arriving at the Daily Post's newsroom, resumes in hand, were skilled young professionals who wanted to make a name for themselves, then move on to the wires or larger newspapers, all the while living and working in a beguiling, faraway city. Many would leverage their work for the Daily Post to inject themselves into mainstream American and British media without slogging away at lower-tier newspapers. They had the same motives that John Sullivan and I had.

For most of the newspaper's reporters, with the exception of Herb Zschech, the Daily Post would be a layover not a destination. Moyra eventually would return home to London to write for a variety of British outlets. Other Daily Post reporters, many of whom had Brazilian spouses, chose to stay in Rio or São Paulo, and after leaving the newspaper would work for English-language media, news wires, or financial outlets, including Dow Jones, Business Week, McGraw-Hill, and later, Bloomberg. Others would create their own

subscription-based newsletters, focused on energy, commodity futures, politics, or tourism. A few, like former *Brazil Herald* manager
editor Walter Colton, who went on to the AP in Rio and São Paulo,
returned to the States but had such *saudades* (affection) for Brazil that
they would move back to translate books, teach, act, and create their
own consulting firms—anything, it seemed, to live in their adopted
country. Eduardo Gentil, the *Daily Post* business editor who had left
the newspaper to go to business school and thereby create the opening I filled, would become a managing director of Goldman Sachs
and later director of Visa's operations in Brazil. Reporter Tom Murphy
would write plays and novels while holding down a variety of financial news positions in Brazil.

Bill Williamson, the jovial newsroom manager who'd been with the
Brazil Heald since his honeymoon in 1959, and *Daily Post* publisher
Mauro Salles ultimately would become embroiled in a series of ac-
rimonious battles over compensation. Salles charged that the *Brazil
Herald's* financial records had been incomplete and inaccurate, and
stopped further payments to Montgomery and to Williamson.

Williamson reacted by abruptly leaving his office one afternoon and
sending his chauffeur to rescue a file cabinet of documents and photographs from the building, which forty-five years later his daughters,
Margaret and Mary Liz, would inherit and give to me to help me in the
preparation of this book. Williamson's lieutenant, aide-de-camp Aldo
Cavaliere, would follow, landing a job at Rio's *O Globo* newspaper.

Williamson eventually hired an attorney to petition Salles for back
wages and other money he said were owed him. By then, Williamson
had become a naturalized Brazilian citizen for tax purposes. The
Williamson-Salles imbroglio would wind its way to a court known in
Brazil as the supreme tribunal of workers' rights. If Williamson pre-
vailed, he would be awarded sufficient assets of the old *Brazil Herald*,
plus a portion of whatever Salles had put into the newly combined
newspapers, along with monetary penalties, to buy out the *Daily Post*.

An expensive and protracted legal battle would fall apart when
Williamson's Brazilian attorney informed him that he could no

longer represent Williamson due to Salles's upcoming scheduled appointment as Communications Minister in the cabinet of Brazil's President-Elect Tancredo Neves in 1985.[3] Williamson contended that Salles had made a preemptive pledge to the attorney that if he would drop the legal case against Salles, Salles would guarantee that the attorney get appointed to a high federal court in the upcoming Neves Administration. Williamson had no proof of any such alleged deal, but steadfastly maintained that it was the reason for his case's collapse against Salles.[4]

Neves would die of an infection stemming from diverticulitis thirty-eight days after he was scheduled to be inaugurated, and thus Salles never got the ministerial appointment he had supposedly sought under the new administration in Brasília; in turn, neither did Williamson's former attorney get appointed to the federal court position. (If this scenario sounds as though it could only happen in a developing country like Brazil, recent US history might indicate otherwise.) The only further recompense Williamson would receive from Salles would be a payment of the equivalent of $30,000 in past compensation due, Williamson told me.[5]

On top of the lawsuit between Williamson and Salles, there would be separate, parallel litigation that Salles would file against the Montgomerys, who in turn would countersue Salles. "The initial lawsuit claimed that we didn't disclose items like unaccrued vacation, lots of undeclared expenses, and other issues," said the junior Montgomery, John Grey. "The money that had been paid from the sale of the *Brazil Herald* went into escrow."[6] The mess of lawsuits sputtered for four years in the Brazilian court system until they were finally settled or adjudicated.

At that point, there was another issue to be resolved: how would the Montgomerys get their proceeds from the sale of the *Herald* out of Brazil? Brazilian law prohibits taking assets from the sale of a Brazilian company beyond the nation's borders. Initially, John Grey Montgomery said the family would invest the proceeds locally "either in real estate or something else."[7] But a local attorney subsequently advised the Montgomerys to invest in a firm that had "export rights," the ability to expatriate funds equal to the amount of the products it imports *into* Brazil. So, the Montgomerys bought an interest in a Canadian religious-book firm, which ostensibly brought into Brazil shiploads of teaching materials. The accrued dollar-equivalent of those imported materials then could be legally exported *out* of Brazil. "You get rid of the books, you make a shell out of the company, and you use 'export rights' to take that money out. It was a common practice at the time," explained Montgomery, who added that his family business paid all applicable US taxes on any revenue from the newspaper's sale.[8]

With Williamson out and Mauro Salles's younger brother, Cláudio, now in charge, in mid-1981 Cláudio Sales called Marilyn Balamaci and me into his spacious second-floor office, the same office that Williamson had occupied. Williamson's former secretary, Marlene,

Fig. 21.1 Stephen G. Bloom in the *Latin America Daily Post* newsroom, São Paulo, 1979. Courtesy of the author.

who now worked for Sales, asked if either of us wanted a cafezinho, a usual and expected offering in any Brazilian business setting.

After several sips, Sales pulled out a white linen handkerchief and covered his nose and mouth, complaining of a *resfriado* (cold). His voice was raspy and sounded labored, but we understood right away what he was telling us.

The newspaper was experiencing a temporary cashflow issue, Sales explained. He emphasized the word "temporary," repeating it several times, *temporário*, saying we would not be getting paid at the end of the month, as usual, but instead by the fifteenth of the next month.

Sales kept the bottom of his face and mouth covered, talking through the linen handkerchief, only lifting it to sip from the demitasse. He must have had a whopper of a resfriado. It crossed my mind that Sales might have been smirking behind the cloth. Or he may have been crying. It was one of those moments when it could have been either, neither, or both.

Our salaries didn't amount to much. That's not why we were working at the newspaper. Since we'd been hired, our wages had free-fallen from the equivalent of $30,000 to $15,000 a year, and the slide was getting more vertical each month as Brazil's inflation kept soaring. Would we ever get paid? If so, when? If the newspaper were experiencing anything more than "a temporary cashflow issue," we likely would be getting laid off.

The paper's financial troubles continued. A British journalist by the name of Stephen Downer had been the *Daily Post*'s Mexico City stringer since the newspaper had started publishing. Yolen had hired him to write four pieces a month for a retainer of $1,000. Downer was one of a half-dozen part-time correspondents Downer would also be expected to report any breaking news.

But Downer said he had never gotten paid. On a trip to Brazil shortly after Cláudio Sales's bare-cupboard declaration to Marilyn and me, Downer visited the *Daily Post* newsroom and demanded that Sales pay him back wages of more than $5,000. In the newsroom, Sales put his arm around Downer's shoulders in an *abraço* and assured him that as soon as he returned to Mexico City, his retainer would be duly deposited in Downer's bank account. That never was to happen, said Downer, who quit the *Daily Post* and got hired by the *Dallas Morning News* as its staff correspondent in Mexico City.[9]

All this was troubling, even after Marilyn's and my paychecks were restored two weeks later, as Sales had promised. We discovered, though, that we were among the lucky staffers. We learned that the Brazilian paste-up crew hadn't been paid in months. These guys got peanuts for wages and were constantly in debt, yet they had continued to show up for work. Their impossible financial straits triggered renewed entreaties for loans from the editorial staff. Considering the circumstances, it was difficult to say no.

Then columnist/oboist Harold Emert got fired. I wasn't sure whether his discharge had anything to do with the newspaper's worsening financial crisis. Emert had never been easy to manage, but he had a loyal following of readers and fans on the newspaper staff, even if some of his columns were misses and veered over-the-top neurotic. His copy was not clean, but that's the case with many talented reporters. He'd been another holdover from the *Brazil Herald*. The editorial direction the more reasoned and sober *Daily Post* had taken ostensibly did not include Emert's assorted personal ruminations on the world.

As Steve Yolen would remember, "Harold had increasingly fallen into disfavor with Ed Taylor, the managing editor and direct newsroom supervisor, and we would have decided together that Harold's relationship with the LADP should be terminated. Ed would have communicated that to Harold, not me. I do remember now that Ed talked to me about Harold's leaving because of the overall body of his reporting and writing, and I agreed. Executive news decision."[10]

Emert's take was different. He said he'd been fired because of a column he had written in which he speculated that someone on the *Daily Post*'s editorial staff likely was a CIA informant. The column was spiked, and shortly thereafter Emert was let go. In addition to Joe Sims's and John Thrall's alleged connections with the CIA, Emert had again raised the perennial "Who's the Company man at the newspaper?"

suspicion that had lurked behind the headlines at the *Brazil Herald* from that paper's founding, now carried over to the *Daily Post*. Emert offered no hard evidence, and he proffered no names. In the iteration he delivered, his column would have had no place at most newspapers, particularly at the newspaper he was accusing of harboring one or more spies.

But if Taylor and Yolen didn't accept Emert's premise or how he had stated it, why not just kill the column? Why can Emert? Why not work with him to deepen and broaden the reporting? Could what Emert had written have hit too close to home? Were there morsels of truth in it?

Yolen and Taylor weathered the fallout from axing Emert. Journalists might project a degree of solidarity, but when it comes to accepting personnel decisions made by their bosses, they're like workers anywhere else. There was grumbling, but no one backed Emert enough to do anything about his firing. Emert was an at-will employee, and his employer had decided that his services were no longer needed.

Emert's firing instead morphed into a general sense of ire directed at Salles and brother Cláudio, who were viewed by the staff more as cruzeiro-pinching opportunists than as reputable, principled publishers. Perhaps Bill Hall had been right to have protested the São Paulo overlords who had swept into the *Herald* newsroom. Maybe Hall had been smarter than anyone had given him credit for.

The dream of creating a visionary global-minded newspaper distributed throughout Latin America began to fade. The cashflow issue that Cláudio Sales had used as the rationale to delay paying Marilyn and me would sooner or later turn into a matter *permanente*. It was just a matter of time. There was no percentage in denying it any longer. Mauro Salles had neither the resources nor imagination to sustain what the newspaper's overworked staff had sought to create.

But that wouldn't necessarily mean the end of the *Daily Post*. Not by a long shot. Salles had simply lost interest in his latest pet project. That might turn out all right, though. Salles had provided the seed money to hire the personnel to launch the *Daily Post*. Yolen's vision was that

Salles was a trailblazer. Maybe he had started the *Daily Post* to flip it for a quick profit. Perhaps Salles wasn't a "closer," as Yolen had put it, but a "starter."

What Salles had financed and Yolen and the staff had launched could now be sold to a more suitable publisher with deeper pockets, someone with the patience to play the long (or longer) game. Perhaps the *Miami Herald* would reconsider buying a smart English-language daily in Brazil, a broadsheet that carried more gravitas than the *Brazil Herald* had. Or maybe *The New York Times*, *The Washington Post*, or *Wall Street Journal* would be in the market to expand south of the border. The *Daily Post* could still become the Latin American equivalent of the *International Herald Tribune*, long-distance sisters separated by a great ocean, each serving a select audience, a bench of talented, multi-lingual reporters and editors employed at both newspapers. What an exciting precedent that would be.

CHAPTER 22

The Letter X

If only.

Apart from whether Mauro Salles had gotten cold feet or not, there were external forces that would make the long-term publication of a comprehensive English-language daily newspaper in Brazil challenging, if not impossible.

The nation had started a headfirst slide into what would become known as the "lost decade," an economic coda to the "lost generation" of literary adventurers who, like me, had chosen to leave America and Britain for Brazil. With the world oil crisis of the 1970s came unpaid bills from the lavish spending sprees by a succession of generals from the late 1960s. International loans had come due, and unless Brazil repaid them, it would default on hundreds of millions in borrowed dollars used for massive public works and megaeconomic expansion. Meanwhile, hyperinflation would undermine the cruzeiro, leading to repeated devaluations, and ultimately a new currency, first the cruzado, then cruzeiro real, and finally the real. The residual impact of relocating the nation's capital from Rio de Janeiro to Brasília in the early 1960s would prove to overwhelm Rio, creating a void that had a ripple effect felt into the 1980s and beyond. The impact would include skyrocketing rates of crime, petty and violent. Unemployment, as well as a collapse of living wages, plagued the country, particularly in Rio, the nation's crown jewel. Hundreds of thousands of Brazilians who could afford to leave Rio relocated to

São Paulo, Miami, or New York. *Cidade Maravilhosa* became a dangerous and difficult place to live. All of these events did not ingratiate international bankers to Brazil.

Ousted by the Salles Brothers, Bill Williamson and his family would leave Rio for Miami, where Williamson would become executive director of the Inter American Press Association, the clubby newspaper lobbying group he and John D. Montgomery had spent so much of their professional lives cultivating.

Despite Moyra's dour assessment of publisher Salles and the newspaper's future, I continued at the *Daily Post* because I enjoyed working there, even with its daily miscues and editorial stumbles. I had worked too hard to get there to leave. Not for a minute was I ever lonely in Rio. I was having too good a time. My facility with Portuguese had taken a quantum leap. I'd go through a growth period, reach a frustrating plateau, and then charge ahead. Speaking was the thing, and the newspaper's ragtag paste-up crew, who had finally gotten paid, guaranteed me opportunities to do so every day and gave me the confidence to conduct interviews in Portuguese and eventually hire myself out as a translator. I knew that no matter how long I'd remain in Brazil, even were it for the rest of my life, I'd never speak like a native. Still, learning a foreign language was a necessary challenge. Nearly all the journalists at the newspaper from Zschech on down spoke two or three with ease. It was wrong for anyone considered reasonably cosmopolitan and learned to go through life knowing just one language. It was the worst of geopolitical, ethnocentric cultural narcissism, resurrecting the joke:

What do you call a person who speaks two languages? Bilingual.

What do you call someone who speaks three languages? Trilingual

What do you call someone who speaks only one language? An American

I didn't have a hankering to return to America. I wasn't homesick. I could live in Brazil for as long as I wanted, provided that my visa allowed it. The chilly reception I'd gotten while looking for newspaper work in the States still unnerved me, and the Milk and Moscone assassinations in San Francisco, along with Jim Jones's final Hail Mary, continued to spook me. It still does.

My staying in Brazil, though, was firmly predicated on the *Daily Post*'s continuing to employ me. I still wanted to be a newspaperman, and without the *Daily Post*, I'd be cooked.

Getting hired by *The New York Times*, *Washington Post*, or any other metro newspaper that had interest in employing a full-time correspondent in Brazil was nearly impossible. Those jobs usually went to reporters as end-of-career sinecures or vetted young staffers. Working for AP or UPI in Brazil held little interest for me. Too much like being a bookkeeper, covering minutia or disasters, usually the former. Teaching English would just be buying time, delaying the making of any decision to stay or leave. Besides, I didn't have the temperament to teach English to Brazilian executives or their teenage children, the prime audiences for such schools or for private tutoring. It'd just be marking my time, a similar feeling to how John Sullivan probably felt, living in Rio and having a blast but feeling guilty about it.

Nor did I want to work for an American multinational in Brazil. Even though I had edited the *Daily Post*'s business pages, I still didn't know much about finance, and I didn't have the patience to learn more. That might sound privileged or brash, but I hated talking money, and writing about it held zero appeal. Ideas were the currency that I hoped could take me places.

I ruled out working for the US government in the Foreign Service or in any other capacity. I had come of age at Berkeley, during the nationwide Vietnam War protests, in the aftermath of the revulsive Kent State shootings. Ronald Reagan and his confederacy of neo-conservatives had just taken over Washington, DC. As an ex-officio member of the California Board of Regents, Reagan had signed my

Berkeley diploma. I knew what four or eight years of the Gipper in the White House could do to America. I didn't want to be a part of that.

I still wanted to be a journalist. "Comfort the afflicted, afflict the comfortable," the credo for generations of American journalists, still held tremendous utilitarian appeal. But despite my continued infatuation with Brazil, if the *Daily Post* were to go under, I'd have no choice. I'd have to move back to the States. Working for a newspaper had been my forever goal, going back to when I stretched out on the carpet in my parents' living room reading the *Newark Evening News*, followed by my years in California, working as a waiter at Giovanni, and beyond. With the *Daily Post* sliding editorially and financially, the news business, which had done little to accommodate me in the States, would sooner or later squeeze me out of Brazil, too.

There was something broken with that economic model. Like A. J. Lamoureux, Mauro Salles had been on the right side of history, but ultimately would emerge as a bit player in a quicksand marketplace that would demonstrate how doomed the newspaper business anywhere would eventually prove to be.

As a hedge to whatever lay around the corner, I picked up the pace of my freelancing to Field News Service, and while I wasn't making much from that side hustle either, Field ran my stories, which began appearing in US newspapers with some regularity. My contributions reflected what it was like to live in Brazil during the early 1980s. I wasn't fixated with reporting conventional news because there wasn't much of it happening in Brazil that would interest Americans. I was more interested in getting at the cultural ethos of such a foreign place, from the minute to the impossibly large. An abbreviated sampling: the popularity of toothpicks (everyone in Brazil used them, and they were cheaper than a visit to the dentist); despachantes (I interviewed Bogie, the red-tape cutter the *Daily Post* had hired to get my work visa, along with a troupe of equally mysterious expeditors); Pope John Paul II's visit to Brazil (during which he celebrated a mass attended by one million supplicants on Copacabana Beach); the ga-ga cult surrounding Carmen Miranda (I visited her grave in a Rio cemetery, where the seriously devoted came with fruit assemblages on their heads to pay their respects); the *esquadrão da morte*, death squads (off-duty cops who avenged petty drug dealers with lurid public executions); how to live with Brazil's triple-digit inflation (by converting your pay check into durable hardgoods as fast as you got paid, which in turn spurred more inflation); Butantã Snake Institute (a medical-venom facility to be avoided by anyone with ophidiophobia); hilarious foreign-language gaffes ("But I didn't mean to say that!"); Rio's ridiculous abundance of mirrors—literally everywhere—a reflection, so to speak, of the city's adoration of youth and beauty (the birthplace of what would become known as the Brazilian butt lift); *abertura* (the Portuguese word for *opening*), the nation's populist-driven transition from dictatorship to democracy, which would resemble the Soviet Union's *perestroika* and *glasnost* a decade later); and the obligatory feature on British train-robber/fugitive Ronald Biggs ("Newspapers would run anything that mentioned his name," the AP's Ed Miller would remember[1]).

I used the dollars I got from those stories to get out of Rio on weekends to report other stories: stark Brasília on its twentieth anniversary; the disappearing rainforest; and while in the Amazon, features on a rubber factory founded by automobile tycoon Henry Ford; industrialist Daniel Ludwig's failed pulp-paper Jari project; Carajás, a hole-in-the-ground filled with the world's largest deposits of iron ore; ecotourism; and the coming market for pharmaceuticals derived from exotic medicinal herbs. I got myself to Paraguay to write about a bizarre time-capsule of a settlement five hours from Asunción called Filadelfia, where old-world Mennonites had recreated a German village and spoke an arcane variant of Plattdeutsch (another Stephen King variation of my Americana story). In Montevideo I recreated a dramatic tick-tock procedural of when Uruguayan revolutionaries kidnapped and killed former Indiana police chief and suspected CIA agent Dan Mitrione.

I'm certain that the other journalists at the *Daily Post* and those who worked for the wires or US and British newspapers in Brazil thought my story selection was as simplistic as when I had written about Confederados Judith and Jim Jones. Viewed against today's journalistic standards, these gee-whiz stories sound dated and sophomoric. I was trying to shine a light into crevasses that were foreign, offbeat, curious, and bizarre (at least to me they were). Wasn't that what a foreign correspondent was supposed to do between covering earthquakes and coups? With each pitch I tried to embody what the popular and middlebrow historians Will and Ariel Durant said historians *ought* to be doing:

> Civilization is a stream with banks. The stream is sometimes filled with blood from people killing, stealing, shouting and doing the things historians usually record, while on the banks, unnoticed, people build homes, make love, raise children, sing songs, write poetry and even whittle statues. The story of civilization is the story of what happened on the banks. Historians are pessimists because they ignore the banks for the river.[2]

In the place of *historians* in the above, I plugged in *journalists* when it came to the stories I was sending back to the States.

Many of these takeouts appeared in fat Sunday metro newspapers since that day's larger number of display advertisements proportionately increased the size of the paper's editorial hole. They also appeared in Monday editions because since relatively little political or breaking news happens on Sundays there also was a greater need for editorial content. The latter stories, often without a news peg, were called "Monday Burgers" at some newspapers. Both days' newspapers were chock-full of such off-news-cycle stories also known as "yarns." This was before newspapers routinely ran those pesky preprinted advertising inserts that did nothing to expand the size of the core product.

Meanwhile, I was writing up a storm, so much so that my sturdy Olivetti Lettera 32 could barely keep up. After an evening of keyboard pounding, the X key started to stick, and even with repeated anointments from a can of Singer All Purpose Sewing Machine Oil, it kept jamming. I'd be typing at a good clip when the X key suddenly wouldn't retract, splayed out on the platen like a wounded soldier, stuck, unable to move. This required an uncoupling of other soldiers that had come to the rescue of the X key, who found themselves similarly immobilized. It was as though they all had been lured into a trap and had been massacred. As anyone who has ever used a typewriter knows, such pileups cause instinctual screaming and a profusion of profanity. I was about to throw my otherwise-sturdy Lettera 32 out the window of my apartment.

The next morning I took my battalion of keys to a repair shop on Visconde de Pirajá, which had a flashing neon sign out front, *Reparação de Máquinas de Escrever*.

After peering inside the Lettera 32 with a jeweler's loupe, the repairman removed his eyepiece and looked up. "You're lucky," he pronounced. "X is the one typewriter key you don't really need."

Maybe in Portuguese, but in English the letter X does appear every once in a while. The medic's diagnosis ultimately proved to be a sublime moment that presaged a turning point. It also was a very Brazilian solution. *Dar um jeito*, if you can't change something, you work around it.

I wasn't ready to give up yet on the letter X.

At that instance, I knew that the *Daily Post* would eventually fold. Maybe in six months, or a year, maybe more, maybe less. It couldn't go on. The actual closing wouldn't be so bad. It would be the slide of getting there that would mean a degradation I didn't want to experience. More publisher interference, fewer pages, a thinner newspaper, more *temporário* cashflow issues, more layoffs. Moyra's prediction come true.

In the typewriter-repair shop, I experienced an epiphany, what the Japanese call *satori*, an awakening or understanding, that rang true.

It was time to make a decision.

Should I follow Teddy Hecht's lead and never return to the United States?

Do I chase Hunter S. Thompson's scramble through South America, then get back to the States, perhaps wiser, perhaps not, and throw out any notion of working for a newspaper?

Do I pack up and try once again to insert myself into the maelstrom of American journalism, wherever it was headed?

I flipflopped for months.

I'd miss the sultry and frenetic life that Rio exuded, an exuberance that had seeped into my psyche, which I knew would never leave. But I needed to give another go at what I had always wanted to do, even though the future of newspapers appeared as bleak in the States as it seemed in Brazil, at least at the *Daily Post*. There were impossible-to-ignore, industry-wide global signs of doom, but nothing like what would happen a decade later: broadband internet, digital classifieds, shorter attention spans, the ubiquity of smart phones and handheld screens, and the habit shift from reading to scrolling online. That would be down the road. Maybe the lesson from the *Daily Post* was that Brazil had been way ahead of what would happen when I'd try to be a newspaperman in the States.

I wanted in now, before it would be too late.

Goodbye, Hello

IN KANSAS, LONGTIME *Brazil Herald* publisher John D. Montgomery died of lung cancer in 1985. Bill Williamson's wife Vânia recalled her last conversation with him: "He called to say goodbye to Bill and me. He said he wished that a train would run him over—he was in that much pain."[1]

Mauro Salles, the man Montgomery had sold the Herald to, soon grew tired of being the publisher of the *Latin America Daily Post*. If the newspaper ever made a profit, it was insignificant. Never truly engaged in running the newspaper, Salles became more and more an absentee publisher. The thrill of being an international newspaper magnate wore off as quickly as it had seized Salles when John Garner and Steve Yolen convinced him to go it alone.

When Gilberto Huber Jr., the man who had approached Montgomery and Williamson a decade earlier to buy the newspaper, would pay a visit to Salles in early 1982, the two would strike a deal, although there is no record of how much money was exchanged. Huber had made sizeable fortunes following his father, Gilbert Jacob Huber Sr., who had moved to Brazil to create its telephone directories, *Listas Telefônicas Brasileiras S.A.* (LTB) and *Paginas Amarelas* (Yellow Pages). The younger Gilberto, who Brazilianized his name by adding the "o," took over his father's company. Huber's goal was vertical integration of the *Listas* with allied print-related businesses.[2] That's where the *Daily Post*'s acquisition came in.

Huber would join the newspaper as a major shareholder and be named president and publisher on the *Daily Post*'s masthead; Salles would still be listed as editor in chief, although neither had much, if anything, to do with the *Daily Post*'s everyday content.[3]

Huber "was a non-entity. He played no role, except maybe talking to Mauro [Salles] privately," said Yolen, who would continue as executive editor.[4] Huber had an unsavory reputation among the foreign press in Rio," said former AP correspondent Ed Miller. "He was a total egomaniac. He was arrogant and self-centered."[5]

Neither Huber nor Salles would be serious about investing additional resources in the *Daily Post*. All the newspaper's stringers would be let go; only a skeletal staff in the old *Brazil Herald* building on Rua do Resende would remain. In 1982, when the Falkland Islands War between Britain and Argentina erupted, the biggest truly international story in South America in half a century, the *Daily Post* sent no correspondent to Buenos Aires. The newspaper's original correspondent there, Robert Lindley, had been laid off, and the *Daily Post* would suffer the ignominy of republishing stories from American and British journalists who had been sent thousands of miles to cover a war happening in the newspaper's southern backyard.

The *Daily Post* limped long, getting smaller and smaller, with less news, fewer ads, and more editorial valentines to attract or assuage advertisers and political influencers. Herb Zschech continued writing his daily column, "Zschech and Double Check," and Rita Davy kept contributing her about-town social-happenings column, as did expat society maven Jo Ann Hein from São Paulo. Zschech and Davy were fixtures that went with the building, and Hein likely would have continued writing for the *Daily Post* even if it meant paying the editors to run her column.[6] Tom Murphy, Betsy Herrington, and Christopher Pickard admirably wrote local features. By then, former foreign editor and São Paulo correspondent Stan Lehman had left for the Associated Press.

Within a year, the *Brazil Herald*'s insert into the *Daily Post* was eliminated, and with it, almost all locally produced news disappeared.

Yolen and Taylor would have little more to do than select international wire copy, write headlines, and pen a local editorial (which some days appeared, and other days did not). Fewer classified and display ads would be published; many showing up on page one, as sure a sign as any, during that era, of a newspaper's imminent demise. What little circulation the *Daily Post* had crumbled. "By then, the newspaper was pretty much just an empty shell," Yolen recalled. "It was clear the newspaper was not going to survive."[7]

In early 1988, Salles and Huber shuttered the *Latin America Daily Post*. In recounting the newspaper's missteps, Yolen's take was that "the *Daily Post* would have survived the 1980s decade had it remained true to its original purpose as a serious pro-business publication based in São Paulo, and not bought the *Brazil Herald* and moved the operation to Rio. The *Herald* would have gone out of business soon enough. The idea of owning a printing press I think tipped the scales, but it probably was a mistake to buy the *Herald* and its liabilities (market, personnel, etc.)."[8] Yolen had become the victim of his own cheery disposition. He blamed the *Latin America Daily Post*'s demise on the acquisition of a newspaper he never believed was the *Daily Post*'s competition. It was more complicated—and ultimately more predictable—than that.

The newsroom on Rua do Resende would soon be cleared out and abandoned, its contents sold or junked, everyone laid off. Within months, graffiti would cover the entirety of a padlocked rolltop gate protecting the building from squatters.

I knew that returning to the United States would bring joys and disappointments. Hearing English everywhere at first sounded strange. I had to recalibrate my brain to seeing billboards, listening to the radio, watching TV, eavesdropping, all in English. I had no need any longer to preemptively translate into Portuguese whatever I wanted to say before I opened my mouth.

I also had to prepare myself for America being centric to everything, a replay of the famous Saul Steinberg *New Yorker* cover, but with California and New York now sharing equal billing, and the rest of the world a bit player, if at all. Brazil—in fact, the entirety of Latin

Fig. Epilogue.1 Shuttered offices of the *Latin America Daily Post* and *Brazil Herald*, circa 2020. Photograph courtesy of Tom Murphy.

America—was on no one's radar. Brazil was large, tropical, and steamy with a rainforest and a lot of political instability—but exactly where, no one seemed to know. It was somewhere out *there*.

Cultural cues jumped out at me as I settled back in. I had forgotten how Americans distance themselves; they don't get as physically close as Brazilians do, in the market, on the bus, in elevators, at the grocery store. This was as true in cities as it was in rural settings. I found that for a lot of Americans, making eye contact, was taboo. Brazilians look strangers in the eye, acknowledging them, perhaps looking out for them. Or maybe for themselves. At least, that was my impression.

Brazilians are much more social than their American counterparts. They eat later and stay out much later. A cross-generational adoration of music infuses Brazil. As I had experienced firsthand at my São Paulo pension, any object could and would be repurposed into a makeshift musical instrument. Brazilian women of a certain age, particularly in Rio, seemed much more forward than their North American counterparts. If they liked you after a brief encounter on the beach or at a party, *they'd* ask for your phone number or address.

Of assorted other bi-national observations, three stood out.

In Brazil, you couldn't get milk in bottles or cartons; it came only in flimsy, bladder-like plastic bags. Small, insignificant, inconsequential.

At American supermarkets, the colossal variety of offerings and choices floored me. Somehow, I had forgotten. You could get everything and anything under one very large roof. As June Erlick, who had also worked for the *Daily Post*, remembered when she returned to the States and went to a market, put it: "When I got to the yogurt case, I saw they had fat-free yogurt, 1% fat, 10% fat, rich and creamy, with sprinkles, without sprinkles, assorted fruit flavors and innumerable brands. I just froze. I couldn't imagine so much choice."[9]

My third observation carried more magnitude, put into sharper focus based on America's cornucopia of plenty: Brazil's unrelenting poverty. The reflexive way to deal with it was to look away. What other ready choice was there? From favelas you could see anywhere in *Cidade Maravilhosa* to whole families sleeping on iron grates covering lights illuminating the city's luxury shopping centers and high-rises, the disparity of income was constantly in your face. The initial shock of seeing homeless children coming up to your table at a soigné outdoor bistro, stretching the bottoms of their T-shirts, begging you to dump a plateful of food onto what they had fashioned into a makeshift bowl, soon wears off. Against instinct, you shoo the beggars away—or others might join them. Some, called *trombadinhas*, prowled too closely and were experts at snatching something of value, often tossing it to an accomplice and disappearing. If you didn't tip a *pivete* (a juvenile thief) to "look after" your car parked on the street, there was a good chance you would return to find it vandalized or not there. I understood why the blackmail was necessary. The tacit agreement never made me feel unsafe. But it did make me feel angry and powerless that such a system existed that so thoroughly undercut the dignity and sanctity of fellow human beings.

I'd been accustomed to seeing homeless people in American cities, the battalions of squeegee men who demanded money after they washed your windshield at a red light, but Brazilian poverty was heartache on a magnum scale. On that score, perhaps Brazil had arrived first at where the United States would be headed: sprawling homeless encampments, tent cities, urban neighborhoods declared off-limits because they had been taken over by habitues with no other place to go.

There was a seemingly unbridgeable divide between those in Brazil who had and the multitudes who did not. I'd gotten accustomed to seeing distant tableaus of mountainside favelas leavened by brightly colored kites, framing some of the most breathtaking scenery in the world. By the time I left Brazil, I didn't see any longer what had so viscerally struck me when I first arrived. Maybe I had gone native.

Critics called this disparity the end game of *capitalismo salvagem* (savage capitalism). Brazil's richest five percent have the same income as the accumulation of the remaining ninety-five percent, making for the second-highest lopsided income distribution in the world (Qatar is first). At its current rate, it would take Brazil seventy-five years to reach Britain's level of income equality and sixty years to meet Spanish standards. Compared to its South American neighbors, Brazil is thirty-five years behind Uruguay and thirty years behind Argentina in the same metrics.[10] No wonder Brazil is such a fertile breeding ground for revolution. Trickle-down economics, the mantra of the Reagan years, would turn into a crueler myth in Brazil than it would become in the United States.

One positive cultural element in which the Brazilians outpaced Americans was relative freedom from race-based discrimination. Brazil was far from prejudice-free. But when I returned to the US, almost instantly I felt how ingrained fear based solely on race was for both white and Black Americans. The palpable terror many Blacks shared of anyone white and in power, particularly police officers, would erupt decades later with the murder of George Floyd, but such race-based terror has long been a cancerous lesion on America's underbelly and continues to fester. Countless times in just a couple of weeks of my return, I saw whites automatically cross the street to avoid passing a group of Black males. In Brazil, that particular alarm doesn't automatically sound.

Discrimination in Brazil seemed, at least nominally, to be more connected to economic class than skin color. Since relatively few second- or third-generation Brazilian families can claim no miscegenation, the notion of racial superiority, inferiority, or stereotyping doesn't readily exist. "Blacks" and "whites" mingle in Brazil, something that infelicitously doesn't often happen in many places in the States. The commonly heard Portuguese-English cognates *mulatto* and *mulatta*, a biracial man or woman, are seldom uttered in the US because the terms are considered offensive slurs, but in nonbinary Brazil they're neutral descriptors since they apply to some genealogical degree to nearly everyone.

I did find in Brazil an uncomfortable social hierarchy, a degree of class entitlement that I rarely had experienced in the States. Maids, *porteiros* (apartment doormen), drivers, anyone lower than you on the economic-social ladder, were seldom introduced in social settings. They had no name, as though they didn't exist as anything more than the service they provided. I saw this repeatedly in Brazil. Perhaps this had something to do with Brazil once being a colony of the imperial Portuguese monarchy. In that sense, pluralistic America, at least the myth of it, played more to my sensibilities, although my perceptions were confined to where I had returned: the San Francisco Bay Area, the original Land of Woke.

Fuzzy cultural perceptions aside, I didn't have a lot of money when I returned to the States, and I had to find work fast. I had barely enough for a month or two of rent. My job at the *Daily Post* hadn't afforded me the luxury of saving much. I could barely afford a dinner at Giovanni, my old employer, and I certainly never risked going to Golden Gate Fields, with or without the career waiters and their surefire betting wheel. As I had realized before I'd left America, journalism might ennoble the mind, but it wasn't a calling that made you more than barely middle-class.

To make matters worse, by the time I had returned in the fall of 1981, the atmosphere was awfully gloomy to be looking for newspaper work. Two great newspapers, *The Washington Star*, which had been acquired several years earlier by Time, Inc., had just folded, and the *Philadelphia Bulletin*, once the largest evening newspaper in America, wobbled on a precipice, about to collapse next. Dozens of newspapers were on the chopping block, and thousands of journalists were out of work. Competing big-city newspapers had no alternative but to merge, which eroded the remaining papers' quality. It was a coda to what the *Daily Post* had done when Mauro Salles had bought the *Brazil Herald* and eventually shuttered it.

All this gave me a counter-intuitive thought: Maybe I could get hired at the *Philadelphia Bulletin* in its waning days before it went under. Someone had to take the places of the droves of journalists exiting. Maybe I could get hired on a short-term basis, which would give me enough experience and stateside credibility to go hat-in-hand somewhere else. The prospect of working for the afternoon Philadelphia newspaper, even if the job lasted only a few months, seemed like an adventure, tame when compared to my Brazil odyssey. Once the *Bulletin* was taken off life support, maybe another newspaper would hire me in a measure of solidarity.

Somehow I wangled an interview with the *Bulletin*'s harried executive editor, Craig Ammerman, whom I quickly realized wasn't about to hire anyone, even though I made certain to mention my Field News story about the *other* Philadelphia, Filadelfia, the remote Mennonite city I had visited and written about in Paraguay. But Ammerman wasn't in the least interested. With apologies, he escorted me out of the *Bulletin*'s huge, eerily empty newsroom on Filbert Street almost as soon I had arrived.

When I got back to Oakland, I pitched a story to *60 Minutes* about Paraguay's crusty despot, Alfredo Stroessner, the world's longest-ruling dictator, and got as far as Mike Wallace and Barry Lando, the show's executive producer, both of whom I talked to. They seemed interested, but balked when it came to sending a team to Asunción to interview *el presidente*.

I tried to contact Harrison Salisbury, the *New York Times* editor who had published my Del Monte assembly-line diary on the Op-Ed page, but by then he had retired. I doubted whether he'd remember me, anyway. Marylois Purdy Vega, the head of *Time*'s fact-checking department, had also retired.

I knew I didn't have a chance at getting hired in a major market like New York, Chicago, or Los Angeles, although I unexpectedly scored an interview with the local New York ABC-TV affiliate as a news writer, but that was canceled because on the morning of my interview, October 6, 1981, Egyptian President Anwar Sadat was assassinated and every station in town was scrambling to get the local angle. The interview never got rescheduled.

It was time to get real. I confined my search to mid-sized American cities with competing newspapers. I'd leverage my work at the *Latin America Daily Post* and Field News Service as a wild-card pedigree.

While that seemed like drawing to an inside straight, I didn't have much else. Although I didn't know it at the time, this was the same strategy that had sunk A. J. Lamoureux's hopeful reentry from Brazil into the US job market eighty years earlier.

I wasn't looking to be a hard-news reporter, so I resurrected the story list I'd come up with before I'd left the States. To that list, which had included odd-ball entries such as tracing a year in the life of a rental tuxedo and interviewing petitioners in the name-change court, I added three dozen more, pitched to each newspaper's demographic. Some were inspired by my time in Brazil, others had been lodged in my brain for too long and needed air: talk to local tropical fish dealers to find out whose collection of black-market piranhas is the largest in town; embed with the NRP *Sagres*, a Portuguese three-masted tall ship that often sailed across the Atlantic; spend a week in a monastery to learn who becomes a monk; share croissants with sex guru Dr. Ruth when she comes to town; interview local crossword/Scrabble/acrostic freaks; write about being a spear carrier, an extra or supernumerary, in a productions at the city opera; interview seventy-year-old-plus professional "gigolos," hired by cruise-ship companies as escorts and dance partners. In retrospect, some of these ideas seem to have sprung from a writer famous at the time, George Plimpton, but all were mine. I threw in some of my original ideas, pre-Brazil, for good measure: a tour of the city's best pastrami sandwiches, cigars, barbers, martinis.

In a seemingly last-ditch effort to pick up relevancy and circulation, newspaper "women's sections" at the time were in the process of being transformed into daily magazines for women *and* men, with upbeat, unisex names like *Style, Tempo, View, Today, Living, High Profile.* Where I wanted to live was less important than where I could find work. I sent my story list to editors in Atlanta, Detroit, and Dallas. Maybe I'd have a shot in those markets.

One morning out of the blue, I got a call from Alvin Shuster, the foreign editor of the *Los Angeles Times*, who asked whether I'd be interested in becoming the *Times* correspondent in El Salvador. I had no idea where Shuster had gotten my name or phone number, and initially I was thrilled. But then I flashed on poor John Sullivan, and after some hesitation, I said no to Shuster, perhaps once again against my best interests. I wasn't prepared to go to El Salvador, nor did I want to. What could I report that other correspondents hadn't? Even if I did come across something new and different, was I ready to expose myself to the dangers in getting that story? Maybe Sullivan had taught me something after all.

In the meantime, I received no word from my job inquiries in Atlanta, a lukewarm response from Detroit, and a curious phone call one morning while brushing my teeth from an assistant managing editor at the *Dallas Morning News.*

"Where'd you get this list of story ideas from?" a man with the hard-to-forget name of Buster Haas asked. "Is this some list making the rounds?" He seemed both amused and miffed.

"They're mine!" I responded defensively and with some edge.

"These are *your* ideas?"

"Absolutely!"

"Really," Hass said, less as a question and more as an accusation.

"Yes," I said, masking how annoyed I was getting.

I didn't want to replay my self-immolation at the *Miami Herald* during my interview with Janet Chusmir. I knew the *Dallas Morning News* was locked in a last-stand-at-the Alamo battle with the city's afternoon paper, the *L.A. Times*-owned *Times-Herald,* and was prepared to do anything to slay the competition. I had read stories about the so-called newspaper shoot-out in *Editor & Publisher.* Only one of the two Dallas newspapers was expected to survive. The fight for which one was under way.

Mollified, Haas seemed pleasant enough. We talked about several ideas on my list, but there were no openings at the newspaper and none was expected. The old story. Haas asked nothing about my experiences working for the *Latin America Daily Post* or Field News Service. My experiences in Brazil seemed to count for little except a mild case of curiosity. "Where was it you said you lived?" Haas asked.

There was something he was holding back. I could feel it. Haas ended our ten-minute back-and-forth with, "Well, if you ever find yourself in Dallas, give me a call and I'll take you to lunch."

I didn't anticipate any such trip and I thanked Haas for his time. At least I hadn't set myself on fire.

But ten seconds after I hung up, I realized what Haas had said—or rather, had not said. He had telegraphed to me a message in code. *"Come to Dallas, let us meet you. We won't pay your way. But if you're interested, we might be, too."*

It was similar to what *Daily Post* executive editor Steve Yolen had written when I first queried him long-distance about a job, and what Bill Williamson had done when Hunter S. Thompson had written and asked about working at the *Brazil Herald*.

I dialed Haas back. "It just so happens that I'm going to be in Dallas next week," I volunteered, almost giddy with my improvisation. "Might I take you up on that lunch invitation?" Besides booking a standby ticket and paying for a cheap motel, what did I have to lose?

I had spent all my savings on the five-stop Líneas Aéreas Paraguayas plane ticket that had gotten me back to the States from Brazil, and my rent money was about to run out. All the more reason to dig in. At the time, Dallas was transitioning into a modern American city from an oil boom town. The eponymous TV show was America's favorite prime time diversion. *The Morning News* was in the midst of transitioning from a regional broadsheet into the makings of a national powerhouse. The newspaper had brought in a slew of talented editors from the East Coast, including Burl Osborne, the former president of AP, as well as a whiz kid feature editor by the name of Ellen Kampinsky.

I scraped together enough to get myself to Dallas the following week, stay at the downtown Holiday Inn, and meet Haas. We ate at a restaurant in a converted train depot, and while walking back to the newspaper office in one of Dallas's skyways, Haas offered to set up meetings with other editors that afternoon. "I can't promise you anything, but as long as you're here, you might as well meet them," Haas said, sounding reasonable.

One was with a very large man, city editor Billy Don Smith (this was Texas, after all), who, strangely enough, clipped his fingernails while interviewing me. I wasn't sure whether this was a Texas thing, Smith was dissing me, or he felt so at home that he did what most people do in private. I thought of mentioning my Confederados story, which the *L.A. Times* had run on page one, but rejected the idea as too chancy. Such story-dropping had done nothing for me with Ammerman at the *Philadelphia Bulletin*, and it likely wouldn't do anything for me here, even though I was in the Lone Star State. Smith handed me off to several assistant city editors. When I said goodbye to Haas at three, he asked me to call him before I left DFW that evening.

This was still the age of payphones, and at the airport gate, I used one to dial Haas, who asked if I wouldn't mind if he put me on hold, which proved to be five, then ten minutes.

"Can you wait another couple of minutes?" Haas asked, coming back on the line. "Hang on. I'll be back."

By then, my Braniff jet had boarded and the gate area was empty.

"Are you coming, sir?" the airline agent asked, pointing to me, holding the telephone receiver, at the far end of the gate area. "We're about to close the airplane doors."

"Can you wait a minute? I replied. "Please!"

"I'm sorry, sir," she shouted back. "Boarding is complete. If you're coming, it has to be now."

At that moment, Haas got back on the phone. "Gimme a minute," he said out of breath. "I'll be back."

Before I could protest, Haas had put me on hold again.

By now, the gate attendant was motioning me furiously to board. She put her index finger and thumb to her throat and pulled them across horizontally in a slashing motion. It was now or never.

"Wait," I pleaded. "Just a minute!"

At that moment, Haas came back on the line.

"Stephen, you still there? Sorry it took me so long. It's awfully hard to corral editors at this time of day. Hope you enjoyed meeting us as much as we enjoyed meeting you."

"I sure did," I replied, trying to sound normal.

"It took some time," Hass drawled.

He paused for what seemed like an eternity.

"Yes, Buster, please go ahead!"

"We'd like to offer you a job. When can you start?"

ACKNOWLEDGMENTS

FOR ALL OF my adult life, I've wanted to make sense of my years in Brazil, working for the *Latin America Daily Post*. The idea gained currency when I read a terrific book about a fictional English-language newspaper, one published in Italy patterned after another expat paper, the *Rome Daily American*, which in real life was published from 1946 to 1984, roughly the same timeframe as the *Brazil Herald*.

Tom Rachman's brilliant 2010 novel, *The Imperfectionists*, started me thinking about writing a nonfiction account of my own days as a young newspaper reporter at the *Latin American Daily Post*. I followed Rachman's book with Ronald Weber's *News of Paris: American Journalists in the City of Light Between the Wars* (2007). Both books gave me a sketchy roadmap to imagine a hybrid book: a story of my own adventures living and working in Brazil, along with an account of that nation's offbeat English-language newspapers, dating back a century earlier. Combining both stories seemed unwieldy and manufactured at first, but as I descended into the material, there seemed to be a common thread that braided both accounts together. *The Brazil Chronicles* is the heartening results of that weaving.

The *Brazil Chronicles* would turn into neither a conventional trade nor academic book, but would borrow characteristics from each. Such a model isn't welcomed by an industry unaccustomed to doing things differently. *The Brazil Chronicles* is a triumph of perseverance with so many agents and editors telling me that this book would fall into neither category, and thus would capture no more than minimal interest.

That was bad enough, but the same agents and editors also advised, "Who cares about newspapers? Who cares about Brazil? Move on." That sentiment troubled me, but with great fortune the manuscript found an enthusiastic and supportive home with Andrew Davidson, the editor in chief at the University of Missouri Press, who seemed instantly charmed by the idea of a young man's coming-of-age story intertwined with the legacy of a multitude of extraordinary English-language newspapers printed in distant Brazil. The press's director, David M. Rosenbaum, quickly got invested in the project, and the three of us formed a team to bring *The Brazil Chronicles* to the public. Both Susan Curtis and Ken McLaughlin offered me their skills as editors; their suggestions greatly improved the manuscript. Production manager Drew Griffith did a masterful job of converting an organic and evolving manuscript into a finished book.

Particularly for Chapter XIII, "Gonzo," I'm greatly indebted to Douglas Brinkley and his edited collection of Hunter S. Thompson's letters, *The Fear and Loathing Letters, Volume One: The Proud Highway, Saga of a Desperate Southern Gentleman 1955-1967* (1997), and Brian Kevin for *The Footloose American: Following the Hunter S. Thompson Trail Across South America* (2014).

An undertaking of *The Brazil Chronicle*'s scope is possible only with encouragement and help from numerous bystanders, all with connections to either the *Brazil Herald* or *Latin America Daily Post*. Thanks to Rob Anderson, Cricket Appel, Moyra Ashford, Reid Baron, Bob Beadle, Don Best, Jim Bruce, Richard Cole, Walter Colton, Stephen Downer, Harold Emert, June Erlick, Liza Fourré, Mark Gruberg, Gilberto Huber, Phylis Huber, David Hume, Janet Huseby, Peter Jarvis, Robin Lai, Stan Lehman, Mary A. Lenz, Marc Lifsher, Susan Lightcap, Maggie Locke, Ramez Maluf, Ed Miller, John Grey Montgomery, Tom Murphy, Brian Nicholson, Joe Novitski, Christopher Pickard, Maya Pijnappel, Rick Smith, and Steve Yolen. Each took time to meet, talk, or exchange emails with me.

Journalists no longer with us who contributed recollections included Jerry Ceppos, Dick Foster, Bob Nadkarni, Joe Sims, John Thrall,

Jean Etsinger, and Bill Williamson. My gratitude goes especially to Bill, who spent scores of hours with me before his death in 2020, as did his late wife Vânia, and their two daughters, Margaret and Mary Liz, who grew up in Rio de Janeiro in the shadow of the *Brazil Herald*. The legacies of many newspeople created the stories in this book. These journalists include Bob Bone, Joseph Brown, Adelina Capper, Rita Davy, Juan de Onís, Pam Deacon, André Fodor, Frank Garcia, J. C. Garritano, Philip Graham, Margaret Grammer, Bill Hall, Otto (Vic) Hawkins, Jo Ann Hein, Betsy Herrington, Alex Kennard, Charles Kuralt, Andrew Jackson Lamoureux, Lee Langley, Garry Marchant, Richard Momsen, John D. Montgomery, Bill Moore, Millie Norman, Charles Obertance, Chris Phillips, Guy Lyon Playfair, Andrew Reid, Ralph Ross, David St. Clair, Mauro Salles, Paul Vanorden Shaw, John Sullivan, Tad Szulc, Hunter S. Thompson, Igor Tsvik, Edwina Hecht Williams, Mary Wynne, and Herb Zschech.

There are numerous others who helped support this endeavor of sharing my excursion into the profession I still love, as well as the jubilation at discovering the sagas of forgotten newspapers and expat journalists in such a distant place. My colleague David Dowling, as usual, was a resourceful guide to the inner workings of academic publishing, and I have a profound appreciation for his knowledge. Chris Cheatum, a chemist with a journalist's heart; Josh Weiner, a biologist with an investigator's drive; Melissa Tully, a communications scholar who loves newspapers; and Sara Sanders, a social worker's social worker, were a quartet any book writer could only hope for. I'm indebted to The University of Iowa, where fine writing of all kinds is supported, nurtured, and genuinely revered.

The librarians at the Newspaper Division of the Library of Congress were nothing short of herculean in retrieving heavy bound volumes, as well as spools of microfilm, of both the *Brazil Herald* and *Latin America Daily Post*. Particular thanks go to Roslyn Waddy at the LOC, who shared my excitement for this undertaking. My appreciation also goes to Tim Noakes, head of public services of the Department of Special Collections at Stanford University, who accessed a trove of letters between Andrew Jackson Lamoureux and his Cornell University classmate and lifelong friend, John Casper Branner. Katy Darr, Special Collections Service Librarian at the Newberry Library in Chicago, resurrected a forgotten cache of letters from Teddy Hecht to her father, the great screenwriter Ben Hecht, which helped illuminate the guts and gaiety of a female reporter working for the *Brazil Herald* in the late 1940s. Added insight into Teddy's life came from her daughter, Mirim, who met with me and responded to myriad questions about her mother. I deeply appreciated the time that Donna Sullivan Igoe spent with me to reminisce about her brother "Johnny," as she called him, who had the horrific bad luck to be in the wrong place at the wrong time and paid the price for it. Donna supplied me with numerous mementos, clippings, letters, and documents, which helped me further understand a young journalist hellbent on coming back with the story. Thanks also to Tim Hodgdon, research librarian at the Louis Round Wilson Special Collections Library at the University of North Carolina, for providing access to newsman Charles Kuralt's papers, as well as to researchers at the Rockefeller Archives Center for accessing correspondence between philanthropist and New York governor Nelson A. Rockefeller and *Brazil Herald* publisher John D. Montgomery.

Much of my research was made possible through the immense electronic archives of Brazil's National Library, which maintains millions of pages of more than two thousand of the nation's current and defunct newspapers accessible at bndigital.bn.gov.br/hemeroteca-digital/.

A note of appreciation to Steve Yolen and Tom Murphy, terrific journalists who have spent the entirety of their professional lives in Brazil, for reading early drafts of the manuscript. Walter Colton, a former managing editor at the *Brazil Herald*, in many ways the glue that continues to bind many former staffers at the newspaper together fifty years later, was unstinting in his encouragement. Walter connected me with many of the journalists whose recollections are recorded in this book. He also vouched for me as a chronicler of their stories, and for that I'm grateful. Former Associated Press reporter

Ed Miller graciously shared with me his meticulous recollections of his own years in Brazil in manuscript form, corroborating key elements contained in this book. Former *Herald* reporter Rob Anderson scanned dozens of articles from the newspaper, which helped narrate the story of several years that had preceded my own in Rio. John Grey Montgomery, the son of longtime *Brazil Herald* publisher John David Montgomery, genially and candidly spoke with me about his father's adventurous thirty-one-year sojourn in Rio de Janeiro.

Thanks also to former *Herald* staff writer Mark Gruberg, who shared with me vintage *Brazil Herald*s he has kept in a cardboard box for fifty years, as well to Mary A. Lenz and Liza Fourré, who allowed me access to personal letters that captured the joys and challenges of reporters' lives in their mid-twenties, more than forty years ago. Liza opened her daily diary as a young journalist at the *Brazil Herald*, which helped recreate the verve of expatriates merrily living in Rio at the time.

There are three titans who continue to guide me, even though all are listed under the journalist's shorthand for an obituary—30—: Hanno Hardt, Buster Haas, and Herb Michelson. Hanno, a German-born colleague at the University of Iowa, who long ago urged me to write a book about expats living in Brazil; Buster, who gave me my first job back in the States at the *Dallas Morning News*; and Herb, who taught me how to know when to leave the honorable profession of daily newspaper work.

I was employed at the *Latin America Daily Post* for a scant two years. But my perceptions aren't based just on those years. They've been augmented by decades of rearview appraisal, as well as reflections from scores of journalists who also worked at the *Brazil Herald* or *Latin America Daily Post*. That I am the reader's guide to represent such memories is the power invested in the storyteller, a responsibility I'm humbled to assume.

The Brazil Chronicles is a wholly subjective report, as, by the way, all journalism is, no matter how "true" and "objective" anyone claims it to be. The history of both the *Brazil Herald* and *Latin America Daily*

Post may very well have happened differently. This is my version of what happened based on my own assessment and the recollections of others on the scene.

Any newspaper has a multitude of editorial employees, some on staff and are regular contributors, others whose work only occasionally appears in the newspaper. Many hardworking journalists never have their names printed in a newspaper. To those whose names escaped mention in this account of *The Rio News, Brazil Herald*, and *Latin America Daily Post*, I offer a profound apology.

A final note: Perhaps David Perlman and Janet Chusmir, the two naysaying newspaper editors I approached for work before leaving America, were having off days when our respective galaxies intersected. That also goes for the others who didn't give me a job before I embarked on my Brazil adventure. I'm sure many of them were terrific journalists and mentors. For me, they were bouncers, barring me from the glittery club I stood in line and awe waiting to enter. But in retrospect, it turned out all right. Without them blocking the entrance, I might never have gotten in through the side door that helped define who I am today.

The Rio News, Brazil Herald and Latin America Daily Post Editorial Staff, 1946–1988

Addams, Dawn	BH society writer, 1951; Suffolk-born English actress, former girlfriend of fashion mogul Oleg Cassini.
Agins, Teri	LADP stringer in Salvador and Belo Horizonte, Brazil, 1981–1984; Wall Street Journal fashion reporter; author, The End of Fashion (2010) and Hijacking the Runway (2014).
Anderson, Rob	BH reporter, 1976–1977; professor of Portuguese, Winston-Salem State University; University of North Carolina; translator of Portuguese-language books into English.
Andrews, Margaret	BH reporter, 1972.
Appel, Cricket	BH editor, late 1960s, early 1970s.
Ashford, Moyra	LADP/BH São Paulo reporter, 1977–1981.
Asheshov, Nicholas	LADP Peru correspondent, former Fleet Street journalist, 1979.
Balamaci, Marilyn	LADP Rio de Janeiro reporter/editor, 1979–1981; chief of correspondents, People Magazine; associate editor at Parade and other magazines.
Barbosa, Kem	BH contributor, 1977.
Barboza, A. M.	BH reporter, 1947.
Baron, Barbara	BH Brasília contributor, 1977.

Appendix

Baron, Reid	BH cultural reporter, movie reviewer, editor, 1976–1977; publisher, managing editor, Washington, DC-based *Galleries* magazine.
Beadle, Bob	BH reporter, 1969.
Belville, Lance	BH reporter, date uncertain.
Berkowitz, Marc	Prolific BH arts critic, 1946–1965; born in Russia; died November 1989, buried in Rio's Cemitério dos Ingleses.
Best, Betty (Kussmaul)	BH photographer and page designer, mid-1970s; Amazon missionary.
Best, Don	BH business editor, 1975–1976; Amazon missionary; author, *The Gravedigger's Dream* (2021) and *The Third Promise* (2022).
Biderman, Sol	BH/LADP art critic, 1982; longtime contributor to *Time* magazine, author, *Bring Me to the Banqueting House* (1969) and *When Elvis Met Che in Denver* (1986).
Bloom, Stephen G.	LADP reporter/editor, 1979–1981.
Bonner, Raymond	LADP Central America correspondent, 1979–1980; lawyer; author; foreign correspondent, *The New York Times*; staff writer, *The New Yorker*; co-owner of Bookoccino Bookstore, Avalon, Australia; author, *Weakness and Deceit* (1984), *Waltzing with a Dictator* (1987), *At the Hand of Man* (1993), and *Anatomy of Injustice* (2012).
Braun, Frank	LADP São Paulo reporter, 1978; contributor, UPI, CBS News, *Space News*, *Business Week*; producer, documentaries on space missions.
Brooke, Jim	BH Reporter, 1976; *Miami Herald*, *New York Times* and Bloomberg News foreign correspondent.
Brown, Joseph Folsom	BH founder, financial manager, 1946–1948, 1953–1954; died, 1973, buried in Rio's Cemitério dos Ingleses.
Bruce, Jim	BH editor/reporter/contributor, 1974–1977; editor of *Brazilian Business*, organ of the American

	Chamber of Commerce in Rio; prolific São Paulo freelancer.
Bullaty, George	BH sports columnist, originator, Bullaty's Bull, 1947.
Bustamante, Jaime	BH São Paulo reporter, 1977.
Cacioli, Claude	BH Brasília social columnist, 1976–1978.
Cacioli, Decy (Vignoli)	BH Brasília social columnist, 1976–1978.
Capper, Adelina	Prolific BH fashion writer, 1962–1970; worked for Brazilian magazines *Manchete, Joia, Fatos e Fotos*, newspapers *Voz de Portugal* and *Jornal da Bahia*, Fairchild Publications' *Women's Wear Daily*.
Christenson, Kristen Ann	LADP proofreader; last editor in chief, 1986–1988.
Cole, Richard	BH/LADP editor/reporter/columnist, 1978–1980; AP wire service reporter.
Collingwood, Michael T.	BH reporter, 1954–1955.
Colton, Walter	BH editor/sports reporter, 1973; BH managing editor, 1975–1977; AP Rio bureau reporter, 1978–1982; Brazil-based import-export consultant.
Compson, Wilbur	BH drama critic, 1951.
Crescenzi, Betty	BH Campinas social correspondent; originator of weekly column, Campinas Capers, 1976–1980.
Curtis, Mike	BH news editor, reporter, 1951–1954.
Daly, Francis, G.	Physician who wrote BH column, Tropical Themes, 1976.
Davenport, Phyllis	BH reporter, 1960.
Davy, Rita	Brit who covered the Rio de Janeiro expatriate social whirl for the BH, 1963–1985; creator of the BH column, Rio Social Spotlight; died 1988, buried in Rio's Cemitério dos Ingleses.
de Onís, Juan	*New York Times, Los Angeles Times* Rio de Janeiro correspondent, who may (or may not) have worked for the BH in early 1950s. See chapter 10, endnote 70.

Deacon, Pamela   BH reporter, 1973.

Diehl, Pamela   BH reporter, 1976.

Downer, Stephen   LADP Mexico City correspondent, 1979–1981.

Dresser, Linda   Possible pseudonym for 1947 BH columnist who wrote Hemline Hijinks.

Dyer, Elisabeth (Betty)   BH staff writer, 1946; reporter and editor, *New York Post* and *PM* newspapers; wrote the lead story in the BH's inaugural edition, February 1, 1946; founder, the *Tico Times*, English-language newspaper in Costa Rica.

Emert, Harold   BH/LADP columnist, Inside Cidade Maravilhosa, in the style of Walter Winchell, but more often of Woody Allen, 1973–1982; world-famous oboe player.

Erlick, June Carolyn   LADP stringer, Bogotá, 1979; head of publications for Harvard University David Rockefeller Center for Latin America Studies.

Etsinger, Jean   BH reporter, managing editor, 1967–1970, author of column, Quebrando o Galho, Portuguese slang for "offering a favor to a friend"; reporter/editor, Associated Press, *Chicago Tribune*, *Miami Herald*, and Virgin Islands Source Newspapers.

Fischer, Paul   BH contributor, 1977.

Fitzgerald, Phyllis   BH reporter in São Paulo, 1974.

Fodor, André   Longtime BH Rio at Day and Night columnist, 1955–1972, often under the byline, André Todor; originator of dubious *Miss Estrangeira* pageant; died 1978, buried in Rio's Cemitério dos Ingleses.

Fourré, Liza   BH editor and reporter turned photographer and artist, 1976–1978; founder, Art Workshops in Guatemala.

Fraser, Kerry   BH reporter, 1976–1978; AP São Paulo correspondent.

Freedman, Jonathan   BH editor/reporter, 1967 Pulitzer Prize winner for Editorial Writing, *San Diego Union-Tribune*; author, *From Cradle to Grave* (1993), *Wall of Fame* (2000), and *The Last Brazil of Benjamin East* (2015).

Frost, Louisa C.   BH art critic, mid-1950s.

Fuad, Kim   LADP Caracas stringer, 1979–1981.

Galanternick, Mary   BH contributor, 1979.

Ganong, Jean   BH proofreader, 1976.

Garcia, Frank M.   BH editor, columnist, associate publisher, original 1946 partner/founder; longtime *New York Times* Brazil correspondent; died 1958, buried in Rio's Cemitério dos Ingleses.

Garner, John   LADP business manager, 1978.

Garritano, J. C.   BH theater critic, 1970–1971.

Gentil, Eduardo   LADP business editor, 1979; executive director, JP Morgan New York and São Paulo; Chief Executive Officer, Visa do Brasil.

Gillette, Alyse   BH arts reporter, 1949.

Gilmore, Jim   BH reporter, 1948.

Goodman, Sue   BH editor, social editor, 1974.

Grammer, Margaret   LADP reporter & editor, 1978–1979; killed in automobile crash in Buenos Aires, 1980.

Gruberg, Mark   BH reporter, 1975–1978; lawyer, novelist, cab driver, manager of San Francisco taxi collective, Green Cab.

Guillen, H.   BH reporter, Brasília, 1979.

Hall, Bill   BH editor; wire editor, 1974–1980.

Harding, Rex   BH reporter; covered ship debarkations in Rio, 1948.

Harnisch, Wolf H. Jr.   BH drama critic, 1946.

Harper, Glen T.   BH São Paulo reporter, 1967.

Appendix

Hawkins, Otto (Vic)	Argentine-born original BH founder/partner; died 1946, buried in Rio's Cemitério dos Ingleses.
Hawryzyswyn, George	BH contributor, 1975–1978.
Hein, Jo Ann	LADP São Paulo society columnist, 1978–1983.
Herrington, Elizabeth (Betsy)	LADP São Paulo reporter; occasional BH restaurant critic, 1980–1982.
Hinrichsen, Albert D.	BH drama and art critic, 1964–1977.
Hinrichsen, Hans Albert	BH music and drama critic, 1955–1960.
Hippeau, Eric	BH managing editor, 1971–1972; 1974–1975; sports reporter; founder, *Data News*, CEO of Ziff-Davis, *Huffington Post*; venture capitalist.
Hoagland, Decy Vignoli	BH society reporter, 1966.
Hobart, John	BH news reporter, 1946–1947.
Hobbs, Nancy	BH São Paulo correspondent, 1973.
Huber, Gilberto	LADP president and publisher, 1981–1985; publisher of telephone books throughout Brazil.
Huber, Phylis	BH reporter/editor, 1974; started Brazilian version of a magazine inspired by *Rolling Stone* in the early 1970s.
Huber, Roberta	BH contributor, 1976–1977.
Hume, David	BH reporter/editor, 1964–1966.
Huseby, Janet	BH reporter/editor, 1972–1973; editor, *The Berkeley Book of College Essays* (2007).
Ivy, Dave	BH sportswriter, 1951.
Jacobsen, Pauline	BH reporter, 1970.
Joan	BH columnist, author of weekly People We've Met feature that carried the byline, By Joan, 1947. Her full name is unknown.
Karrer, Barbara	BH contributor, 1977.
Kennard, Alex	BH film and cultural critic, 1964–1971.

Klagsbrunn, Kurt	BH photographer, 1946–1970.
Kraft, Pearl	BH society reporter, 1951.
Krull, Felix	BH record/music reviewer, pseudonym of Brian Nicholson, 1978–1979.
Kuralt, Charles	CBS South American correspondent, 1962, shared offices with the BH; storyteller who pioneered TV news with his On The Road series.
Lamoureux, Andrew Jackson	Founder/editor, *The Rio News*, 1879–1901, precursor to BH and LADP.
Langley, Lee	BH editor,1947, joined founders of BH as equity partner; ABC correspondent in Brazil; professor of physiology, University of Alabama, University of Missouri medical schools.
Latuszynski, Susan	BH São Paulo social correspondent, 1976-1977; originated column, Suzi says.
Lee, Ira	BH film writer, 1978.
Lehman, Stan	LADP foreign editor/reporter in São Paulo, 1978–1984; UPI, AP reporter.
Leitão, Sergio	BH sports reporter, 1966.
Lenz, Mary A.	BH reporter, 1975, AP Rio reporter, 1976–1977; AP Anchorage reporter; reporter, *Tundra Drums, Dallas Morning News, Dallas Times Herald, Texas Observer, Houston Post, Austin America-Statesman.*
Lies, George M.	BH reporter, 1976–1977.
Lindley, Robert	BH/LADP Buenos Aires correspondent, 1976–1980.
Locke, Maggie	BH reporter/editor, 1974–1976; reporter, *Washington Post, Los Angeles Times*; marriage and family therapist.
Lopes, Tim	BH reporter, 1978.
Lowe, Karen	LADP São Paulo reporter, 1979; Washington-based correspondent, Agence France Presse; senior editor, Marketplace Radio; senior podcast producer/editor, Wondery.

Machado, Ney   BH Rio by Night columnist, 1977.

Mackenzie, Eileen   BH contributor, 1975–1977; *Time* and McGraw-Hill
                           correspondent.

Mahoney, Bert   BH sports reporter, 1952.

Maluf, Ramez B.   BH managing editor, 1971–1972, 1973–1974;
                           president, AZM University, Tripoli, Lebanon.

Marc, Steven   BH reporter, 1971.

Marchant, Garry   BH managing editor, 1973; peripatetic, award-
                           winning Canadian travel writer.

Mathes, Libbie S.   BH/LADP contributor, 1976–1979.

Marron, Lupe   BH translator, proofreader; Guatemalan native,
                           1973–1975.

McGilly, Elly   BH cultural reporter and graphic artist, 1975–1976.

Menezes, Millicent   BH Rio society correspondent, 1957.

Meyer, Babs   BH reporter, 1978–1979.

Merrick, Jill   BH Belo Horizonte correspondent, 1974.

Miller, Ed   AP Rio correspondent, 1961–1966; returned to
                           Brazil for AP in 1973, AP chief of Caribbean
                           services in San Juan; occasional BH contributor.

Miller, Jean   BH contributor, creator of Brazil Devalued column,
                           1976.

Moir, Phyllis   BH São Paulo society correspondent, 1956.

Motley, Diana   BH Woman's Page contributor, 1951.

Montgomery, Harry E.   Publisher, *Junction City Daily Union*; father of John
                           D. Montgomery, who bought BH in 1948.

Montgomery, John David   Kansas-based publisher; principal partner, BH,
                           1948–1978; publisher of Montgomery Publications,
                           Inc., which included the *Junction City Daily Union,
                           Lindsborg News-Record, Chapman Advisor, Fort
                           Riley Post, Wamego Smoke Signal*; founded *The
                           Coral Gables Riviera, Miami Beach Daily Tropics*;

publisher, *Miami Beach Sun, Miami Beach Sun-Star, Havana Post.*

Montgomery, John Grey   Son of John D. and Mary Liz Montgomery; BH and Montgomery Publications, Inc. publisher, sold family interest of BH in 1978; assistant to the president, vice president, San Francisco Newspaper Agency, 1964–1973; returned to Kansas to take over as publisher of family newspapers, 1973.

Montgomery, Mary Liz   Wife of John D. Montgomery; her column, Incidentally..., occasionally ran in the BH.

Moore, Bill   BH cultural reporter, 1971–1977.

Morrissey, Patrick   BH book reviewer, 1977.

Morris, Greta   BH reporter, 1948–1949.

Morrison, H. Stuart   BH editor & director,1949–1954; died 1964, buried in Rio's Cemitério dos Ingleses.

Morrison, Margaret Miles   BH managing editor, columnist, 1949–1953; editor, *Miami Herald, Milwaukee Sentinel* and *Chicago Daily News.*

Morrow, Patrick   LADP Washington-based correspondent, 1979.

Mourisco, M.   BH reporter, 1977.

Munk, Judith   BH photographer, 1960–1970.

Muniz, Paulo   BH photographer, 1977.

Murphy, Tom   BH/LADP reporter, 1978–1982; Brazil-based reporter, Associated Press, Dow Jones, Knight-Ridder Financial News, *O Estado de São Paulo*; author of the novel, *Deadlock* (2020), short stories, and dramatic plays.

Nadkarni, Bob   BH proofreader and reporter, 1972; globe-trotting cameraman; owner, Maze jazz club, Rio de Janeiro.

Netto, Sieiro   BH Rio by Night columnist, 1977.

Newman, George H.   Nominal BH editorial director, 1948–1979; Brazilian attorney; BH "editor responsável," editor

in chief, due to laws outlawing foreigners from
holding executive positions within operating
Brazilian media companies.

Nicholson, Brian   BH/LADP staff editor/reporter, 1978–1979; stringer
for Reuters and the BBC; UPI chief Brazil corre-
spondent; founder/publisher, *Village News*, a São
Paulo ex-pat newsletter.

Norman, Mildred (Millie)   BH arts critic, 1966–1977, occasionally wrote about
the New York art/dance/theater scene.

Obertance, Charles   BH contributor and São Paulo advertising representative, 1971; McGraw-Hill executive; *Brazilian
Business* editor; *Wall Street Journal* reporter.

Page, Diana   BH night editor, 1970; UPI reporter, Rio, Buenos
Aires; *St. Petersburg Times* El Salvador corre-
spondent; author with El Salvador President Jose
Napoleon Duarte, *Duarte: My Story* (1986); US
Foreign Service officer.

Pagom, Paulo   BH automotive reporter, 1970.

Paladino, Paulo   BH reporter, 1976–1977.

Patureau, Alan   BH reporter/editor, 1970; reporter, *Newsday, St.
Petersburg Times, Atlanta Journal-Constitution*.

Patron, Jean   BH arts contributor, 1950.

Phillips, Chris   Longtime chief BH/LADP proofreader, occasional
columnist, 1968–1983; US Air Force pilot; liaison
officer, US Air Force in Recife and Fernando de
Noronha, and for Lockheed Aircraft.

Phillips, Maria   BH reporter, 1971.

Phillips, Susan   BH reporter, late 1960s.

Pickard, Christopher   LADP reporter, early 1980s; restaurant critic;
author, numerous guidebooks on Brazil and Rio,
including the definitive *Insider's Guide to Rio de
Janeiro*; ghost writer for Ronald Biggs's autobiogra-
phies and a novel, *Keep on Running* (1995).

Pimentel, Monica   BH copy editor, 1985–1987.

Playfair, Guy Lyon   BH feature, arts writer, 1965–1968; author, *The Indefinite Boundary* (1976), *This House is Haunted* (1980), *Medicine, Mind and Magic* (1987) , *Twin Telepathy* (2002), and *The Flying Cow* (2011),

Proctor, John   BH theater and music critic, 1964–1977.

Purchia, Randi   BH reporter, 1976–1978.

Raphael, Alison   BH reporter, 1975–1977; *Time* contributor, Rio, 1977; Ph.D. in History of Latin America, Columbia University; UNICEF consultant.

Rambo, W. Preston   BH manager in the late 1940s, affiliated with the US State Department as vice-consul at various consulates in Brazil.

Ramos, Elisa, M.   BH food and theater writer, 1976.

Reid, Andrew   BH/LADP Rio de Janeiro staff editor and bon vivant, 1978–1983; Laura Reid's brother. Author of several pornographic novels.

Reid, Laura   BH/LADP Rio de Janeiro-based reporter/editor, 1973–1984; Andrew Reid's sister.

Risser, Mary Jo   BH cultural reporter, 1978.

Ritchie, Susan Davis   BH night editor, 1969.

Ross, Ralph B.   One of four original BH founders, 1946; BH editor.

Rusk, Hugh Parks   BH technical director, 1947–48; manager, *Miami Beach Tropics* and *Sun*; reporter, *Atlanta Constitution*, and Atlanta city councilmember; brother of Dean Rusk, US Secretary of State during Kennedy Administration.

St. Clair, David   BH reporter/editor, 1962–1967; wrote weekly arts column and became noted collector of Brazilian art; psychic; author, *Drum and Candle* (1971), *How Your Psychic Powers Can Make You Rich* (1975), *Instant ESP* (1978), *Child Possessed* (1983), and *Say You Love Satan* (1987).

Appendix

Sales, Cláudio	LADP financial manager, 1981–1984; youngest brother of Mauro Salles; president of São Paulo-based energy thinktank, Instituto Acende Brasil.
Salles, Mauro	Mercurial founder/publisher of LADP, 1979–1985.
Sanchez, Wes	BH reporter, 1975.
Sandlin, Donna	BH/LADP contributor, 1982.
Sausser, Betty	BH Potpourri columnist, 1973–1974.
Schertel, Diki	Short-lived LADP executive, 1978.
Schmitz, Ernest	BH reporter, occasionally wrote racetrack news, 1951–1953.
Scott, Leslie Jyl	BH contributor, 1977.
Scott, Victor	LADP tourism editor, 1981.
Seaton, David	BH reporter, date unknown.
Serafino, Nina	LADP correspondent, Santiago, Chile, 1978–1979.
Shannon, Don	BH reporter/editor, 1947–1948; *Los Angeles Times* bureau chief/reporter, Paris, Africa, Tokyo, United Nations, Washington, DC.
Shaw, Paul Vanorden	BH political columnist, late 1950s–1970; Brazil stringer, *Christian Science Monitor, Baltimore Sun*; professor, University of São Paulo.
Shaw, Sandra	BH reporter, 1978.
Shepard, John	LADP/BH reporter, 1982.
Sinclair, Ted	BH Rio by Night reporter, 1948.
Sims, Joseph	BH managing editor, 1966–1967, listed on BH masthead as Assistant General Manager; Rio de Janeiro UPI bureau chief, 1963-1965; public relations, Pan Am; paid CIA asset.
Singleton, Jane	BH reporter, copy editor, mid-1970s.
Smith, Harley	BH Porto Alegre correspondent, 1949–1950.
Smith, Linda	BH social/copy editor, 1974–1976.

Smith, Rick	BH reporter, started working at age fifteen, collecting BH subscription remittances, 1969.
Staeblein, Paola	BH Proofreader, 1981.
Stein, Mark	BH reporter, 1953.
Straker, D. G.	BH contributor, 1977.
Stransky, Ted	BH Rio by Night columnist, 1950–1955.
Sullivan, John	BH/LADP reporter and columnist; killed in El Salvador while on assignment for *Hustler* magazine, 1981.
Swarthmore, Burle	BH reporter, 1978.
Szulc, Tad	BH columnist, author of news column, World Today, 1946; *New York Times* reporter who broke the 1961 Bay of Pigs story; freelance writer; author of many books, including *Compulsive Spy* (1974), *Diplomatic Immunity* (1981), *Pope John Paul II* (1995), *Chopin in Paris* (1999), and *Fidel* (2000).
Taylor, Ed	LADP managing editor, 1978–1988.
Terry, Wayne	BH reporter, 1978.
Thomas, Angie	BH news and arts reporter, 1974.
Thrall, John	BH assistant editor, 1975; claimed to be CIA operative in Central America and Brazil; author of several thrillers and science fiction novels.
Thompson, Hunter S.	BH reporter, 1962; self-styled journalist, author, touted creator of Gonzo journalism; author of many books, including *Hell's Angels* (1967), *Fear and Loathing in Las Vegas* (1971), *Fear and Loathing on the Campaign Trail* (1973), *The Great Shark Hunt* (1979), *The Rum Diary* (1998).
Todor, André	see André Fodor.
Thevenot, Sherry	BH reporter, 1977–1978.
Torres, Lui	BH reporter, 1978.
Trierweiler, Betty	BH contributor, 1950–1951.

Appendix

Tucker, Beryl	BH society reporter, author of short-lived column, Heraldry, 1955.
Tupy, Dulce	BH cultural reporter, 1978.
Typhoon	BH pseudonymous race track columnist; originator, Rio Racing News, 1946–1949.
Vergniaud, Luis	BH business reporter, 1970.
Warner, Louise	BH contributor, creator of column, São Paulo Shoppers' Guide, 1976–1977.
Watson, Don	BH sportswriter, 1950.
Weaver, Anderson	Author of short-lived 1947 BH column, Kindred Words; died 1955, buried in Rio's Cemitério dos Ingleses.
Weldon, Marybelle	BH women's page writer, 1946; wrote column …Did You Know…
Wertheim, Peter Howard	LADP business editor, 1982.
Wheeler, Ted	BH reporter, 1978.
Williams, Wally	BH restaurant critic, 1970s; creator of That's Dining; minister at English-language Protestant church, Rio de Janeiro.
Williamson, Bill	BH General Manager, 1960–1963; BH Editor/ Managing Partner, 1963–1979; editor of American Chamber of Commerce publications in Brazil; executive director of Miami-based Inter American Press Association; sailed thirty-two-foot sloop solo across the Atlantic and back, 1995.
Woodward, Chuck	BH society writer, 1955.
Wright, Dennis	BH reporter, 1973.
Wynne, Mary	BH society and arts columnist, 1960–1974.
Yolen, Steve	Executive Editor, LADP; 1978–1987; UPI correspondent; Fairchild Publications; Brazil-based business consultant.

Zschech, Herbert   German-born BH/LADP editor, crime and political
                          columnist, 1946–1984; one of the first BH editorial
                          employees; creator of columns Probex, It Happened
                          Yesterday, and Zschech and Double Check; various-
                          ly listed on BH masthead as Assistant Supervisor
                          and Editorial Manager.

ENDNOTES

Chapter 5 - Confederados

1. See Eugene C. Harter, *The Lost Colony of the Confederacy* (College Station: Texas A&M University Press, 2000); Cyrus B. Dawsey and James M. Dawsey, eds., *The Confederados: Old South Immigrants in Brazil* (Tuscaloosa: University Alabama Press, 1995); William Clark Griggs, *The Elusive Eden: Frank McMullan's Confederate Colony in Brazil* (Austin: University of Texas Press, 1987); Alan P. Marcus, *Confederate Exodus: Social and Environmental Forces in the Migration of U.S. Southerners to Brazil* (Lincoln: University of Nebraska, 2021); and Stephen G. Bloom, "Brazil's Secret History of Southern Hospitality," *Narratively*, July 7, 2014. https://narratively.com/brazils-secret-history-of-southern-hospitality/.

2. See Rita Lee 2023 obituary, Alex Williams, "Rita Lee, Brazil's Queen of Rock, Is Dead at 75," *New York Times*, May 10, 2023. https://www.nytimes.com/2023/05/10/arts/music/rita-lee-dead.html?smid=nytcore-ios-

Chapter 7 - The Ark of the Southern Journalistic Covenant

1. Oliver Marshall, *The English-Language Press in Latin America, Institute of Latin American Studies* (London: University of London Press, 1996), 21.

2. Amanda Peruchi, "Os periódicos franceses na imprensa carioca oitocentista: Uma leitura dos editoriais de primeira edição," *Almanack*, (Guarulhos) (18 Abr. 2018): 489–516; Lúcia Granja, "A circulação dos impressos no Brasil do século," XIX (atores do mundo dos livros) *Olho d'água* 13.1 (Jan.–June 2021): 1–195.

3. *Rio Herald*, March 8, 1828, 1.

4. *Rio Herald*, April 5, 1828, 2.

5. *Rio Herald*, July 5, 1828, 2, 3.

6. *The Literary Intelligencer and Universal Gleaner*, April 7, 1831, 4.

7. *Commercial Formalities of Rio de Janeiro* (Rio de Janeiro: T. B. Hunt & Co, 1834).

8. Anais da Biblioteca Nacional, Sumario, *Catálogo de Jornais e Revistas do Rio de Janeiro (1808–1889)*, Divisão de Publicações e Divulgão, Vol. 85, 1965. *O Mutuca Picante*, which translates to The Spicy Horsefly, was a humorous political journal.

Endnotes for Chapter 7

9. Nachman Falbel, *Judeus no Brasil, Estudos e Notas* (São Paulo: Editora Humanitas, 2008), 281; Elias Salgado, "Respirando Liberdade Sob os Ares do Império: Os Judeus Precursores no Brasil do Século XIX," 3, https://www.academia.edu/30093590/judeus_no_imp%C3%A9rio_Elias_Salgado_doc; Brito Aranha, *Diccionario Bibliographico Portuguez*, X (Lisbon: Imprensa Nacional, 1883), 95–6.

10. *The Anglo-Brazilian Times*, February 7, 1865, 1. Note use of the Arabic word, salaam, which signifies a gesture of greeting or respect.

11. *New York Daily Herald*, "South America," December 23, 1866, 6.

12. Miguel Alexandre de Araujo Neto, "Great Britain, the Paraguayan War and Free Immigration in Brazil, 1862-1875." *Irish Migration Studies in Latin America* 4.3 (July 2006): 115–31.

13. See Sergio Pinto-Handler, "The Dream of a Rural Democracy US Reconstruction and Abolitionist Propaganda in Rio de Janeiro, 1880–1890," in *Freedoms Gained and Lost: Reconstruction and Its Meanings 150 Years Later*, edited by Adam H. Domby and Simon Lewis (New York: Fordham University Press, 2022), 213–30.

14. *The Preston Chronicle and Lancashire Advertiser*, May 25, 1867, 2.

15. Araujo Neto, Miguel Alexandre de, "An Anglo-Irish Newspaper in Nineteenth-Century Brazil: The Anglo-Brazilian Times, 1865-1884" in *Newsletter of the Brazilian Association for Irish Studies*–ABEI, N° 8, August 1994, University of São Paulo; Edmundo Murray, "William Scully (d. 1885): Irish Journalist and Businessman in Rio de Janeiro," *Irish Migration Studies in Latin America* 4.3 (July, 2006): 175–6.

16. "A Memphian Abroad," *Memphis Daily Appeal*, August 26, 1869, 4; "Mrs. Shippey, Confederacy's Heroine, Dies," *The Pasadena Post*, February 19, 1937, 5.

17. *The American Mail*, December 25, 1873, 1; "Charles F. de Vivaldi naming Isaac Goodnow as newspaper agent," March 11, 1860, in *Kansas Memory*, Kansas Historical Society; *The Bay City Press*, September 7, 1861, 3.

18. Helen de Oliveira Silva, "As Ilustrações de Charles F. de Vivaldi - apontamentos de um projeto de pesquisa." https://www.academia.edu/36082926/As_Il ustra%C3%A7%C3%B5es_de_Charles_F_de_Vivaldi_apontamentos_de_um_ projeto_de_pesquisa; *Green Bay Press-Gazette*, July 13, 1891, 3.

19. See "Hesch History ... from Bohemia to Buckman, Who was Francis de Vivaldi," February 19, 2011, http://heschistory.blogspot.com/2011/02/who-was-francis-de-vivaldi.html; and A de Vivaldi Timeline, August 23, 2012, http://heschistory.blogspot .com/search/label/de%20Vivaldi; Tim Hoheisel, "Enigmatic priest created controversy in 1800s," *SC Times*, December 4, 2014, https://www.sctimes.com/story/life /2014/12/05/enigmatic-priest-created-controversy/19910653/; *Green Bay Press-Gazette*, July 13, 1891, 3.

20. *The British and American Mail*, August 17, 1877, 2.

21. *The British and American Mail*, August 17, 1877, 2.

22. *The British and American Mail*, August 17, 1877, 2.

23. Elaine Maria Santos, "James Edwin Hewitt, E O Ensino de Ingles no Século XIX," *Rev. Tempos Espaços Educ.* 13.32 (jan./dez.2020): 1–14; see *The New York Times*, December 13, 1878, 3.

Chapter 8 - Not All Beer and Skittles

1. *The Ten-Year Book of the Cornell University, 1868–1878* (Ithaca: B. Herman Smith, 1878), 86.

2. Ancestry.com.

3. *Star-Gazette* (Elmira, New York), February 11, 1907, 6.

4. "Quaint Humor and Homely Philosophy In the Prosaic Advertiser's World," *Kansas City Star*, June 28, 1926, 22; *The Ten-Year Book of the Cornell University, 1868–1887*, 86; William Sheafe Chase, *Delta Upsilon Quinquennial Catalogue* (Whitefish, MT: Kessinger Publishing, 2010), 424.

5. From *Anais da Biblioteca Nacional* 85 (1965), 119. See http://docplayer.com.br/88385775-Anais-da-biblioteca-nacional-vol-85-divisao-de-publicacoes-e-divulgacao-1965.html.

6. *The Rio News*, and more than two thousand other newspapers, can be accessed digitally from an archive of Brazilian newspapers, Hemeroteca Digital Brasileira, bndigital.bn.gov.br/hemeroteca-digital.

7. *The Rio News*, August 24, 1879, 2.

8. *The Rio News*, November 15, 1880, 2.

9. *The Rio News*, May 24, 1880, 4.

10. *The Rio News*, November 15, 1880.

11. Thomas E Skidmore, *Brazil, Black into White: Race and Nationality in Brazilian Thought*, (Raleigh: Duke University Press, 2003), 44-45.

12. Lamonte Aidoo, "Diluting the 'African' Nation: European Immigration, Whitening, and the Crisis of Slave Emancipation," *Alter/natives Latin American Cultural Studies Journal* No. 8 (2018):1–18. https://alternativas.osu.edu/en/issues/spring-8-2018/miscellany2/aidoo.html.

13. *Revista Illustrada*, Anno 9, No. 395, 3.

14. *The Rio News*, September 24, 1880, 2; see also Handler, "The Dream of a Rural Democracy," 213–30. *The Gazeta da Tarde* ostensibly exaggerated the support the local English-language community in Brazil gave Lamoureux and *The Rio News*.

15. *The Rio News*, January 5, 1881, 4.

16. *Daily Journal* (Ithaca, New York), "Town Talk," November 18, 1886, 7.

17. Antonio Penalves Rocha, "The Rio News de A. J. Lamoureux: Um Journal Abolisionista Carioca de un Norte-Americano," *Projecto História* No. 35 (December 2006): 144; *The New York Times*, February 20, 1888, 3.

18. Brasil Silvado, *Primary Teaching in Rio de Janeiro* (Rio de Janeiro: A. J. Lamoureux & Co. (Rio de Janeiro), 1892. *The Hand Book of Rio de Janeiro* is available for download through Stanford University Libraries at https://searchworks.stanford.edu/?q=%22+Rio+news%2C+Rio+de+Janeiro.%22&search_field=search_title;

19. 18 "Dr. Frank Cowan Dead, Physician, Lawyer, Journalist, Traveler, Lecturer, and Author," *The New York Times*, February 13, 1905, 7.

20. *The Hand Book of Rio de Janeiro* (Rio de Janeiro: A. J. Lamoureux & Co., 1887).

21. Ruy Barbosa, *Martial Law: Its Constitution, Limits and Effect: Application Made to the Federal Supreme Court for Habeas-Corpus on behalf of the Persons*

arrested in virtue of Decrees of April 10 and 12, 1892 (Rio de Janeiro: Aldina de A. J. Lamoureux & Co., 1892).

22. Henry George, *Progress and Poverty: An Inquiry into the Cause of Industrial Depressions, and of Increase of Want with Increase of Wealth.* (New York: D. Appleton and Company, 1880).

23. Joaquim Nabuco, *Henry George: Nacionalisação do Solo, Apreciaçao da Propaganda para Abolição do Monopolio Territorial na Inglaterra*, (Rio de Janeiro: A. J. Lamoureux & Co., 1884).

24. *The Rio News*, July 5, 1879, 2.

25. Carlos Manoel de Hollanda Cavalcanti, "Angelo Agostini e seu 'Zé Caipora' entre a Corte e a República," *História, Imagem e Narrativas* No 3, ano 2 (setembro/2006).

26. "A. J. Lamoureux—Editor—Owner of the Rio News— May 13, 1888—The Brazilian Abolitionists."

27. *The New York Times*, September 11, 1888.

28. *The Rio News*, September 5, 1888, 3.

29. *The Rio News*, December 15, 1879, 4.

30. *The Rio News*, January 25, 1880, 4; February 15, 1880, 4, February 24, 1880, 4, March 6, 1880, 4, October 15, 1880.

31. *The Rio News*, June 15, 1880, 2.

32. *The Rio News*, August 15, 1888, 3.

33. *The New York Times*, "South America's War Cloud," December 19, 1884, 2.

34. *Detroit Free Press*, "A French Brazilian Yankee," January 22, 1885, 4.

35. *The Illustrated American*, "Two Sides of a Medal," May 2, 1891, 534.

36. John C. Branner, *A Brief Grammar of the Portuguese Language with Exercises and Vocabularies*, (New York: Henry Holt, 1910).

37. Herculano Alexandre, *History of the Origin and Establishment of the Inquisition in Portugal*, translated by John C. Branner (Palo Alto: Stanford University Publications, 1926).

38. A. J. Lamoureux to John Casper Branner, May 7, 1893, John Casper Branner Papers, The Department of Special Collections, Stanford University Libraries, (hereinafter JCBP) SC0034, Series 1, box 26, folder 105.

39. Lamoureux to Branner, December 20, 1893, JCBP, SC0034, Series 1, box 26, folder 105.

40. Lamoureux to Branner, August 20, 1900, JCBP, SC0034, Series 1, box 26, folder 105.

41. Lamoureux to Branner, September 15, 1892, JCBP, SC0034, Series 1, box 26, folder 105.

42. Lamoureux to Branner, June 21, 1899, JCBP, SC0034, Series 1, box 26, folder 105.

43. Lamoureux to Branner, September 15, 1892, JCBP, SC0034, Series 1, box 26, folder 105.

44. "Resumption of the Rio News," *The Evening Post* (New York), January 24, 1895, 7.

Endnotes for Chapter 8

45. "Hard Lines in Brazil," *The Pittsburgh Press*, November 8, 1893, 4.

46. James Gordon Bennett, "Foreigners Angry with Peixoto: His Extension of Martial Law in Rio Condemned," *Chicago Tribune*, October 25, 1893, 5.

47. Lamoureux to Branner, December 20, 1893, JCBP, SC0034, Series 1, box 26, folder 105.

48. Lamoureux to Branner, April 23, 1894, from Careañá, Argentina, JCBP, SC0034, Series 1, box 26, folder 105.

49. Lamoureux to Branner, December 20 1893, from Rio de Janeiro, JCBP, SC0034, Series 1, box 26, folder 105.

50. Commercial Editor.

51. Lamoureux to Branner, February 28, 1895, from Rio de Janeiro, JCBP, SC0034, Series 1, box 26, folder 105. Com Editor likely refers to Community Editor.

52. Lamoureux to Branner, October 27, 1895, from Rio de Janeiro, JCBP, SC0034, Series 1, box 26, folder 105.

53. Lamoureux to Branner, July 27, 1895, from Rio de Janeiro, JCBP, SC0034, Series 1, box 26, folder 105.

54. Lamoureux to Branner, January 22, 1896, from Rio de Janeiro, JCBP, SC0034, Series 1, box 26, folder 105.

55. Lamoureux to Branner, January 22 and 26, April 24, 1896, from Rio de Janeiro, JCBP, SC0034, Series 1, box 26, folder 105.

56. Lamoureux to Branner, July 12, 1896, from Rio de Janeiro, JCBP, SC0034, Series 1, box 26, folder 105.

57. Lamoureux to Branner, April 18, 1897, from Rio de Janeiro, JCBP, SC0034, Series 1, box 26, folder 105.

58. Lamoureux to Branner, June 20, 1897, from Canterbury, England, JCBP, SC0034, Series 1, box 26, folder 105.

59. Lamoureux to Branner, May 7, 1898, from Rio de Janeiro, JCBP, SC0034, Series 1, box 26, folder 105.

60. Lamoureux to Branner, March 23, 1899, from Rio de Janeiro, JCBP, SC0034, Series 1, box 26, folder 105.

61. Lamoureux to Branner, August 18, 1899, from Rio de Janeiro, JCBP, SC0034, Series 1, box 26, folder 105.

62. Lamoureux to Branner, June 14, 1899, from Rio de Janeiro, JCBP, SC0034, Series 1, box 26, folder 105.

63. Lamoureux to Branner, June 21, 1899, JCBP, SC0034, Series 1, box 26, folder 105.

64. Lamoureux to Branner, September 1, 1900, JCBP, SC0034, Series 1, box 26, folder 105. The reference to "a white man's country" is curious, especially considering Lamoureux's stalwart advocacy for emancipation, as well as his friendship with African-Brazilians, in particular, engineer and abolitionist André Rebouças. In another letter, dated April 24, 1896, Lamoureux made an ostensible anti-Semitic reference to an American be said reneged on a loan. Lamoureux wrote, "(by name, Jacobs!—I ought to have known better!"). Lamoureux's letters to Branner were private; he had no idea they would someday be collected and be available to the public.

419

65. Lamoureux to Branner, Rio de Janeiro, September 12, 1900, JCBP, JSC0034, Series 1, box 26, folder 105. Lamoureux to Branner, Rio de Janeiro, December 20, 1893, JCBP, SC0034, Series 1, box 26, folder 105.

66. "List of Passengers: Departures," *The Brazilian Review*, August 6, 1901, 560.

67. Harold Dane L'Amoureux, ed., *The Lamoureux Record: A Study of the Lamoureux Family in America*, No. Two, April 1939, Mesa Arizona Family Search Library, available through Family Search Digital Library.

68. *The Rio News*, August 27, 1901, 4.

69. "A. J. Lamoureux Dies; Brazil Honored Him," *Ithaca Journal-News*, February 25, 1928, 5.

70. *The Rio News*, December 3, 1901.

71. *The Rio News*, December 3, 1901, 8.

72. *Boston Evening Record*, February 15, 1902—March 24, 1902.

73. A. J. Lamoureux, "The Regeneration of South America, XIII," *Boston Evening Transcript*, May 24, 1902, 19.

74. A. J. Lamoureux, "A contradiction in Politics," *Out West*, July, 1902, 77–80.

75. Genealogical notes, including children, occupation, and residence, are taken from US Census data, available from Ancestry.com.

76. *The New York Times*, letters to the editor, A. J. Lamoureux, July 27, 1902; May 11, 1903; June 28, 1903; November 8, 1903; November 22, 1903; October 11, 1905; December 10, 1905; January 14, 1906; March 1, 1906; May 16, 1906; June 2, 1906; June 16, 1906; August 4, 1906; October 3, 1906.

77. A. J. Lamoureux, "Keep to the Subject," *The Ithaca Daily Journal*, February 14, 1910, 5; October 26, 1914, 6; October 30, 1920, 4.

78. L'Amoureux, ed., *The Lamoureux Record*, 219.

79. "A. J. Lamoureux Dead; Funeral This Afternoon," *The Cornell Daily Sun*, February 27, 1928, 1–2.

80. "He Stopped Slavery in Brazil," *The Western Outlook*, March 10, 1928, 8.

81. "A. J. Lamoureux Dies; Brazil Honored Him," *Ithaca Journal-News*, February 25, 1928, 5.

Chapter 9 - Ralph, Betty, Zschech, Vic, Lee, Joe, and Frank

1. Fittingly, when Runyon died on December 11, 1946, the *Brazil Herald* ran a frontpage, boldfaced, headlined AP story with this appreciation: "Broadways 'guys' and 'dolls' became fabulous with the touch of Damon Runyon's gifted pen. He knew the habitues of the famous street—the gamblers, managers, promoters, fighters... the shills and pitchmen...the big shots. And hangers-on... the plain everyday citizens. And they knew him and sometimes provided the inspiration for his short stories, many of which became motion pictures."

2. As quoted in Ronald Weber, *News of Paris: American Journalists in the City of Light Between the Wars* (Chicago: Ivan R. Dee, 2006), 19, 20.

3. "New Argentine Weekly," *The Fourth Estate*, July 19, 1924, 25; "Folks Worth Knowing," *Editor & Publisher*, August 4, 1923, 27.

4. "Seeks Foreign Favor: Argentina Plans Propaganda to Show Its Advantages," *Washington Post*, April 3, 1919, 5; "Argentine Nation Is Stable, Though Hit Hard, Says Ralph E. Ross, Visitor in Mobley," *Moberly Monitor-Index*, January 2, 1932, 4; "W. C. Ross Leaves for Buenos Aires," *Moberly Monitor-Index*, August 31, 1932, 5; "Ralph B. Ross Stops in City on Way Home to Argentina," *St Louis Post-Dispatch*, March 15, 1936, 11; "Foreign Language Press Is Doomed in Brazil," *Miami Herald*, February 9, 1941, 13; Ernie Hill, "U.S. Papers Are Revived in Brazil," *Miami Herald*, December 16, 1945, 25.

5. Tania Regina de Luca and Margaret Alves Antunes, "A presença de jornais em lingua estrangeira em algumas bibliotecas paulistas e na Biblioteca Nacional do Rio de Janeiro," *Revista Escitos* ano 9, n. 9 (2015): 223–87.

6. "30 Years: Optimism Pays Off," *Brazil Herald*, January 2, 1976, 2.

7. "Otto Inskipp (Vic) Hawkins," *Brazil Herald*, May 7, 1946, 1.

8. From a letter written to John D. Montgomery from William D. Pawley, dated April 14, 1966, and shared with the author.

9. Joseph F. Brown, "Historic," *Brazil Herald*, February 1, 1971.

10. Herbert Zschech, "Historic," *Brazil Herald*, February 1, 1971.

11. Pamela Deacon, "Brazil Herald History," *Brazil Herald*, February 1, 1973; Eurico Gaspar Dutra, Brazil's former minister of war, succeeded Vargas in a general election. Vargas had been president since 1930 (and would return as president, 1951–54).

12. *PM* was published from 1940 to 1948. It was singular at the time since it wasn't supported by advertising, used larger photos, and was bound with staples. It never became financially viable with a circulation that averaged 165,000. Noted journalist I. F. Stone was *PM*'s Washington, DC correspondent; photographer Arthur Fellig, known professionally as Weegie, was a frequent contributor, as were photographers Margaret Bourke-White, Walker Evans, Edward Steichen, Edward Weston, Ralph Steiner, and Robert Capa. Other longtime contributors included cartoonist Theodor Geisel, later to be known as Dr. Seuss, writers Erskine Caldwell, Heywood Hale Broun, James Thurber, Dorothy Parker, Ernest Hemingway, Ben Hecht, and Malcolm Cowley.

13. See Nancy Bilyeau's comprehensive article on Oakes and 1940s Bahamas in *DuJour* magazine, https://dujour.com/culture/mysterious-death-of-sir-harry-oakes -in-the-bahamas/.

14. "Tico Times is Proof: No Such Thing as an 'Ex-Journalist,'" *The Tico Times*, May 19, 2006, https://ticotimes.net/2006/05/19/tico-times-is-proof-no-such-thing -as-an-ex-journalist; "Veteran Newsman Leaves," *Brazil Herald*, August 10, 1951, 7.

15. "Brazil's Only English Language Daily Makes Initial Appearance," *Brazil Herald*, February 1, 1946, 1.

16. "How the Washington Post in 1946 Hailed the Appearance of the Brazil Herald in Rio," *Brazil Herald*, February 1, 1959, 3.

17. "Blonde Lana's Good-Will in Brazil Chilled," *Charleston Gazette*, March 8, 1946, 6.

Endnotes for Chapter 9

18. "Goldwyn Girls Coming to Rio!" *Brazil Herald*, March 4, 1947, 3.
19. "The Goldwyn Girls Are Here..." *Brazil Herald*, March 7, 1946, 3.
20. "The Brazil Herald Meets Bob Hope," *Brazil Herald*, June 14, 1947, 3.
21. "A Fitting Title," *Brazil Herald*, September 28, 1947, 9.
22. *Brazil Herald*, October 17, 1946.
23. "Boston Contract Team in Second-Place Tie," *The Boston Globe*, July 14, 1934, 18.
24. See *Brazil Herald*, November 14, 1946, 3. An elementary school in Rio de Janeiro, Escola Municipal Charles Anderson Weaver, is named after Weaver. His wife, Eunice de Sousa Gabbi Weaver, became famous for founding boarding schools for those suffering from leprosy. She was commemorated with a Brazilian stamp in 1972, although the schools she founded were subsequently condemned as sites of abuse and experimentation.
25. Examples of the "By Joan" and "Window Shopping" columns, *Brazil Herald*, March 16, 18, 1947.
26. "A Inauguração do Instituto Scientifico de Belleza 'Cosmetica Alemã LTD,'" *O Jornal*, May 9, 1936, 6; "O que ha de novo para a belleza?" *O Jornal*, May 16, 1937, 10; *Jornal do Brasil*, November 8, 1936, 22.
27. Tom Murphy, "Chronicler Herb Zschech: A View from Inside," *Brazil Herald*, February 11, 1981.
28. Herbert Zschech, "Historic," *Brazil Herald*, February 1, 1971, 9. Considering Zschech's physical height, it may have been he who wrote the copy in the *Herald*, touting the Goldwyn Girls' arrival in Brazil.
29. Zschech,"Historic," 10.
30. "Slaying Orgy," *Brazil Herald*, January 9, 1947, 5.
31. "Because of a Pair of Hands," *Brazil Herald*, September 6, 1947, 2.
32. "Otto Inskipp (Vic) Hawkins," *Brazil Herald*, May 7, 1946, 1. Hawkins is buried at Rio's Cemitério dos Ingleses; https://www.ancestry.com/family-tree/person/tree/133411/person/392138790316/facts.
33. Zschech, "Historic."
34. L.L. Langley, "Highlights of Brazilian Medicine," *Brazil Herald*, May 26, 1946, 3.
35. "ABC Will Cover Foreign Ministers Meeting in Rio," *Battle Creek Enquirer*, July 24, 1947, 12; "Moss, Langley Named Branch Chiefs in NIH Extramural Programs," *The NIH Record*, June 30, 1964, 6; "Dr. Langley Joins NLM as Associate Director," *The NIH Record*, April 14, 1970, 1; Leroy Langley 2006 obituary, https://www.legacy.com/us/obituaries/kansascity/name/leroy-langley-obituary?id=4472803.
36. Rockefeller would become a seminal political and business force in Latin America and especially in Brazil until his death in 1979. Rockefeller would lead the US delegation for Brazilian President Getulio Vargas's inauguration in 1951. He had a cordial and personal relationship with Vargas.
37. *The New York Times* obituary, Joseph F. Brown, August 10, 1973; "Honor Former Vine City Man in Brazil," *Elmira Star-Gazette*, October 15, 1960, 3.

38. Rotary Global History Fellowship, Rotario Club of Rio de Janeiro, First Club of Brazil, https://www.rghfhome.org/first100/global/southamerica/rio/index.htm#.Xs q8E8Z7lp9.

39. "Frank R. Garcia, Times Reporter," *The New York Times*, June 21, 1958; http://www.toponimiainsulana.com.br/frank_garcia.html.

40. "Brazil Herald: Historic," *Brazil Herald*, February 1, 1971, 5.

41. "Merry Christmas," *Brazil Herald*, December 25, 1947, 1.

Chapter 10 - Cuba, Teddy, Dawn, Tad, and Marc

1. As quoted in Richard M. Caldwell, "Globe-Trotting Secretary Married Her Boss," *The Tulsa Tribune*, March 29, 1944, 13.

2. *Brazil Herald*, May 12, 1946, 1.

3. *Association for Diplomatic Studies & Training*, interview, John Howard Burns, https://adst.org/wp-content/uploads/2012/09/Brazil1.pdf 39.

4. Time-Life would play a huge role in Brazilian media. Time-Life bought a small TV station in Rio de Janeiro in the late 1950s, imported its own manager from San Diego, American Joe Wallach, to run it, and within two decades the station turned into Brazil's largest television network, O Globo, the fourth largest in the world.

5. "General Eisenhower Arrives Today as Guest of Brazilian Government," *Brazil Herald*, August 4, 1946, 1.

6. "Defeatists Have No Place in New World Fight for Peace, Eisenhower Tells Reporters," *Brazil Herald*, August 10, 1946, 1.

7. Ralph Ross, "Technical Help in Its Many Phases Is Shown in Assistance Given Peru," *The Kansas City Times*, December 10, 1952, 34. See Thomas G. Paterson, *Meeting the Communist Threat: Truman to Reagan* (New York: Oxford University Press, 1988).

8. "President Truman Arrives," *Brazil Herald*, September 2, 1947, 1.

9. "Senora Peron Arrives," *Brazil Herald*, September 3, 1947, 1.

10. Herbert Zschech, "Historic," *Brazil Herald*, February 1, 1971.

11. This was not surprising, particularly since Columbia Pictures was one of the shareholders of the newspaper, joining twenty-two other local affiliates in bailing out the newspaper in its first year.

12. Bob Simpson, "Seaplane's Dubious 1911 Debut in Brazil Recalled," *Fort Worth Star-Telegram*, October 20, 1966, 7; Ernie Hill, "Envoy to Brazil Congratulates Hill," *Miami Herald*, December 20, 1946, 5.

13. "Ex-President Vargas, As Senator, Tells Brazil Herald his Role in Present Government Is that of Observer," *Brazil Herald*, June 4, 1946, 1.

14. "Nobel Prize Asked for Oswaldo Aranha," *Brazil Herald*, December 25, 1947, 8. The Peace Prize Award for 1948 went to no one.

15. "The Miracle of the Brazil Herald," *Brazil Herald*, January 12, 1947, 1.

16. Zschech, "Historic."

17. Edwina Hecht and Russell Maloney, "Anonymous," *The New Yorker*, February 23, 1935, 9.

Endnotes for Chapter 10

18. See Richard Koszarski, *Hollywood on the Hudson: Film and Television in New York from Griffith to Sarnoff* (New Brunswick: Rutgers University Press, 2008), 290.

19. Hecht and Maloney, "Anonymous."

20. The *Sombra* cover created by Saul Steinberg, December, 1940-January, 1941, is a magnificent drawing of a woman licking an ice cream cone with the backdrop of a reclining sunworshipper, beach umbrellas, colorful clothing-changing stalls, and a brilliant orange sun. Steinberg also created two drawings for the inside of the same issue of *Sombra*. The *New Yorker* Steinberg cover, instantly recognizable as iconic, originally appeared March 29, 1976.

21. Edwina Hecht, "Impressões do Rio," *Sombra*, June/July, 1941, 25, 26. See Stela Kaz, "Um Jeito Copacabana de Ser: O Discurso do Mito em *O Cruzeiro e Sombra*," (PhD diss.., Pontifícia Universidade Católica do Rio de Janeiro, 2010), 152, 165. http://www.rio.rj.gov.br/dlstatic/10112/1806097/DLFE-237571.pdf/umjeitocopaca banadeser.pdf.

22. "...Num Domingo do Sol, um Gropo de Americanos pela Guanabara," *Sombra*, July, 1941, 28. "Find New Way of to Roast Coffee," *The New York Times*, January 25, 1942, 84. In a letter to her father about the outing, Teddy refers to Polin as "Herbert the Sherbert." See also John Gunther, *Inside Latin America* (New York: Harper & Bros. 1940), 393. In 1943, Polin had come up with a patented process in Brazil to create plastic from coffee grinds, called *cafelite*, an effort that apparently went nowhere.

23. Nasht was a fascinating person in his own right. He worked for the OSS, the forerunner of the CIA in Europe during World War II, then as the Washington, DC correspondent for the Brazilian newspaper, *Correio da Noite*. Following his stint as *Newsweek*'s Latin America correspondent, Nasht went on to a career as a movie and stage producer. Fittingly, he was the producer of the 1959 film, *The Treasure of San Teresa* (also titled *Hot Money Girl*), co-starring ex-*Brazil Herald* reporter Dawn Addams, about a cache of gems hidden in a Czech convent by a Nazi general. Addams plays Hedi von Hartmann, the daughter of the general and co-star Eddie Constantine's ex-lover in the Alvin Rakoff-directed thriller. According to film scholar Rebecca Prime, Nasht had a notorious reputation for hiring American blacklisted actors and directors who had fled to Europe, then reneging on paying them, citing their black-listed status as an excuse. Walter Winchell, "Notes of an Innocent Bystander," *Charlotte Observer*, February 25, 1946, 20. See also Edwina Hecht letter, dated January 3, 1945 from the Ben Hecht Papers., Series 4: Family, Correspondence, 1915-1976, Newberry Library, Box 75, folder 2305, 06, 07, (hereinafter BHP).

24. All letters from Edwina Hecht to her father are contained in Chicago's Newberry Library, which houses her father's voluminous papers.

25. All letters cited are from the BHP. This letter is dated August 20 (no year).

26. Edwina Hecht letter, January 23 (no year).

27. Edwina Hecht letter, June 22 (no year).

28. Edwina Hecht letter, October 22 (no year).

29. Edwina Hecht letters, October 22 and December 8 (no year).

30. Edwina Hecht letter, November 5 (no year).

31. Edwina Hecht letters, October 22 (no year).

32. Edwina Hecht letter, December 8, (no year).

33. Edwina Hecht letter, November 5, (no year).

34. Edwina Hecht letter, December 8 (no year). Dorothy was a fellow expat American friend, who, when Teddy Hecht died in 1971, her widower, Dee Jackson, married (per Mirim Jackson Tullis, Dee and Teddy Hecht Jackson's daughter).

35. Edwina Hecht, December 8 (no year). The declaration that Rio de Janeiro's cost of living rivaled New York's seems an exaggeration.

36. Edwina Hecht letter, December 8 (no year).

37. Edwina Hecht letter, December 8 (no year).

38. "Edwina Jackson: 'A destramento produz provas mutio bonitas,'" *A Gazeta Esportiva* (São Paulo), December 4, 1956, 16.

39. "Auspicioso Inicio Teve a Temporada de Hipismo," *Correio Paulistano* (São Paulo), April 11, 1957, 7 (2 caderno).

40. Edwina Hecht letter, October 22 (no year).

41. Edwina Hecht letter, January 3 (no year).

42. Edwina Hecht letter, December 7 (no year).

43. Edwina Hecht letter, May 27 (no year).

44. Edwina Hecht letter, September 21 (no year).

45. Edwina Hecht letter, January 26 (no year).

46. Edwina Hecht letter, June 9 (no year).

47. Edwina Hecht letter, February 8 (no year).

48. Edwina Hecht letters, June 9 (no year)..

49. Email and text communications from Teddy Hecht's daughter, Mirim Tullis, to author, March 1, 2023; author interview with Mirim Tullis at her home in Boulder Creek, California, March 26, 2023.

50. Edwina Hecht letter, no date.

51. Edwina Hecht letter, February 8 (no year).

52. Genealogical information about Teddy Hecht comes from Ancestry.com, as well as letters from the Newberry Collection, and interviews with Hecht's daughter, Mirim Tullis, January 29 and February 21, 2023, and text messages, March 1, 2023.

53. André Fodor, "Rio by Day and Night," *Brazil Herald*, February 1, 1971, 12.

54. Marjory Adams, "'Priscilla' Had Possibilities, Actress Sawn Addams Decides," *Boston Globe*, September 4, 1952, 18; Walter Waggoner, "Dawn Addams, 54, Actress Is Dead," *The New York Times*, May 9, 1985, 30; Albert Watson, "A New Dawn," *Evening Post* (Reading, Berkshire, England), February 10, 1972, 7; "Brazil Scenes in 'The Moon is Blue' Are Nothing New to One of its Stars," *Norfolk Virginian-Pilot*, July 12, 1953, Part 2, 15; http://www.glamourgirlsofthesilverscreen.com/show/4/Dawn+Addams/index.html; https://www.findagrave.com/memorial/6382540/dawn-addams.

55. Joseph Novitski email to the author, May 17, 2020.

56. João Gilberto Neves Saraiva, "Para Ler a América Latina: Tad Szulc, as Relações InterAmericanas e a Política Externa dos Estados Unidos (1955–65)" (PhD diss., Universidad Federal Fluminese, 2019), 111–12.

Endnotes for Chapter 10

57. Zschech, "Historic."

58. Tad Szulc, "World Today," *Brazil Herald*, July 8, 1946, 3.

59. Szulc's first article that appeared with his byline for the Associated Press was a November 1945 profile of former Brazilian President Getúlio Vargas in what turned out to be a short-lived retirement before he was elected president once again.

60. Szulc's first France Press story appeared May 22, 1947, about a potential intervention and mediation by Argentina, Bolivia, and Brazil in an ongoing conflict in neighboring Paraguay. Tellingly, Szulc's reporting was based on "informed sources," within the government. See Tad Szulc, "Mediação do Brasil e da Argentina," *A Noite*, 1.

61. Declassified CIA dispatch from Chief of Station, Rio de Janeiro, June 20, 1962, https://www.archives.gov/files/research/jfk/releases/2018/104-10103-10103.pdf.

62. "Viajantes," *Jornal do Brasil*, February 15, 1958, 1.°Caderno, 6; "Correspondente do 'Times' de Nova Iorque no Rio Ganhou o Prêmio Cabot-58," September 9, 1959, 1.°Caderno, 9.

63. Daniel Lewis, "Tad Szulc, 74, Dies; Times Correspondent Who Uncovered Bay of Pig Imbroglio," *The New York Times*, May 22, 2001.

64. Harrison E. Salisbury, *Without Fear or Favor: The New York Times and its Times*, (New York: Times Books, 1980), 148–50.

65."Obituário, Rio de Janeiro, Marc Berkowitz," *Jornal do Brasil*, November 25, 1989, 12.

66. Marc Berkowitz, "Latin American Slant at the Bienal, " *ArtNews* (February, 1976): 11–102.

67. As a result of the trip, Norris wrote an essay for *Life* Magazine (Sept. 2, 1946), in which he noted, "Most Americans who survive Brazil more than five years never want to leave it."

68. Marc Berkowitz, "Cultural Activities," *Brazil Herald*, June 7, 1946, 7.

69. Marc Berkowitz, "Cultural Activities," *Brazil Herald*, January 6, 1947, 7. "The Human Fly" appeared in the January 1947 issue of *The Atlantic*.

70. Although future *Brazil Herald* managing partner Bill Williamson insisted to the author in several interviews that he was "hundred-percent certain" Juan de Onís worked at the newspaper, an interview with his daughter, as well as an examination of thousands of yellowed pages of the newspaper, didn't reveal that the well-known journalist ever was employed there, or at least ever had a byline. A graduate of Columbia University Journalism School, de Onís certainly had the literary lineage to make sense of the daily crush of news in Latin America. He was the godson of Spain's most famous poet, Federico García Lorca and Encarnación López Júlvez, better known as La Argentinita, a revered Spanish-Argentine flamenco dancer. His parents were Federico de Onís, a professor who started the Instituto de las Españas at Columbia University (known today as the Department of Latin American and Iberian Cultures), and Harriet de Onís, a celebrated translator of Latin American novelists who would become international literary stars, including Brazilian Jorge Amado and Cuban Alejo Carpentier. While attending Columbia, young de Onís joined a coterie of New York beat writers that included Jack Kerouac, Allen

Ginsberg, and Lucien Carr. Although he was a journalist, not a novelist or poet, de Onís brought to his work a literary bearing where word choice and rhythm mattered. It was an unusual talent for a newspaperman. In Brazil, de Onís, his wife, Marcia, and their first born, Paco, lived in Niterói, across Guanabara Bay from Rio. De Onís moved to UPI's Rio Bureau, then to UPI's Buenos Aires bureau, and later joined *The New York Times*, where he was appointed bureau chief in Rio, then in Mexico City, and years later in Beirut. After sitting out of journalism for a decade in rural Chile, de Onís returned to Rio as the *Los Angeles Times'* bureau chief. Joseph Novitski, *The Washington Post* and later, *The New York Times*, correspondent in Rio, called de Onís "a Brazilian at heart, and a really, really good reporter." That sentiment was shared by Ed Miller, the Rio AP correspondent at the time. "Juan was the best reporter I ever met. A great reporter, the best." If de Onís did work for the *Brazil Herald*, it was between other jobs, as a freelancer, and for a short period of time.

71. *Congressional Record*, 1961—Appendix, "Ambassador Pawley's Grave Reservations, Extension of Remarks of Hon. George A. Smathers," April 18, 1961, A2581, citing *Brazil Herald's* Paul Vanorden Shaw's column, March 1, 1961.

Chapter 11 - John D., Hugh, Stu, and Margaret

1. Leonard Sloan, "Kansan's Daily in Brazil: Good Business, After All," *The New York Times*, February 15, 1979.

2. "Late Amb. Pawley Called Montgomery To Save Herald," *Brazil Herald*, February 1, 1977.

3. Author interview with John Grey Montgomery, John D. Montgomery's son, May 2, 2023. The author examined every available issue of the *Brazil Herald* from its first edition to twenty-one months later when Montgomery purchased the newspaper and no photograph ever appeared of substandard Chicago housing, or for that matter, any so-called "slums" in the United States.

4. Joseph F. Brown, "Historic," *Brazil Herald*, February 1, 1971. 7.

5. From a letter written to John D. Montgomery from William D. Pawley, dated April 14, 1966, shared with the author.

6. "Admiral Halsey Maps Stringent Plans for Dealing with Japanese," *The Charlotte News*, April 20, 1945. 2; "Halsey Wins Praise for His Job as Envoy," *Miami Herald*, August 25, 1946, 1.

7. L. L. Langley, "On Second Thought," *Brazil Herald*, July 21, 1946, 5.

8. From a letter written to John D. Montgomery from William D. Pawley, dated April 14, 1966, shared with the author.

9. Author interview with John Grey Montgomery, May 2, 2023.

10. "Late Amb. Pawley Called Montgomery to Save Herald," *Brazil Herald*, February 1, 1977.

11. "Late Amb. Pawley Called Montgomery to Save Herald," *Brazil Herald*, February 1, 1977; "7 Persons Due KU Distinguished Citations," *Lawrence Daily Journal-World*, May 3, 1971, 2.

12. "US Partners Visit Herald," *Brazil Herald*, January 2, 1976, 1.

13. Robert H. Clark, "John Montgomery Bids for Congress," *The Kansas City Times*, April 9, 1964.

14. Wesley Stout, "The Beachcomber," *Fort Lauderdale News*, March 10, 1959, 8; Marge Clark, "Homemaker, Writer, Civic Worker Mrs. John Montgomery Visits Wichita," *The Wichita Eagle*, November 4, 1956, 56.

15. Pamela Deacon, "Brazil Herald History," *Brazil Herald*, February 1, 1973.

16. FGV Instituto Brasileiro de Economia, http://portalibre.fgv.br/main.jsp?lum ChannelId=402880811D8E34B9011D97C18E8F0195.

17. Author interview with John Grey Montgomery, May 2, 2023.

18. An example of acitivity in such society circles was that in June 1949, Pawley's son, William Pawley Jr., twenty-eight, was romantically involved with a seventeen-year-old film sensation by the name of Elizabeth Taylor. The two had been introduced in Miami Beach, and their romance had blossomed; the couple was engaged to be married—only to have young Pawley's five-carat diamond engagement ring returned by Taylor. The next year, Taylor married Nicky Hilton, heir to the hotel chain.

19. Despite assertions from business associates close to Montgomery, in an interview with the author, former Pan Am publicity director Jeff Kriendler, January 13, 2020, disagreed that Montgomery got free passage on the airline's carriers. He said, "I can't verify Montgomery's Pan Am pass. I don't think that's right."

20. *New York Tribune*, October 28, 1921, 13. Momsen's wife was an heir to the Singer Sewing Machine fortune.

21. Bill Williamson interview with the author, January 6, 2020; Bill Williamson email to the author, July 14, 2020.

22. "Brazil Herald Read by Americans," *Miami Herald*, July 16, 1948, 12; "Miami Editor Takes Over Brazil Paper," *Tampa Tribune*, July 13, 1948, 4.

23. "Brazil Herald Read by Americans," *Miami Herald*, July 16, 1948, 12.

24. Ultimately, Rusk became publisher of the *Miami Beach Sun* in 1954. He had also managed public relations for the Biltmore Hotel chain and was named to the Executive Advisory Board of the Miss Universe Beauty Pageant. He died in Atlanta in 1986 on his eighty-fifth birthday.

25. Ernie Hill, "Miami Newsman, Wife Succeed in Rejuvenating Paper in Rio," *Miami Herald*, November 2, 1949, 21.

26. *Brazil Herald*, June 25, 1949, 5; August 10, 1951, 7.

27. *Brazil Herald*, "Place Just Right For You? Sounds OK, But Where Is It?" by Margaret M. Morrison, July 31, 1948, 4.

28. Margaret M. Morrison, "Critics May Groan But Never As Well as I and Only Bing," *Brazil Herald*, August 28, 1949.

29. *Brazil Herald*, July 28, 1949, 2.

30. *Brazil Herald*, August 2, 1948, 3.

31. *Brazil Herald*, August 21, 1949, 3.

32. *Brazil Herald*, February 1, 1950, 2.

33. *Brazil Herald*, March 11, 1950, 3.

34. *Brazil Herald*, April 20, 1950, 3.

35. *Brazil Herald*, July 1, 1950, 3.
36. *Brazil Herald*, August 22, 1950, 3.
37. *Brazil Herald* August 24, 1950, 2.
38. *Brazil Herald*, August 26, 1950, 3.
39. *Brazil Herald*, August 31, 1950, 2.
40. *Brazil Herald*, September 22, 1950, 3.
41. *Brazil Herald*, October 28, 1950, 2.
42. *Brazil Herald*, December 10, 1950, 3.
43. *Brazil Herald*, January 30, 1951, 3.
44. *Brazil Herald*, April 26, 1951, 3.
45. *Brazil Herald*, May 3, 1951, 2.
46. *Brazil Herald*, April 3, 1954.
47. *Brazil Herald*, September 24, 1954, 3.
48. Richard O'Connell, "Brazilian Happenings," *The New Yorker*, September 17, 1966, 58; October 22, 1966, 60; and November 19, 1966, 62. O'Connell's observations were also published as *Brazilian Poems* (Rio de Janeiro: Editorial Sul America SA, 1960).
49. Johnson's official title was Ambassador Extraordinary and Plenipotentiary.
50. *Brazil Herald*, February 1, 1953, 1.
51. Letter from Herschel V. Johnson, *Brazil Herald*, February 1, 1953, 1, and Stuart Morrison, "Brazil Herald Pledges Always to Stand for Causes of Freedom," *Brazil Herald*, February 1, 1953, 4.
52. Margaret M. Morrison, "Women, Too, Want to Find Their Place In This Busy World," *Brazil Herald*, April 7, 1951, 4.
53. *Brazil Herald*, November 5, 1950, 1.
54. Internal correspondence between aide Francis A. Jamieson and Nelson A. Rockefeller, December 4, 1950; correspondence between Frederick G. Mayor and Howard Knowles, aide to Nelson A. Rockefeller, May 26, 1949; Rockefeller Archive Center, Nelson A. Rockefeller personal papers, Box 14, Folder 99.
55. "Nelson Rockefeller Silent about Post in State Department," and "Rockefeller Pleased with Ike's Victory," *Brazil Herald*, November 13, 1952. 1.
56. *Brazil Herald*, August 12, 1951, 1.
57. Author interview with John Grey Montgomery, May 2, 2023.
58. *Brazil Herald*, February 1, 1951, 1.
59. *Brazil Herald*, July 24, 1951, 1.
60. *Brazil Herald*, August 12, 1951, 1.
61. United States Congress, Hearings before the Subcommittee on International Organizations and Movement of the Committee on Foreign Affairs, *Winning the Cold War: The U.S. Ideological Offensive*, U.S. Government Printing Office, 1963, 588, 619.
62. Edgar Miller email to the author, July 5, 2020; Miller interview with the author, January 29, 2021.
63. Bill Williamson email to the author, July 14, 2020.
64. Ancestry.com.

65. As quoted by former *Latin America Daily Post* executive editor Steve Yolen, from the *Brazil Herald's* 25th anniversary edition, in an email to the author, February 5, 2020.

66. David Hume email to the author, April 19, 2020.

Chapter 12 - Senhor Bill

1. "John Montgomery Announces Plan to Run for Congress," *Brazil Herald*, March 31, 1964, 1.

2. "Named to Board of Regents," *Atchison Daily Globe*, January 7, 1974, 1; "John Montgomery Bids for Congress," *Kansas City Times*, April 9, 1964, 65; Lew Ferguson, "Pressure Building for Roy-Keys Battle," *Parsons Sun*, December 10, 1975, 18; "John D. Montgomery, JC publisher, dead," *Manhattan Mercury*, October 16, 1985, 1; Ellen Wells, "It's Inaugural No. 2," *Miami Herald*, January 29, 1961, 2-E.

3. Brown, "Historic."

4. Frank Garcia, "Brazil Herald Eleven Years Old," *Brazil Herald*, February 1, 1957, 4.

5. Joseph F. Brown, "Frank M. Garcia—A Tribute," *Brazil Herald,,* June 21, 1958, 4.

6. Author interview with Vânia Tôrres Nogueira Williamson , January 7, 2020.

7. While in Kansas City, Bill and Vânia Williamson drove to Columbia, Missouri, so Bill could visit with Bill Taft, his journalism professor at Memphis State, who had been hired at the University of Missouri.

8. Noted American printer's devils include Mark Twain, Walt Whitman, Ambrose Bierce, and Bret Harte.

9. Bill Williamson interviews with the author, January 6 and 7, 2020; *The Courier* (Waterloo, Iowa), May 30, 1965, 10.

10. Brown, "Historic."

11. Author interview with Bill Williamson interview, January 7, 2020.

12. Ralph Grizzle, *Remembering Charles Kuralt* (Asheville, NC: Kenilworth Media, 2000), 147–48.

13. Paige Williams, "A Double Life on the Road," *The Washington Post*, May 31, 1998.

14. Author interview with Ed Miller, January 29, 2021; Kuralt would be followed in the Latin America bureau by CBS correspondent Bob Schakne, from 1964 to 1966.

15. The story aired Sunday, March 25, 1962, 12:15 - 12:30 p.m. on a public affairs show called "WCBS Views the Press with Charles Collingwood." Kuralt was introduced by stentorian-voiced CBS correspondent Collingwood, who opened with, "You can tell a lot about a place from its newspapers. Among the many things about Latin America that we in the United States don't know much about are its newspapers, so we have called on Charles Kuralt, CBS correspondent in Rio de Janeiro, to tell us about the press in that part of the world today." The WCBS transcript is contained in the Charles Kuralt Collection, 1935–1997, No. 04882, Folder 62. It is housed at the Louis Round Wilson Special Collections Library, University

of North Carolina, and quoted with permission. In the transcript, Dear Abby is spelled incorrectly.

16. The author examined more than fifty letters exchanged between Williamson and Montgomery between 1967 and 1979; author interview with John Grey Montgomery, May 2, 2023.

17. *The New Yorker*, August 25, 1956, 77; November 9, 1957, 52; December 1, 1962, 134; May 15, 1965, 198; and August 7, 1978, 75.

18. At the time, telephone numbers were so hard to procure that the *Brazil Herald* ran this classified ad on October 11, 1959: "Distinguished gentleman in Copacabana owns telephone. Will trade for nice furnished room."

19. Author interview with Ed Miller, January 29, 2021.

20. Author interview with Walter Colton, April 12, 2020.

21. Mary A. Lenz email to the author, May 10, 2020. For more than a hundred years, -30- was the traditional way American newspaper reporters ended their stories, alerting typesetters that no more copy would follow. It also was a popular headline in newspaper trade publications for journalists' obituaries.

22. Eric Hippeau and Janet Huseby "The New D'&? a Machine," *Brazil Herald*, February 1, 1973.

Chapter 13 - Gonzo

1. Douglas Brinkley, ed., *The Proud Highway: Saga of a Desperate Southern Gentleman, 1955-1967, Hunter S. Thompson* (New York: Ballantine Books, 1997), 290.

2. Brinkley, ed., *The Proud Highway*, 315–18.

3. Brinkley, ed., *The Proud Highway*, 330–31.

4. Jann S. Wenner and Corey Seymour, *Gonzo: The Life of Hunter S. Thompson*, (New York: Little, Brown and Company, 2007), 38–39.

5. John Morton, "Great While It Lasted," *American Journalism Review*, December, 2002.

6. Ridley stayed with the *National Observer* until it folded in 1977, then became a critic with *The Philadelphia Inquirer*. He published an anthology of arts reporting from the *National Observer*, titled *The Arts Explosion* (Princeton, NJ: Dow Jones, 1972).

7. Tanya Schevitz, "Hunter S. Thompson: 1937–2005," *San Francisco Chronicle*, February 21, 2005; https://www.sfgate.com/news/article/hunter-s-thompson-1937-2005-original-gonzo-2728840.php; Wenner and Seymor, *Gonzo*, 44.

8. Wenner and Seymour, *Gonzo*, 44.

9. Brinkley, ed., *The Proud Highway*, 345–47.

10. Brinkley, ed., *The Proud Highway*, 350. In an interview with the author, Williamson said he has no recall that he wrote anything in his reply to Thompson about salary or cost of living.

11. Brinkley, ed., *The Proud Highway*, 349.

12. Brinkley, ed., *The Proud Highway*, 354.

13. Ernest Hemingway, *Moveable Feast: Sketches of the Author's Life in Paris in the Twenties* (New York: Charles Scribner's Sons, 1964), 101.

14. Ed Miller emails to the author, May 17–18, 2020.

15. Brinkley, ed., *The Proud Highway*, 359.

16. Jann S. Wenner and Corey Seymour, "Hunter S. Thompson: Growing Up Gonzo," *Rolling Stone*, October 4, 2007, 44, 59; Robert W. Bone, *Fire Bone! A Maverick Guide to Life in Journalism* (Walnut Creek, CA: Peripety Press, 2017), 149–53.

17. Hunter S. Thompson, "Sen. Talmadge Stresses Self-Help, Voices Concern Over L America," *Brazil Herald*, October 23, 1962, 2.

18. Zschech, "Historic."

19. Author interview with Williamson, January 7, 2020,

20. Zschech, "Historic."

21. Brian Kevin, *The Footloose American: Following the Hunter S. Thompson Trail Across South America*, (New York: Broadway Books, 2014), 253.

22. Recollections are from Bill Williamson's unpublished manuscript, "Madeira Memories," undated, supplied to the author.

23. As quoted in Wenner and Seymour, *Gonzo*, 60.

24. Brinkley, ed., *The Proud Highway*, 315; Sasha Siemel, *Tigrero!*, (New York: Prentice-Hall, 1953).

25. As quoted in Kevin, *The Footloose American* 342.

26. Thompson was referring to the editorial style adopted by both *Newsweek* and *Time* magazines of not using a byline atop staff-written stories, with the exception of columns.

27. Czech-born Milan (Mike) J. Kubic was a *Newsweek* correspondent from 1958 to 1989, including stints as bureau chief in Rio de Janeiro (1963), Beirut, Vienna, West Germany, and Jerusalem. He died in January, 2020.

28. An exceedingly minor quibble; "Tchau" is how the Brazilians spell the word for "bye."

29. Bone, *Fire Bone*, 150.

30. The Thompson-Graham letter exchange is contained in Brinkley's *The Proud Highway*, 370–73.

31. "Philip Graham, 48, Publisher, a Suicide," *The New York Times*, August 4, 1963, 1.

32. "Hemingway's Suicide Gun," *Garden & Gun*, October 20, 2010, https://garden andgun.com/articles/hemingways-suicide-gun/. See also, Silvio Calabi, Steve Helsley, and Roger Sanger, *Hemingway's Guns: The Sporting Arms of Ernest Hemingway*, (Rockport, Maine: Down East Books, 2010).

33. Douglas Brinkley, "Football Season Is Over," *Rolling Stone*, September 8, 2005. https://web.archive.org/web/20080619074031/http://www.rollingstone.com/news /story/7605448/football_season_is_over.

Chapter 14 - André, Rita, Eddie, Humphrey, and Jean

1. André Fodor, "Rio By Day and Night," *Brazil Herald*, February 1, 1971, 12. See also https://www.theshipslist.com/ships/lines/creunis.shtml.

2. André Todor, "Joint Advertising to Boost Tourism In South America," *Brazil Herald*, December 29, 1955, 5.

3. André Fodor, "Rio by Night," *Brazil Herald*, December 11, 1955, 11.

4. Harold Emert email to the author, May 8, 2020; Fodor's wife was Claire Fodor. André died in 1978, and Claire in 2001; both are buried in Rio's Cemitério dos Ingleses.

5. Fodor, "Rio by Day and Night," February 1, 1971, 12.

6. Author interview with Bill Williamson, January 7, 2020.

7. https://bcsrio.org.br/bcs-history/. "Rita Davy BH Social Columnist," *Brazil Herald*, February 1, 1974, 3. Davy died in 1988, leaving her sister, Marjorie, and their cat, Topsy, whose names are also inscribed on her tombstone at Rio's Cemitério dos Ingleses.

8. Tom Murphy email correspondence with the author, June 29, 2020.

9. "U.S. Air Pioneer Killed in Brazil," *The New York Times*, December 11, 1974, 12.

10. "New York Financier Says He Took $2 Million to Protect Self, Firm," *San Antonio Express and News*, June 16, 1962, 16-C, author interview with Williamson, January 6, 2020.

11. Jerry W. Markham, *A Financial History of Modern U.S. Corporate Scandals: From Enron to Reform* (New York: Routledge, 2006), 618; John Pryor, "Wall Streeter Gilbert Gets Four Years for Stock Fraud," UPI, July 31, 1981; William Stadiem, *Jet Set: The People, the Planes, the Glamour, and the Romance in Aviation's Golden Years,*" (New York: Random House, 2014); Bryan Taylor, "Eddie Gilbert: The Boy Wonder of Wall Street," *Global Financial Date*, February 18, 2016. Gilbert died at age ninety-two in Santa Fe, New Mexico, on December 23, 2015.

12. Bob Simpson, "Seaplane's Dubious 1911 Debut in Brazil Recalled," *Fort Worth Star-Telegram*, October 20, 1966, 7.

13. From a letter (and news clipping) Bill Williamson sent John Montgomery, September 5, 1969, obtained by the author.

14. "Kidnap U.S. Envoy in Rio," *Kansas City Times*, September 5, 1969, 1; author interview with Vânia Williamson, January 6, 2020.

15. "1969: Presos políticos embarcam para o México em negociação pela liberdade de embaixador," *Folha de S. Paulo*, September 7, 2019, 1.

16. See David Randall, "'Third minister in 1970s sex scandal, says Norma Levy," *The Independent* (London), January 28, 2007, 1; John Ezard, "Norma Levy Charged in London," *The Guardian* (London), July 16, 1973, 1.

17. "U.S. Air Pioneer Killed in Brazil."

18. "Humphrey W. Toomey Congratulated on Anniversary Flight," *Brazil Herald*, November 20, 1955, 10.

19. One of many examples was "New Million Dollar Tourism Compaign [*sic*] Announced by PAA," *Brazil Herald*, August 24, 1951, 1.

20. See Felipe Fernandes Cruz's fascinating story of the rescue mission in "Amazonia 1952: Found," *The Appendix*, December 21, 2012. http://theappendix.net/issues/2012/12/field-notes,-amazonia-1952:-found.

21. American Foreign Service, "Report of the Death of an American Citizen," Grace Cecilia Strelow Toomey, March 31, 1954. "Mrs. H.W. Toomey Dies Suddenly,

Endnotes for Chapter 15

Service at Christ Church Today," *Brazil Herald*, March 23, 1954, 1; "Mrs. H. W. Toomey, Wife Of PAA Chief," *The Miami News*, March 22, 1954, 20. Toomey married the former Frances Williams in San Francisco in 1929.

22. André Fodor, "Rio by Night," *Brazil Herald*, December 11, 1955, 11.

23. André Fodor, "Rio by Day and Night," *Brazil Herald*, October 1956.

24. See https://www.imdb.com/name/nm0079174/?ref_=ttfc_fc_wr1; https://www.themoviedb.org/movie/438876-miss-o-matar.

25. Jorge César Wamburg, "A Morte do Americano Tranquilo," *Manchette*, December 28, 1974, 8–13; "Mulher é suspeita pela morte do director da Pan Am," *Jornal do Brasil*, December 11, 1974, 14; "Buscas sobre a morte de Toomey se voltem para 'infrminhos' da Zona Sul," *Jornal do Brasil*, December 15, 1974, 50; "Preocupação no caso Toomey agora é apurar os passos de Huber no dia do crime," *Jornal do Brasil*, December 20, 1974, 26; "Jogo de milhões em terra illegal na Barra envolve o assassínio de Humphrey," *Diario de Noticias*, December 18, 1974, 6.

26. Harold Emert email to the author, August 8, 2020.

27. Jean Etsinger email to the author, June 5, 2020.

28. Jean Etsinger email to the author, June 5, 2020; Cricket Appel email to the author, June 3, 2020; Bill Williamson interview with the author, January 6, 2020.

29. Author interview with Walter Colton, April 12, 2020.

30. Mark Gruberg's many finely crafted stories appeared in the *Times of Brazil*, the weekend supplement of the *Brazil Herald*, including "Turf: A Day at the Races," August 8, 1976; "The Man Who Invents Himself," January 16/17; 1977; and "Sports: The Maracanã Experience," May 23,/24/1976.

Chapter 15 - Censors and Spooks

1. See J. Patrice Mcsherry's *Predatory States: Operation Condor and Covert War in Latin America* (Lanham, Maryland: Rowman & Littlefield), 2005 and John Dinges's *The Condor Years: How Pinochet and His Allies Brought Terrorism to Three Continents* (New York: The New Press), 2005; along with accounts published in the Brazilian newspaper *Folha de São Paulo* and the Brazilian magazine *Carta Maior*, among other media outlets.

2. CIA FOIA documents, https://www.cia.gov/library/readingroom/docs/CIA-RDP91-00901R000700060125-0.pdf.

3. In the past, the *Herald* convention was to translate editorials from local newspapers and not announce its own political stance. The citations are all from the *Brazil Herald*, April 1–4, 1964.

4. Brazil's landmass is 3,287,357 square miles compared to Cuba's 42,803 square miles, South America's 6,878,000 square miles, and the US's 2,995,064 square miles; https://database.earth/population/by-country/1964.

5. Cited in "American Papers Stress Brazil Events' Significance," *Brazil Herald*, April 4, 1964.

6. Unpublished recollections, "Chapter 7, Brazil: The First Time," shared with the author by Ed Miller; author interview with Miller, January 29, 2021.

7. "Jules Dubois, 56, Journalist, Dead," *The New York Times*, August 17, 1966, 31.

Endnotes for Chapter 15

8. John M. Crewdson and Joseph B. Treaster, "C.I.A. Established Many Links to Journalists in U.S. and Abroad," *The New York Times*, December 27, 1977, 1.

9. Hal Hendrix, "Brazil Herald Is Set by Printers Who Can't Read Their Copy," *The Kansas City Star*, October 29, 1954, 10.

10. Vi Murphy, "Music To Remember By," *Moline Dispatch*, January 14, 1969, 17.

11. Crewdson and Treaster,"C.I.A. Established Many Links to Journalists in U.S. and Abroad."

12. Joseph Sims email to author, January 22, 2020.

13. Joseph Sims email, sent to Edgar Miller, retired AP reporter, March 23, 2011, shared with the author.

14. Joseph Sims email to the author, January 22, 2020.

15. John Thrall email to Walter Colton, July 22, 2012, shared with the author.

16. Susan Lightcap email to Walter Colton, February 20, 2023, shared with the author.

17. FOIA requested July 14, 1951, letter from William D. Pawley to CIA director Allen W. Dulles. Ever connected to politics and business, Pawley in 1965 tried to interest his longtime friend and Brazil enthusiast, Nelson A. Rockefeller, while governor of New York, in investing in a venture of his, the Talisman Sugar Corporation, a ten-thousand-acre farm in south Florida, but Rockefeller demurred. Pawley would remain a hardline anti-communist for the rest of his life. In 1958 Pawley conceived of a plan to replace faltering Cuban President Fulgencio Batista with a four-person anti-Castro provisional government. Pawley presented the plan to President Eisenhower, who approved of it, sending Pawley on a secret mission to convince Batista to abdicate one month before Castro would assume power, but the Cuban leader would not agree. Two years later, Pawley hosted meetings in Miami with CIA officials and Cuban refugees alarmed at Castro's growing power, laying the groundwork for the failed Bay of Pigs affair under President Kennedy's administration, to be exposed by former *Brazil Herald* reporter Tad Szulc, at the time working for *The New York Times*.

18. CIA letter from Mark Lilly, Information and Privacy Coordinator, to author, December 5, 2019.

19. Author interview with Bill Williamson, January 6, 2020.

20. Author interview with Bill Williamson, January 6, 2020.

21. From 1960 through 1964, Mestre was joined by numerous other CIA operations officials in Brazil attached to diplomatic missions in the country. They included: Lewis P. Achen; Charles L. Acree Jr.; Thomas J. Barrett Jr.; Thomas A. Brady; Brendan A. Burns Jr.; Stuart D. Burton; Thomas E. Carroll; Albert M. Clearman; George T. Colman Jr.; Charles R. Cookson; Stephen F. Creone; Walter C. D'Andrade; Joaquin B. De Castro; Timothy J. Desmond; Louis V. Ebert III; Robert L. Fambrini; Arthur P. Frizzell; Jack M. Forcey; Robert D. Gahagen; L. Keith Gardiner; Maurice J. Gremillion; Vernet L. Gresham; Claris R. Halliwell; Gardner H. Hathaway; John W. Hennessey; Russell G. Hibbs; Herman J. Jelinek; Robert E. Jones, Joseph Y. Kiyonaga; Arthur Kamm; Donald K. Kanes; Star M. King Jr.; James N. Lawler; Lawrence C. Laser; John O. Lawrence; Wesley L. Laybourne; Paul A. Maggio; Victoria

Endnotes for Chapter 15

Mathews; James L. McMahon; Michael Marchese Jr.; Donald C. Marelius; Antonio L. Neves; Walter J. O'Lone; Lawrence A. Penn; John B. Perkey Jr.; Robert Reynolds; Carlton A. Rood; Richard S. Sampson; Gil M. Saude; Calvin M. Smyth; Lawrence M. Sternfield; Richard D. Van Winkle; Leonard Whistler; and David L. Yelton. The list was compiled by Vincente Gil da Silva and included in his doctoral dissertation for the Federal University of Rio de Janeiro, 2020, titled "Planejamento e organização da contrarevolução preventiva no Brazil; atores e articulaçõs transnacionais (1936–1964)." The list was compiled primarily from Philip Agee's *Inside the Company* (New York: Penguin Books, 1975), government archives, including documents from the US State Department, Foreign Service, CIA Electronic Reading Room, as well as obituaries published in *The New York Times* and *Washington Post*. It does not include CIA assets employed as part-time informants, or contract employees, and is neither thorough nor complete.

22. Per an email Bill Williamson sent the author, January 21, 2020. Lee Gwynne Mestres died May 13, 2010, of a heart attack. See CIA reference in obituary in the *Princeton Alumni Weekly*, https://paw.princeton.edu/memorial/lee-g-mestres-sr -%E2%80%9957. Peter Rodenbeck was born in Michigan but became a naturalized Brazilian citizen.

23. The connection between US-financed right-wing political activism and the *Brazil Herald* and ultimately, the *Latin America Daily Post*, is tantalizingly suggestive. Apart from the two *Herald* staffers, Joe Sims and John Thrall, who claimed they had at one time worked for the CIA, personnel who would take on management roles at the *Daily Post* also had alleged financial ties to covert US involvement with internal Brazilian affairs.

In 1959, the CIA backed a newly formed anti-communist group, the Brazilian Institute for Democratic Action. IBAD became a well-funded umbrella organization of more than a dozen political-action groups that enlisted as members business leaders, professionals, housewives, and students. It financed pro-military candidates and organized opposition rallies to defeat left-wing politicians, including João Goulart. IBAD published a monthly circular, *Ação Democrática*, which at the time circulated to more than two hundred and fifty thousand Brazilians. An allied group, also with backing from the CIA and the US State Department, was the Institute for Social Research Studies (IPES). Printing much of IBAD and IPES's propaganda was a private company that also published the country's telephone books and yellow pages, owned by an American-Brazilian, Gilberto Huber. A public-relations firm called Salles Promotions, Inc. handled much of the organizations' national publicity and circulation efforts. That company was run by three brothers from a prominent Brazilian family, the Salleses. Mauro Salles, along with family members, would later start the *Latin America Daily Post*, the newspaper I joined in 1979. Gilberto Huber would ultimately become its major shareholder in the mid-1980s.

24. *Brazil Herald* column from October 23, 1962, as reprinted in *Nieman Reports*, December 1962, 9.

25. David Hume email to the author, April 19, 2020.

26. Marisa Bittar and Amarilio Ferreiro Jr., "The History of Education in Brazil; The Formation of the Field and Theoretical Influences," *Espacio, Tiempo y Educación*, 3.1 (2016): 61–84; http://dx.doi.org/10.14516/ete.2016.003.001.5. Rodrigo Carro, "Brazilian Newspapers: The Risk of Becoming Irrelevant," Reuters Institute for the Study of Journalism, 2016, 16.

27. The WCBS transcript is contained in the Charles Kuralt Collection, 1935–1997, No. 04882, Folder 62. It is housed at the Louis Round Wilson Special Collections Library, University of North Carolina, and quoted with permission. In the transcript, Dear Abby is spelled incorrectly.

28. Bob Nadkarni email to the author, June 28, 2020.

29. Lisa Fourré email to the author, April 21, 2023.

30. Jean Etsinger email to the author, June 5, 2020.

31. Jean Etsinger email to the author, June 5, 2020.

32. Author interview with Ramez Maluf interview, January 1, 2021.

33. Mark Gruberg email to the author, June 7, 2020.

34. Author interview with Walter Colton, May 1, 2021.

35. Maggie Locke email to the author, May 29, 2020.

36. See Jim Bruce, "Opinião Seeks Own Free Reins," *Brazil Herald*, April 1, 1977, 1, for a discussion of the weekly and increasing censorship.

37. Don Best email to the author, May 14, 2020.

38. Author interview with Walter Colton, April 22, 2020.

39. "Our Easter Present," *Brazil Herald*, March 8, 1964, 8.

40. See Will Savive, "Jim Jones: Mystery Man, Mystery Trip," in the website Alternative Considerations of Jonestown & the Peoples Temple, sponsored by the Special Collections of Library and Information Access at San Diego State University, https://jonestown.sdsu.edu/

41. Per an email Bill Williamson sent to the author, January 21, 2020.

42. "Building a Better Thumbscrew," *New Scientist*, July 19, 1973, 139–41.

43. It remains curious that all three alleged CIA operatives, Joe Sims, Dan Mitrione, and Jim Jones, had Indiana connections: Sims graduated from Indiana State University and lived just over the Illinois-Indian state line, Mitrione worked as a police officer in Richmond, Indiana; and Jones was a native of Crete, Indiana.

44. Directed by French filmmaker Marcel Camus and based on a play by Brazilian writer Vinicius de Moraes, the film recounts the Greek tragedy of Orpheus and Eurydice, set in a Rio favela during Carnival. The soundtrack features scores by Brazilian bossa nova musician Antonio Carlos Jobim. *Orfeu Negro* won the Palme d'Or at the 1959 Cannes Film Festival and Best Foreign Language Film at the 1960 Academy Awards.

45. Author telephone interview with Bob Beadle, March 21, 2023; email exchanges with Peter Jarvis, March 20, 21, 2023.

46. Peter Jarvis email shared with the author, April 6, 2023.

47. Author interview with Ramez Maluf, January 1, 2021.

Chapter 16 - Merry Pranksters

1. Garry Marchant, "Rio de Janeiro," in *Away From Home—Canadian Writers in Exotic Places*, ed. Kildare Dobbs (Toronto: Deneau, 1985), 201–16.The "John" mentioned was John Thrall; "Laura" was Laura Reid, "Pamela" is unknown (perhaps a composite), "Walter" was Walter Colton, and "Betty" was Betty Sausser.

2. Per an email from Thrall's former wife, Susan Lightcap, February 20, 2023, to Walter Colton, shared with the author.

3. John York, "Dope Inside Case; Man Gets 5 Years," *The Atlanta Constitution*, October 10, 1969, 9.

4. Keeler McCartney, "$20,000 in Drugs Seized on 2 Here," *The Atlanta Constitution*, February 15, 1969, 1; Achsah Nesmith, "Prisoner in Solitary Sues Jail as Hurting Sanity," *The Atlanta Constitution*, August 27, 1970, 35.

5. Barry Henderson, "Lee's Killing Canceled Plan to Raid His House," *The Atlanta Constitution*, November 9, 1974, 1; "Shooter in Lee Case," *Sun-Herald* (Biloxi), September 15, 1990, 9; Susan Lightcap email.

6. Author interview with Walter Colton, with whom Thrall shared video clips from Thrall's and Hall's performance in Brasília, April 12, 2020.

7. John Thrall email to the author, May 18, 2020. Thrall died in 2020.

8. Don Best email to the author, May 14, 2020.

9. Bob Nadkarni email to the author, June 28, 2020.

10. Walter Colton email to the author, April 21, 2020; author interview with Janet Huseby, June 7, 2023.

11. Susan Lightcap email to Walter Colton, April 21, 2020, shared with the author.

12. Marchant, "Rio de Janeiro," 201–16,

13. Author interview with Walter Colton, April 3, 2020.

14. Marchant, "Rio de Janeiro," 201–16.

15. Betty Sausser, "Potpourri," *Brazil Herald*, March 18, 1973.

16. Mary A. Lenz email to the author, May 10, 2020. Lenz shared with the author a trove of letters she sent from Brazil to her parents.

17. Mary A. Lenz email to the author, May 10, 2020, along with copies of letters sent to her parents.

18. Liza Fourré letter to her father, April 22, 1976, shared with the author.

19. Jean Etsinger email to the author, June 5, 2020.

20. Diana Page, *Looking for Love in All the Wrong Places: A Memoir for My Stepdaughters*, (Tucson: Wheatmark, 2016), 122. Page went on to work for UPI in Rio and Buenos Aires, as well as the *St. Petersburg Times*, followed by a career in the US Foreign Service.

21. Email shared with the author, from Jonathan Kapstein, April 11, 2023.

22. Diana Page, *Looking for Love in All the Wrong Places: A Memoir for My Stepdaughters*, 199–12.

23. John D. Montgomery letter to Bill Williamson, May 4, 1970.

24. Bill Williamson letter to John D. Montgomery, November 24, 1969.

25. Bill Williamson letter to John D. Montgomery, November 27, 1969.

26. Bob Nadkarni email to the author, April 11, 2020. Patureau died in Fort Lauderdale in 2012. Nadkarni died in 2023.

27. Not-for-attribution quote from a former *Herald* staffer. Hippeau did not respond to the author's multiple requests for comments or reflections about his employment at the *Brazil Herald*.

28. Marchant, "Rio de Janeiro," 201–16; "The Boss," as told to Patricia R. Olsen, *The New York Times*, March 21, 2010, Business section, 9.

29. Harold Emert email shared with the author, February 17, 2023.

30. Walter Colton email to the author, February 16, 2023.

31. Don Best email to the author, February 19, 2023.

32. Maggie Locke email to author, May 12, 2020.

33. Don Best email to the author, May 14, 2020.

34. "Army Grabs BH Editor," *Brazil Herald*, undated, 4.

35. Don Best email to the author, May 14, 2020.

36. Mary A. Lenz email to the author, citing correspondence with her parents, May 10, 2020.

37. Mary A. Lenz email to the author, May 10, 2020.

38. Mark Gruberg email to the author, June 7, 2020.

39. Author interview with Janet Huseby, June 7, 2023; Janet Huseby email to the author, April 24, 2020.

40. Author interview with Janet Huseby, June 7, 2023; Janet Huseby email to the author, April 24, 2020. Huseby ultimately quit the AP within two years, she said, when she discovered that another AP correspondent in the bureau, a man, with the same job responsibilities, was earning twice as much as she was. When Huseby confronted her supervisor about this, she recalled he shrugged his shoulders and explained that the male correspondent was intending to make a career as a wire-service reporter while she would "get married, quit, and be having babies."

41. Janet Huseby, "Carnival Mood Begins to Be Felt in Guanabara," *Brazil Herald*, January 30, 1974.

42. Alison Raphael, "History of the Samba Schools," *Brazil Herald*, January 12–13 February 13–14, 1977, *Times of Brazil* insert, 1.

43. Liza Fourré email to the author, April 21, 2023.

44. The traditional soccer rivalry between the two Rio teams, Fluminense vs Flamengo, is akin to competition between the Chicago White Sox and Chicago Cubs or the New York Yankees and New York Mets.

45. Equal Rights Amendment, designed to guarantee equal legal rights for all American citizens regardless of gender, introduced to Congress in 1923, but despite approval by 35 state legislatures, still has not been adopted.

46. Diary entries shared by Liza Fourré with the author, April 29, 2023. Something else worth sharing: When rain washed out a beach day, Fourré and others occasionally played bridge—another sign of the times.

47. Author interview with Robin Lai, December 13, 2020.

48. Author interview with Robin Lai, December 13, 2020.
49. Eric Hippeau and Janet Huseby "The New D'&? a machine," *Brazil Herald*, February 1, 1973.
50. Eric Hippeau and Janet Huseby, "YOUR NEWSPAPER: 27 YEARS OLD AND GETTING NEWER: The new D'&? a machine," *Brazil Herald*, February 1, 1973.
51. Editôra Mory Financial Statements (unaudited), year ended July 31, 1976, and January 31, 1977.
52. Author interview with Bill Williamson, January 7, 2020.
53. Author interview with John Grey Montgomery, May 2, 2023.
54. Author interview with John Grey Montgomery, May 2, 2023.
55. Undated letter on *Brazil Herald* stationery from Bill Hall to Liza Fourré, shared with the author by Fourré.
56. Liza Fourré letter to her parents, December 24, 1977, shared with the author.
57. Jim Bruce email to the author, February 15, 2021.
58. Brian Nicholson email to the author, June 22, 2020.
59. Thomas Mann, *Confessions of Felix Krull, Confidence Man: The Early Years* (New York: New American Library, 1957).
60. Brian Nicholson email to the author, June 22, 2020.
61. Brian Nicholson email to the author, June 22, 2020.

Chapter 17 - "Just Put Your Lips Together and Blow"

1. The apartments were part of a New York City Housing Authority project called the Lillian Wald Houses, located between East Third and Houston Streets.
2. Background to Harold Emert's early life comes from emails sent to the author, January 2, January 22, 2021, February 25, 2023, along with author interviews with Emert.
3. Harold Emert, "Reporter Gets Green Baptism from Architects," *The Ithaca Journal*, March 18, 1966, 11; "Drivers, Pay Attention City's Radar Listening," *The Ithaca Journal*, February 18. 1966, 9; "College Singers Find Germans to Be Excellent Hosts on Tour," *The Ithaca Journal*, July 26, 1966, 5; "Last Gathering for No 2s In Historic Fire Building," *The Ithaca Journal*, July 3, 1966, 9; and "Professor Gets 10-Day Jail Sentence, Appeals," *The Ithaca Journal*, June 9, 1966, 13.
4. Emert email to the author, February 25, 2023.
5. Emert emails to the author, January 2, January 22, 2021, February 25, 2023.
6. Author interview with Ramez Maluf, January 1, 2022.
7. Harold Emert, "Inside Cidade Maravilhosa: "Marriage, Brazilian Style," *Brazil Herald*, February 12–13, 1977, 2.
8. https://www.barrypopik.com/index.php/new_york_city/entry/a_schlemiel_is_the_guy.
9. Harold Emert repost on Facebook, December 31, 2022.
10. Harold Emert, "A Wild Dream Comes True," *Brazil Herald*, April 19, 1980. The hit song of the same era, Chega Mais, was sung by Brazilian megastar Rita Lee, whose family came from Americana, Brazil, the city where US Confederates settled after the American Civil War.

11. At the time, the number of attendees who went to the Sinatra concert made it into the *Guinness Book of World Records*, only to be broken eight years later when Tina Turner appeared at Maracanã and drew 180,000 fans, per Brian Nicholson, "Mini-skirted Tina Turner claims record audience," UPI, January 17, 1988, https://www.upi.com/Archives/1988/01/17/Mini-skirted-Tina-Turner-claims-record-audience/7848569394000/.
12. Author recollection from Emert, January, 1980.
13. Per Emert email to the author, March 16, 2023.
14. Recalled in Emert email to the author, April 13, 2020.
15. Harold Emert, "Inside Cidade Maravilhosa," *Brazil Herald*, April 18–19, 1976, 7.
16. Emert email to author, November 15, 2020.
17. "Brazil Herald Managing Partner Received Award," *Brazil Herald*, February 1, 1975, 8.
18. Maluf interview with the author, January 1, 2021.
19. Williamson email to the author, April 9, 2020.
20. Agreement of stock assignment, transfer and purchase of the *Brazil Herald* from John D. Montgomery, John G. Montgomery, and Bill Williamson to São Bento Administração e Participações Ldta, dated February 8, 1979, a copy of which came into the possession of the author.
21. Williamson letter provided to the author.
22. See endnote 22 in Chapter 15, Censors and Spooks.
23. Author interview with Williamson, January 6, 2020.
24. Williamson email to the author, April 9, 2020.

Chapter 18 - Manic
1. Garner eventually moved to Ocala, Florida, where he owned a horse farm, and later to Jacksonville.
2. Ed Miller email to the author, May 18, 2020.
3. See Steve Yolen's Spanish-language account of covering the Chilean coup for UPI, "400 balas: el 11 de septiembre chileno," in the online magazine, *Ciper*, https://www.ciperchile.cl/2023/09/07/400-balas-el-11-de-septiembre-chileno/.
4. Steve Yolen email and memo to the author, May 12, 2020. All quotes from Yolen in this chapter are from the email and memo.
5. Mauro Salles's brother name was spelled "Sales" with one "l" instead of two because of a mistake when their parents registered Luiz at birth; the notary blundered on the birth certificate, and it was never corrected in later life. The same thing happened with another one of Salles brothers, Cláudio, as well). In 1989, Luiz Sales was to make headlines when he was kidnapped and held for ransom by urban guerrillas for several months. He was eventually released after an undisclosed sum was paid.
6. The decision, Latin America or Latin American, recalled Yolen "would cause confusion for years to come — hardly anybody ever got the name right."
7. Curiously, the Monumento às Bandeiras, or Monument to the Flags, designed by Italian-Brazilian sculptor Victor Brecheret, would become hugely controversial,

renounced, and repudiated, particularly in the wake of the murder of African-American George Floyd by Minneapolis, Minnesota police in 2020. The statue depicts men on horseback forging a path into Brazil's interior. Critics charge that the settlers the monument seeks to commemorate killed or enslaved multitudes of Brazil's indigenous people, as well as African-Brazilians. The statue often is the target of graffiti, and is the subject of ongoing debates about removing it.

8. Newspapers have historically employed such slogans to denote their vaunted claims to fame. Examples include *The New York Times* "All the News That's Fit to Print," *Toledo Blade* "One of America's Great Newspapers," *Chicago Daily Tribune* "The World's Greatest Newspaper," *Denver Post* "Climate Capital of the World," *Atlanta Constitution* "Covers Dixie like the Dew," *Miami News* "The Best Newspaper under the Sun," *Miami Herald*, "Florida's Most Complete Newspaper," and *San Francisco Examiner* "The Monarch of the Dailies."

9. Mark Gruberg letter to Liza Fourré, December 9, 1978, shared with the author.

10. Williamson's reason for becoming a Brazilian, he wrote, "large as it looms in my personal life, is trifling retribution for what this great country has given me—in love (a Bahiana-Carioca wife and three bi-national children), friendship (hundreds if not thousands of warm and wonderful friends), professional fulfillment (20 years working for Brazilian-America understanding on a newspaper devoted mainly to this country's expatriate English-language community." Williamson also wrote, "I publicly admit taxes were one of many influencing my decision," citing the United States' "unique, and absurd, laws taxing its citizens living abroad on their incomes earned overseas." From Bill Williamson, "The Making of a Brazilian," *Brazil Herald*, September 7/8, 1979, 2.

11. The closest reference to São Marcelo comes from the thirtieth Catholic Pope who lived from AD 304 to 309 . São Marcelo also is the name of a cylindrical maritime fort located in the bay of Salvador da Bahia in northeast Brazil, originally built in 1623.

12. *O Estado de São Paulo*, while editorially at times boring and plodding, was considered the most respectable newspaper in the city, if not the country at the time.

13. Stanley Lehman email to the author, June 29, 2020.

14. From the four-page broadsheet promotional copy of the *Latin America Daily Post*, dated November 1978.

15. "Welcome Colleague," *Brazil Herald*, original typewritten version appeared in Bill Williamson's private papers, no date.

16. "The Latin American Daily Post and the Brazil Herald—A comparison, some thoughts, and a statistical analysis," by Brian L. Nicholson, October 30, 1978. A copy of the internal report commissioned by the *Brazil Herald* was acquired by the author.

17. Myron Kandel and Philip Greer, "A Business Newspaper in English for Brazil," *Chicago Tribune*, May 6, 1979, 31.

18. David F. Belnap, "English-Language Newspaper Planned in Brazil," *Los Angeles Times*, October 31, 1978, 45.

19. Gentil's maternal grandfather was Ellsworth F. Bunker, a businessman and diplomat, who had been the US ambassador to Argentina, Italy, India, Nepal, and South Vietnam.

20. Author interviews with John Grey Montgomery, May 2 and June 4, 2023.

21. Author interview with John Grey Montgomery, May 2, 2023.

22. The cruzeiro-dollar exchange rate on the day of the sale was twenty-one cruzeiros to one dollar. The cruzeiro became obsolete in July 1994, when the real became the legal currency in Brazil.

23. Richard Cole email to the author, March 3, 2020.

24. Brian Nicholson email to the author, June 22, 2020.

25. Mark Gruberg email to the author, April 24, 2023. When asked about the issue, Williamson maintained to the author he had no recall of this story or headline he had written.

26. Richard Cole email to the author, March 23, 2020. In addition to his editing duties, Cole wrote a popular column for the *Brazil Herald* and *Latin America Daily Post*, exploring the life of an expat in Rio de Janeiro. Whimsical columns included one about "sidewalking," in which he pointed out that Brazilians wander erratically on the sidewalk, making passing them an adventure, and another in which he speculated what it would be like if Rio workers commuted in hot air balloons above the heavily trafficked Zona Sul route downtown, the Aterro do Flamengo. Another memorable Cole column was more dystopian, speculating on Brazil's role in the new world order once the Soviet Union and the United States had destroyed each other in preemptive nuclear attacks.

27. Richard Cole email to the author, March 3, 2020.

28. Agreement of stock assignment, transfer and purchase of the *Brazil Herald* from John D. Montgomery, John G. Montgomery, and Bill Williamson to São Bento Administração e Participações Ldta, dated February 8, 1979, a copy of which came into the possession of the author; author interview with Bill Williamson, January 7, 2020. Williamson contended that the remainder of scheduled compensation was stalled and ultimately never paid him, even after a lengthy litigation process. At the time, monthly inflation in Brazil was in excess of ten percent, so any timed payouts based in cruzeiros, even with built-in indexed escalators, would be greatly reduced.

29. "What We Believe," *Latin America Daily Post*, April 26, 1979, 1.

30. Stan Lehman email to the author, June 22, 2020.

31. Brian Nicholson email to the author, June 22, 2020.

32. Brian Nicholson email to the author, June 22, 2020.

33. Brian Nicholson email to the author, June 22, 2020.

34. Brian Nicholson email to the author, June 22, 2020.

Chapter 19 - Sharpened Pencils

1. "Goodbye, Hello," *Brazil Herald*, April 7, 1979, 4.

2. Steve Yolen email to the author, February 5, 2020.

3. Brian Nicholson email to the author, June 22, 2020.

4. Jim Bruce memorandum to the author, February 15, 2021.

5. Maya Pijnappel email to the author, February 24, 2021. Pijnappel, a Rio de Janeiro resident, had been married to Reid.

6. *Masturbating Missies* is available at numerous online bookstores; *The Porto Rican Call Boy* appears out of print.

7. Stroppiana was a well-known producer of such Brazilian films as *Capitães da Areia* (2011), the novel by Jorge Amado, the most famous of Brazil's twentieth century writers, and *Por Incrível Que Pareça* (1986). Padovani was a cinematographer best known for the 1983 Brazilian film, *Tormenta*.

8. Harold Emert email to the author, December 23, 2020.

9. John Thrall email to the author, May 18, 2020.

10. Author's recollection from a conversation with Reid, in the fall of 1980. Reid was to die in February 2009, in Santa Cruz de la Sierra, Bolivia, of lung congestion, his widow, Mary Pijnappel wrote the author in a February 24, 2021. At the time, Reid was writing a script about Amazon women warriors in the future, in Mad Max style, she wrote.

11. Maggie Locke email to the author, May 12, 2020.

12. Marchant, "Rio de Janeiro," 201–16.

13. Chris Phillips, "Adventures in Bumming," *Brazil Herald*, no date available.

14. Recollection from *Brazil Herald* editor Walter Colton shared with the author, July 20, 2020.

Chapter 20 - Without Spurs

1. From John Sullivan's untitled book proposal, dated November 22, 1980, shared with the author by Sullivan's sister, Donna Sullivan Igoe. Chapter title taken from Stan Godlewski's *New York Times* story, "John Sullivan: Gone but Not Forgotten," March 27, 1983.

2. Bogota (New Jersey) High School Yearbook, *Purple B, Class of 1973.*

3. As quoted in Rod Allee, "Memorial for a Young Byline," *The* (Hackensack) *Record*, June 2, 1996, 97–98.

4. Several of Sullivan's *Brazil Herald* columns appeared in United States newspapers. This one was published by the *Spokane Spokesman-Review*, "Dirty Harry Getting Too Clean," December 2, 1979, 74.

5. John Sullivan, "St. Joan of the Nukes," *Latin America Daily Post*, date unavailable.

6. John Sullivan, "Special Magic of Brazil's Monarchy Lives On," *Brazil Herald*, September 4, 1979, 1; John Sullivan, "GM Chief Gives Brazil High Marks," *Latin America Daily Post*, December 5, 1979, 1; "São Paulo Metalworkers Bury Comrades as Strike Continues," *Latin America Daily Post*, November 1, 1979, 1; John Sullivan, "Economy Reform Is Announced By Figueiredo," *Latin America Daily Post*, December 8, 1979, 1.

7. From "The John Sullivan Project," a documentary film proposal based on incidents from Sullivan's life, copyright 1985 by Bonime Associates, Ltd., shared with the author by Donna Sullivan Igoe.

8. As quoted in Meg Lundstrom, "A Life Lived Hard, a Death Too Soon," *The* (Hackensack, N.J.) *Record*, February 27, 1983, 17, 19.

9. As quoted in Lundstrom, "A Life Lived Hard, a Death Too Soon."

10. Steve Yolen email to the author, March 16, 2023.

11. (New York) Daily News, October 22, 1976, 1.

12. Richard Cole email to the author, March 23, 2020.

13. Richard Cole email to the author, March 26, 2020.

14. Brian Nicholson email to the author, June 29, 2020, in which he amplified his memory by sympathetically adding about Sullivan, "I'm sure he deserves to be remembered for more than that!"

15. Richard Cole interview with the author, March 27, 2020.

16. Bob Gima, "Friend Wonders Why Nothing Is Being Done About Missing Reporter," *The Wilkes-Barre Citizens' Voice*, March 11, 1982, 27, 34.

17. Lundstrom, "A Life Lived Hard, a Death Too Soon."

18.Tony Scherman, "Bogota Family's Agony: Son Lost in El Salvador," *The* (Hackensack, N.J.) *Record*, April 19, 1981, 1.

19. Donna Sullivan Igoe interview with the author, January 31, 2024.

20. Scherman, "Bogota Family's Agony."

21. Rogers Worthington, "Family Won't Take 'Missing' for an Answer," *Chicago Tribune*, April 15, 1982, 35, 40, 41.

22. Harold Emert email to author, March 15, 2023.

23. Scherman, "Bogota Family's Agony."

24. Richard Cole, "A Missing Friend," *Brazil Herald*, date unavailable.

25. See Frederick Zugibe and David L. Carroll's account of identifying Sullivan's body, in *Dissecting Death: Secrets of a Medical Examiner*, (New York: Broadway Books, 2005), 209–25.

26. "Journalist missing in El Salvador," *Berkeley Gazette*, (AP story), January 8, 1981, 28.

27. *The Boston Globe Magazine*, "The Strange Case of John Sullivan," by Pat Williams, October 10, 1982, 14, 15, 16, 18, 20, 22, 24, 28.

28. Worthington, "Family Won't Take 'Missing' for an Answer."

29. Memorandum for Deputy Director of Central Intelligence from National Intelligence Office for Latin America, July 27, 1982; approved for released June 29, 2007, Intelligence Community Assessment, SECRET, signed Constantin C. Menges, item 25.

30. Worthington, "Family Won't Take 'Missing' for an Answer."

31. Resolution on John R. Sullivan, Jr. Missing American Reporter in El Salvador, International Council of Lithographers & Photo-Engravers' Union, January 27, 1981.

32.Mike Kelly, "A Death in El Salvador," *The* (Hackensack) *Record*, November 30, 1989, 4; "Study by Retired U.S. Judge Finds Salvadorans Attempted Cover-up," *Richmond Times-Dispatch*, May 25, 1984, 4. See also Joan Didion, "In El Salvador," *New York Review of Books*, November 4, 1982.

33. "2nd Man Says He Saw Reporter in El Salvador," *Asbury Park* (NJ) *Press*, July 15, 1982, 5; "Keansburg Man Still Not Convinced Sullivan Is Dead," *Asbury Park* (NJ) *Press*, February 21, 1983, 2.

Endnotes for Epilogue

34. "State Reps Ask Duarte to Intensify Slay Inquiry," *The Paterson News*, June 25, 1984, 2.
35. "Torricelli Fought for the Truth," *The* (Hackensack) *Record*, May 31, 1995, 42.
36. "State Reps Ask Duarte to Intensify Slay Inquiry" ;June 25, 1984, 2; "Body Identified as Writer Who Disappeared," *Los Angeles Times*, February 25, 1983, 2.
37. Rod Allee, "Memorial for a Young Byline."
38. Worthington, "Family Won't Take 'Missing' for an Answer."
39. Donna Sullivan Igoe email to the author, February 28, 2024.
40. Donna Sullivan Igoe email to the author, February 28, 2024.
41. Dave Marash's eulogy shared with the author by Donna Sullivan Igoe.
42. The 1982 film *Missing*, starring Jack Lemon, Sissy Spacek, and John Shea is about Charles Horman, an American writer who disappeared in Chile following the overthrow of that country's president, Salvador Allende, in 1973.
43. "Memorial Service for Slain Journalist," *Newsday*, March 13, 1983, 23. Sullivan is buried next to his father in Tappan Cemetery in Rockland County, New York.

Chapter 21 - Murmurs

1. Moyra Ashford manuscript titled "Chapter Ten—Latin America Daily Post LADP)," shared with the author, June 16, 2020.
2. Moyra Ashford email to the author, May 30, 2020.
3. Mauro Salles had been named communications director for the incoming Tancredo Neves administration, which would give the publisher control over government advertising that would ostensibly appear in the *Daily Post*.
4. Author interview with Bill Williamson, March 23, 2020.
5. Bill Williamson email to the author, April 24, 2020.
6. Author interview with John Grey Montgomery, May 2, 2023.
7. "Montgomery Publications Sells Brazilian Firm," *The Wichita Eagle*, February 15, 1979, 24.
8. Author Interview with John Grey Montgomery, June 4, 2023.
9. Stephen Downer email to the author, March 23, 2020.
10. Steve Yolen email to the author, March 16, 2023.

Chapter 22 - The Letter X

1. Ed Miller email to the author, August 5, 2023.
2. As quoted in Jim Hicks, "More History from the Will Durants: Spry Old Team Does It Again," *Life*, October 18, 1963, 92.

Epilogue - Goodbye, Hello

1. Interview with Vânia Williamson, January 6, 2020. Vânia Williamson died shortly after our interview.
2. Ed Miller email with the author, January 28, 2024, along with excerpts from Miller's unpublished manuscript on his experiences as a wire-service correspondent

in Brazil, in the chapter titled, "A Venture in the Business World." Gilberto Huber email to the author, January 28, 2024. Huber died in August of 2024

3. "Daily Post Creates Council, Huber Named as Publisher," *Latin America Daily Post*, January 7, 1982, 1.

4. Steve Yolen email to the author, May 4, 2023.

5. Ed Miller interview with the author, January 29, 2021; excerpts from Miller's unpublished manuscript.

6. In a letter from Jo Ann Hein to Bill Williamson, dated December 19, 1984, Hein wrote, "I need every word of encouragement you can give me. I find it hard to get wrapped up in free-lancing, but the paper isn't paying anyone. Oh, Bill, they cut back to printing only 5 days a week. On Sundays we have a WE (Weekly Edition) of TV schedules, events, and social news with pictures, printed in the tabloid size. No news at all!" By then, Williamson had left the Brazil for Miami to become the executive director of the Inter American Press Association. In her letter, Hein asked, "Is this anything I should join? Would I benefit from it? S.O.S. I'm looking for contacts."

7. Steve Yolen email to the author, May 4, 2023.

8. Steve Yolen email to the author, May 22, 2023.

9. June Carolyn Erlick email to the author, March 27, 2024.

10. See Oxfam International, https://www.oxfam.org/en/brazil-extreme-inequality-numbers#:~:text=Brazil%20is%20decades%20away%20from,as%20the%20remaining%2095%20percent, and *Harvard Political Review*, https://harvardpolitics.com/brazil-social-inequality/.

INDEX

Page number in italics indicate images

Index

Confederate enclave in, 45–60, 61–63, 75, 80, 83; coup, 235–41, 247–48, 255–56; cultural differences with US, 381–86; democratic transition of, 63, 375; demographics of, 84; entry and visa requirements, 21–22, 29–30; expats' interest in, 68–69; Jewish settlement in, 149–50; ownership requirements for media, 165, 192, 304; population of, 84; poverty in, 383–84

Brazil economy: and coup, 238; expats and economic development, 68; growth after WWII, 164; and income inequality, 384–85; and inflation, 323, 366, 371, 375; and journalist strike, 315; and lost decade, 371; and slavery, 74, 80, 83

Brazil Herald: arts coverage, 153–54, 232; and broadsheet format, 293; as career way station, xvi, 19–20, 106–7, 109, 267; and censorship, 248, 250–53; and CIA, 106, 241–47, 339–40; circulation of, 115, 189, 194, 293; and communism concerns, 157–58, 312; and crime news, 89, 122–23, 169–71, 223–29; daily operations, 257–58; on *Daily Post*, 306–8; *Daily Post* as competition for, 19, 20, 107–8, 298, 301–2, 303, 306–8, 310; *Daily Post* merger, 63–64, 105–6, 108–9, 313–14, 321–27, 357; distribution of, 136, 177–78, 194, 358; and fugitive stories, 223–29; Hollywood coverage, 114, 115–17, 174; Kuralt on, 188; litigation, 363–64; locations of, 135, 136, 176, 192, *382*; Montgomery acquisition, 157–66; Montgomery coverage in, 173, 180, 292, 359; origins of, 105, 109–11, 113–15; ownership requirements, 165, 304; and Pawley, 129, 131–37, 157, 159, 160–61, 163, 245–46; printing and production of, 128, 135–36, 177, 192, 193–94, 268, 274, 276; printing of other materials, 194; as pro-American, 133–35, 137, 157, 164, 171, 208, 245, 247–48; as Rio-focused, 302; salaries

and compensation, 132, 142, 154, 182–83, 202–3, 277, 323; sale of, 293–95, 310–14, 363–64; society coverage, 167, 175, 220–21, 260; staff as Bohemian, 176–77, 181, 257–58, 260, 268–69, 279; style of, 105–6, 108–9, 118, 123, 231; and tabloid format, 154; *Times of Brazil* incorporation, 191–92; and typos, 109, 114, 115, 122, 128, 137–38, 177, 193, 288; and wire copy, 114, 279. *See also* Garcia, Frank Mario; Montgomery, John D.; Williamson, Bill; *individual contributors*

Brazil Herald and politics: and coup, 235–41, 247–48; coverage, 133–35, 137, 159–60, 165–66, 174, 235–41, 247–48; Emert columns, 291; Langley writings, 159–60; political activism by staff, 230, 255–56; Szulc writings, 150–51; Zschech columns, 121, 150–51, 169, 263

Brazil Herald finances: and broadsheet format, 293; and John Grey Montgomery, 274–77; and Morrisons, 167; and Pawley, 136–37; as precarious, 127–29, 138, 154, 264–65; records, 178, 180–81; and sale to *Daily Post*, 310–13; and tabloid format, 154; and Williamson, 185–86, 189, 264–65, 292–93

Brazilian American, 105

Brazilian Business, 126, 183, 199

The Brazilian Immigrant, 69

Brazilian Institute for Democratic Action (IBAD), 294, 436n23

Brazilian Reflector, 69

Brazilian World, 69, 75

Brecheret, Victor, 441n7

Breslin, Jimmy, 340

The British and American Mail, 76–77, 81. See also *The Rio News*

British and Foreign Anti-Slavery Society, 84

Brooke, Jim, 281, 400

Brooks, Carroll, 117

Broun, Heywood Hale, 421n12

Index

Index

Index

Downer, Stephen, 366–67, 402
Dresser, Linda, 402
drugs: and Beadle, 255; and Bloom, 8; at
    Daily Post, 356; and Garritano, 232;
    and Lightcap, 260; and Nicholson, 280;
    and Reid, 260; and Thrall, 257, 258, 259
Duarte, José Napoleón, 349
Dubois, Jules, 239, 242
Dulles, Allen, 246
Duo Publiçidade, 218
Durant, Ariel, 376
Durant, Will, 376
Dutra, Eurico Gaspar, 111, 155
Dyer, Betty, 111–13, *112,* 402
Dyer, Elisabeth Townsend. *See* Dyer,
    Betty
Dyer, Richard, 111, 112, 113

Eastwood, Clint, 340
Easy Rider (1969), 5
Edgar (paste-up guy), 328
Edison, Thomas, 92
Edward VIII, 113
Eisenhower, Dwight D., 133, 435n17
Eisenstaedt, Alfred, 297
Elbrick, Charles Burke, 225
E. L. Bruce Co., 223
El Salvador: correspondent position,
    388–89; and Sullivan, 343–52, 389
El Suplemento Semanal, 109
Embraer, 360
Emert, Edith, 285
Emert, Fred, 285–86
Emert, Harold: on Andrew Reid,
    330; background, 282, 283–87; as
    columnist, 287–91, 334–35, 355; and
    compensation, 334–35; firing of, 367–
    68; on Fodor, 219; on Hippeau, 266;
    hiring of, 282; images, *284;* and Maluf,
    283–85, 287, 288; marriage, 288–89; as
    nerdy, 338; in roster, 402; and Sullivan,
    344, 347–48
Emigration Reporter, 69
Encyclopedia Britannica, 103
Erlick, June Carolyn, 383, 402
Estes, Elliott M., 340

ethics: and side deals, 182–83, 188,
    222–23, 357; and smuggling in printer
    equipment, 276
Etsinger, Jean, 229–30, 250–51, 254, 263,
    402
Evans, Walker, 421n12

Fairchild Publications, 299
Falkland Islands War, 380
Fallon, Mavis, 208
Fallon, Richard, 206–7, 208
Farber, Barry, 9
FBI, 246–47
feijoada, 31, 360
Felker, Clay, 286
Fellig, Arthur, 169, 421n12
Ferlinghetti, Lawrence, 6–7
Field, Marshall, II, 113
Field News Service, 21, 45, 61–63, 199,
    374–76
Figueiredo, João, 340
Filadelfia, 375
Fischer, Paul, 402
Fish, Richard L., 228
Fitzgerald, Phyllis, 402
fixers. See *despachantes* (fixers)
A Flag Is Born (Hecht), 145
Florida Star, 162
Florida State Advertising Commission,
    163
Florida State Racing Commission, 163
Florida Sun, 162
Floyd, George, 385, 442n7
Flying Down to Rio (1933), 162
Flynn, Errol, 331
Flynt, Larry, 349
Fodor, André: and Addams, 148; and
    beauty pageants, 218–19; and *Brazil
    Herald,* 217–20; death of, 432n4; and
    Gilbert, 224; images, *218;* in roster,
    402; and side deals, 217, 219, 222; and
    Toomey, 226–27, 228; and Williamson,
    275
Fodor, Claire, 432n4
Folha de São Paulo, 305, 314
Fonda, Jane, 340

Index

food: and Andrew Reid, 330; and
  Berkowitz, 153; *caipirinhas*, 18;
  churrasco, 147; and Confederate
  enclave in Americana, 48, 51; *cozido*,
  36; and Davy, 220, 355; *feijoada*, 31,
  360; and Fodor, 219; food poisoning
  fear, 41–42; and Szulc, 152
Forbes, Malcolm, 338, 354
Ford, Henry, 375
Forgione, Vincent, 352
Four Point Program, 134
Fourré, Liza, 250, 263, 271–72, *273*,
  277–78, 402
France Presse, 151
Fraser, Kerry, 402
Freedman, Jonathan, 403
Free Speech Movement, 5–6
Freitas, Alípio Cristiano de, 255
Freligh, J. H., 75
Friendly, Al, 214
The Front Page (Hecht and MacArthur),
  20, 138
Frost, Louisa C., 403
Fuad, Kim, 403
fugitive stories and *Brazil Herald*, 223–29

Gabor, Zsa Zsa, 148
Galanternick, Mary, 403
Galbraith, John Kenneth, 362
gambling, 14, 20, 35
Gandhi, Indira, 263
Ganong, Jean, 403
Garcia, Frank Mario: background,
  126–27; and *Brazil Herald* acquisition
  by Montgomery, 160–61, 165; and
  Brazil Herald ownership, 110, 111,
  115, 117, *117*, 126–27, 137; on *Brazil
  Herald* staff, 181; and *Brazil Herald*
  writing, 127, 137, 165–66, 180; death
  of, 181–82; and Momsem, 165; and
  Pawley, 135; in roster, 403; and US
  intelligence, 245
Garcia, Mabel, 126
García Lorca, Federico, 426n70
Garner, John Hills, 298–303, 403
Garnero, Mário, 306

Garrett, Kelly, 343, 344
Garritano, J. C., 232, 403
Gasparian, Fernando, 194
Gaylord, Karen X., 116
Gazeta da Farmárcia, 194
Gazeta da Tarde, 84–85
Gazette (Rio), 71
Geisel, Theodor, 421n12
Geller, Uri, 272
Gentil, Eduardo, 28, 30, 31, 309, 363, 403
George, Henry, 86–87
Getty, J. Paul, 225
Gilbert, Eddie M., 223–24
Gilbert, Rhoda, 223
Gillette, Alyse, 403
GIL Modas, 194
Gilmore, Jim, 403
Giman, Bob, 344
Ginsberg, Allen, 426n70
Giovanni (restaurant), 12–14, 20, 22, 309
Gira da Umbanda, 194
Godleswki, Stan, 341
Goldberg, Sidney, 345
Gone With the Wind (Mitchell), 52
Goodman, Sue, 403
Gordon, Lincoln, 206, 235–36, 241, 248
Gosteleradio, 241
Goulart, João Belchior Marques, 206,
  235–41, 436n23
Graham, Katharine, 215
Graham, Philip L., 209–15
Grammer, Margaret, 309, 403
Granger, Farley, 148
Grant Advertising, 146
The Great Speckled Bird, 258
Great Train Robbery, 228–29, 291, 375
Greer, Philip, 308
Grizzle, Ralph, 186
Gruberg, Mark, 232, 269, 303, 312–13,
  403
Gugs, 192, 343
Guillen, H., 403
guns and Thompson, 208, 209
Gustafson, Ralph, 154

Haas, Buster, 389–92

Index

Hall, Bill: demotion of, 325–27; as editor, 277–79, 355; images, *326*; and machismo, 337; and Nicholson, 280; in roster, 403; and sale of *Brazil Herald* to *Daily Post*, 313, 325–27, 368; and Thompson, 259

Halsey, William F. "Bull," Jr., 159–60

Halsman, Philippe, 297

Handler, Bruce, 271

Harbor Springs Republican, 103

Harding, Rex, 403

Harnisch, Wolf H., Jr., 403

Harper, Glen T., 403

Harpers, 6

Harris, Gibson, 55

Harris, Maglin, 55

Harte, Bret, 430n8

Havana Daily Post and Evening Telegraph, 162

Hawkins, Otto "Vic," 110, 111, 123–24, 181, 404

Hawryzyswyn, George, 404

Hayworth, Rita, 174

Hecht, Ben, 13, 19, 109, 138, 145, 421n12

Hecht, Edwina "Teddy," 19–20, 109, 138–48, *139*

Hecht, Marie, 141

Hein, Jo Ann: Bloom's meeting of, 28; and merger, 64, 322; in roster, 404; and society beat, 35, 69, 221, 356, 380

Hemingway, Ernest, 4, 203, 215, 421n12

Hendrix, Hal, 239, 242, 243

Herald. See Brazil Herald; Herald (Paris); *Rio Herald*

Herald (Paris), 19, 108–9, 135

Herrington, Elizabeth "Betsy," 380, 404

Hewitt, Edwin, 76–77

Hilton, Nicky, 428n18

Hinrichsen, Albert D., 404

Hinrichsen, Hans Albert, 404

Hinton, Deane R., 350

Hippeau, Claude, 265

Hippeau, Eric Jean Charles, 20, 109, 260, 265–68, 274, 277, 404

Hoagland, Decy Vignoli, 404

Hobart, John, 404

Hobbs, Nancy, 404

Holden, William, 148

Holliger, Heinz, 287

Hollywood coverage in *Brazil Herald,* 114, 115–17, 174

Hope, Bob, 117, *117*

Horman, Charles, 354

horses, 144, 147, 299

hospitals, 43–44

housing: and Andrew Reid, 329–30; and Bloom, 26, 30–31, 36–40, 64, 329; and Hecht, 142–43; and Lamoureux, 92, 97; and Morrisons, 168; and Szulc, 190; and Thompson, 203; and Thrall, 260; and Williamson, 189–90

Howe, Marvine, 267

Huber, Bill, 228

Huber, Gilbert Jacob, Sr., 294, 379, 436n23

Huber, Gilberto, Jr., 294, 379–80, 381, 404

Huber, Phylis, 404

Huber, Roberta, 404

Huffington Post, 20

"The Human Fly" (Gustafson), 154

Hume, David, 176–77, 248, 404

Hunt, Thomas B., 69–72

Hunter, Tab, 148

Huseby, Bill, 270

Huseby, Janet, 260, 270–71, 274, 404

Hustler, 343–45, 349

IAPA. *See* Inter American Press Association (IAPA)

IBAD (Brazilian Institute for Democratic Action), 294, 436n23

Igoe, Donna Sullivan, 345, 349, 350, 351, 352, 353

The Illustrated American, 92

Ilustração do Brasil, 75–76

Ilustração Popular, 76

In Cold Blood (Capote), 4–5

income inequality, 384–85

Independent News Alliance, 344–45

inflation, 323, 366, 371, 375

Institute for Social Research Studies (IPES), 436n23

456

Index

Krock, Arthur, 152
Krull, Felix, 405
Kubic, Milan, 213
Kuralt, Charles, 186–88, 222, 249, 405
Kuralt, Suzanna "Petie" Baird, 186, 187
Kussmaul, Elizabeth "Betty," 277, 400

La Argentinita (Encarnación López
   Júlvez), 426n70
Lacerda, Carlos, 236
La Gorce Country Club (Miami), 163,
   166
Lai, Robin, 232, 273–74
Lamoureux, Andrew Jackson:
   background, 81; Bloom comparison,
   78, 104, 388; Branner correspondence,
   92–99; career in US, 81, 85–86,
   100–104; death of, 103–4; health of,
   81, 96–97, 99, 103; on honorific titles,
   90–91; images, 80; and Ithaca papers,
   81, 85–86, 103–4; marriage and family,
   97–98; Miller comparison, 241; other
   publishing by, 86, 194; in roster, 405;
   and slavery, 83–85, 86, 87–88, 103. See
   also The Rio News
Lamoureux, Mabel, 98, 99
Lamoureux, Sarah, 98, 99, 103, 104
Lamoureux, Vincent, 98, 99
La Nación, 109
Lando, Barry, 387
Laney, Al, 108
Langley, Lee: background, 125; and Brazil
   Herald acquisition by Montgomery,
   160–61, 165, 166; as Brazil Herald
   partner, 124–25, 127; and Hope, 117,
   117; later career, 125; and Pawley, 135,
   158, 159–60, 241; in roster, 405
Langley, Mrs. Lee, 125
Lardner, Ring, Jr., 285–86
Latin America Daily Post: ambitions of,
   33, 164, 298–99, 300, 358–59; Bloom,
   hiring of, xv, 20, 27, 28, 31, 199, 317;
   Bloom's duties, 28, 31, 327, 334–35;
   Bloom's learning about, 14–15, 309;
   Bloom's meeting of staff, 27–28; Bloom
   story ideas, 21, 38, 327; Brazil Herald as

competition, 19, 20, 107–8, 298, 301–2,
   303, 306–8, 310; Brazil Herald merger,
   63–64, 105–6, 108–9, 313–14, 321–27,
   357; Brazilian ownership of, 304; as
   career way station for journalists, xvii,
   362; circulation of, 325; closing of,
   381; decline of, 380–81; distribution
   of, 33, 358–59; finances, 308, 325, 358,
   359, 365–69, 371, 374; first hires, 305,
   309; and gossip, 34; inaugural issue,
   314; International Herald Tribune as
   model for, 14, 33, 302–3, 369; locations
   of, 304–5, 382; name selection, 302;
   operations overview, 33–35; origins
   of, 105, 298–303; page design, 302–3;
   paste-up staff, 34, 35, 327–29, 367,
   372; political coverage, 121; printing
   and production, 304–5; promotion
   of, 305–6, 308–9; Rio transfers, 64,
   321; salaries and compensation, 323,
   366–67, 368; sale of, 379–80; slogan,
   303; and society columns, 35, 69,
   221, 356; staff, competition among,
   61–63; staff as professional, 107–8;
   staff as quirky, 355; and strike, 30, 314,
   316–17, 323, 324; style of, 33, 324; and
   US intelligence, 367–68, 435n23; and
   wire services, 33, 305, 314, 325. See also
   Salles, Mauro; Yolen, Steve; individual
   contributors
Latuszynski, Susan, 405
Lawford, Peter, 148
Lee, Ira, 405
Lee, Rita, 58, 440n10
Lee, Stephen Jeffrey, 259
Lehman, Stan: and Bloom friendship,
   30–31, 44; Bloom's first meeting of, 28;
   and Confederate enclave story, 63; and
   Daily Post, 35, 64, 305, 306, 322, 356,
   359; later career, 380; and merger, 64,
   322, 356; in roster, 405; and strike, 30,
   314
Leitão, Sergio, 405
Lemmon, Jack, 354
Lenz, Mary A., 192, 262, 268–69, 405
Lessing, Doris, 362

Index

Index

Index

Pedlar & Ryan, 173
Peixoto, Floriano Vieira, 95
Pelé, 264, 289
Pepper, Claude, 164
Perlman, David, 10
permuta. *See* side deals
Perón, Evita, 135
Perón, Juan, 115, 135, 150
Peru, Bloom's travels in, 17
Pfeffer, Frederick, 99
Philadelphia Bulletin, 386–87
The Philadelphia Inquirer, 431n6
Phillips, Chris, 330–34, *333*, 355, 408
Phillips, Maria, 408
Phillips, Susan, 408
phones, 190, 269–70
photography: in early English-language journalism, 76; and *Life*, 297; vanity photos of Montgomery, 173; and Veder, 8–9
Pickard, Christopher, 380, 408
Pijnappel, Maya, 444n5
Pimentel, Monica, 409
Pitanguy, Ivo, 362
Plancher, Pierre, 69
Plattdeutsch, 375
Playfair, Guy Lyon, 409
Plimpton, George, 388
PM, 113
poetry and censorship, 249–50
Polin, Herbert S., 140
politics: activism by journalists, 230, 255–56; and censorship, 248–53; and *Daily Post*, 121; and early English-language journalism, 77, 84, 87; and Emert, 291; and Lamoureux, 84, 87, 93–96; and Langley writings, 159–60; and Montgomery, 179–80, 359; and *The Rio News*, 87, 93–96, 151, 241; and Salles, 325; and Scully, 74; and Szulc, 150–51, 159; and Zschech, 121, 150–51, 169, 263. See also *Brazil Herald* and politics; coup
Ponseele, Rogelio, 351
Ponzi, Charles, 106
Por Incrível Que Pareça (1986), 444n7

pornography: and Andrew Reid, 329; *Hustler* and Sullivan story, 343–45, 349
Portuguese: and Bloom, 18–19, 21–22, 25, 36, 38, 372; and Branner, 92; and Brown, 127; and Emert, 284; and Garcia, 127; and Hecht, 147; and Miller, 240; and pronunciation, 25, 30; slang, 25, 38, 217, 328; and Szulc, 150; and Williamson, 184
The Postman Always Rings Twice (1946), 116
Power, Tyrone, 117
power outages, 268, 283
Prager, Karsten, 9
Prenzlauer, Edwin, 44
printer's devils, 185
"Prisoner of Sex" (Mailer), 6
Proctor, John, 232, 409
Progress and Poverty (George), 86–87
Public Ledger, 126, 127
Purchia, Randi, 409

Quadros, Jânio, 179, 249

race and racism: and Confederate enclave, 58; and discrimination in Brazil, 385. *See also* slavery
Radical Chic & Mau-Mauing the Flak Catchers (Wolfe), 7
radio: and Bloom, 3–4, 9; and censorship, 249; Gosteleradio, 241; and Sevareid, 135
Rambo, W. Preston, 409
Ramos, Elisa M., 409
Rangle, Darcey, 292
Raphael, Alison, 271, 409
Reagan, Ronald, 52, 53, 54, 373–74
Rebouças, André, 86, 419n64
Rector, James, 5–6
Reid, Andrew, 329–30, 355, 409
Reid, David, 329
Reid, Judy, 174
Reid, Laura, 257, 260, 265–66, 279, 329, 330, 355, 409
Reston, James "Scotty," 281
Reuters, 118, 329

Index

Index

Schmitz, Ernest, 410
Schroeder, Rotraud, 226–27, *227*, 228
Scott, Leslie Jyl, 410
Scott, Victor, 410
Scripps Howard, 239, 242
Scully, William, 72–74
Seaton, David, 410
Semonin, Paul, 198, 201, 209
Senhorita, 140
Serafino, Nina, 410
Sevareid, Eric, 108, 135
Shannon, Don, 20, 109, 410
Shannon, Pat, 187
Shaw, Irwin, 4
Shaw, Paul Vanorden, 247–48, 410
Shaw, Sandra, 410
Shepard, John, 410
Shepherd, Jean, 3
shoe sales, 4, 11
Shuster, Alvin, 388–89
side deals: and compensation, 182–83,
    188, 222–23, 357; and Fodor, 217, 219,
    222
Siemel, Sasha, 209
Silva, Luiz Inácio "Lula" da, 315–16
Simon, William, 306
Simonsen, Mário Henrique, 306
Simpson, Wallis, 113
Sims, Joseph Stanley, 242–45, *243*, 246,
    339, 367, 410, 436n43
Sinatra, Frank, 290, 347–48
Sinclair, Ted, 410
Singleton, Jane, 410
Sirotsky, Nahum, 150
60 Minutes, 387
Skofic, Milko, 149
slavery: abolishment of, 87; and Brazilian
    economy, 74, 80, 83; and *Brazilian
    World,* 75; and Confederate enclave
    in Brazil, 46, 50, 52, 75, 80, 83; and
    Lamoureux and *The Rio News,* 79, 83–
    85, 86, 87–88, 103; and Monumento
    às Bandeiras, 441n7; and *Revista
    Illustrada,* 84, 87; and Scully, 73
Slocum, Bill, 285
Smith, Billy Don, 391

Smith, Harley, 410
Smith, Linda, 410
Smith, Rick, 411
soccer, 194, 232, 269, 272
society columns: and *Brazil Herald,* 167,
    175, 220–21, 260; and *Daily Post,* 35,
    69, 221, 356; and Liz Montgomery, 162
Solomon, Digby, 309
Solters, Lee, 290
Sombra, 140, 143
The South American Mail, 75–76
Staeblein, Paola, 411
State of Siege (1973), 254
Station Daily News Bulletin, 184
St. Clair, David, 409
Steichen, Edward, 421n12
Stein, Mark, 411
Steinberg, Saul, 140
Steiner, Ralph, 421n12
Stewart, Kenneth, 108
St. Louis Dispatch, 109
St. Louis Republic, 109
Stone, I. F., 421n12
Straker, D. G., 411
Stransky, Ted, 411
Strelow, Grace Cecilia, 226
Strick, Stan, 11
Stroessner, Alfredo, 387
Stroppiana, Bruno, 330
sugar, 80
suicide, 215
Sullivan, Debbie, 349, 350
Sullivan, Donna. *See* Igoe, Donna
    Sullivan
Sullivan, John, Jr., 340, 346, 350, 351, 353
Sullivan, John Joseph, III: background,
    340, 342; Bolivia trip idea, 341–42;
    charisma of, 337, 338–39; and CIA,
    339–40, 350; and *Daily Post,* 337–43;
    death of, 351–52, 355; disappearance
    of, 346–52, 389; El Salvador trip,
    343–52, 389; fighting and temper, 337,
    340–41; images, *339*; in roster, 411;
    talent and ambition of, 337–38, 341
Sullivan, Lorraine, 340, 349, 350, 353
surfing, 254

464

Index

Index